John Henry Overton

The English Church in the Nineteenth Century, 1800-1833

John Henry Overton

The English Church in the Nineteenth Century, 1800-1833

ISBN/EAN: 9783337002923

Printed in Europe, USA, Canada, Australia, Japan

Cover: Foto ©Lupo / pixelio.de

More available books at **www.hansebooks.com**

THE
ENGLISH CHURCH

IN THE

NINETEENTH CENTURY
(1800–1833)

BY

JOHN H. OVERTON, D.D.

CANON OF LINCOLN AND RECTOR OF EPWORTH
JOINT AUTHOR OF "THE ENGLISH CHURCH IN THE EIGHTEENTH CENTURY"

LONDON
LONGMANS, GREEN, & CO.
AND NEW YORK: 15 EAST 16th STREET
1893

THE ENGLISH CHURCH

IN THE

NINETEENTH CENTURY

(1800–1833)

PREFACE

IT was impossible to investigate the history of the English Church in the eighteenth century without being carried forward into the nineteenth, especially when one loved, and believed in, the Church's system, and could not fail to see, towards the close of the earlier period, indications of the dawn of a brighter day. Hence, the materials for this volume have been accumulating for more than twenty years. During the whole of that time the subject, though amid many interruptions, has never been wholly absent from the writer's mind; and his notes upon it swelled into such a vast mass, that they began to be in danger of becoming unmanageable. Nearly five years have elapsed since he began to put the mass into shape; and the result is at last presented to the public.

J. H. O.

EPWORTH RECTORY, DONCASTER.
MDCCCXCIII.

CONTENTS

CHAPTER I.
THE GENERAL STATE OF THE CHURCH.

French Revolution and war—Low state of morals and religion—Pluralities and non-residence—Improvement as years went on—Abuse of the Church and clergy—" The Church in danger"—Church unprepared for new emergencies—The Church in Wales   1

CHAPTER II.
THE 'ORTHODOX.'

The party had not died out—Evidences of its existence—Jones of Nayland —William Stevens—Joshua Watson—J. J. Watson—H. H. Norris— Christopher Wordsworth—C. Daubeny—T. Sikes—Hugh James Rose —Sympathetic prelates—Other prominent sympathizers—Old and new types of High Churchmen   24

CHAPTER III.
THE 'EVANGELICALS.'

Charles Simeon—Isaac Milner—William Farish—Other Cambridge residents—Clapham sect—W. Wilberforce—H. Thornton—Z. Macaulay— J. Stephen—John Venn—Thomas Gisborne—Abolition of the Slave Trade—Evangelicals in London—Evangelicals in the country—Evangelical bishops—Evangelical laity—Weak points in the system—Views of "the world"—Views of "the Church"—Alleged degeneracy— Views of "human learning"—Literature and art—Strong points— Summary   51

CHAPTER IV.
THE 'LIBERALS.'

William Paley—Samuel Parr—Sydney Smith—Henry Bathurst—Edward Stanley—The Oriel Noetics—Richard Whately—Thomas Arnold—No united action   110

CONTENTS.

CHAPTER V.
CHURCH SERVICES AND CHURCH FABRICS.

Holy Communion—Irregularities tolerated—Psalmody—Preaching—Sunday evening services—Week-day services—Want of church accommodation—Pew system—Proprietary chapels—The war prevented church-building—State and voluntary efforts—Difficulties about church-building—Ugliness and costliness of new churches—First free church in England—Squalor of country churches—" A Clergyman's Work, A.D. 1825 " . **127**

CHAPTER VI.
CHURCH LITERATURE.

Evidential writings—Practical and devotional works—Biblical literature—Liturgical literature—The Calvinistic controversy—Baptismal Regeneration—Biography—Church history—The Roman controversy—Religious periodicals—Religious poetry—General Literature—Summary . . . **163**

CHAPTER VII.
THE CHURCH AND EDUCATION.

Oxford—Cambridge—Other institutions—public schools—Dr. Arnold—Elementary Education — Bell and Lancaster controversy — The National Society—Efforts of the parochial clergy—Sunday schools—Jesus Lane Sunday school—Training and infant schools **219**

CHAPTER VIII.
CHURCH SOCIETIES.

Society for the Propagation of the Gospel—Church Missionary Society—Sierra Leone—India—The " five chaplains " — Alarm about proselytizing—Lord Teignmouth—Renewal of Company's Charter—Bishop Middleton—Bishop Heber—Four lives sacrificed—Society for Promoting Christian Knowledge—Society for Suppression of Vice—Mixed societies — The Church and the Bible Society — Private religious societies. **253**

CHAPTER IX.
CHURCH AND STATE.

Acts of 1801 and 1802—Acts of 1803 and 1804—Services of Mr. Perceval and Lord Liverpool—Acts between 1811 and 1819—Roman Catholic Relief Bill—Repeal of Test and Corporation Acts—The case of Queen Caroline—" The Church in danger " **295**

CHAPTER X.
INTERCOURSE WITH SISTER CHURCHES.

Ireland—Scotland—America **313**

THE ENGLISH CHURCH

IN THE

NINETEENTH CENTURY.

CHAPTER I.

THE GENERAL STATE OF THE CHURCH.

THE first thirty years of the nineteenth century naturally divide themselves into two equal parts; the first fifteen, when the national mind was occupied with the one subject of the war with France; the next fifteen, when it was adjusting itself to the new condition of things which a period of settled peace brought about. In no department is this division more clearly marked than in the most important of all—that of religion; and, therefore, for a right understanding of the general state of the Church in the early years of our period, the first thing to be done is to inquire how it was affected by the all-absorbing topic of the day.

When the nineteenth century dawned, the eyes of all England were turned across the Channel. The ardent sympathy which had been felt by many generous minds with the earlier efforts of the French to throw off oppression had been followed by a violent reaction in the opposite direction. It is true that different opinions existed as to the expediency of continuing the war with France; but there were few bold enough to own that they objected to the war because they approved of the doings of the French in the later stages of the Revolution. A very small minority dared to utter such sentiments with bated breath; but the vast majority were in favour either of war with France to the knife, or else of leaving her to settle her own affairs without interfering in so odious a business. This feeling towards France affected the attitude of Englishmen towards their own Church in more ways than one. It undoubtedly increased their attachment to that Church, simply because she was a type of all settled institutions; and settled institutions were at all hazards to be upheld when the unsettlement of them in France was giving so fearful a warning. Not undeservedly was the Church regarded as the great bulwark of stability in England. She had been inactive; but there was a *vis inertiæ* in her very inactivity which constituted an effectual barrier against all dreaded change. Moreover, her professional inactivity led to her being brought more into contact with the secular life of the nation. Her clergy were, for the most part, no separate caste, but men who mixed freely in social life; not perhaps giving a high spiritual tone to it, but on the whole influencing it for good. The great majority of them were University men, better educated than others of the same social status; and as a body they threw themselves enthusiastically into the anti-French scale.

It is curious to observe how the French Revolution affected the work of the Church in two diametrically opposite ways. On the one hand, it acted as a sort of drag upon her, by rendering men suspicious of any improvement, which was apt to be regarded as a dangerous innovation, savouring of that dreaded thing, Jacobinism. On the other hand, it indirectly, but very really, stimulated her to increased activity. The revolutionary ideas, which in the later years of the eighteenth century undoubtedly leavened the minds of the lower classes, and in some cases led to violent disturbances, showed the Church how little real hold she had upon the masses. In fact, she began to feel rather ashamed of herself for not having done more to instil sound principles, which might have prevented them from becoming the prey of the first charlatan who promised them liberty, equality, and fraternity.

In another way the Revolution affected the history of the Church during the early years of the nineteenth century; because the Revolution led to the war, and the war swallowed up the available resources of the nation. After all, Church work cannot go on without money, and money was not forthcoming. And the war monopolized not only the money, but also the interest, of the nation. During the whole of the first fifteen years of the century men's minds were engrossed by the great struggle which was almost incessantly going on. The clergy shared to the full the excitement which was everywhere prevalent. Their pulpits were always ready to stimulate their countrymen to patriotic endeavour, to celebrate a victory, or to pronounce the funeral eulogium upon a hero. They were sometimes blamed for acting as fuglemen of war when their office was to be messengers of peace ; but they would have been still more generally blamed if they had acted otherwise, for there is little doubt that the line they took was strictly in accordance with the feelings of the majority of the nation. A hit at Tom Paine, a side glance at Voltaire and Rousseau, a denunciation of Buonaparte, was only what was expected ; and bishops and archdeacons in their Charges, as well as clergy in their pulpits, were quite ready to meet the demand. In fact, the French Revolution and the war with France at once aroused men to a sense of the need of greater activity on the part of the Church, and also, for the reasons above mentioned, were hindrances to the exertion of that activity. And this appears to me to explain, in part at least, a curious double phenomenon which may be observed all through our period, viz. a steadily growing improvement in every department, side by side with a steadily growing odium against the Church, which reached its climax in the events connected with the Reform Bill.

The Church had reached low-water mark before the eighteenth century closed, and the dawn of the nineteenth century synchronized approximately with the turn of the tide. Abuses which had been allowed to go on for nearly a century without a remonstrance began then, at any rate, to be recognized *as* abuses, though, of course, it took some time to apply any effectual remedy to them. The fatal soporific of Sir R. Walpole, "Quieta non movere," was losing its efficacy, and the Church was beginning to rouse herself from her long slumber.

The very first year of the new century[1] witnessed a stirring

[1] Perhaps it would be more correct to say the last year of the old, but the effects of the Report of 1800 would not be observed till 1801.

of the dry bones in the shape of a remarkable document, entitled, "A Report from the Clergy of a District in the Diocese of Lincoln, convened for the Purpose of considering the State of Religion in the Several Parishes of the said District (1800)." "It is to be feared," says the advertisement, with only too much truth, "that this interesting statement of facts existing in the district to which the Report relates will be found, upon examination, to be applicable to a great part of the kingdom." The Report gives a sad picture of the indifference to religion, as shown by statistics about Church services, education, and so forth, and then suggests remedies.

The wail was repeated with melancholy monotony. "Loud," writes a reviewer of Dr. Hugh Blair's "Sermons," in 1802, "are the daily complaints of the irreligion and depravity of the age, and we are afraid they are not louder than just" (*British Critic*). The preface to the famous Lenten lectures, preached by the Bishop of London (Dr. Beilby Porteus) in four successive years, from 1798 to 1801 inclusive, tells us that they were delivered because "the state of the kingdom, political, moral, and religious, was so unfavourable as to excite the most serious alarm in every mind of reflection"—with more to the same effect. "No crisis," says Bishop Horsley, in his Charge to the clergy of the diocese of Rochester in 1800, "at any period of time since the moment of our Lord's departure from the earth has more demanded than the present the vigilant attention of the clergy of all ranks, from the prelate to the village curate, to the duties of the weighty charge to which we are called. . . . For the last thirty years we have seen in every part but little correspondence between the lives of men and their professions, a general indifference about the doctrines of Christianity, a general neglect of its duties."

Such general complaints might be quoted *ad infinitum ;*[1] and they are certainly justified by the details which have come down to us. The disgraceful opposition which Hannah More and her sisters met with in their single-minded efforts to elevate a degraded people at Cheddar and the neighbourhood, began in the eighteenth century, but did not reach its

---

[1] See, *e.g.*, the Charges of the Bishop of Rochester in 1803, of the Bishop of Hereford in 1792, the preface to Sydney Smith's *Sermons* in 1801, etc.

climax until the nineteenth.[1] William Wilberforce, when visiting Brigg in 1796, found "no service on Sunday morning, and the people sadly lounging about."[2] At Stamford, in 1798, he records, "This seems a sad, careless place. I talked to several common people. I found the butchers' shops open [on Sunday]. At church, miserable work. Remnant of Sunday school, only eight children. I have seldom seen a more apparently irreligious place. A shopkeeper said none of the clergy were active, or went among the poor."[3] When Daniel Wilson went to Worton, a village near Banbury, as curate, in 1804, he found "everything had fallen into sad neglect. The curate had been a keen sportsman, and kept hunters. The neighbouring clergy were like-minded, and the discussions at clerical parties turned chiefly on country sports. Very few attended church."[4] When Venn Elliott made a pilgrimage, in 1813, to Yelling, the scene of his grandfather Henry Venn's later labours, he found the church almost in ruins, and the steeple taken down by the clergyman's orders.[5] Legh Richmond, when he went to Turvey, in 1805, found the parish had been greatly neglected before the time of his immediate predecessor, Erasmus Middleton, who only held the living for a year.[6] Wilberforce writes, in 1809, that he had "heard but a very melancholy account of Olney," the scene of John Newton's and Thomas Scott's labours.[7]

These accounts all come from members of the Evangelical party; but earnest men of other schools tell the same tale. When Edward Stanley entered upon the vicarage of Alderley, in 1805, he found that "the parish had, from the long apathy and non-residence of the previous incumbent, been greatly neglected. The clerk used to go to the churchyard stile to see whether there were any more coming to church, for there were seldom enough to make a congregation. The rector

---

[1] See *Hannah More*, by Miss Charlotte M. Yonge, in the Eminent Women Series, *passim*, especially pp. 80–89.
[2] *Life of William Wilberforce*, by his son, revised and condensed from the original edition, p. 155.
[3] *Id.*, p. 193.
[4] *Life of Daniel Wilson, Bishop of Calcutta*, by Josiah Bateman, i. 120, 121.
[5] *Life of H. V. Elliott*, by Josiah Bateman, p. 31.
[6] *Life of Legh Richmond*, by T. S. Grimshaw, p. 112.
[7] *Life*, p. 304.

used to boast that he had never set foot in a sick person's cottage." This was in a parish containing thirteen hundred inhabitants.[1] When Charles Daubeny took the living of North Bradley, towards the close of the eighteenth century, he found the church "in a state of shameful dilapidation," and the "people so barbarous that they opposed all improvements; and would pull down the walls [of church and vicarage] which were building, and cut down and destroy the trees recently planted." [2] When Bishop Burgess was appointed to the see of St. David's, in 1803, "the churches," we are told, "and ecclesiastical buildings were generally in a ruinous condition. Many of the clergy were incompetently educated, and disgraced their profession by inebriety and other degrading vices." [3]

Many other evidences to the same effect might be given; [4] but the point is most forcibly illustrated by the low standard which even thoroughly good clergymen took of their duties, and the little that was expected of them even by good men.

Dr. Van Mildert, for instance, was one of the ablest and best clergymen who flourished during our period; and yet, in 1807, when he was rector of a large and important London parish, St. Mary-le-Bow, Cheapside, he thought it no harm to apply also for the living of Farningham, near Sevenoaks, "as an agreeable retreat within a convenient distance from town;" and the Archbishop of Canterbury (Dr. Manners-Sutton), also an excellent man, thought it quite right to give it him for this purpose.[5]

Dr. Valpy, of classical fame, an earnest Christian man, was Rector of Stradishall, in Suffolk, at the same time that he was Head-master of Reading School, that is, for twenty years at the close of the last and the early part of the present

---

[1] *Memoir of Edward Stanley, Bishop of Norwich*, by A. P. Stanley, p. 9.

[2] *Life of Charles Daubeny*, prefixed to the third edition of the *Guide to the Church* (1830).

[3] Address of the St. David's clergy to the bishop, on his leaving the diocese in 1825. See *Life of Thomas Burgess, Bishop of Salisbury*, by John S. Harford, p. 361.

[4] See, *inter alia*, the account of the diocese of Norwich in Bishop Bathurst's time, in the *Memoir of Bishop Stanley*, p. 31; Southey's account of the Lakes, given to Wilberforce, *Life of Wilberforce*, p. 379.

[5] See *Memoir of William Van Mildert, late Bishop of Durham*, prefixed to his *Sermons and Charges*, by Cornelius Ives.

century. He salved his conscience by writing to his parishioners an address of a very plain, practical, sensible character, in which he remarks, with delightful *naïveté*, "My absence from you for the greatest part of the year was a strong reason to induce me to form this engagement. I lament the necessity of that absence; and, though my place is ably supplied, I shall receive great comfort from the consideration that this address will give me, at least, an imaginary presence among you." And so far was he from apprehending any episcopal interference in the arrangement, that he had the audacity (as we should now deem it) to dedicate the address to the very man who should have prevented its being necessary—the Bishop of Norwich.

But the fact is, bishops, as a rule, were not in a position to be over-strict; they were wont in their Charges to make some faint general protests against the incumbents' non-residence in, and consequent neglect of, their parishes; but it was not likely that their protests would be of much effect when some of their own body were among the most glaring offenders.[1] Thus the rich living of Stanhope had been held by three successive prelates when its rector, Dr. Phillpotts, was made Bishop of Exeter in 1830. Bishop Courtenay held the living of St. George's, Hanover Square, with a population of 43,396, Bishop Pelham a living in Sussex, and Bishop Bethell a living in Yorkshire, each with the see of Exeter.[2] Two such conscientious men as Bishops Ryder and Blomfield were both pluralists for a time—the one holding the deanery of Wells, the other the living of Bishopsgate *in commendam*, in conjunction with his bishopric. Bishop Copleston held the deanery of St. Paul's with the see of Llandaff. The arrangement was not so difficult with many, because their proper episcopal duties must have sat very lightly upon them. We hear strange tales of one bishop examining his candidates for ordination in a tent on a cricket-field, he himself being one of the players; of another sending a message, by his butler, to the candidate, to write an essay; of another per-

---

[1] This does not apply to the particular bishop mentioned above, for Bishop Bathurst was not a pluralist.

[2] See *Life, Times, and Writings of H. Phillpotts, Bishop of Exeter*, by R. Shulte, i. 290.

forming the difficult process of examining a man while shaving, and, not unnaturally, stopping the examination when the examinee had construed two words.[1]

At the same time, though to the end of our period there was still a very wide margin for further improvement, there is no doubt that matters did steadily improve as the years of the century rolled on, and that the Church in 1833 showed a very different record from that of the Church in 1800. The evidence to this effect is strong and varied. In 1817 Robert Southey wrote to John Jebb, afterwards Bishop of Limerick, "Unless I deceive myself, the state of religion in these kingdoms is better at this time than it has been at any other since the first fervour of the Reformation. Knowledge is reviving as well as zeal, and zeal is taking the best direction."[2] This seems an exaggerated estimate, but it must not be lightly passed over, as it comes from one of the foremost and most intelligent laymen of the day. A correspondent of Hannah More, in 1815, contrasts most favourably the then state of religion with that of twenty years before, "when the poor lived in vicious ignorance, and the rich in presumptuous apostasy."[3] A clever, anonymous writer, in 1824, affirms that "the last twenty years may be termed an epocha of a further revival of religion. More has been effected for the diffusion of religious knowledge, at home as well as abroad, than has ever occurred in the annals of any country. A very real increase of piety has manifested itself in our Church," etc.[4] Another, in 1827, calls attention to "the astonishing advancement of the sacred profession, within the last half-century, and the steady and vigorous pace with which it is still going forward."[5] Lord Liverpool, in 1813, declared in Parliament that "the subject of the efficiency of the Church had long occupied his attention, and that he was

---

[1] The names of all these bishops are given, but I purposely abstain from mentioning them, because such stories are apt to be exaggerated, and it would be unnecessarily cruel to gibbet individuals except on the strongest evidence.

[2] *Life and Correspondence of Robert Southey*, iii. 285.

[3] See *William Wilberforce, his Friends and his Times*, by J. C. Colquhoun: "Hannah More."

[4] *A Letter to a Friend, with some Observations on the Present State of the Established Church*, by a Layman.

[5] *British Critic*, April, 1827.

of opinion that, however, some years ago, there might be a deficiency in the performance of their duties by the clergy, they had of late improved; that both residence and performance of duty among the lower orders of the clergy had increased."[1] William Wilberforce, on his return from a tour in Yorkshire, in 1827, expressed himself "highly gratified with the opening prospects, and," he continues, " I can add, who knew the aspect of things forty years ago, with the highly improved state of the clergy, especially in the East and West Ridings."[2]

Perhaps one ought not to lay too much stress upon the utterances of bishops about their own clergy, whom they would naturally be inclined to regard in the most favourable light, while, of course, the clergy themselves would be on their very best behaviour in the presence of their diocesans. Still, the testimony of such men as Bishops Howley, Van Mildert, and Sumner cannot be lightly passed over. Bishop Howley, in his primary Charge to the diocese of London, in 1814, speaks of his clergy as "respected and respectable as a body for piety, for learning, and conscientious attention to their pastoral care, and abounding with members distinguished in an eminent degree by all the qualifications which bestow attraction or dignity on intrinsic worth;" and in 1818 he affirms that his "anticipations had been realized by the experience of five years." He has "no personal ground of complaint against his clergy; and can regard with satisfaction the general complexion of their professional conduct and attention to their sacred duties." "A body," he adds, "more truly respectable for learning and piety than the clergy of this diocese will not easily be found." In 1833 Bishop Van Mildert said, in the House of Lords, "I may say of my clergy [in the diocese of Durham] in general, that they are a valuable body of men, attentive to their duties, and ready to adopt any improvement that may be recommended."[3] Bishop J. B. Sumner, in his primary Charge to the clergy of the Chester diocese in 1829 admits, "Such has been the

---

[1] *Memoirs of the Public Life and Administration of the Earl of Liverpool*, p. 453.
[2] *Recollections of William Wilberforce*, by J. S. Harford, p. 187.
[3] *Memoir of Bishop Van Mildert*, by Cornelius Ives.

activity and ability of my predecessors, and so cheerful the compliance which has been paid to their regulations, that in the administration of the diocese there is no accumulation of abuses requiring to be noticed or crying for correction. My wishes will be fully gratified if I can maintain and complete the system which I find generally established." Not to weary the reader with evidences of improvement, which might be multiplied *ad libitum*, let it suffice to end as we began, by quoting Robert Southey, who, in 1833, wrote again to the Bishop of Limerick, "There is a comfort in knowing that the Church of England and Ireland could never at any time have been better able to bear hostile inquiry, and to defend themselves than now;" and to John Miller in the same year, "Among the many ominous parallelisms between the present time and those of Charles I., none has struck me more forcibly than those which are to be found in the state of the Church; and of those, this especially, that the Church of England at that time was better provided with able and faithful ministers than it had ever been before, and is in like manner better provided now than it has ever been since. . . . No human means are likely to avert the threatened overthrow of the Establishment."[1]

If we cannot quite agree with Southey that the Church was at its best, we can at any rate agree with him when he implies that it had reached the climax of apparent popularity. For, side by side with its growing efficiency, there was, oddly enough, a growing odium against it, and that for just those very faults which it was doing its best to amend. When the Church was doing next to nothing, it was popular enough; when it began to do something, it was unpopular because it was supposed to be doing nothing. This curious paradox was noted by several writers besides Southey. "The Church and clergy," writes one in 1823, " were never worse spoken of, and never less deserved it. The Church, as a body, was never so free from secular views; its clergy, as individuals, never so distinguished for general morals, learning, and industry."[2] In 1831, Bishop Kaye, having shown that the Church was

---
[1] *Life and Correspondence of Robert Southey*, vi. 222.
[2] *An Appeal to the Gentlemen of England on behalf of the Church of England*, by Aug. Campbell, Rector of Wallasey, Cheshire, p. 57.

denounced not merely as worthless, but as positively injurious, as obstructing instead of advancing the interests of true religion, adds, "There never was, perhaps, a time when the clergy stood in less need of being urged to a diligent performance of their duties, when they entertained juster notions of the responsibility attaching to the ministerial character."[1] A very abusive book appeared in 1820, entitled "The Black Book," the writer of which quite lashes himself into a fury when he thinks of the iniquities of the Church. It is "that ulcerous concretion," "that foul and unformed mass of rapacity, intolerance, absurdity, and wickedness;" the Church Catechism is "this poisonous production;" a "Church of England priest" is "a furious, political demon, rapacious, insolent, luxurious, having no fear of God before his eyes;" and so forth, and so forth, in language which, one would have thought, would carry its own confutation with it. After the lapse of eleven years matters do not seem to have improved. the "Extraordinary Black Book," published in 1831, is quite as abusive as its predecessor. The charges are absurdly exaggerated, and the statistics on which they are founded are often false or misleading;[2] but the books reflect only too truly the feelings with which the Church was then regarded. In fact, both friend and foe agreed that there was every probability of its being swept away, as a national institution, by the besom of Reform, when that implement had done its work in the political world. One can scarcely now conceive the state of things when a Prime Minister could tell

[1] See *Nine Charges*, etc., by John Kaye, late Lord Bishop of Lincoln, edited by his son.
[2] For instance, we find among the pluralists gibbeted in the *Extraordinary Black Book*, "Chaplin, W. : Raithby R., Hallington R., Maltby C., Haugham V.," implying that this clergyman held four pieces of preferment, some of which he would be bound to neglect. As a matter of fact, the whole population of the four did not exceed four hundred. Hallington consists simply of two farms in the little village of Raithby, Maltby of a single farm in the little village of Haugham. Raithby and Haugham are two small adjoining parishes, and an able-bodied man would scarcely find enough work in both put together to occupy his time. Again, "Massingberd, F. C. : Driby R., Ketsby R., South Ormesby C." Here are three cures which practically are well within the compass of one man. Driby is one of those very small parishes in which Lincolnshire abounds, and which it would be absurd to give as the sole work for a man in health and strength; Ketsby is simply a farmhouse in South Ormsby. The writer knew personally both Mr. Chaplin and Mr. Massingberd ; both were excellent clergymen.

the bishops in the House of Lords that they must set their house in order; and when a member of Parliament could stand up in the House of Commons and gravely say, "I had hoped that these foolish ordinations would terminate. But these young gentlemen must bear in mind that, though the nation will feel itself bound to make a provision for such as in past years have entered into orders; though it would doubtless be unjust that a corporation like the Church, which was set up by Parliament nearly three hundred years ago, and is older, therefore, than either the East or West India Company, should be abolished without adequate compensation to those who have wasted their youth in its service; yet by those who enter this body now that it is condemned by the country, when its charter is on the eve of being cancelled by the authority which gave it, when it is admitted on all hands to be not useful only, but absolutely detrimental, neither indulgence nor compensation can fairly be expected. They choose to invest their time and property in a condemned building, and can expect no more pity than the man who bought the Borough of Gatton after the publication of Schedule A, or a West India estate after Mr. Burton's motion."[1] Mr. Joseph Hume, the utterer of these remarkable words, had not exactly the gift of prophecy; this doomed institution which was "older than either the East or West India Company" managed to outlive both; but his forebodings were not more ominous than those of several bishops. "When," writes the Bishop of Lincoln, in 1831, "in former times, the clergy spoke of the dangers impending over the Church, they were charged with exciting a cry of which they knew the falsehood, from interested motives; but now that its adversaries declare it to be in danger, and exultingly tell us that it is tottering to its fall, we cannot be accused of childlike proneness to alarm, if we suspect that their confident anticipations are not merely the suggestion of their wishes, but that they intend their prediction to work its own accomplishment."[2] In the same year the Bishop of Durham expressed his opinion that the Church had never had to contend with so many open and avowed enemies; and, after quoting some of the violent

---

[1] Quoted in the *Christian Remembrancer* for 1841, pp. 422, 423.
[2] *Nine Charges, ut supra.*

abuse which was poured upon it, he appeals with proper indignation to the laity of Durham, to look and see whether their own clergy deserved this abuse. The Bishop of Lichfield is all the more depressing because he *will* hope against hope. "I am not," he says, in 1832, "one of those, even in these days of change and innovation, who despair of the safety of the Established Church. But that it is a crisis—perhaps even a fiery ordeal for our Church—I will not deny. It may possibly prove little less so than it was at those marked and trying periods of her history—the Rebellion, the Revolution. Four years must elapse now before we meet again on a similar occasion, and I feel that a more than common uncertainty hangs over such a prospect. If we are spared thus to meet once more in this life, it may be under altered circumstances. But whether the outward state of our Zion be prosperous or adverse, may we ever recollect that our vows of allegiance to her, in and through her Divine Head, are upon us, and that we have to be followers of her as she is of Christ, whether it be through famine, through fire, the sword, or the cross. Her altars we cannot desert, her people we cannot abandon."

The fury of the attack fell upon the bishops, chiefly owing to their opposition to the Reform Bill. Some of them were burnt in effigy; the Bishop of Bristol's palace was burnt to the ground by an infuriated mob; the Bishop of London was warned that it was dangerous for him to preach in a London church, and actually gave up his engagement in consequence; the Bishop of Lichfield was in danger of his life after he had been preaching in London; and the Archbishop of Canterbury was mobbed in his own cathedral city.[1] The inferior clergy were only less the objects of attack because they were less prominent.

But all this while there was a quiet stream of attachment to the Church, which, to the surprise of many, suddenly swelled into a mighty torrent, carrying all opposition before it. When the fate of the Established Church seemed trembling in the balance, a little band of her devoted sons made an appeal to the nation, the result of which cannot better be described than in the words of one who took a

[1] See *Memoir of Bishop Blomfield*, p. 169; *Life of Bishop Samuel Wilberforce*, vol. i. (by Canon Ashwell), p. 61, etc.

leading part in it. "From every part of England," he writes, "and every town and city, there arose a united, a strong, an emphatic declaration of warm and zealous and devoted loyalty to the Church of England. The national feeling, long pent up, depressed, despondent, had at length obtained freedom to pour forth; and the effect was amazing. The Church suddenly came to life. The journals daily were filled with reports of meetings, in which sentiments long unknown to the columns of newspapers were expressed. . . . The Church, to its astonishment, found itself the object of warm, popular affection and universal devotion. Its enemies were silenced."[1]

We are thus brought face to face with two curious paradoxes: first, a growing improvement in the Church side by side with a growing odium against the Church; and then an overwhelming and unexpected demonstration of attachment to the Church, quite bearing down all this odium, and rendering it harmless. How are we to account for the phenomena?

A closer investigation will show us, first, that the undoubted improvements in the Church were really the work of one or the other of two classes of Churchmen, which, both together, only constituted a small minority among her members; and, secondly, that all this odium against the Church was more apparent than real, or, at any rate, that it only existed among a small but noisy body in certain great centres, and did not reflect the general feeling throughout the country, which, when at last called forth, showed itself most strongly in favour of the National Church.

To make good these two points, we must try to throw ourselves back in thought, into the state of affairs in which the Church found herself at the beginning of the century. She was in a position for which, if one may use so homely a phrase, she had never bargained. From the accession of George III. to the close of the eighteenth century, she was in a most prosperous, peaceful, and, to tell the truth, sleepy state. The men who were ordained in the early years of the nineteenth century expected that they were to go on just as

[1] "The Oxford Movement of 1833," by Sir William Palmer, in the *Contemporary Review* for May, 1883.

their fathers and grandfathers had done. But that was not to be. A change had come over the spirit of the dream. There was a general and "sudden increase of the vital energy of the species. Humanity assumed a higher mood ; a deep agitation, as if from a fresh discharge out of celestial space into the solid body of our planet, shook the soul of the world, and left it troubled and excited."[1] At any rate, to narrow the matter a little, it had that effect upon the Church, and her officers were brought face to face with the most tremendous difficulties, the most violent changes, when they were not in the least prepared for the emergency. There were only two classes that could at all cope with it, and that because they both had a strong lever to wield, which the easy-going mass had not. The one was the Evangelical party, the other that of the distinctly High Churchmen, both of whom had to do with the improvements which ultimately occurred ; but both together were far outnumbered by the many who were neither one thing nor the other ; some inclining to the high and dry, some to the low and slow ; some whose creed consisted mainly in a sort of general amiability ; some who were mere worldlings ; some, alas ! who were absolutely immoral. The vast majority both of clerical and lay Churchmen fell under one or other of these last heads, not of the two first ; and it is a great mistake to suppose that they were either unpopular on the one hand, or at all a potent spiritual force on the other. These facts are brought out quite as strongly, though perhaps unconsciously, by their eulogists as by their detractors. Take, for example, Mr. J. A. Froude's graphic description of the Church in the times immediately preceding the Oxford Movement. " As the laity were, so were the clergy. They were gentlemen of superior culture, manners, and character. The pastor in 'The Excursion' is a favourable but not an exceptional specimen of a large class among them. Others were country gentlemen of the best kind, continually in contact with the people, but associating on equal terms with the squires and the aristocracy. . . . The average English incumbent of sixty years ago [this was written in 1881] was a man of private fortune, the younger brother of the

[1] *Wordsworth, Shelley, Keats, and other Essays*, by David Masson : "Wordsworth," p. 19.

landlord perhaps, and holding the family living; or, it might be, the landlord himself, his advowson being part of the estate. His professional duties were his services on Sundays, funerals and weddings on week-days, and visits when needed among the sick people. In other respects he lived like his neighbours, distinguished from them only by a black coat and white neckcloth, and greater watchfulness over his words and actions. He farmed his own glebe, kept horses, shot and hunted moderately, and mixed in general society. He was generally a magistrate; he attended public meetings, and his education enabled him to take a leading part in county business. His wife and daughters looked after the poor, taught in the Sunday school;" and so forth.[1] I have no doubt that this picture is drawn from the life; indeed, I am old enough to remember many specimens of the class. And the account is fully borne out by others. Mr. Jerram, for instance, a good Evangelical, thus describes the Surrey clergy of a few years earlier (1810): "Most of them were branches of the aristocracy and gentry with which Surrey abounds; they were, with one or two exceptions, very respectable characters; they regularly discharged their clerical functions; preached against vice and profligacy; taught the necessity of attending to all the decencies and services of religion, and of rectifying what was deficient in morality; and the duty of carefully avoiding infidelity on the one hand, and enthusiasm on the other. They mixed freely with the gentry around them, associated with them in their amusements, and generally formed a goodly number at their balls and assemblies. Races never lacked their presence, nor any scene of gaiety wanted the sanction of their attendance. Yet on all these occasions they maintained that decency of deportment which made them careful not to transgress the bounds of moderation, and to avoid the imputation of dishonouring their profession by those moral delinquencies which disgraced not a few of the clergy in other places."[2]

A precisely similar account is given in a thoughtful article

---

[1] See article in *Good Words*, by J. A. Froude, 1881. Republished in *Short Studies on Great Subjects*, 4th series: "The Oxford Counter-Reformation."

[2] *Memoirs of the Rev. Charles Jerram*, p. 262.

which appeared in *Blackwood's Magazine* in 1887,[1] does it at all differ from that given by Sir William Palmer, a leader of the early Oxford Movement, in his generous defence of the old times.

Now, it is not denied that such men did much good. They had many advantages, in being in touch with the laity, which are lacking in the more exclusively professional characters of their successors. But in times of a great upheaval, when the population was increasing with unexampled rapidity; when first principles were being discussed on all sides; when the godless notions imported from France on the one hand, and the wildest fanaticism emanating from the extreme left of Methodism on the other, were rampant; when constant supervision and a distinct and definite faith were absolutely necessary to produce any permanent effect,—they had not the ποῦ στῶ from which they could move the world. One can perfectly well understand how, in an age when everything was to be reformed, an outcry would be raised against a Church which was manned by such officers; but one can also perfectly well understand how, when serious danger threatened the Church, its friends, who under such a *régime* would be numerous, should rally round it. The real spiritual force of the Church, however, belonged not to the class just described, but to the two classes which will form the subjects of the next two chapters.

But before closing this sketch of the general state of the Church, it may be well to say all that need be said separately about those four dioceses which lay in the principality of Wales. It appears to me to have been perfectly well understood all through the eighteenth and the early part of the nineteenth centuries that these dioceses were as integral a part of the Church of England as London or Yorkshire. This should be remembered when complaints—and perfectly just complaints—are made of Englishmen unacquainted with the Welsh language being appointed to ecclesiastical dignities in the principality over the heads of the native clergy. The fact is, the dioceses of St. David's, Llandaff, Bangor, and St.

---

[1] "The Country Parson as he was and as he is," in *Blackwood's Magazine* for September, 1887. The whole of this most interesting and suggestive article deserves to be carefully studied.

Asaph were treated just like any other four dioceses in the province of Canterbury. From the historical and ecclesiastical point of view, this was right enough; there was no more reason why a Welshman should necessarily be chosen for a Welsh diocese than a Yorkshireman for a Yorkshire diocese. But practically it was a very different matter. Though ecclesiastical Wales was as much a part of the great National Church of England as civil Wales was a part of the great nation of England, yet, as a matter of fact, the Welsh people were of a different race, different language, different habits and temperaments; and it was the greatest source of weakness to the Church that these differences were so long ignored. But it is not in the least surprising that they were. In days when, unhappily, men's special fitness for the special posts they were to occupy was far less considered than it is now, it seemed quite natural that the favoured candidate for promotion should succeed, as a matter of course, to the next see, deanery, or whatever it might be, that was vacant, whether it happened to be on the east or the west side of the Welsh border. Indeed, the border was not necessarily the dividing line, for of one of the four dioceses, part is on one side of the line and part on the other. No doubt it was wrong to appoint a bishop or any other dignitary in Wales who knew nothing about the Welsh; but it was wrong only in the same sense, though in a greater degree, in which it would be wrong to appoint a Londoner, who knew nothing whatever about country life, to a purely agricultural diocese. The quickened sense of a duty to be performed as well as a privilege to be enjoyed, which, broadly speaking, was coincident with the new century, brought about a great change of feeling on this point; and there was no part of the country in which the curious paradox noticed in this chapter was more conspicuous than in Wales. There, more than anywhere else, when the Church was doing next to nothing, there appear to have been few complaints; but when she began to do something the complaints were loud against her for doing nothing. It does not seem to have outraged public feeling very much that Bishop Hoadly should have held the see of Bangor seven years without setting foot in the diocese, or that Bishop Watson should have accepted the see of Llandaff, and then settled himself comfortably "in the beautiful district on the banks of Lake Windermere."[1] But when there was certainly a higher standard of episcopal duty, when the first really successful attempt was made to raise the character of the Welsh clergy, and to render the Church more efficient, then the Church received a more serious blow than she had ever received in the days of her apathy, by the secession of the large and increasing body of Calvinistic Methodists. This took place in the year 1811, and the circumstances of it remind us painfully of a similar event which took place in England nearly thirty years earlier, the only difference being that in Wales the logical results occurred at once, while in England they were delayed for several years. The Methodist movement in the eighteenth century had been, in Wales even more markedly than in England, the work of Churchmen; and the man who, apparently against his will, originated the secession in Wales was an Oxford graduate, who had been duly ordained by the Bishop of Oxford, and had been an intimate friend of the leading Evangelical clergy in England. This was *Thomas Charles*, an earnest and active clergyman, the father of Welsh Sunday schools, and the cause of the foundation of the Bible Society. Having met with the opposition which fell to the lot of the early "Methodist clergy" in two or three curacies in England, he settled himself at Bala, as a sort of free lance, but still retaining his position as a clergyman of the Church of England. Like John Wesley, he was induced by pressure from without to "ordain" eight lay members of the Calvinistic Methodist body in 1811; and Calvinistic Methodism became, and has ever since continued, a separate organization.

The history of the Church in Wales during our period is certainly not one of which any churchmen need be ashamed. She numbered among her prelates some highly distinguished men, who strove to do their duty to the flocks over which they were called to preside. Let us take the greatest first. Bishop Horsley was Bishop of St. David's from 1788 to 1793, and Bishop of St. Asaph from 1802 to 1806, and was very far from being a *roi fainéant* in either capacity. At St. David's he began to do the work which was most of all needed in

[1] See Bishop Watson's *Anecdotes of his own life*.

Wales—that of raising the status of the Welsh clergy. He helped them both by his purse and by his counsel, and successfully insisted upon the minimum stipend of a curate being raised from £7 to the not extravagant sum of £15 per annum. It appears also that candidates for holy orders had been accustomed to receive the whole of their training in a Dissenting academy! No imputation is intended against the efficiency of this academy in its way; but how could it possibly train clergymen to present the Church's system in its fulness to their people? Bishop Horsley refused to receive certificates from Castle Howell, the name of this Carmarthen college, as guarantees for the eligibility of candidates; and surely no right-minded Dissenter could blame him for so doing. He was in his seventieth year when he was translated from Rochester to St. Asaph; but in spite of his years, the old man set himself bravely to do the uphill work of a Welsh diocese, and was not content with being a mere cipher. Some of his great Charges, which rank among the finest compositions of the age, were in the first instance delivered in Wales.

Dr. Copleston, the highly distinguished Provost of Oriel, having been Dean of Chester for a few years, was appointed Bishop of Llandaff in 1828. It is true that he also held with the bishopric the deanery of St. Paul's, and that the duties of the two offices ought to have been incompatible; but it was the interests of St. Paul's, not those of Llandaff, that were sacrificed. He was a working bishop, setting himself especially to the sorely needed task of bringing about the restoration of churches and the erection of glebe houses; twenty new churches and fifty-three glebe houses were built during his incumbency. This does not seem a large number, according to our modern notions, but, judged by the standard of the eighteenth century, it was gigantic. Bishop Copleston also set the wholesome example of requiring a knowledge of the Welsh tongue from the clergy whom he instituted to livings. This was all the more creditable to him, because he did not feel so strongly as some did the necessity of the accomplishment, arguing that as in Wales all public business was conducted in English, most Welsh people could easily train themselves to understand the English services.

Again, Dr. Herbert Marsh, who, in my opinion, ranks, in point of ability, next to Bishop Horsley among the prelates of the period, occupied the see of Llandaff from 1816 to 1819, and worked conscientiously in his diocese. But the bishop who of all others made his mark upon the Church in Wales was Thomas Burgess, who held the see of St. David's from 1803 to 1825. Those twenty-two years were really a memorable era in one at least of the Welsh dioceses. Nothing was more wanted than the supply of a better education, especially to the future clergy. Few of them could afford the expense of an English University, and bishops had to be content with candidates for holy orders who had gained such a smattering of knowledge as the Welsh grammar schools could supply. In the first instance, Bishop Burgess wisely tried to improve the grammar schools themselves. He licensed four of them, and required seven years' study at one of them before he would accept a candidate at all. But this was, of course, only a partial remedy of the evil; and the bishop set himself, with a dogged determination, to establish a college, to be managed on the lines of those at Oxford and Cambridge, both for a general and for a specially theological training. This was a thing that could not be done in a day or in a year. So the bishop regularly set aside a part of his own income for the purpose, and persuaded many of his clergy to set aside a tenth of their own wretched stipends for the same end. The result was that in seventeen years £11,000 was collected; and the bishop, being able to show what the Welsh had been willing to do for themselves, felt justified in appealing for aid to the king and to the English Universities. The appeal was not made in vain; and in 1822 the foundation of St. David's College at Lampeter was laid.[1] The college was not ready for opening until 1827, by which time Bishop Burgess was translated to Salisbury; but he still took a deep interest in the scheme, and to him above all others belongs the chief credit of the first adequate effort to supply a higher education to the Church in Wales which had been made for more than a thousand years. In other respects also Bishop Burgess showed himself a most active and

[1] Mr. Harford, of Blaise Castle, who afterwards wrote a *Life of Bishop Burgess*, gave the site.

efficient prelate. The very year after his appointment (1804) he established a "Society for promoting Christian Knowledge and Church Union in the Diocese of St. David's," the aims of which were "to raise the standard of classical education, to provide English and Sunday schools for the poor, to spread religious books, and to found libraries and a superannuation fund for the poorer clergy." He was most particular in the conducting of his Confirmations and Ordinations; he refused to induct clergy ignorant of Welsh into Welsh-speaking parishes; in fact, he did all that an earnest and energetic bishop could do to advance the cause and raise the standard of the Church in Wales.[1]

Though all this refers only to one of the four dioceses, it must be remembered that St. David's was still virtually the metropolitan see of the principality; that it was almost equal in area to the three other dioceses put together; that it claimed as its founder the patron saint of Wales; and that its cathedral was by far the largest and most imposing of all the Welsh cathedrals. It might, therefore, claim to lead the way and give the tone to the rest.[2]

But practically Llandaff was the most important. There alone the difficulty occurred which has been noticed in this chapter in connection with the Church in England. Wales was even worse prepared than England to meet the emergency caused by an immense increase of trade, and the consequent rise of vast centres of population. The discovery of iron ore and coal in the beautiful hills of Glamorganshire changed a quiet, pastoral, and sparsely populated district into a busy centre of industry, with a population which doubled and trebled itself with marvellous rapidity. In its most active time it would have been difficult for the Church to keep pace with the rapid increase of work which devolved upon it; but the Church in Wales had been as inactive as it had been in England, while it was embarrassed in a way that England was not, by the bilingual difficulty. This necessitated in

---

[1] How highly Bishop Burgess's achievements were appreciated in his diocese may be seen from an address presented to him on his leaving it, which has been quoted on p. 6. See Harford's *Life of Bishop Burgess*, p. 361.

[2] See *Four Biographical Sketches*, by Rev. John Morgan, p. 69. Mr. Morgan gives many very interesting details of Church life and work at a rather later period than we are concerned with.

many places a double staff of clergy, one for the Welsh-speaking, and the other for the English-speaking, population.

But it is needless to follow further the history of the Church in Wales separately. The history of the Church of England *is* the history of the Church in Wales. They were one and the same Church, and had been so for more than six hundred years—ever since the Welsh bishops gave in their allegiance to the Archbishop of Canterbury, in 1172. No doubt there are special circumstances in connection with the Church in Wales, some of which have been noticed; but so there are in connection with the Church, say, in Cornwall, or in Lincolnshire, or in the Black Country; but to make these the subject of a separate chapter would only be to foster the notion that there is a difference between the Church on the one and on the other side of the " Marches," and thus to falsify history.

CHAPTER II.

THE ORTHODOX.

BEFORE entering upon the subjects of this and the two following chapters, it is necessary to explain why the titles of them—"Orthodox," "Evangelicals," "Liberals"—have been chosen in preference to the more obvious ones—"High Churchmen," "Low Churchmen," "Broad Churchmen." The choice has not been made without much hesitation, much deliberation, and much consultation with those who appeared competent to give an opinion. The reasons of the decision finally arrived at are as follows: To describe the parties treated of in Chapters III. and IV. simply as "Low Churchmen" and "Broad Churchmen" respectively would be utterly misleading. In the nomenclature of the eighteenth and early nineteenth centuries the Broad Churchman would be the Low Churchman. Burnet, Hoadly, Blackburn, and Paley would be called Low Churchmen; but they had very little in common with the typical Evangelical. As for the term "Broad Churchmen," it did not, so far as my reading enables me to judge, exist. "High Churchmen" was, of course, a well-known title, and the party which is the subject of the present chapter would doubtless fall under that designation. But to term them "High Churchmen," in contradistinction to "Evangelicals" and "Liberals," would be a cross-division, "low" and "broad" being the natural correlatives to "high." Moreover, there would be a danger of confounding them with the "Church and State" men, who were also called *par excellence* "High Churchmen." The adoption of the term "Orthodox," by which they were at least as frequently designated in their own day, obviates both those objections; and hence it is, with some misgivings, chosen.

It is frequently said that the old Orthodox or High Church party was fast asleep, if it had not entirely died out, before it was revived by the Oxford Movement. But this mode of stating the case is far too strong. The High Church party had never ceased to exist or even to be active. It had suffered a grievous loss—far more grievous than the mere counting of heads would indicate—by the retirement of the Nonjurors in 1689 and 1714; but it was beginning to recover from that loss before the nineteenth century commenced. It suffered, perhaps, still more severely from being mixed up with another party, with which it really had only an accidental connection. There was no reason in the nature of things why the true High Churchmen should have been specially identified with the maintenance of "our happy constitution in Church and State," to use a familiar phrase of the day. Indeed, their principles rendered them more independent of any connection with the State than any other party in the Church could be. If "our happy constitution" had been entirely broken up, it would not have made the slightest difference to the essential position of the High Churchman. This is so obvious to us now that it sounds like a truism, but it would have sounded strangely in the ears of our forefathers. To them a High Churchman meant one who was the strongest supporter of Church and State; and so indeed he *was*, as a matter of fact. None supported the established constitution more ably and consistently than the High Churchmen. They were better equipped for the task than any other party. Valuing deeply the science of theology, they studied it more thoroughly and systematically than any other class did. Indeed, strange as it may sound to some, I venture to think that the majority of competent divines in the early part of this century were what we should now call distinctly High Churchmen.

A few passages selected from writers of note, written in a way which shows that they did not regard their doctrines as innovations, but such as would command the assent of all who called themselves Churchmen, will serve to illustrate this. Bishop Horsley was, beyond all question, the ablest and most eminent prelate still living at the commencement of the nineteenth century; and this is the way in which he expresses his Church principles : " To be a *High Churchman* in the only sense which the word can be allowed to bear as applicable to any in the present day—God forbid that this should ever cease to be my public pretension, my pride, my glory ! . . . In the language of our modern sectaries, every one is a High Churchman who is not unwilling to recognize so much as the spiritual authority of the priesthood ; every one who, denying what we ourselves disclaim, anything of a divine right to temporalities, acknowledges, however, in the sacred character, somewhat more divine than may belong to the mere hired servants of the State or of the laity ; and regards the services which we are thought to perform for our pay as something more than a part to be gravely played in the drama of human politics. My reverend brethren, we must be content to be High Churchmen according to this usage of the word, or we cannot be Churchmen at all ; for he who thinks of God's ministers as the mere servants of the State is out of the Church, severed from it by a kind of self-excommunication."[1] Next to Bishop Horsley, Bishop Van Mildert was perhaps the ablest theological writer during our period. In his Bampton Lectures (1814), when he was Regius Professor of Divinity, he dwells upon what he considers " the *essential* doctrines of the Church," among which he includes "the ordinances of the Christian Sacraments and the Priesthood ; " and then he adds, " We are speaking now, it will be recollected, of what in ecclesiastical history is emphatically called THE CHURCH ; that which has from age to age borne rule upon the ground of its pretensions to Apostolical Succession." Archdeacon Daubeny, again, was a man of considerable mark in his day, and his testimony is equally explicit. " If," he says, " the title of High Churchman conveys any meaning beyond that of a decided and principled attachment to the apostolic government of the Church, as originally established under the direction of the Holy Spirit by its Divine Founder (from whom alone a commission to minister in holy things can properly be derived), it is a meaning for which those must be answerable who understand and maintain it ; the sense annexed to that title, in my mind, containing in it nothing

---

[1] First Charge of the Bishop of St. David's, 1790.

but in what every sound minister of the Church of England ought to glory."[1] And again, "I could have wished to see the Church described in its independence of every human establishment; vested with those spiritual powers which it possesses in itself; in the exercise of which every individual ought to be governed by the authority from which alone those powers are derived."[2] "To God," writes Archdeacon Wrangham, in 1823, "and not to a patronizing Crown or to an electing people, we authoritatively refer our origin as a ministry. For Christ, we are expressly told in Scripture, sent His apostles with a power to send others, thus providing an unbroken succession for all coming ages, and promised to be with them always, even to the end of the world."[3]

It would be easy to multiply instances to the same effect,[4] but enough, perhaps, has been quoted to show that the High Churchmen had not died out. How is it, then, that the idea that they had has so generally prevailed?

Perhaps one reason is that, so far from being too diffident, they were too confident in their cause. They took it for granted that their views would be understood and accepted, and that there was no need to do more than simply to state them. But, as a matter of fact, this was not so. Englishmen recognized, and were proud of, the Church of England as a great national institution; but, as Sir W. Palmer says most truly, " the notion of the Church as a spiritual body possessing a faith and a conscience like other religious bodies, had died out."[5] It had died out, that is, among the main body of the nation, upon the mind of which the High Churchmen had certainly failed to impress their own convictions. Indeed, they themselves laid too much stress upon the fact of their

[1] *Guide to the Church*, i. introd. xliv., 2nd edit., 1804. (The first edition was published in 1798.)
[2] *Id.*, i. 307.
[3] Charge to the archdeaconry of Cleveland, 1823.
[4] See, for instance, S. T. Coleridge, *On the Constitution of the Church and State, according to the Idea of each*, pp. 65, 126, 135, 136; H. J. Rose's sermon before the Suffolk Society, *The Churchman's Duty and Comfort in the Present Time*; *Life of Bishop Jebb*; A. Knox's *Remains, passim*; and, above all, the remarkable prophecy of Thomas Sikes, quoted in Dr. Pusey's *Letter to the Archbishop of Canterbury*, 1842, pp. 33, 34.
[5] *A Narrative of Events connected with the Publication of the Tracts for the Times*, introduction to the edition published in 1883, p. 39.

belonging to an established Church. The circumstances of the times tempted them to do so. When established institutions were being violently upset in neighbouring countries, it was natural that they should dwell upon the duty of maintaining in its integrity the great establishment of which they were officers; and hence the higher view of their office, though it was never ignored by them, was, as a rule, kept too much in the background. There is another kindred reason, which is so admirably stated by a thoughtful writer in 1841, that I cannot do better than quote his words. "The difference," he writes, "between the High Churchmen of the present day [that is, after the Oxford Movement] and their immediate predecessors, does not consist so much in the formal enunciation of doctrine, as in the fact that, just before our own day, those Church principles were only held negatively which now are put forward positively. Their abettors were then but too apt to use them for no purposes but defensive ones. Such negative and defensive views never could tell greatly on the public mind or produce influence on the heart."[1]

At any rate, be the cause what it may, it is to be feared that the very names of a number of Churchmen, who were not only men of the highest character and attainments, but also did practical work, the benefits of which the Church is reaping at the present day, are all but forgotten; and, in common gratitude, it should be one of the first duties of any historian of the Church of the period to bring such men prominently before his readers.

The year 1800 witnessed the death of one of the ablest and best among them. *William Jones, Vicar of Nayland* (1726–1800), never rose to a higher dignity than that of a country parson, but he was a man of greater eminence than most of the dignitaries of his time. He was the chaplain and devoted friend of Bishop Horne, who died in 1792, whose works he published, and whose biography he wrote. His influence was a little impaired by the fact that, like his patron, he adopted the views of the Hutchinsonians, who, among other things, attempted the hopeless task of upsetting the Newtonian philosophy. But these views, though eccentric and untenable, did not touch any vital point of the faith;

[1] *Christian Remembrancer*, preface to vol. ii., July—December, 1841.

they were, in fact, held by many of the soundest Churchmen of the day. Jones's own writings, with the exception of their Hutchinsonianism, are most valuable. With considerable power of humour, he defended the Church, not only in a very able way, but also in a way which caught the popular ear; and personally he was regarded as one of the chief leaders of the Orthodox party. Nayland Vicarage became a sort of rallying-point for them;[1] and their respect for its owner was unbounded. Both the life and writings of William Jones, of course, belong to the eighteenth, not to the nineteenth century; but it is necessary to notice him because, above all others, he gave the tone to the true High Churchmen of the later period. It is not without a feeling of righteous indignation that one hears of such a man being in indigent circumstances in his last years. His good friend and biographer, William Stevens, kindly came to the rescue, taking upon himself the expense of a curate for "the old boy," as Jones was familiarly called by his friends, and writing to the Archbishop of Canterbury on his behalf. Archbishop Moore responded nobly. He allowed Jones £100 a year out of his own pocket, and, with rare delicacy, obviated any feeling of dependence which the recipient might have entertained, by calling it "a sinecure." He was not, however, taxed for long. It was in 1798 that Mr. Stevens wrote to him, and on the Feast of the Epiphany, 1800, William Jones entered into his rest. Posterity has appreciated him better than his contemporaries did; his works are still regarded as classics in their way; at any rate, their reputation is greater than that of most of the works published during our period. The foremost prelate of the day, Dr. Horsley, paid a deserved tribute to William Jones's memory, describing him as "a faithful servant of God, of whom he could speak both from his personal knowledge and his writings.... He was," adds the bishop, "a man of quick penetration, of extensive learning, of the soundest piety, and had, beyond any other man I ever knew, the talent of writing upon the deepest subjects to the plainest understanding."[2]

---

[1] See Churton's *Memoir of Joshua Watson*, i. 28; Stevens's *Life of William Jones*; *Life of William Kirby*, by John Freeman, 36.

[2] See Horsley's Charges: *Second Charge of the Bishop of Rochester*, 1800.

The death of William Jones was a grievous loss to the High Churchmen, and there was no one who could exactly take his place. But he left behind him many friends—one might almost call them disciples—and these formed the nucleus of by far the most active section of the party during the whole of the period with which this work is concerned.

First and foremost among these was his biographer, editor, and one may really add, benefactor, *William Stevens* (1732–1807). Mr. Stevens never took holy orders, thinking that he could do the Church better service, and would be less suspected of interested motives, by continuing a layman. Like Mr. Jones and Bishop Horne (whose near kinsman he was), he was a Hutchinsonian; and he unfortunately devotes a considerable space in his "Life" of Jones to a defence of Hutchinsonianism—a subject which has ceased to have even an historical interest in the present day. He had, of course, nothing like the literary talent of his friend Mr. Jones, but it is wonderful, considering the little education which he enjoyed, how good a scholar and theologian he made himself. He was taken from school at the age of fourteen, and apprenticed to a hosier at 68, Old Broad Street, in the city of London, and here he found a home for the remainder of his life, being taken into partnership in 1754. It will, of course, be remembered that the social distinction between trades and professions was not so marked then as it is now; so there is nothing extraordinary in the fact of his mixing, though a tradesman, on terms of perfect equality with the clergy and the gentry. He continued "active in business" until 1801, within six years of his death; but this did not prevent him from being also "fervent in spirit, serving the Lord." Many of the agencies for good which employed the energies of the other High Churchmen who will come before us did not exist in Stevens's day; in fact, many of them arose, indirectly but very really, through his influence; but with such as did exist he identified himself thoroughly. He was an active supporter of the Societies for Promoting Christian Knowledge and for the Propagation of the Gospel, and treasurer of Queen Anne's Bounty— an office which naturally brought before him the poverty of the clergy, which he endeavoured to relieve privately in the most liberal yet most unostentatious way. The Clergy Orphan School was an object of his special support. He warmly advocated the claims of the Scotch Episcopal Church; in fact, he was always employing his pen, his tongue, and his purse in furthering Church work. A man of quaint humour, which was continually leaking out, he must have possessed a singularly attractive personality, and his great delight was to assemble his many friends around him in his own bachelor establishment. When the infirmities of age rendered this arrangement inconvenient to him, these friends determined to form a sort of club which should meet elsewhere, but of which he should be the chief; hence the formation of "Nobody's Club," or the club of "Nobody's Friends," in 1800. The origin of the name was this. William Stevens was wont to give familiar appellations to his friends, and he gave himself the name of "Nobody." At the solicitation of his friends, he collected, in 1777, his writings into one volume, which he styled Οὐδενὸς ἔργα, and by the appellation of "Nobody" he was ever afterwards known among his friends. Varying his language, he published a "Defence" of his friend Jones under the name of "Ain," the Hebrew for "nobody." The original members of the club of "Nobody's Friends" and their immediate successors were the backbone of the Orthodox party during the whole of our period, and the club still remains to keep fresh the memory of the good old Churchman who was the occasion of its foundation.[1]

If William Stevens's mantle can be said to have fallen upon any man, that man would certainly be *Joshua Watson* (1771-1855). There were some curious resemblances between the outer lives of the two men and their surroundings, which are well brought out by an intimate friend of both, Sir John Richardson, himself one of the Church worthies of the period. "It has often struck me," he writes, "that there was a remarkable, I might say a providential, similarity between the lives, the fortunes, and the characters of the bishop (Horne) and his cousin (William Stevens) on the one hand

---

[1] *Memoirs of the late William Stevens, Esq.*, by Sir James Allan Park. I have thought it well to quote the account of the name "Nobody" in the biographer's own words, because a slightly different account is given in the *Memoir of Joshua Watson*, i. 32, 33.

and the archdeacon (Watson) and his brother (Joshua Watson) on the other. In each case the first-named was destined to the clerical profession, and the last-named to mercantile life; they respectively left school at the same age, and became members, two of the University of Oxford, and two of mercantile counting-houses in London. The most unbroken friendship and the most confidential intercourse ever continued; and when the clerical students devoted themselves to the study of divinity, the mercantile assiduously imitated their example, and became not at all their inferiors in the soundness of their principles, or in their devoted attachment to our holy Church. The two mercantile men, having succeeded in their respective walks to the extent of their wishes, and realized competent fortunes, retired from their counting-houses; but, instead of giving themselves up to idle lives, or endeavouring to crown 'a life of labour with an age of ease,' continued ever after to devote all the energies of their minds, all their knowledge of business, and very large portions of their fortunes, towards the prosperity of every institution connected with the Church, and other portions equally large to acts of charity and kindness." [1]

But the points of difference between the two men were also very marked. The younger, though full of quiet humour, was a calm, staid, decorous man, with little of the quaintness —not to say eccentricity—which was characteristic of the elder. Though it was quite a mistake, one can understand one who did not know him well writing of Joshua Watson thus: "I remember so well, as a lad, case-hardening myself against the name of Joshua Watson, which I was continually hearing quoted as a final authority in all Church matters, and I pictured to myself a hard, dry, impenetrable man, who had no sympathies beyond a committee-room." [2] So far from being hard and dry, he was the most genial and lovable of men, with strong domestic affections, and an unusual number of attached friends whom he loved; but it is hardly an exaggeration to say that he was regarded as a final authority in all Church matters. His calm judgment, his absolutely settled convictions, which prevented him,

---

[1] See Churton's *Memoir of Joshua Watson*, i. 47.
[2] *Memoir of Joshua Watson*, ii. 308.

among other things, from being captivated by the Hutchinsonian theories, as many of his friends were; his clear head, not only for business, but also for literary matters and for theology, which caused Van Mildert, one of the best writers of the day, to consult him and to defer to his opinion in the matter of his very important writings, gave him an influence which has rarely if ever been attained in the Church by one in his position. In many respects he less resembles William Stevens than another no less devoted layman of a hundred years earlier. He might with some truth be termed the Robert Nelson of the nineteenth century. But the schemes which Robert Nelson only devised were, many of them, actually carried out, greatly through the influence of Joshua Watson. Happily, there was no such barrier to his practical usefulness as there was to that of Robert Nelson through the Nonjuring dispute. Had there been, Joshua Watson would probably have acted as Robert Nelson did; for he felt a deep interest in the earlier Nonjurors, and a strong sympathy with them.[1] On the other hand, Robert Nelson did useful work with his pen, while Joshua Watson's modesty prevented him from attempting much in that direction, though there is little doubt that he was quite competent to do it. This, however, is not the place to discuss historical parallels; let us be content with seeing what Joshua Watson was in himself. He belonged, as we have seen, to that great middle class which is the backbone of England, and was, in fact, himself engaged in business as a wine-merchant until he reached middle life. But in 1814 he determined to devote himself to the practical work of the Church, and for more than forty years was incessantly occupied in that work. There was no scheme of usefulness conducted on strictly Church principles, and scarcely any scheme in which he could join without sacrificing any of those principles, in which the name of Joshua Watson does not come prominently forward. He was one of the founders, and for many years the treasurer, of the National Society. He was also treasurer of the Society for Promoting Christian Knowledge, and took a leading part in the marvellous revival of the energies of that society which occurred in the early years of the nine-

[1] *Memoir*, ii. 292.

teenth century. He was treasurer of the Clergy Orphan School, which of all good projects was, perhaps, the one to which he was most attached. He was one of the chief agents in the foundation of the Church Building Society in 1817–18, for which, with the aid of his uncle, Archdeacon Daubeny, he drew up the first rules. The revived life in the Society for the Propagation of the Gospel and the rapid rise of the Colonial Church were greatly due to his efforts; and he was on terms of intimacy with almost all the then few colonial bishops. His munificence to these and other efforts of piety and benevolence was unbounded, and the moral weight of his character and his various talents, all devoted to the Church's service, were still greater helps.[1] He survived our period for more than twenty years, and there is a singular interest in the fact that in his old age he had many interviews at Brighton with Dr. Pusey, who afterwards wrote to him: "One had become so much the object of suspicion that I cannot say how cheering it was to be recognized by you as carrying on the same torch which we had received from yourself and from those of your generation, who had remained faithful to the old teaching. We seemed no longer separated by a chasm from the old times and the old paths, to which we wished to lead people back; the links which united us to those of old seemed to be restored. It seems hard to wish to keep you from a greater rest; yet I trust you will be for some time spared to us, finding rest in diffusing peace amidst our troubled waters, and a witness yet further to the principles you have brought down to us."[2] This was in 1843. Joshua Watson lived till 1855, and it is fair to add that he shared the alarm which, as we shall see, his friends felt at the later development of the Oxford school, and especially at the secession of Newman and others. But he greatly admired Newman's sermons, one volume of which is dedi-

---

[1] Perhaps one of the best instances of his clear-headedness may be found in his memorial to the Archbishop of Canterbury, Dr. Manners-Sutton, advising that the missionary work of the S.P.C.K. should be handed over to the S.P.G. This was done, with great benefit to both societies. Speaking of the committee meetings of the great Church societies, Archdeacon Pott declares that Joshua Watson was "a thousandfold the best adviser." See Churton, *Memoir of Joshua Watson*, i. 267.

[2] *Memoir*, ii. 83.

cated to him; and Keble's "Christian Year" was his constant solace and delight. Joshua Watson died at Clapton, where he had lived for a great part of his life;[1] and hence the little coterie of which he was the leading spirit was sometimes termed the "Clapton sect," with reference, no doubt, to another coterie of good men of a very different school of thought, the " Clapham sect."

John James Watson, his elder brother, who was for forty years Rector of Hackney, and for some time also Archdeacon of St. Albans and Vicar of Diggeswell, a small country living in Hertfordshire, did not come so much to the front in general Church work as the younger; partly because he was for many years an invalid, and partly for the excellent reason that his time was fully occupied in his own large parish; but he was an important member of the group. The two brothers always lived in perfect harmony, and saw very much of one another; in fact, Joshua Watson took up his abode at Clapton because his house was within five minutes' walk of Hackney Rectory. The archdeacon died at Hackney, in 1839, and the demonstrations of respect which were shown at his funeral prove that, though High Churchmanship was not then generally popular, it was no bar to a clergyman gaining the love of his people.

A far more prominent member of the little band was the archdeacon's brother-in law, *Henry Handley Norris* (1771-1850). Like the Watsons, he was the son of a London merchant, from whom, as well as from his grandfather, he inherited a competent fortune, which enabled him to carry out the noble purpose of devoting his whole life to the service of the Church without remuneration. He served for two years as assistant curate to the Rev. John Sawbridge, Vicar of Stretton, a notice of whose work will be found on another page, and in 1810 settled himself at South Hackney as a sort of perpetual curate to his brother-in-law, Archdeacon Watson, and there he continued, relieving the rector of the south part of his large parish for nearly forty years.[2] In 1816 the Bishop of

---
[1] For some years he shared a house with his friend, Van Mildert, in Park Street, Westminster, that he might be nearer to his work on the Church Commission. Here he lived for sixteen years (1823-1839).

[2] The living was subdivided in his time, and Mr. Norris became incumbent of the south part of it.

Llandaff (Dr. Herbert Marsh) offered him the first prebendal stall in his gift. Mr. Norris hesitated about accepting it; "for," he said, "when I take preferment I cease to be a volunteer in the service of the Church, and perhaps it is conducive to the effect of my service that I should not lose this character." But his friends very sensibly represented to him the other side of the question. He was already a great power in the Church, and it would seem that some foolish persons had actually objected that too much confidence was placed by men in high quarters in one who, after all, was only a subaltern; if he were a dignitary, however humble, he would put to silence such objections. So he accepted the prebend, which was of small value; and for the same reason, in 1825, he also accepted a non-residentiary stall in St. Paul's from Bishop Howley, because it would give him a standing in London, where most of his work lay. But when the Additional Curates Society was founded, in 1837, "I shall," he said, "return to the Church, in this her need, all that my two dignities have put into my pocket;" and he did so.

As Joshua Watson was the most prominent layman, so Henry Handley Norris was the most prominent clergyman, among the group of Churchmen now before us. The two worked shoulder to shoulder, and it is really difficult to say which of them was most influential. Norris was called "The Bishop-maker," because Prime Ministers were supposed to consult him frequently about episcopal appointments. Bishop Lloyd of Oxford went further, and was wont to address him as "The Patriarch," for "your care," he said, "of all the Churches is more than an archbishop's."[1] No man did a more varied amount of work than H. H. Norris. He was an active parish priest, and never rested until he had a handsome church built in his parish—an achievement far more difficult then than now; he was one of the three founders of the National Society, and its first honorary secretary; he took as regular and active a part in the working of all the other great Church societies as Joshua Watson himself did; he was the friend and correspondent of almost all the colonial bishops; having succeeded, at great expense, in conjunction with Joshua Watson, in rescuing the *British Critic* from what he deemed a not sufficiently

[1] *Memoir of Joshua Watson*, i. 279.

Church management, he took an active share in editing it, though he was not the actual editor,—the letters he received from Bishop Lloyd on the subject are a positive proof of this.[1] He projected, and gathered materials for much literary work; and it is a pity he did not carry it out, for his correspondence and other remains show that he had not only an original mind, but a good literary style; one work which he planned, on the decline and fall of the Nonjurors, would have been especially valuable. But when a man does so much, it is unreasonable to complain that he does not do more; and few men did more efficient service for the Church than H. H. Norris. He was of a more combative spirit than his brother-in-law, and we are not surprised to hear that the Hackney Dissenters liked the archdeacon better than they liked Mr. Norris,[2] who equally objected to Dissent and Romanism, and was in the habit of speaking out his mind with remarkable plainness. "I scarcely know," he said, "whether from popery or fanaticism we have at present [1824] most to fear; and I should not be surprised to see them confederate for the accomplishment of their purposes."[3] Bishop Jebb gives an interesting account of the impression which the Hackney phalanx,[4] and especially Mr. Norris, made upon him when he paid a visit to England in 1820: "With Mr. N—— I passed a day, and there met the editor of the *British Critic*,[5] and some other High Churchmen. Their minds are too controversially bent on one class of subjects, but some of them are amiable and estimable men. Mr. N—— I particularly like. He is a very munificent dispenser of a large private fortune, and has a disposition full of friendship." A few days later, writing to the same correspondent, he describes Mr. Norris more at length. "I like Mr. N——. He appears a most friendly and good-natured man. His notions, in High Churchmanship, are, perhaps, rather too rigid; but I think him a simple-

---

[1] See Churton's *Memoir of Joshua Watson*, i. 279–287.
[2] See *Religion in England*, 1800–1850, by John Stoughton, D.D., i. 100: "He [Norris] was not at all popular with the Hackney Dissenters."
[3] Letter to Archdeacon Daubeny, respecting his *Protestant's Companion*. See *Life of Daubeny*, prefixed to the third edition of his *Guide to the Church*, 1830.
[4] This, like "the Clapton sect," was a name given to the party because two of its chiefs lived at Hackney.
[5] Dr. Van Mildert.

hearted, right-forward man, without any by-end to serve, and without any other intention than that of supporting with all his power that which he thinks the cause of true religion. His private fortune is considerable, his Church preferment next to nothing, and he is princely in his contributions for good and useful purposes. As a specimen of the way in which he does things, I will just mention that, finding an able and industrious young clergyman in want of a library, he purchased for him a complete one, comprising the most expensive and valuable works in theology—the complete apparatus, in short, of a learned divine."[1] This is a wonderfully accurate portrait of the man, considering that it is drawn by a stranger; but it is somewhat curious to find one who is generally and rightly regarded as one of the chief precursors of the Oxford Movement alleging as his only complaint against Mr. Norris, that he was rather too High Church. Bishop Jebb, however, was a High Churchman of a different type from Mr. Norris; the one was an anticipation of the new school, the other a typical representative of the old.

Among those who threw themselves heart and soul into the general Church work of the Hackney phalanx was one whose name is in some respects more illustrious than that of any of the others. *Christopher Wordsworth* (1774–1846), as brother of the greatest living poet, as chaplain and confidential friend of the greatest ecclesiastical dignitary (Dr. Manners-Sutton, Archbishop of Canterbury), and then as head of the greatest college in England, could speak and act with an authority which his own personal character fully bore out. He had all the characteristic features of the Wordsworths, a rugged and manly independence joined with a guileless simplicity and disinterestedness, and a very extensive knowledge of divinity; a calm and judicial habit of mind joined with a courage and outspokenness which made him ever ready to combat error and defend truth; while his great experience of parish work both in town and country placed him more in sympathy with the working clergy than a mere college dignitary could be. Dr. Wordsworth had, in common with his son, the Bishop of Lincoln, the rare gift, art, or quality—one hardly knows what to call it—of expressing

[1] *Correspondence between Jebb and Knox*, ii. 438 and 443, 2nd edit., 1836.

with the utmost courtesy and yet with the utmost plainness his disagreement with what he regarded the mistakes of good men,—a task which requires much greater courage and tact than to rebuke the evil. It is rather difficult to put what is meant into words, but an instance or two will illustrate it. When he was asked to take part in the formation of the Colchester branch of the Bible Society, he was not content with simply declining, but entered fully into his reasons for doing so, without the slightest disguise and without the slightest discourtesy. He showed the same moral courage—for it *is* moral courage of the highest sort—when some papers to be put forth by the S.P.C.K. were submitted to him. In that rather peremptory tone, which is also a Wordsworth characteristic, he drew attention to " a species of phraseology almost new to the society, in which these papers somewhat largely indulge." "We have," he says, "'members of the Established Church,' 'well affected to Church and State,' 'the friends of the Church,' 'all friends of the Established Church,' and 'members of the Established Church,' again repeated. Now, I will venture to express myself freely. There is a great deal too much of all this. First, the habit of our society has been to act, and not to talk ; these professions are beneath its dignity. Its principles are well known, its character does not need these ostentatious testimonies. Pray let us continue, as much as may be, grave and sober, and catch as little as is possible of the character and temper of this pragmatical, factious, and professive age." And, after much more to the same effect, he concludes, "The subject is important, and ought not to be treated lightly."[1]

Dr. Wordsworth's services to the High Church party were, it seems to me, greater than appeared on the surface. In the first place, I have no doubt that he greatly influenced his patron, Archbishop Manners-Sutton, in this direction. Little circumstances, trifling in themselves, but all pointing to the same conclusion, show this. It was, for instance, confessedly through Dr. Wordsworth that the archbishop was led to place implicit confidence in Joshua Watson ; it was through Dr. Wordsworth that he went out of his way to preside over a meeting of the S.P.C.K. when a critical

[1] Quoted in Churton's *Memoir of Joshua Watson*, i. 130, 131.

question between the Orthodox and Evangelical members was to be discussed, and threw all the weight of his great authority into the Orthodox scale.

Again, when Wordsworth was appointed Master of Trinity, in 1820, Cambridge was, of all places, the one in which piety was most identified with Evangelicalism; and he set himself, with all the Wordsworth determination, to cultivate in his own college a spirit of piety of the Orthodox type, which might thence spread through the rest of the University. And once more, I have little doubt he influenced his brother, the poet, and, through him, numbers whom the mere ecclesiastic could never have reached. On the death of Bishop Middleton, the see of Calcutta was offered to him; but he declined it. He left his mark in many ways and in many places. It is to him that Joshua Watson gives the chief credit of setting on foot the system of district committees of the S.P.C.K., which was the main cause of the great advance made from about the year 1811 by that venerable society. It was he again, more than any one else, who brought about the custom of issuing Royal Letters, which for forty years drew large sums into the coffers of the great Church societies. It was he who was mainly instrumental in having four new districts formed and four new churches built in the great parish of Lambeth; and it was he who helped largely in transferring the India Fund of the S.P.C.K. to the S.P.G., to the great advantage of the work in India.

Another important though distant member of the group was *Charles Daubeny* (1745–1827), who, like the Watsons and Stevenses, was the son of a merchant, but of Bristol, not London. In the neighbourhood of Bristol he lived all his life with the exception of his Oxford career, and two years at Winchester when he was a Fellow. He then took the living of North Bradley, the value of which was £50 a year; but he had a private fortune, and, like H. H. Norris, he determined to serve the Church for nothing, or rather, less than nothing, for what he spent on North Bradley was far more than what he received from it. The restoration of the church and rebuilding of the vicarage cost him personally £3000. He built and endowed an "asylum" and a school in North Bradley, about 1810; and a "poor-house" for twelve persons, in 1818; and in 1824 a church at Road, an outlying part of North Bradley, which cost above £12,600, more than £4000 being given by himself; and at Bath he brought about the erection of the first free church in England,[1] where he officiated for fifteen years. The Bishop of Salisbury (Dr. Shute Barrington) was a great friend of Daubeny in his early ministerial life, and gave him a prebend in Salisbury Cathedral, saying, what he probably knew would be an inducement to him to accept it, "It is one of the least valuable of my prebends." In 1804 he was made Archdeacon of Sarum by Bishop Douglas, the successor of Bishop Barrington. He was an intimate friend of Joshua Watson, who married his niece. His services to the Church cause were chiefly exercised by his pen, which was a busy and effective one. His distance from London prevented him from taking a prominent personal part in the good works of which the metropolis was necessarily the centre; but it was a distinct advantage to the men of Hackney to have sympathizers like Daubeny in different parts of the country. Archdeacon Daubeny is said, like several other High Churchmen, to have been a Hutchinsonian; but his Hutchinsonianism does not appear prominently in his writings, which were among the most plain and direct expositions of Anglicanism, as opposed to Dissent of all sorts on the one hand, and Romanism on the other, that appeared during our period; so much so that he was sometimes humorously called, after the title of his most celebrated work, "The Guide to the Church."[2]

Another outpost of the Hackney phalanx was Guilsborough, a country living in Northants, held, for many years, by *Thomas Sikes* (1767–1834), who, although he lived there in great retirement, was, in his way, an important member of the group. He was the nephew of Daubeny and brother-in-law of the Watsons, and his views were in the main identical with theirs; but he seems to have realized more vividly than any of them the great defect of the Church of his day, viz. its tendency to stop short at the idea of a national establishment, or, at any rate, to bring too little into pro-

[1] See chapter on "Church Fabrics."
[2] See *Life of Charles Daubeny, Archdeacon of Sarum*, prefixed to the third edition of *The Guide to the Church*, by H. Daubeny, 1830, *passim*.

minence the idea of a spiritual society, of which establishment and endowment were, after all, only "accidents," and not even "inseparable accidents," to use the terms of logic. He was beyond question an "advanced Churchman," in the modern sense of the words, and, though his position would be perfectly intelligible now, it was not so then. "I propose," writes C. J. Blomfield, in 1823—that is, before his elevation to the episcopate—"going to see Mr. Sikes, brother-in-law of Joshua Watson. He is not in very good odour here, on account of his very High Church notions. He is called in this neighbourhood *The Pope.* I rather expect to find the Norrises there."[1] It has been suggested that these "very High Church notions" (they were not really higher than would be held by every one who called himself a High Churchman at all in the present day) arose partly from a reaction against the training he had received at St. Edmund Hall, then the head-quarters of the few Evangelicals at Oxford, and his very retired life did not render it at all necessary that he should tone them down. A remarkable prophecy is quoted by Dr. Pusey, in his "Letter to the Archbishop of Canterbury," in 1841, as having been uttered by Mr. Sikes, some years before the Oxford Movement began. It is too long to quote in full, especially as it probably does not give the *ipsissima verba* of the prophet; but the gist of it is that there was a universal want of definite teaching on the subject of the Holy Catholic Church, and that as soon as ever that article in the Creed should be brought prominently to the front, which he thought would not be in his own day, but very soon afterwards, the result would be at first endless misunderstanding, and one great outcry of "popery" from one end of the country to the other.[2] How soon and how

---

[1] *Memoir of Bishop Blomfield*, edited by G. A. Blomfield, 1813, i. 94.

[2] *Letter to the Archbishop of Canterbury on some Circumstances connected with the Present Crisis in the Church of England*, by E. B. Pusey, 1841. Archdeacon Churton thinks that Dr. Pusey wrote "from the memory of a narrator, who probably intended to relate the substance rather than the words, as the wisdom of his age seldom indulged in long speeches;" but he does not in the least impugn the substantial accuracy of Dr. Pusey; on the contrary, he confirms it. "He (Sikes) used sometimes to speak," he says, "in almost prophetic terms of the dangerous reaction which he anticipated, and which has since been too fully realized, from the kind of zeal and revenge with which men are impelled to contend for long-neglected truths."—*Memoir of Joshua Watson*, i. 51, 52.

literally this striking prediction was fulfilled, it is needless to say. Mr. Sikes himself lived just long enough to hear the first faint rumblings of the approaching storm, but was called to his rest some years before it burst out in all its fury, raising such a commotion as had not been felt since the time of the Reformation.

Least of all must we omit to give a prominent place among the Orthodox worthies of our period to *Hugh James Rose* (1795–1838). As he was only five years old at the beginning of the century, he may seem to belong to a later generation; but he came into note early, and, alas! was not spared to see more than the dawn of that later era which commenced with the Oxford Movement. Moreover, he was brought into very close relations with several of the older group of High Churchmen; he was the intimate friend and frequent correspondent of Joshua Watson; the assistant-curate at Lambeth of Christopher Wordsworth; the *spes gregis* of Van Mildert in his cherished scheme of a new University at Durham; and the *protégé* of two archbishops, who were, as we shall see, more than friendly to the cause. Hugh James Rose seems to me to have done more than any single man *before* 1833 to bring English Churchmen at large to a sense of what English Churchmanship is. His four sermons at Cambridge, in 1826, "On the Commission and Consequent Duties of the Clergy," and still more, the eight sermons delivered before the same University, in 1829, in his double capacity of Christian Advocate and Select Preacher, were perhaps the most rousing and widely influential of any preached during our period. Even to read them now in cold blood without being impressed is impossible; but to do so must be to gain a very feeble idea of the effect they produced. A striking presence, a peculiarly musical voice, and, above all, a certain attractiveness about the personality of the preacher, enhanced rather than diminished by his obvious ill health, lent a charm to them which cannot be reproduced in print.[1]

[1] See Burgon's *Twelve Good Men; The Restorer of the Old Paths;* also *Autobiographic Recollections of Professor George Pryme*, whose testimony is the more remarkable because his views would not altogether accord with those of Mr. Rose. He knew him well, and writes, "It is difficult to convey the full effect of his eloquence to those who never heard his sweet deep-toned voice, or saw his tall and dignified figure, his calm yet earnest manner," etc. (p. 173).

The "Clapton sect," or "Hackney phalanx" (for it was called by both names, from the residences of its lay and clerical chiefs respectively), was not wanting in what its principles would lead it to regard as of the first importance —episcopal sanction. The Archbishop of Canterbury, Dr. Manners-Sutton, was more than sympathetic; he was its warm supporter. He chose for his chaplains men who were either members of the group or in thorough sympathy with its objects. On more than one critical occasion he lent all the weight of his authority to it when it was opposed, and the party highly appreciated his aid. "Seldom," writes the biographer of Joshua Watson, "has any primate presided over the English Church whose personal dignity of character commanded so much deference;"[1] and when the archbishop died, in 1828, Joshua Watson himself bore warm testimony to the "extraordinary services he was graciously permitted to render to the Church of England."[2] His successor, Archbishop Howley, though, perhaps, less inclined to identify himself with the party, was distinctly favourable, and chose for his chaplain and confidential friend its most distinguished member, Hugh James Rose, who spoke in the most enthusiastic terms of the primate's merits. Then, again, they could not only claim the full sympathy of the ablest prelate of a past generation, Bishop Horsley, but also that of the two ablest prelates of their own day, Bishop Herbert Marsh and Bishop Van Mildert. Bishop Marsh was thoroughly at one with them, though he does not appear to have come much into personal contact with their leaders; but Bishop Van Mildert was actually one of the phalanx, having joined it long before he was raised to the bench, and keeping up his connection with it after he became a bishop. He was a member of Nobody's Club; editor for a short time of the *British Critic*, after it had become the property of Joshua Watson and H. H. Norris, in 1811;[3] and was one of the founders of the *Churchman's Remembrancer*,[4] which was published expressly to advocate Church principles; the intimate personal friend of almost all the leading members

---

[1] Churton, i. 254.   [2] *Id.*   [3] *Id.*, i. 96.
[4] This was not a Review, but a republication of Tracts, etc., as *The Scholar Armed* had been before it.

of the party; and, in fact, thoroughly identified himself with the movement in every way without reserve.

The same may be said of *Thomas Fanshawe Middleton* (1769-1823), Bishop of Calcutta, who was an intimate friend of the members of the Hackney phalanx, and also for a short time editor of the *British Critic*. Before his elevation to the episcopate, he was Rector of St. Pancras, and in that large and important London parish was a valuable factor in the High Church movement. Nor was it a disadvantage to the cause when he was appointed the first Bishop of Calcutta, in 1814; for the High Churchmen all took a deep interest in foreign mission work; and the appointment of a man who sympathized with them, and whose high reputation and moral courage enabled him to make his opinions felt in so important a centre, more than counterbalanced the loss which the party sustained by his removal from home. Another prelate who went heart and soul with the High Churchmen was Charles Lloyd, for a short time (1827-8) Bishop of Oxford. As Regius Professor of Divinity, he had been a worthy successor of Bishop Van Mildert, and his influence was not at all diminished by a rugged and rather eccentric humour, which was of a character to make him both popular and effective with the young men who were being prepared for holy orders. His premature death in 1828 was a great blow to the cause. There were several other English bishops, who, if they cannot be said to have completely identified themselves with the party, were yet more inclined to sympathize with it than with any other party in the Church. This was certainly the case with Dr. John Randolph, Bishop of Oxford until 1806, when he succeeded Dr. Beilby Porteus as Bishop of London ; his sympathy with the High Churchmen being emphasized by the fact that his predecessor in London had made a nearer approach to the Evangelicals than any other prelate had yet done. Dr. Pretyman, again (afterwards Tomline), whose episcopate, first at Lincoln and then at Winchester, extended over the whole of our period, was so far a High Churchman that his able theological works were more in harmony with the views of the Orthodox than with those of any other party in the Church ; Dr. Kaye, Bishop first of Bristol and then of Lincoln, did yeoman's service to the cause by the impetus he gave to the revival of patristic studies, while his own interesting Charges are of a distinctly Orthodox type; and towards the close of our period two bishops were appointed, Bishop Phillpotts to Exeter, Bishop Blomfield to London, the former of whom very decidedly, the latter more guardedly, showed at any rate great sympathy with the High Churchmen.

Besides these English bishops there were Bishops Mant and Jebb in Ireland, and Bishops Hobart, Inglis, and others in sister Churches across the seas, who were in full accord with the party.

Descending a step or two in the ecclesiastical ladder, we find Archdeacon (afterwards Dean) Lyall, Archdeacons Cambridge, Pott, and Baily, thoroughly identifying themselves with the principles and work of the Hackney phalanx; we have Dr. Routh, President of Magdalen, who threw the whole weight of his learning and reputation into the Orthodox cause, and, in words which are now historical, was "reserved to report to a forgetful generation the theology of the Fathers;"[1] we have Dr. (afterwards Archdeacon) D'Oyly, the biographer of Sancroft, and joint-editor of D'Oyly and Mant's Bible; we have Edward Churton, afterwards Archdeacon of Cleveland, to whom High Churchmen ought to be everlastingly grateful, because to him more than to any other man, living or dead, they owe that intimate knowledge of their predecessors supplied in the "Memoir of Joshua Watson;" we have the three Bowdlers, rather a confusing group for more reasons than one. First there was John Bowdler the elder, best known as the energetic advocate of the claims of the Episcopal Church in Scotland; then there was his son, Thomas Bowdler, writer of a memoir of his father, but better known for his meritorious though rather hazardous attempt to expurgate or "Bowdlerize" Shakespeare; and, finally, the ablest of the three, John Bowdler the younger, another son of the elder John, who became curiously mixed up with the Evangelical party, but who was from first to last a very pronounced and, indeed, advanced High Churchman. He never made the slightest

---

[1] J. H. Newman's dedication of his *Lectures on the Prophetical Office of the Church* (1837) to Dr. Routh.

secret of his opinions, and if he had not been prematurely cut off in, or rather before, his prime, he would probably have been one of the pioneers of the Oxford school. The same may be said of Thomas Rennell the younger, who also died very young, but not before he had made for himself a great reputation as scholar and divine; he was the son of Thomas Rennell, Dean of Winchester, who was also a High Churchman. The High Church party can claim two judges, Sir John Richardson and Sir James Allan Park; one of the most eminent naturalists of the day, the Rev. William Kirby; two very well-known authoresses, Mrs. Trimmer and Miss Agnes Strickland; almost all the Lake poets, who, to say the least, had very strong sympathy with them, while the most original, if the most faulty of all, S. T. Coleridge, shares with Alexander Knox the distinction of anticipating the Oxford Movement more than any other man. Of course, the list might be greatly extended, but it is already long enough to show, it is hoped, that the High Churchmen in the early years of this century formed no effete party, but one which was respectable even in point of numbers, and much more than respectable in point of intellectual attainments, moral earnestness, and spiritual activity.

And yet, in spite of this, it is perfectly true that with all their merits they did not exercise a wide, practical influence over the Church and nation at large. The views which they held about the Church were not held generally. Even many of those who valued most deeply the Church of England valued it chiefly as a great national institution, the preserver of order and decorum, and the home of culture. Inward spiritual religion was tacitly assumed by some, loudly proclaimed by others, to be the almost exclusive possession of quite another school of thought. To be "serious" meant to be a Low Churchman, not a High Churchman. When any one professed to be a High Churchman, and was also "an enthusiast," people did not know what to make of him. The following passage in Alexander Knox's "Remains" is almost startlingly true :—

"Those movements of piety, which belong to the mind and heart, have been rather suspected and discountenanced than explained or cultivated ; until, from its being caricatured by vulgar advocates, inward religion is little less than systematically exploded. It is in this spirit that the present champions for what they think High Church orthodoxy are combating their 'Evangelical' opponents. They involve in their attack all that is venerable and valuable, with that which is really exceptionable and justly to be resisted; and, in doing so, they preclude all aid to their cause, either from Divine grace or from human nature. Were these men acquainted with the chain of traditional truth, which Divine providence kept alive through the darkest ages, they would discover in the prayers which they continually read or hear the well-digested substance of that which, certainly in an ill-digested form, they combat and vilify. They would find, to their confusion, that Gregory, the chief author of those prayers, was what they in their ignorance would call a Methodist; that is, one who prized and cultivated and dwelt upon, in all his writings and discourses, those interior effects of Divine grace which designate their nature to the happy possessor, by a strength which no human effort could possess, and by a purity of which God only could be the Author. Until our Churchmen make this discovery, they will injure what they mean to defend."[1]

This would not fairly represent the attitude of such Churchmen as have come before us in this chapter; but it *did* represent only too faithfully the attitude of many, perhaps the majority, of those who passed under the name of High Churchmen. And the day for such a kind of Churchmanship was past. With an eye to this class, the same thoughtful writer says, with perfect truth, in 1816, "The old High Church race is worn out. The conscientious members are too generally under an opposite bias; and the majority are men of the world, if not men of yesterday; and therefore on every account caring for none of these things."[2] Two years earlier Dr. Copleston had made a very similar remark respecting the Oxford High Churchmen.[3] But Copleston was never in any sense really a High Churchman. Alexander Knox *was*,

---

[1] *Remains*, i. 65.   [2] *Id.*, i. 54.
[3] See *Memoir of Edward Copleston, Bishop of Llandaff*, by W. J. Copleston, ch. i.

though of a very different type from that of the Hackney phalanx. In his own day he was almost *sui generis;* but he was, far more distinctly, the precursor of the later High Churchmen trained under the Oxford Movement, than any of those already mentioned. As he very conveniently belonged to the sister Church of Ireland, I gladly seize upon the pretext thus offered for dwelling upon his position and that of his disciple, Bishop Jebb, in connection with that branch of the Church; for it would be really misleading to group them with the High Churchmen of an earlier date. Equally attached to the Church, they yet looked at it from a different standpoint; and if anywhere "coming events cast their shadows before," the shadows of what was coming from Oxford must be looked for in the writings of Knox and Jebb and S. T. Coleridge, rather than in those of any of the good men who have been described in this chapter. The latter were survivors of the old, the former antepasts of the new type of Churchmanship. The latter have fallen more or less into oblivion; the former come before us with an ever-fresh interest. They were never thoroughly understood in their own day; but, studied in the light of after-events, they have all the interest which attaches to prophets. It would, however, be out of place to treat of them here, when the history of the men of the time, rather than of those who anticipated a future time, is the subject before us.

To those who take an interest in the careers and work of the good men who represented the best side of High Churchmanship in the early part of this century, there is something very sad in that chapter in Mr. T. Mozley's "Reminiscences," entitled "Norris of Hackney."[1] It describes a meeting of the S.P.C.K. about the appointment of a new committee, in which Norris's party was beaten, and it speaks of him as "a dethroned potentate." This was just after "The Tracts for the Times" had appeared, and it was undoubtedly the beginning of a new era, in which High Churchmanship, though, of course, in essentials the same, was entering upon a new phase, in which it gained a hold upon the Church and nation

[1] *Reminiscences, chiefly of Oriel College and the Oxford Movement,* by the Rev. T. Mozley, vol. i. ch. liii.

which, under the phase we have been regarding it in this chapter, it never had gained. But men like Norris, and the Watsons, and Wordsworth, and Daubeny, and Van Mildert, did noble work in their day; and any record of the Church of England in the nineteenth century would be most imperfect if it failed to give a full recognition to that work.

CHAPTER III.

THE EVANGELICALS.

REGARDED purely as a spiritual force, the Evangelicals were undoubtedly the strongest party in the Church during the first thirty years of the nineteenth century. So much was this the case, that spiritual earnestness was in itself a presumption that a man was an Evangelical; and some were placed in that category simply because they were spiritually minded, though in point of fact they were out of sympathy with many of the distinctive tenets of Evangelicalism.

When the nineteenth century opened, the fathers of the Evangelical Revival were fast passing away. Henry Venn, Joseph Milner, William Romaine, John Thornton, John Berridge, and John Wesley, had all been called to their rest in the last decade of the eighteenth century, while William Cowper had just lived to see the dawn of the nineteenth. Those who still survived were regarded with the veneration which is naturally felt for men who have borne the burden and heat of the day, and left the fruits of their labours to be reaped by a new generation. John Newton was still at St. Mary Woolnoth, where he was consulted as a sort of oracle, holding meetings of what he used to call, with characteristic quaintness, "parsons, parsonets, and parsonettas."[1] Richard Cecil was still at St. John's, Bedford Row; Thomas Scott also was still in London, though he soon removed to Aston Sandford; and Thomas Robinson was still at Leicester. There were some who were connecting links between the first and second generations of Evangelicals. Thomas Scott was one of them; and still more markedly Isaac Milner,

[1] But there are painful evidences that he stayed on too long, and that it would have been much better if he had retired.

William Wilberforce, and Hannah More. As far as date goes, this would also apply to Charles Simeon, who was the exact contemporary of Wilberforce; but as his work was more connected with the Evangelicalism of the nineteenth than with that of the eighteenth century, he must occupy the very foremost place in the present sketch.

Charles Simeon (1759–1836) was in some respects an instance of what has been remarked above, viz. that pious men naturally gravitated to that party which was, more than any other, identified with the spirit of piety; for it is curious to notice, in his own account of his spiritual development, how he derived his first serious impressions from sources which were not Evangelical, in the technical sense of that term. He was first aroused from religious indifference by being told that, as an undergraduate at King's College, Cambridge, in 1779, "he *must* attend the Lord's Supper." "I thought," he says, "Satan himself was as fit to attend as I; and that if I *must* attend, I *must* prepare for my attendance there. Without a moment's loss of time, I bought the old 'Whole Duty of Man,' and began to read it with great diligence; at the same time calling my ways to remembrance, and crying to God for mercy. . . . From that time to this, thank God, I have never ceased to regard the salvation of my soul as the one thing needful." "The Whole Duty of Man" was, from the time of the Restoration onward, the most valued book among High Churchmen next to the Bible and the Prayer-book; but among the Evangelicals it was considered much too legal and unspiritual, one of their leaders publishing a book with a similar title, expressly to correct its errors and supplement its defects.[1] Then Simeon became a member of the S.P.C.K, because he thought their books would be the most useful he could procure, and that he might do good to others by the circulation of them. The venerable society was, of course, much more in favour with High Churchmen than with Low Churchmen, but there is not a word to show that he was dissatisfied with it. "The first book," he proceeds, "I got to instruct me in reference to the Lord's Supper was Kettlewell on the Sacrament; but I remember that it required of me more than I could

---

[1] *The Complete Duty of Man*, by Henry Venn.

bear, therefore I procured Bishop Wilson, which seemed to
be more moderate in its requirements." John Kettlewell
and Bishop Wilson were both High Churchmen, but
Simeon took no exception against either of them on that
ground. On the contrary, he goes on: "In Passion Week,
as I was reading Bishop Wilson on the Lord's Supper, I
met with an expression to this effect: 'That the Jews knew
what they did when they transferred their sin to the head
of their offering.' The thought rushed into my mind—
What! may I transfer all my guilt to another? . . . Then,
God willing, I will not bear my sins on my own soul one
moment longer. Accordingly, I sought to lay my sins upon
the sacred head of Jesus, and on the Wednesday began to
have a hope of mercy; on the Thursday that hope increased;
on the Friday and Saturday it became more strong; and on
the Sunday morning (Easter Day, April 4) I awoke early
with these words upon my heart and lips, 'Jesus Christ is
risen to-day, Hallelujah!' and at the Lord's Table in our
chapel I had the sweetest access to God through my blessed
Saviour."[1] During the vacation he "attended regularly the
parish church at Reading," and there he "used to find sweet
seasons of refreshment and comfort," not, so far as he informs
us, from the sermons of the preacher, Mr. Cadogan, a leading
Evangelical, but "in the stated prayers." We next find him
reading James Hervey, the most popular devotional writer
among the Evangelicals; but he was "much perplexed about
saving faith," so he borrowed "Archbishop Sharp's third
volume, containing his casuistical sermons;" and "these,"
he says, "I read with great profit. They showed me that
Hervey's view of saving faith was erroneous; and from that
day to this I have never had a doubt on the subject."[2] Sharp
was one of the very best of the High Churchmen in Queen
Anne's days. All this looks like the experience of a High
Churchman in embryo. After his ordination, in 1782, he was
introduced to John Venn; and "here," he says, "I found a
man after my own heart." John Venn took him over to
Yelling, and introduced him to "his own dear and honoured
father, Henry Venn;" and "oh," he exclaims, "what an

[1] Carus' *Life of Simeon*, pp. 14-16.
[2] Quoted in Carus' *Life*, p. 20.

acquisition was this! In this aged minister I found a father, an instructor, and a most bright example; and I shall have reason to adore my God to all eternity for the benefit of his acquaintance." The meeting between Henry Venn and Charles Simeon, the Evangelical of the generation that was passing away and the Evangelical of the generation that was coming on, would form a good subject for a picture. But it was not by the Venns nor by any human being that Simeon's spiritual character was formed; that had taken place before. "God, no doubt for wise and gracious reasons, had kept far from me all spiritual acquaintance; by which means He made it appear the more clearly that the work in me was 'not of man or by man,' but of God alone."[1]

How he undertook the charge of Trinity Church, a college living, at a merely nominal stipend; how he was opposed by churchwardens, parishioners, and afternoon lecturers; in what a Christian spirit he bore it all, keeping constantly before him and frequently quoting the text, "The servant of the Lord must not strive;" how, after twelve weary years, he lived down all opposition; how he began to attract gownsmen as well as townsmen to his church, and exerted a religious influence over the former such as had never been exercised by any clergyman for many a long year;[2]—all this belongs to the history of the eighteenth century. At the commencement of the nineteenth he had firmly established himself as a real power in the University—a power which continually increased until his death, thirty-six years later. His success is a striking proof that pure goodness must tell in the long run. For he had other difficulties to contend with besides those which "a Methodist"—and especially a Methodist in a University town—must have necessarily found. We have manifold evidence from those who knew him there in his early days that many little points in his own character were against him. Canon Carus quotes Mr. J. J. Gurney's im-

[1] Carus, p. 26.
[2] Bishop Charles Wordsworth is of opinion that Simeon "had a much larger following of young men than Newman, and for a much longer time." This will probably be disputed by many, but the sentence which precedes it is indisputable: "It is a great mistake to suppose Simeon was careless about Church ordinances."
—*Annals of my Early Life* (1806-1846), by Bishop Charles Wordsworth.

pressions: "Like many other good and devout men, he was not without his superficial imperfections; slight symptoms of irritability, great particularity about a variety of little matters. His manners, though invariably refined and courteous, were sometimes so ardent and grotesque as to excite in those whom he was addressing an almost irresistible propensity to laugh."[1] But others use far stronger language than this. "Simeon," writes Mr. Jerram, who knew him in the later years of the eighteenth century, "was naturally of a haughty, impatient, impetuous temper, and over-punctilious of what he conceived to belong to the address and manners of a gentleman. He sometimes gave offence by imperiousness. His besetting sin was pride; he was sensitive and excitable, and in his earlier career imprudent."[2] Mr. Dykes, who knew him a little earlier, was still more struck by the drawbacks to his success. "Among his [Dykes'] first and best friends was Charles Simeon. This extraordinary man— extraordinary in his appearance, his manner, his piety, his zeal, and his success—was at first deemed by Mr. Dykes (a shrewd observer) one of the most unlikely persons to become extensively useful he had ever known. He had much zeal, but not according to knowledge; preached the most crude and undigested discourses, abounding in incorrect statements, and in allusions offensive to good taste. There was an apparent affectation of manner, a fastidiousness about personal appearance, an egotism and a self-importance which seemed likely to bear down the piety of his spirit, or at least to neutralize any good effect which might be produced by his ministry, especially among persons trained to academic modes of thinking."[3] The letters quoted by Simeon's latest biographer from those wary veterans of Evangelicism, John Thornton and John Newton, addressed to their young brother in the first fervour of his ministerial life, bear out, when we read between the lines, these descriptions.[4] But Simeon toned down with years, and being not only a devoted Christian, but also a thorough gentleman, was able to make

[1] Carus, p. 479.
[2] *Memoirs of the Rev. Charles Jerram*, by the Rev. James Jerram.
[3] *Memoir of the Rev. T. Dykes*, by the Rev. J. King, pp. 8, 9.
[4] See the Rev. J. C. Moule's *Simeon* (English Religious Leaders Series), pp. 40–42.

a mark upon the fresh young life of piously disposed undergraduates such as few clergymen have made before or since. He himself notices, with a surprise which we cannot share, the ever-growing number of gownsmen who flocked to his church, attended his "conversation parties," and submitted themselves to his counsel. Nor did his influence over them cease when they had taken their degrees. He found for them curacies with kindred spirits or Indian chaplaincies, corresponded with them frequently, kindling their zeal, but checking their indiscretions in the kindliest and quaintest fashion. An enthusiastic Churchman himself, he kept them firm in their allegiance to their spiritual mother; and we may well understand how true is the remark of one of his most distinguished disciples, that "his enlightened and firm attachment to the Church of England added, in a degree it is difficult to measure, to his weight of character in the country."[1] In fact, his prominent Churchmanship caused a slight dissatisfaction to some of his followers. It was said, we are told, in the religious periodicals of the day, "Mr. Simeon is more of a *Churchman* than a *Gospel-man*."[2] He was wont to say, "The Bible first, the Prayer-book next, and all other books and doings in subordination to both."[3] One marked feature in Simeon's character, which is not found in some reformers, was his uniform respect for dignitaries. In fact, he may almost be said to have been a martyr to the feeling; for it was a visit to Ely to pay his respects to the new bishop that was the cause of his death. "If," he said, "this is to be the closing scene, I shall not at all regret my journey to the bishop; it was of vast importance to you all, and I shall be glad to close my life from such a circumstance." Long before his death he had become universally respected at Cambridge; and when the end came, the whole University felt that it had sustained an irreparable loss. How

---

[1] *Recollections of Simeon*, by Daniel Wilson, Bishop of Calcutta, appended to Carus' *Life*, p. 597.

[2] *Recollections of the Conversation Parties of the Rev. C. Simeon*, by Abner W. Brown, Introduction, p. 11. This is an extremely well-written and interesting book. Canon Abner Brown saw more of Simeon than most undergraduates did, because he was at Cambridge during the vacations as well as term-time from 1827 to 1830.

[3] *Id.*, p. 12.

could it be otherwise in any place where all appreciation of pure, unselfish goodness was not entirely lost? For, again to quote Bishop Daniel Wilson, "Here is a man who labours for nothing, for absolutely no emolument whatever, for more than half a century. Here is a man who passes by and refuses all the livings in his college which in succession were offered to his choice, and some of which every other person almost that could be named would have accepted as a matter of course. Here is a man who, in order to retain his Fellowship and his moneyless station at Trinity Church, persuades his elder brother not to leave him the property which would compel him to vacate it." And all this simply for the sake of doing good in a place where reform was sorely needed.

Those who have any idea at all of what Cambridge was before Simeon tried to infuse a really religious element into it, will indeed be slow to condemn or even to depreciate his efforts. At the same time, it is only fair to remember that there is no need to go beyond Simeon's own words to learn that there was a weak as well as a strong side to his influence. He evidently raised a spirit which he could not lay, and was at times perplexed and dismayed at what he had done. The following account which he gives of his prayer-meetings speaks for itself. In 1812 (that is, after he had been at Trinity Church nearly thirty years) he writes thus about a complaint from the parishioners to the bishop: "One of the malcontents, knowing that the prayer-meeting among my people was still kept up, had declared publicly that he would inform against it. Now, though I did not attend it, the obloquy would all fall on me; it would be in vain for me to say that I had repeatedly testified my disapprobation of it on account of the evil effects that I had seen arising from it, or that I had laboured very earnestly to prevail on my people to lay it aside; it would have been sufficient for my enemies to say that I had once countenanced it; nor would they have believed that my influence among my people was insufficient to put it down; the matter would have been brought before the public, all manner of odium would have been cast upon me and my ministry; and the bishop would have put an end to my evening lectures, if not have removed me from the church which I hold only during his pleasure. . . . I told them that I had long seen and lamented the state of mind to which many of them had been brought by means of that room; for instead of merely reading the Scriptures and praying, they had become expounders of Scriptures and preachers; and instead of confining the assembly to those who had been invited to my societies, they had extended it to others, and made the place really and truly a conventicle in the eye of the law; and instead of retaining their original simplicity, many of them were filled with a high conceit of their attainments and with a contempt for their authorized instructors." He told them that they must meet in smaller numbers, but they would not consent; they said he was giving way to the fear of man and dissembling with God; God had commanded His people not to neglect the assembling themselves together, and they would do it in spite of him.[1]

After this painful account, it is difficult to follow Mr. Simeon in what he immediately adds: "What, after all this experience, is my judgment in relation to private societies? My judgment most decidedly is that without them, where they can be had, a people will never be kept together; nor will they ever feel related to their minister as to a parent." Nor is the difficulty at all diminished by what he writes to his valued friend Mr. Thomason shortly after, in the same year: "I found that five of them [the young men in his societies] were still in the toils of Mr. ———, who is indefatigable in his exertions to pervert and embitter their minds. . . . There is such a self-sufficiency in Mr. ———, and such an obstinacy in Mr. ———, and such a rooted determination in both to make divisions in the Church, that there never can be union amongst us again till God shall be pleased either to change their dispositions, or to separate them from us."[2] It is fair to add that, six years later (1818), he writes to the same correspondent: "Those who greatly disturbed and distressed me are gone, and my Church is sweetly harmonious."[3]

But his private societies were not his only difficulty. We have his own word for it that he sometimes involved himself in great embarrassment with regard to the young men who were being trained, or who had been trained, at Cambridge for the ministry under his auspices. He writes to Wilber-

[1] Carus, pp. 238-240.   [2] *Id.*, p. 247.   [3] *Id.*, p. 346.

force in 1814, complaining that many used his name whom he did not sanction, and then adds, 'The truth is, that young men act very imprudently, and in a *very bad spirit*, and compel the bishops to proceed against them, and then they call it persecution ; and having destroyed their character among all who know them, they use my name as a passport. This must be checked, and I feel the more need to check it, because I feel more than ever the necessity of being *sober-minded.*"[1] His correspondence is full of such "checks," or, to use a more significant term, "snubs" to young men. "Why," he asks one, "should you stand out about the hymns? You are very injudicious in this. You should consider that, when a storm is raised, you are not the only sufferer. Pray study to maintain peace, though you make some sacrifices for it. I stated that your pamphlet was 'somewhat objectionable ; ' but, if I had not been afraid of wounding your feelings, I should have said '*very* objectionable ; '" and then he gives the young clergyman some excellent advice.[2] To an undergraduate he writes, "It is evident that you have been in the habit of writing in the books of the College Library. This, not to speak of the presumption, is a most flagrant breach of confidence, and deserves the most serious reprehension. . . . You are not at all aware how contrary your conduct in this matter has been to the modesty that becomes a young man, and a religious professor in particular."[3] To a curate who had been requested by his incumbent to leave him: "As an abstract question, I think that for a man professing piety to force himself upon his principal against his will is no very Christian act. There are a set of people in the Church who would recommend and encourage such a step ; but they are not the most humble and modest in our flock."[4] To another: "I know you will forgive me, if I say that the very account you give of yourself, in relation to controversy, is a dissuasive from embarking in it."[5] And so one might go on ; but it will be sufficient to quote a passage from his own "Inward Experience," which shows, not only his particular attitude towards individuals, but his general impressions : "My joys are tempered with contrition, and confidence with fear and

[1] Carus, p. 283.   [2] Moule, pp. 182, 183.   [3] *Id.*, p. 185.
[4] *Id.*, p. 188.   [5] Carus, p. 445.

shame. I consider the religion of the day as materially defective in this point; and the preaching of pious ministers defective also. I do not see, so much as I could wish, an holy, reverential awe of God. The confidence that is generally expressed does not sufficiently, in my opinion, savour of a creature-like spirit, or of a sinner-like spirit."[1]

Simeon himself was absolutely free from the spirit which in the above passage he so properly condemns, and the counsel he gives to those whom he thought possessed by it is uniformly excellent; but one cannot add with confidence that the course he pursued did not tend to produce it. It is not an unmixed advantage to gather, at a place like Cambridge, young men into cliques, which from the nature of the case keep them more or less aloof from the general life of the University; still less so, when they come to fancy that the reason why they hold aloof is because *they* are the pious ones, while all the world around them lieth in wickedness. It is no use disguising the fact that outside their own circle the "Simeonites," or "Sims," were looked down upon; and the mischievous result was that many who regarded piety and Simeonism as synonymous terms were repelled from religion altogether.[2]

But in spite of these drawbacks Simeon's work at Cambridge was a noble work; it influenced for good not only the many who came into contact with him, but, through them, untold numbers. The spiritual father of such men as Henry Martyn, Daniel Wilson, Venn Elliott, etc., would indirectly affect thousands whom he never saw or heard of. "As for Simeon," writes one, whose testimony is all the more significant because, personally, he had not the slightest

---

[1] Carus, p. 364.

[2] "At that time" (about 1808-10), writes the biographer of Professor Scholefield, "there was a sort of stigma attached to frequenting Trinity Church, and he had not overcome the feeling of shame at being seen to enter it, and used to look every way before he ventured to pass the gate. This feeling was far from being uncommon with many who really valued Mr. Simeon's ministry." Of a few years later (about 1816), when Scholefield was Simeon's curate, a Mr. Chatfield, Scholefield's first pupil, writes, "He used to take me with him to dear old Simeon's church; and often, as we walked with him thither, we heard the coarse abuse he met with from the idle undergraduates, who rejoiced in nothing more than hooting at Simeon and his curate."—*Memoir of Professor James Scholefield*, by his widow, pp. 18, 19, 27.

sympathy with Simeon's views, "if you knew what his authority and influence were, and how they extended from Cambridge to the most remote corners of England, you would allow that his real sway over the Church was far greater than that of any primate."[1] As to his personal character, we may echo the words of one who was no more a disciple of Simeon than was Macaulay himself, and say that he deserved to be called "St. Charles of Cambridge."[2]

Cambridge was a great centre of Evangelicalism. It was the home of the men who formed the intellectual backbone —always rather weak—of the system. First and foremost amongst these men stands the burly figure of "the Dean," as he was called *par excellence*—*Isaac Milner* (1750–1820), who divided his time between Carlisle and Cambridge, being dean of the former, and president of Queen's College in the latter.[3] Isaac Milner was a sort of Evangelical Dr. Johnson, whose mind, like his body, was massive and powerful, and who also, like the doctor, concealed under a rough exterior a singularly warm and tender heart. He had been in the confidence of all the great men of the first generation of Evangelicals, and was naturally regarded as a tower of strength to their cause by the men of the second generation; a sort of *Deus ex machinâ*, to be summoned when any *dignus vindice nodus* occurred. Full of *bonhomie*, an admirable conversationalist (again like Dr. Johnson), "in wit a man, simplicity a child," an Evangelical of Evangelicals, but withal a man of the world, in the good sense of the term, he was in some respects the most striking of all the figures in the Evangelical group. He was regarded by some as an indolent man; and the fact that he did not write very much, or take any prominent part in the many works of piety and benevolence which were originated and carried out by the Evangelical school, lent colour to the charge. But he was ready to come to the front when any great occasion required it, and could do battle when a foeman worthy of his steel—such as Dr. Herbert Marsh—appeared on the field; and during his

---

[1] Lord Macaulay, quoted in Sir G. Trevelyan's *Life*, i. 67, note.
[2] Sir James Stephen, *Essays on Ecclesiastical Biography*, ii. 375.
[3] For an account of Isaac Milner's early life, see the chapter on "The Evangelical Revival" in *The English Church in the Eighteenth Century*.

residence he preached regularly and with tremendous effect in Carlisle Cathedral. Grotesque as it may sound, I believe it is true, that this great, strong man—strong in every sense—the only dignitary and the acknowledged intellectual Coryphæus of the party, was deterred by nervousness rather than indolence from taking a more active part in its work. In a letter, written in 1813, to the Bishop of Carlisle (Dr. Goodenough), with whom he was on the most intimate terms, though the two did not agree on all points of theology, he describes his feelings in reference to his controversy with Dr. Marsh : "Your lordship admires my nerves. I will tell you how that is. With great appearance of strength, I am as poor a nervous being as ever existed ; and were I to ruminate on contentious matters, I might bid adieu to sleep and appetite. But the fact is, I endeavour to form my resolution as carefully and on as good grounds as I can, and when that is formed, I go straight forward without talking to any one about it. It is the talking to busybodies and the listening to tittle-tattle of all sorts that keeps the mind in a perpetual heat and fret. Never before in my life was I in a controversy, except the petty business with Dr. Haweis ; and I have been remarkably slow to enter this."[1] To this another reason may be added—an extreme dislike which this hearty, genial man had to be at enmity with any. "I abominate," he said, "fendings and provings—they make me miserable ; so does the least alienation of mind in the case of those with whom I am anxious to stand well."[2] Alas! when one excepts all the controversial divinity which comes under these heads, how much remains?

The fact that Isaac Milner was president, of course attracted to Queen's College numbers of the young men who were sent to the University wholly or partly by the help of such societies as the Elland, Dunham, etc. ; but I doubt whether Sir James Stephen is quite accurate when he says that "under the shelter of his [Dean Milner's] name his college flourished as the best cultured and most fruitful nursery of Evangelicals."[3] The description would apply at

---

[1] *Life of Isaac Milner*, by Mary Milner, p. 328.
[2] *Id.*, p. 324.
[3] *Essays on Ecclesiastical Biography* : "The Evangelical Succession."

least as well to Magdalen College, where many Evangelicals who afterwards came to the front were educated.[1] Of one of them, Thomas Dykes, of Hull, his biographer tells us that, "after taking advice of Joseph Milner, he went (1786) to Magdalen College, Cambridge, which was then the general resort of young men seriously impressed with a sense of religion."[2] A leading Evangelical, *William Farish* (1759–1837), was tutor of Magdalen and Jacksonian Professor of Chemistry. Professor Farish had almost as high a reputation for abilities and attainments as Dean Milner himself. Both had been senior wranglers, and both continued their mathematical and other intellectual pursuits all through their lives; and, curiously enough, both were connected with Carlisle—Milner as dean, and Farish because it was his native place. He was son of the Rev. James Farish, lecturer at the cathedral, and was born in the prebendal house just opposite the deanery. He received the whole of his education at Carlisle until he went to Cambridge, in 1765; and there he remained until his death, that is, for more than sixty years. The mere fact of his long residence in the University gave him great weight there: for he did not, as some resident Fellows did, sink into a mere vegetable; on the contrary, the older he grew the more active he seems to have become. Next to Simeon—*longo sed proximus intervallo* —he perhaps exercised more influence than any man over the evangelically disposed undergraduates. Milner was a sort of Grand Llama at Queen's, ruling the college strictly, but, from the nature of his position, being brought into comparatively little contact with the young men; but Farish was their guide, philosopher, and friend. Like Simeon, he took the charge of a parish in Cambridge, being Vicar of St. Giles'. In this he worked on the same lines as Simeon, and with almost equal success. "Professor Farish," writes Simeon

---

[1] Mr. Henry Gunning, in his *Reminiscences of Cambridge*, groups the two colleges together in a passage in which he pays "the Dean" rather a doubtful compliment: "Among the moderators and examiners of that day Milner had, and continued to have during many years, a prodigious influence, and was frequently called upon to settle the places of men in the higher brackets. . . . *Except when a man of his own college or Magdalen was concerned* (!), I do not recollect to have heard any well-founded charge of partiality brought against him" (pp. 92, 93).

[2] *Memoir of the Rev. Thomas Dykes*, by the Rev. John King, p. 6.

to Thomason in 1817, "is doing great things. He has built two schoolrooms, one for four hundred boys, and another for three hundred girls; and is now enlarging his church, so that it will seat as many as mine."[1] Simeon had a great respect for Farish, and submitted his compositions on critical occasions to the professor's judgment.[2] Like Simeon, Farish had some of those little peculiarities which men who pass all their lives in college are apt to contract. "He was," writes the biographer of his pupil, Thomas Dykes, "a man of singular simplicity of manners, often of ludicrous absence of mind, but of astonishing mathematical powers, joined with a benevolence of heart which won the esteem and confidence of all, and a fervour of piety which glowed more brightly as he advanced in age."[3] Like many men who are conspicuous for their modesty and simplicity, Professor Farish was firm as a rock when he thought principles were at stake, and manfully supported the promoters of the Church Missionary and Bible Societies at Cambridge when both were unpopular, and when some who were friends to them at heart hung back. He was a thorough partisan, but a most amiable and large-hearted one, and his schemes for doing good were by no means confined to those which belonged exclusively to the Evangelical school. Perhaps his most active exertions were in behalf of the education of the poor. Such a man was a tower of strength to the Evangelical cause, not only in Cambridge, but in all parts of the world where his Cambridge disciples were scattered abroad; and we may fitly conclude this notice of the good man by a quotation from a sermon preached by a Cambridge clergyman in a Cambridge church on the occasion of his death: "The children taught through the late Professor Farish's influence; the young men encouraged to go forth to arduous labours and services, notwithstanding misgivings and difficulties; those whose path has been cleared by his counsel, and whose hands have been strengthened by his interposition, and whose faith and charity have been enlivened by his example and his patience,—have already borne testimony that he was a good man, and full of the Holy Ghost; while the beneficial effect of his labours, his

---

[1] Carus, p. 329.   [2] *Id.*, p. 201.
[3] *Memoir of Dykes*, by King, p. 6.

counsel, his prayers, is doubtless far greater than we can estimate."[1]

Several other Cambridge residents of high standing in the University threw themselves heart and soul into the Evangelical cause. Among these may be mentioned Thomas Thomason, Simeon's curate and lifelong friend, who entered at Magdalen in 1792, was fifth wrangler in 1796, and was then elected Fellow of Queen's, where he was for some years a college tutor, being also curate to Simeon; he is best known for his noble work in the mission-field, but his earlier work at Cambridge as a pillar of the Evangelical cause must not be forgotten. Another eminent resident who thoroughly identified himself with the Evangelicals, and was a power at Cambridge both among graduates and undergraduates, was *James Scholefield* (1789–1853). He was ordained in 1812, before he took his degree, as assistant curate to Simeon at Trinity Church, and in 1815 was elected Fellow of Trinity College. In 1823 he became Incumbent of St. Michael's, and in 1825 Regius Professor of Greek. Though a more formidable and less accessible man than Simeon or Farish, he attracted, like them, gownsmen to his church, where he presented to them, more than either of the other two, the intellectual side of Christianity, in a manner "calculated," says a reviewer of his life, "to arrest and keep the attention of a cultivated mind. In a congregation composed so largely of intelligent young men, the rising hopes of our Church, who were preparing for future usefulness, he occupied a position the most interesting and important to which an able minister of the New Testament can be called. He thus fell into the very niche of the temple which, by his piety, learning, and eloquence, he was best fitted to occupy."[2] The two Jowetts, *Joseph Jowett* (1752–1813) and his nephew *William Jowett* (1787–1855), were also leaders of the Evangelicals at Cam-

---

[1] Sermon preached at St. Botolph's, Cambridge, January 22, 1837, on occasion of the death of the late Rev. William Farish, B.D., Rector of Stonham Parva, Suffolk, Vicar of St. Giles', Cambridge, and Jacksonian Professor of Chemistry in that University. By Thomas Webster, B.D., rector.

Professor Farish accepted the little living of Stonham shortly before his death, and retired and died there.

[2] *Christian Observer* for July, 1855. See also the *Memoir of Professor James Scholefield*, by his widow.

bridge. The former, who is the hero of the delightful epigram on "the little garden that little Jowett made," was Fellow and Tutor of Trinity Hall and Regius Professor of Civil Law He was the intimate friend of Dean Milner, who regularly spent two evenings in every week alone with him until his death. The latter was Fellow of St. John's—a noted writer in his day, and the first English clergyman who undertook foreign mission work for the Church Missionary Society. Finally (though the list might be further extended), among those who acquired both an academical and an evangelical reputation, must be noticed *William Dealtry* (1775-1847), who was resident Fellow of Trinity until 1813, when he succeeded John Venn as Rector of Clapham. Friend and foe concur in bearing testimony to the high repute in which Dr. Dealtry was held by his co-religionists at Cambridge. Simeon speaks with rapture of his "electrifying a whole congregation by his preaching," and frequently alludes to him with respect ; and Herbert Marsh, his antagonist in the matter of the Bible Society at Cambridge, complains with some bitterness (1812) that "the very circumstance that an argument is used by Mr. Dealtry is regarded by many as a presumption in its favour, and this presumption is heightened by his confidence in himself and contempt of his adversaries."[1]

The mention of Dr. Dealtry reminds us that it is time to go on to another great centre of the Evangelicals. The "Clapham sect," or the "Claphamites," became a name for the whole party. This is misleading, but there was some pretext for the nomenclature ; for most of the schemes of piety and benevolence which distinguished the second generation of Evangelicals either originated from Clapham, or found their strongest supporters there. The names of Wilberforce, Thornton, Teignmouth, Stephen, Macaulay, and Venn are all closely connected with Clapham. Most of them lived there, and all worshipped, more or less regularly, at its parish church.[2] The scene is vividly brought before us in

---

[1] *An Inquiry into the Consequences of neglecting to give the Prayer-book with the Bible: interspersed with remarks on some late speeches at Cambridge, and other important matters relative to the Bible Society, by Herbert Marsh, Margaret Professor of Divinity,* 1812.

[2] Lord Macaulay said truly that "Thackeray introduced too much of the

a word-picture drawn by one who knew them all. "On Sunday they [the Thorntons] sit in the old church with the Wilberforces' and Macaulays' and Stephens' pews close to their own ; and in the front gallery the Teignmouths ; and listen to the wise discourses of Venn, or sit enchanted under the preaching of Gisborne."[1]

William Wilberforce (1759–1833) was unquestionably the central figure of the group.[2] He had many advantages which none of the rest possessed in an equal degree. Gifted with extraordinary powers both of oratory and of conversation, he was calculated alike to shine in public and in private life. He had become a real power in Parliament in days when Parliamentary eloquence was at its zenith, and was able to hold his own with men like Pitt, Fox, Sheridan, and Burke. He won the admiration of men who were very far from sharing his religious views. Of his many eulogists, not one was more enthusiastic than Lord Brougham, who describes him as in some respects more illustrious than Pitt or Grenville.[3] It was not among the least of his powers that he could, when necessary, use with tremendous effect weapons which were frequently employed against the party which he represented. To sneer or laugh at "the saints" was a very common, but very improper course ; and on one occasion when, in this spirit, a member of the House of Commons with execrable taste designated him as "the honourable and religious gentleman," Wilberforce answered him in a strain of sarcasm which none who heard it could ever forget. Sir Samuel Romilly remarked, "It is the most striking thing I almost ever heard."[4]

Dissenting element into Clapham in *The Newcomes*." The leading people were, as Sir G. O. Trevelyan remarks, all staunch Churchmen, though they worked with Dissenters.—See *Life of Lord Macaulay*, i. 62. Otherwise, the account of Sophia Alethea Newcome is wonderfully lifelike, doing full justice to the real goodness, generosity, and self-denial which, in the midst of their affluence and narrowness, certainly characterized the Claphamites.

[1] *William Wilberforce, his Friends and his Times*, by J. C. Colquhoun, p. 309.

[2] For an account of Wilberforce's early life, see the chapter on "The Evangelical Revival" in *The English Church in the Eighteenth Century*.

[3] See *Statesmen in the Time of George III.:* "Mr. Wilberforce," vol. i. p. 96, etc.

[4] *Id.*, p. 99.

No less striking were his conversational powers. Prejudices vanished during a personal interview with him, like dew before the sun. His son's account of his marvellous gift of fascination might be suspected of filial partiality (though he quotes several instances which could have been immediately contradicted if untrue),[1] but what he asserts is fully borne out by quite independent witnesses. Bishop Jebb, for instance, who belonged to quite a different school of theology, writes in 1809, "We had the happiness of meeting Mr. Wilberforce, not only the worthiest and ablest, but the pleasantest of men. There is something to me peculiarly delightful in the almost boyish playfulness of a great and good mind; and this I never saw more fully exhibited than in Mr. Wilberforce. He absolutely overflows with vivacity; and the easy current of his most fluent conversation, every now and then, is diversified by flashes of eloquence, or by classical allusions, or poetical imagery; and the whole is so clearly the emanation of a guileless and benevolent heart, that not to be charmed with him, I at least conceive to be impossible."[2] Reginald Heber was distinctly prejudiced against Wilberforce, but when he saw him he said, "An hour's conversation can dissolve the prejudice of years."[3]

In fact, so great were Wilberforce's advantages, personal and adventitious, that there was a little danger, especially in his later years, of his being spoilt by adulation; and perhaps it was well for him that Nemesis ("the goddess of retribution, who brings down all immoderate good fortune, and checks the presumption that attends it") haunted him by making him, more than most men, the butt of gentle raillery and depreciation among those who disliked the Evangelical party.

When such gifts as Wilberforce possessed are combined with a boundless liberality, to which great wealth enabled him to give full scope, a devoted attachment to what he believed to be the truth, a dogged perseverance in carrying

---

[1] *Life of William Wilberforce*, p. 417. Among others, the writer quotes Sir James Mackintosh, who certainly had no sympathy with Wilberforce's peculiar views.
[2] *Life of Bishop Jebb*, by the Rev. C. Forster, p. 164.
[3] *William Wilberforce, his Friends and his Times*, by J. C. Colquhoun, p. 170.

out his purposes which no difficulties could daunt, and an absolute disregard for all personal advancement, it need not surprise us that he should have been a most mighty engine for the spread of Evangelicalism.

That is, so far as he *was* an Evangelical ; but here again we have an instance of one who joined the party because it seemed to him to be the most in earnest about spiritual things ; for from some of its most distinctive characteristics Wilberforce differed. For example, the Evangelicals were decidedly, though moderately, Calvinistic ; Wilberforce was as decidedly anti-Calvinistic.[1] The Evangelicals were opposed to the doctrine of baptismal regeneration ; Wilberforce appears to have advocated it.[2] The Evangelicals were Protestant to the core, and opposed, as a body, to any favour being granted to Roman Catholics ; Wilberforce was a friend, and, from his position in Parliament, a very powerful friend, of Roman Catholic Emancipation. But, in spite of all this, the Evangelicals may fairly claim William Wilberforce as their own ; and though it is not quite correct to term him, as Lord Brougham does, "the head, indeed the founder, of a powerful religious sect,"[3] he was unquestionably the most influential layman who belonged to the party.

Next to William Wilberforce come his kinsmen, the Thorntons. John Thornton, the father, belonged to an earlier generation, but his mantle fell upon a worthy son, Henry Thornton. The Thorntons were wealthy London bankers, and their princely liberality in behalf of all those objects which the Evangelicals had at heart rivalled that of Wilberforce himself. Henry Thornton was, like Wilberforce, a member of Parliament, and both represented powerful constituencies ; the one Yorkshire, and the other Surrey.

[1] "'You and I who are no Calvinists,' is an expression which occurs repeatedly in his letters," says Canon Ashwell, *Life of Bishop S. Wilberforce*, i. 38, note. "Disputed with Milner about final perseverance," is an entry in his diary for August 25, 1799.

[2] "Papa defended *most strongly* baptismal regeneration against the two clergymen [Daniel Wilson and Cunningham of Harrow, both leading Evangelicals]. His ground was that we are told that no man can see God without a change of heart. We believe that infants do see God, and therefore he did not doubt that their hearts were changed at baptism."—Letter from Henry Wilberforce to his brother Samuel, quoted by Canon Ashwell in his *Life of Bishop S. Wilberforce*, i. 46.

[3] *Statesmen in the Time of George III.* : "Mr. Wilberforce."

Thornton rendered valuable service to his religious friends in Parliament; for though he had none of the oratorical powers of Wilberforce, he had great talents, was an excellent man of business, and won that respect which perfect rectitude of purpose and a stainless private character seldom fail to command. The father and son were good representatives, respectively, of the first and second generation of Evangelicals. John Thornton belonged to the period when they were almost forced to fraternize with Dissenters, who welcomed them while their own Church looked upon them with suspicion as mere Methodists. In Henry Thornton's time the Evangelicals had become recognized as a power in the Church. They were still stigmatized as Methodists in some quarters, but the line of demarcation was more distinctly drawn. At any rate, those who, like Henry Thornton, desired to keep closely within the pale of the Church might easily do so without finding any lack of sympathizers. Indeed, the men themselves were more exclusively Churchmen than their predecessors had been. These facts may explain a remark made by one who never spoke without knowing what he was saying, but which otherwise might be difficult to comprehend. "I have often thought," said John Bowdler, on Henry Thornton's premature death in 1814, "it was almost an evidence of the Christian religion that so commanding a mind as his, prejudiced as it was in early life, by a Methodistical circle in which he lived, against enthusiasm of all kinds, should quietly and soberly examine the subject for himself, and end in becoming not only convinced of the truth of religion, but one of its most warm and devout followers. How we are to go on without him, I cannot understand; as a standard to look up to he was invaluable!"[1] The last sentence is very strong, but hardly too strong for the facts of the case. Henry Thornton was Wilberforce's right-hand man in the crusade against the Slave Trade; he was one of the chief founders of the Church Missionary Society, and its first treasurer; he was the life and soul of that cherished project, connected with both, the foundation of the colony at Sierra Leone; he was one of the first promoters of, and a most voluminous and

---

[1] *William Wilberforce, his Friends and his Times*, p. 532. John Bowdler himself died within a fortnight of uttering these words.

valued contributor to, the *Christian Observer;* and the first treasurer of the British and Foreign Bible Society. In fact, there was not a scheme that was dear to the Evangelical mind in which he did not take a leading part.[1]

Another member of the group was *Zachary Macaulay*, to whom a special interest is attached as the father of a still more illustrious son. He was editor of the *Christian Observer* after the first few numbers, and managed it for fifteen years with singular tact, prevailing upon persons to write in it whom none but he could have persuaded.[2] Like the rest of his party, he took the deepest interest in the foundation of the Church Missionary Society, and especially in the Sierra Leone project ; was an ardent abolitionist, and one of the original founders of the Bible Society. A more complete contrast than that between Zachary and Thomas Babington Macaulay it is difficult to conceive. The father was a silent, severe man, with more of the old Puritan in him than most of the Evangelicals had ; a man of no great brilliancy, but of great strength of character and rectitude of purpose. He was not, perhaps, adapted to be a leader, but he made an admirable lieutenant, and was an important member of what has been termed Wilberforce's "interior cabinet."[3]

A somewhat similar *rôle* was played by Macaulay's friend and neighbour, *James Stephen*, who was also the father, and we may add the grandfather, of men more brilliant than himself. But Stephen introduced a new and an important element into the Clapham councils. He was a lawyer, and his legal acumen was of great service to the cause which he espoused, especially in its relation to the abolition of the Slave Trade, to which branch of the work, above all others, he devoted himself. The fact that he was an intimate friend of a Prime Minister (Mr. Perceval) did not tend to diminish his influence.

Lord Teignmouth, first president of the Bible Society, and formerly Governor-General of India, may fairly be reckoned as a member of the Clapham sect ; for he was an occasional

---

[1] Colquhoun, p. 253. [2] *Id.,* p. 182.
[3] There is a vivid account of Zachary Macaulay in Mr. J. Cotter Morison's very able monograph on *Macaulay* in the English Men of Letters Series ; also, of course, in Sir George Trevelyan's *Life of Lord Macaulay*.

resident of Clapham, worshipped at its parish church, from which he could not be allured even by the preaching of Robert Hall, and rendered valuable service to one of the causes which the Claphamites had at heart, the propagation of the gospel in India. His Indian experience stood him in good stead when that object was violently attacked. Nor must we forget *Granville Sharp*, an abolitionist even before Wilberforce,[1] the inheritor of a name which is noted for piety and benevolence all through the eighteenth century. He was not a man of Clapham, but his deep interest in the abolition of the Slave Trade, and also in the Bible Society, at the first meeting for the foundation of which he was chairman, and his general though not perhaps entire sympathy with the views of the Evangelicals, led him frequently to this Evangelical centre. To a similar extent, *Thomas Babington*, a pious country gentleman of Northumberland, may be regarded as a Claphamite; while Simeon and Milner were also occasional visitors and constant advisers among the Claphamites.

Among a body of men who were brought together chiefly by their agreement in religious matters, of course the clerical element was of vital importance. To their credit be it said, the Claphamites do not seem, like some amateur theologians, to have wasted their time and temper in disputes with their clergy. Of course they took all the pains they could to have a clergyman of their own school, otherwise it would have been miserable both for them and him. They were peculiarly fortunate, in more ways than one, in having for the Rector of Clapham *John Venn* (1759–1813), the worthy son of a worthy father. The very name of Venn would be sufficient to command respect, for had not Henry Venn stood in the first rank of the early Evangelical fathers? John and Henry Venn were very different types of men; but for the position which he had to fill at Clapham the son was decidedly better adapted than the father. This, if one reads between the lines, appears in the characters of the two, as drawn by two Evangelicals,

[1] "It ought," said Bishop Porteus, "to be remembered, in justice to one no less remarkable for his modesty and humility than for his learning and piety, Granville Sharp, that the first publication which drew the attention of the country to the horrors of the African Slave Trade came from his pen." See Hodgson's *Life of Bishop Beilby Porteus*, p. 218.

who both evidently thought the father the better man. "John Venn," writes Mr. Jerram, "possessed his father's talents, but not in all their splendour; partook of his piety, but not of its fervid character."[1] "John Venn," writes Mr. King, "the excellent Vicar of Clapham, son of the still more celebrated Vicar of Huddersfield, ... possessed a remarkable soundness of judgment, combined with a rare intellectual power, which was duly appreciated by such men as Wilberforce and Henry Thornton, as well as by the large assemblage of rank and talent which met together in the spacious church at Clapham, and which might have been far more extensively felt but for a certain diffidence of character, which often caused him to shrink from services which few persons were more competent to discharge than himself."[2]

John Venn at Clapham was the right man in the right place. Such a congregation as his did not so much require to be roused from spiritual apathy—that had been done already—as to be edified or built up in their holy faith, to be instructed, to be guided. Now, John Venn, besides being a very earnest, was also a highly cultured man, and was particularly distinguished for his clear, calm judgment, and, if one may use such an expression, sanctified common sense. This comes out very strongly in his admirable management as chairman of the first meeting, in 1799, which led to the establishment of the Church Missionary Society, or, as it was at first called, "The Society for Missions in Africa and the East." More than any single man, he may be termed the father of the society, and the detailed account of his doings and suggestions fully justifies the glowing eulogy which is passed upon him in the Jubilee volume of the society (1849)—"a man of such wisdom and comprehension of mind, that on that memorable occasion he laid down before a small company of fellow-helpers those principles and regulations which have formed the basis of the society." From the

---

[1] *Memoirs of the Rev. Charles Jerram*, by the Rev. James Jerram, p. 270. It is a pity, by the way, that this most interesting volume is not better known; it contains one of the best accounts extant of the Evangelicals of the second generation. A similar description of the relative merits of the two Venns is given in *The Later Evangelical Fathers*, by M. Seeley, pp. 30–38.

[2] *Memoir of the Rev. Thomas Dykes*, by the Rev. John King, p. 7. This, too, is a book well worth reading.

nature of the case, it is of course impossible to adduce similar proofs of his wisdom in managing his almost unique parish; but we may well conceive how invaluable his well-balanced mind would be, not only for informing, but also for checking any excesses into which earnest laymen, who have not made any special study of theology, are apt to fall. The Clapham congregation seem thoroughly to have appreciated the merits of their pastor; not one word of complaint do we hear from any quarter, but we are expressly told that "in purely ecclesiastical matters Wilberforce always consulted John Venn or Simeon." John Venn died at the comparatively early age of fifty-four, in 1813, having been Rector of Clapham for twenty-one years, succeeding another noted Evangelical, Dr. Stonehouse, in 1792. It was an anxious crisis for the men of Clapham, but they found the very successor they desired. "The parish," writes Zachary Macaulay to Simeon after John Venn's death, "to a man are hoping and praying for Dealtry." And their hopes were realized and their prayers heard; for Dr. Dealtry, who, as we have seen, stood in the first rank of Evangelicals at Cambridge, was appointed, and continued to minister to them until he was made, by Bishop Sumner, Chancellor of Winchester and afterwards Archdeacon of Surrey. "Clapham," writes Mr. Colquhoun, "was highly favoured, as both in John Venn and his successor, Dr. Dealtry, they possessed clergy of zeal and wisdom,—with the special characteristics of their Church,—learning, earnestness and a wise moderation."[1]

But there was another clergyman connected with Clapham, who, to judge by contemporary report, made a greater sensation than either of its two rectors. This was *Thomas Gisborne* (1758-1846), who was what would now be vulgarly called a "squarson." He lived at Yoxall Lodge, in Needwood Forest, where he undertook the charge of the populous village of Barton, and worked diligently among the poor. His appearance in the Clapham pulpit was always looked forward to as a rich intellectual treat, and the rapturous terms in which he is spoken of would lead us to regard him as one of the greatest geniuses of the age. Thus Sir James Stephen, who had, no doubt, often seen and heard him, when

[1] *William Wilberforce, his Friends and his Times*, p. 323.

he was a boy at Clapham, writes, "He contributed largely to the formation of the national mind on subjects of the highest importance to the national character. He was the expositor of the 'Evangelical' system to those cultivated or fastidious readers who were intolerant of the ruder style of his less refined brethren. He addressed them as a poet, as a moralist, as a natural philosopher, and as a divine. His *sermons* were regarded by his contemporaries as models in a style of composition in which the English has scarcely a single specimen of excellence."[1] One is tempted to ask whether the writer had ever read South, Jeremy Taylor, Barrow, or, to come nearer his own times, Horsley; and, if so, whether he found in them no specimens of excellence, and whether he seriously thought Mr. Gisborne was superior to them? Even when he adds, "Mr. Gisborne approached more nearly than any Anglican clergyman of his time towards the ideal of that much-neglected art," one cannot help thinking of Van Mildert, Mant, Isaac Milner, and many others, and feeling half amused, half provoked, at the extravagance of the estimate. For, unfortunately, Mr. Gisborne's sermons and other writings are still accessible to those who will take the trouble to disinter them from the dusty shelves in which they repose. Like much of the Evangelical literature, they are very disappointing from an intellectual point of view; though the sermons are plain, sensible, and spirited, and would probably sound better when heard than they appear when read.

It is only fair to add that there were others, and those highly competent judges, who formed the very highest opinion of Mr. Gisborne. "Gisborne," writes Henry Thornton to a young friend, "is the man of almost all others whom I could wish you implicitly to follow. The longer we live, the more shall we discover the value of his sobriety, candour, openness, and kindness." Alexander Knox, when speaking of the want of "unction" in English sermons, declares that any preacher who has it will be called Methodistical, "as," he adds, as if it were a monstrous supposition, "I dare say, when I inquire, I shall find to be the case with the excellent Mr. Gisborne."[2] Reginald Heber, in a letter to John Thornton

[1] *Essays in Ecclesiastical Biography:* "The Clapham Sect."
[2] *Remains of Alexander Knox,* iv. 104.

the younger, in 1809, after praising highly, but not at all too highly, the very striking pamphlet entitled "*Zeal without Innovation*," asks, "Is Gisborne the author?" as if no one else was worthy of the authorship.[1] "The appearance," we are told, "of a new volume [by Mr. Gisborne] was hailed by Hannah More, and other persons of taste, as a spiritual and intellectual treat."[2] If the virtue appears now to have gone out of this once admired writer, it is perhaps because the present generation does not know the man, about whose personality there must have been something singularly fascinating.

Before we quit Clapham a word must be said about the numerous schemes of piety and charity, the success of which was mainly due to the good men who were connected with that place. It may seem to be a grovelling view to take of the matter; but, after all, in this work-day world of ours, money and business talents are very important elements in the successful carrying out of practical projects for good. The men of Clapham possessed both. Clapham was not then, as now, a part of London, but it was near enough to make it a very convenient home for business men. The Claphamites were able and willing to spend almost any amount of money on the projects which they had at heart; but, as men of business, they liked to have their money's worth for their money. They were not worldly men, but they knew perfectly well what they were about, in dealing with matters in which a knowledge of the world makes all the difference between success and failure. And so they could contribute, not only money, but what would make money effective for their objects. Wilberforce contributed his eloquence, Thornton his monetary experience as a banker, and both their Parliamentary influence; Stephen his legal knowledge, Lord Teignmouth his knowledge of men as governor of a great province; and these, added to their money, made them irresistible.

The most conspicuous and arduous of their achievements was the abolition of the Slave Trade in 1807, and the abolition

---

[1] *Life of Bishop Heber*, by his widow, i. 359. Mr. Gisborne was *not* the author of *Zeal without Innovation*. It was written by Mr. Bean.
[2] Colquhoun, p. 203.

of slavery itself in 1833. For, while we must give full credit to the assistance which they received from men who were not Claphamites, such as Henry Brougham, Bishop Porteus, and, above all, Thomas Clarkson, it must yet be admitted that a thoughtful modern writer has hardly exaggerated the matter in saying, "The men who with the hard labour of twenty years won from England the abolition of slavery, a step which cost so much in actual expenditure, and by which the nation ventured nobly upon a great sacrifice of effort for abstract right with doubtful results, belonged without exception to this straitest of religious communities."[1] We may go a step further, and say that they not only *belonged* to this community, but that they derived from it the stimulus which urged them, and the fulcrum which supported them; speaking broadly, it was not only Evangelicals, but Evangelicalism, which abolished the Slave Trade and emancipated the negro. The testimony quoted above is all the more striking, because it comes from one who is very far from being an indiscriminate eulogist of the Evangelicals; and the same may be said of another, whose vivid account of the magnitude and unselfishness of the work I cannot possibly improve upon, and will therefore venture to borrow in full. "The Slave Trade Association," writes Sir Erskine May,[2] "was formed to forward a cause of noble philanthropy, the abolition of the Slave Trade. It was almost beyond the range of politics. It had no constitutional change to seek; no interest to promote; no prejudice to gratify; not even the national welfare to advance. Its clients were a despised race, in a distant clime,—an inferior type of the human family, for whom natures of a higher mould felt repugnance rather than sympathy. Benevolence and Christian charity were its only incentives. On the other hand, the Slave Trade was supported by some of the most powerful classes in the country —merchants, shipowners, planters. Before it could be proscribed, vested interests must be overborne, ignorance

---

[1] *Literary History of England in the End of the Eighteenth and the Beginning of the Nineteenth Century*, by Mrs. Oliphant: "The Evangelicals," p. 370.

[2] *Constitutional History of England*, vol. ii. pp. 128-130. It is fair to add that the Slave Trade Association did not *originate* with the Evangelicals; but it is no less true that if the Evangelicals had not taken the matter up, it would never have succeeded.

enlightened, prejudices and indifferences overcome, public opinion converted. And to this great work did Granville Sharp, Wilberforce, Clarkson, and other noble spirits devote their lives. Never was cause supported by greater earnestness and activity. The organization of the society comprehended all classes and religious denominations. Evidence was collected from every source, to lay bare the cruelties and iniquity of the traffic. Illustration and argument were inexhaustible. Men of feeling and sensibility appealed, with deep emotion, to the religious feelings and benevolence of the people. If extravagance and bad taste sometimes courted ridicule, the high purpose, just sentiments, and eloquence of the leaders of this movement won respect and admiration. Tracts found their way into every house; pulpits and platforms resounded with the wrongs of the negro; petitions were multiplied; ministers and Parliaments moved to inquiry and action. Such a mission was not to be soon accomplished. The cause could not be won by sudden enthusiasm, still less by intimidation, but conviction must be wrought in the mind and conscience of the nation. And this was done. Parliament was soon prevailed upon to attempt the mitigation of the worst evils which had been brought to light; and in little more than twenty years the Slave Trade was utterly condemned and prohibited. A good cause prevailed, not by violence and passion, not by demonstration of popular force, but by reason, earnestness, and the best feelings of mankind."

It is not necessary to dwell here upon the painful controversy which arose, on the publication of the "Life of William Wilberforce," about the respective shares of William Wilberforce and Thomas Clarkson in the great work of the abolition of the Slave Trade. Let it be granted that Mr. Clarkson and Mr. Granville Sharp were first in the field, it can still scarcely be denied that but for the work of the Clapham sect, with Wilberforce as "the Agamemnon of the host,"[1] and James Stephen, Zachary Macaulay, and Henry Thornton as his lieutenants, the grand result would never have been effected. And if, in the later work of abolishing

---

[1] Sir J. Stephen's expression: "The Clapham Sect," in *Essays in Ecclesiastical Biography*, p. 298.

slavery, Wilberforce gave place to younger men, notably Sir T. Fowell Buxton,[1] his was still the name to conjure with; and there is a certain dramatic propriety in the fact that one of the last public utterances which reached his ears was the announcement, in 1833, that the British nation had spent a sum of twenty millions of pounds, and that from August 21, 1834, slavery was to cease.

How large a share the men of Clapham had in the institution of the Church Missionary Society, the British and Foreign Bible Society, the Indian Episcopate, and other agencies for good, has been already hinted at in the notices of individuals, and will appear more at length in a future chapter. But these large general undertakings do not by any means exhaust the list of their labours. In the words of one who knew them well, "schools, prison discipline, savings banks, tracts, village libraries, district visitings, and church building, each for a time rivalled their cosmopolitan projects. In short, they, if any men could, might bear the test, ' By their fruits ye shall know them.' "[2]

Making a short journey from Clapham, we find the metropolis itself an increasingly important centre of Evangelicalism. Perhaps the most prominent and important post was the proprietary chapel of St. John's, Bedford Row. The high reputation of its minister, Richard Cecil, who was the most cultured and refined of the early Evangelical leaders, and who lived on, an honoured veteran, through the first ten years of the nineteenth century, made it a natural rallying-point for the party, and attracted rising men for assistant-ministers. On Cecil's death, in 1810, he was succeeded by a no less distinguished Evangelical, Daniel Wilson, under whom the traditions of the place were fully kept up. In his time St. John's throve wonderfully. "Among the regular attendants," we are told, "were John Thornton and his sons; Charles Grant and his two distinguished sons, one of whom afterwards became Lord Glenelg, and the other Sir Robert Grant, Governor of Bombay; Zachary Macaulay and his son."[3]

[1] Sir T. Fowell Buxton was also an Evangelical, who owed his religious views to the Evangelical preacher Josiah Pratt.
[2] Sir James Stephen, "The Clapham Sect:" *Essays*, etc.
[3] *Life of Daniel Wilson, Bishop of Calcutta*, by Josiah Bateman, p. 178.

There is something rather puzzling in this account; for John Thornton the elder died twenty years before Daniel Wilson's incumbency, and the Thorntons and Macaulays worshipped, as a rule, at Clapham. The statistics of St. John's remind us of the figures of the present day, in the number of communicants, and the amount of the contributions to religious and charitable objects.[1] But it had more than a local interest. "The vestry of St. John's Chapel," says Mr. Wilson's biographer, "is a place from whence numberless schemes of benevolence and Christian charity have emanated. It was the head-quarters of *The London Clerical Education Society*, formed for the purpose of carrying young men of promise and piety, but of straitened means, through the University, by defraying their expenses in whole or in part. Daniel Wilson was secretary. There, also, a society assembled for many years, called *The Eclectic Society*, which will be noticed in a future chapter.

At the beginning of the century there was a sort of antiquarian interest to Evangelicals in the parish of St. Mary Woolnoth, where good old John Newton had been working for more than twenty years, and where he still held on, though his day was nearly done; but after his death, in 1806, St. Mary Woolnoth does not appear to have been prominent among Evangelical centres. It was otherwise with the chapel of the Lock Hospital, where Newton's spiritual son, Thomas Scott, remained for the first two years of the new century. This chapel had been founded by Martin Madan, an early Evangelical, and always remained in the hands of the party. Scott's successor was Mr. Fry, a man of some eminence in his day, but long since forgotten. Clerkenwell, again, had among its clergy one who had not only a reputation in himself, but was interesting as being a link between the first and second generations of Evangelicals. This was Henry Foster, who had formerly been an assistant to William Romaine, and still continued to be a great friend of Richard Cecil. Charles Jerram gives us an interesting account of an interview with Mr. Cecil and Mr. Foster, to whom, after having been accepted as a candidate for help at Cambridge from the Elland Society,

[1] *Life of Daniel Wilson*, pp. 182, 183.

he was sent "for examination as to fitness, in piety and talents, to receive the benefits of the society's patronage."[1]

Links with the Evangelicals of the past might also be found in two other London churches—St. Ann's, Blackfriars, and Bentinck Chapel, Marylebone. The rector of the former was the Rev. W. Goode, who had been curate to William Romaine, and succeeded to the living on the death of that Evangelical father in 1795. There he remained until his death in 1816. The committee meetings of the Church Missionary Society were all held in his study, and its anniversary sermons preached in his church.[2] At Bentinck Chapel was the Rev. Basil Woodd for no less a space than forty-six years (1785-1831), a most active parish priest, who worked on what we should now call distinctly Church lines, laying great stress on the fasts and festivals of the Church, on the duty of public catechizing, and of supporting the old Church societies, but at the same time casting in his lot decidedly with the Evangelical party.[3]

Josiah Pratt (1768-1844) has been already mentioned, but he was far too distinguished a man among the Evangelical clergy in London to be dismissed with a passing notice. In all the distinctive works of the Evangelicals he took a leading part. He was one of the founders of the Bible Society, and its first Church of England secretary; the main projector of the *Christian Observer*, and its first editor, though he only held the office for a few months; and one of the originators of the Church Missionary Society, of which he was the most effective secretary for many years. He had been engaged in business with his father at Birmingham

---

[1] *Memoirs of the Rev. Charles Jerram*, p. 47.

[2] *Memoir of the Rev. William Goode*, by his son, Dean Goode, especially pp. 47 and 61.

[3] See *Memoir of the Rev. Basil Woodd, late Rector of Drayton Beauchamp, and Minister of Bentinck Chapel, Marylebone*, by the Rev. S. C. Wilks; reprinted from the *Christian Observer*, 1831. Mr. Wilks was for thirteen years the curate, and then the successor, of Basil Woodd at Bentinck Chapel. To his interesting memoir of his chief the reader is specially referred, because it is felt that justice is scarcely done in the text to the memory of Basil Woodd. The writer would fain have dwelt longer on the history of this good man, but space is limited, and the number of exemplary Evangelical clergymen so great, that it is absolutely necessary to exercise self-restraint in dealing with those who were not obviously in the first rank.

before he received Holy Orders; and, like many of the Evangelicals, he showed great business talents, which were most valuable in the management of their various projects. He was a man of a singularly unobtrusive character, and was rather forced by circumstances, than led by his own choice, into prominence. We shall find more than one instance of his being content to labour and see other men entering into the fruits of his labour. Without at all approaching to the stature of a really great divine, he had a very competent knowledge of divinity, and was a pleasing writer. But his forte was practical wisdom, and it was in no slight degree owing to his management that the Church Missionary Society's business arrangements were placed on that excellent footing which they have never lost. Though distinctly a party man, Josiah Pratt was not narrow-minded, a remarkable instance of which was shown in 1819, when a royal letter was obtained for the Society for the Propagation of the Gospel. Mr. Pratt's sympathies were, of course, all with the sister—we will not say rival—society, but he took infinite pains to bring together a selection of passages taken from the S.P.G. reports, and especially the anniversary sermons for more than a century, in order to inform the public (which did not then know much about missionary work) of the merits of the society, and to stimulate their zeal in its behalf. In the same spirit he successfully used his influence to persuade his own society (C.M.S.) to make a munificent grant towards the Bishops' College at Calcutta, though he would not agree entirely with the High Church views of its founder, Bishop Middleton. His connection with the bishop was of earlier date, for he resided in the parish of St. Pancras when Archdeacon Middleton was vicar: "The archdeacon and he had always been on the most friendly terms; at the vestry meetings of the parish Mr. Pratt was one of the main supporters of his vicar, for whose talents and active benevolence he entertained the highest regard." When it is remembered how shamefully Middleton was thwarted in his attempts to do good at St. Pancras, a special significance will be attached to this account. Josiah Pratt was quite one of the best in every way of the Evangelical clergy in London, and it is not to the credit of the dispensers of Church preferment that he remained unbeneficed until he had reached the mature age of fifty-eight. One hears with a feeling akin to indignation of the heavy hackwork (no milder term will express it) which this good and able man had to go through. "His ministry," said a brother clergyman, "was such as might fully have occupied many. At one time he preached in the morning of the Lord's day at Wheler Chapel, in the evening at St. Mary Woolnoth, and on Wednesday at St. Lawrence, Jewry. Besides all this, he was occupied in the missionary work at the Missionary House, often from ten in the morning till after ten or later at night."[1] He was Cecil's curate till 1804, when he became Newton's curate at St. Mary, Woolnoth, where, as John Newton was quite worn out, he had to do all the work. In 1809 he was appointed, through the influence of his friends, to the incumbency of Wheler Chapel in Spital Square ; and it was not until 1826 that he was presented to the living of St. Stephen's, Coleman Street. Even for this tardy piece of preferment he was indebted to that very unsatisfactory method of appointing an incumbent by the votes of the parishioners. For once the method worked well ; and it is something to set against the many scandals which the system of popular election has caused, that it enabled a measure of justice to be done to so excellent a clergyman as Josiah Pratt.[2]

Another London clergyman, who was most popular both as a preacher and as a devotional writer, was *Henry Blunt* (1794-1843), who, after having, like many of the Evangelical clergy, distinguished himself both as a mathematical and a classical scholar at Cambridge, lived in the country village of Clare, in Suffolk, dividing his time between parochial work and private pupils. In 1824 he took the curacy of St. Luke's, Chelsea—an extensive and laborious charge ; and in 1830 was presented to the new church of Holy Trinity, Upper Chelsea Though his health was always delicate, he was an indefati-

[1] Funeral sermon, preached at St. Mary, Coleman Street, by Rev. John Harding.
[2] See *Memoir of the Rev. Josiah Pratt, B.D.*, late Vicar of St. Stephen's, Coleman Street, and for twenty-one years secretary of the Church Missionary Society, by his son, Josiah Pratt, Vicar of St. Stephen's, Coleman Street, and John Henry Pratt, Chaplain to the Bishop of Calcutta, 1849.

gable worker. He is said to have "drawn around him the most influential congregation in London or its neighbourhood. Nobles, peers, commoners, tradesmen, and the poor alike hung upon his fascinating discourses."[1] His writings passed through many editions, and are still quoted by collectors of devotional extracts. He was also a good parish priest; and it is not surprising that his feeble frame prematurely gave way under these multifarious labours. A short time before his death he was appointed Rector of Streatham; but it was at St. Luke's, and afterwards at Trinity Church, Sloane Street, both in Upper Chelsea, that he made his great reputation.

Another proprietary chapel in Marylebone, St. James's, Welbeck Street, or, as it was generally called, Welbeck Chapel, was also in Evangelical hands. In the early part of the century we find at Welbeck Chapel Claudius Buchanan, an Evangelical to the core, whose noble efforts in after-years were the chief cause of the interest taken in the Christianization of India. Dr. Jennings, afterwards Archdeacon of Norfolk, ministered at Welbeck Chapel during the later part of our period, and "by his faithful and evangelical discourses instructed and edified large and attentive congregations." But for seven years—from 1826 to 1833—there was an assistant-minister of greater fame than Dr. Jennings. This was T. Hartwell Horne, the well-known author of the "Introduction to the Critical Study of Holy Scripture," and other works. It is his description of Dr. Jennings, whom he calls "my kind and eloquent friend," that has been quoted above. He adds, "The most serious portion of the aristocracy were at that time attendants at Welbeck Chapel. Among these were Lord Teignmouth, president of the Bible Society, Mr. Wilberforce, and, for a time, Sir Edward Parry."[2] It was while he was at Welbeck Chapel (1829) that Hartwell Horne published his "Manual of Parochial Psalmody," which was adopted in many churches, with the sanction of several bishops, including the primate, Dr. Howley. Though inferior to many modern collections, it was, at any rate, superior to Tate and Brady. Hartwell Horne left Welbeck Chapel in

---

[1] Funeral sermon by the Rev. F. Close.
[2] *Reminiscences of T. Hartwell Horne*, p. 55.

1833, on his appointment to the rectory of St. Edmund-the-King with St. Nicholas-Acons, in the City of London.

1824 is an era in the history of Evangelicalism in London, for in that year Daniel Wilson became Vicar of Islington, and made it, what it has been ever since, a stronghold of the party. It was high time that something should be done to stir up spiritual life in that vast parish; for in 1824 Islington had thirty thousand inhabitants, and only one church and one chapel of ease. Even the one church was not overburdened with work, for there were but two services on the Sunday— one in the morning, for which the vicar was responsible, and the other in the afternoon, which was supplied by a lecturer. This was not a state of things that Daniel Wilson was used to at St. John's, Bedford Row, and he soon began to inspire life into the dry bones of Islington. By 1828 he had established "three full services in the church on Sundays and great festival days, and one in the week, besides morning prayers on Wednesdays and Fridays and saints' days. An early sacrament at eight, in addition to the usual celebration, had been also commenced." Then, "for an expenditure of £12,000, the parish was enriched by three large and noble churches, which had in reality cost £30,000."[1] The Low Churchmen were, after all, better Churchmen than the No-Churchmen.

It is, of course, impossible to enumerate all the Evangelical clergy in London during our period. There was, for instance, Thomas Dale, Vicar of St. Bride's, Fleet Street, who rose to great eminence at a later date; there was Mr. Budd, of whose efficiency Edward Bickersteth, when he lived as a layman in his parish during the early years of this century, gives us a pleasing impression;[2] there was Cornelius Neale, father of a still more distinguished son, John Mason Neale, a clergyman in Conduit Street; there was Edward Bickersteth himself; there was Gerard Noel, for a few years Incumbent of Percy Chapel, another proprietary chapel in Evangelical hands; and his brother, Baptist Noel, who took the lease of St. John's, Bedford Row, in 1826.

But enough has been mentioned to show that the

[1] *Life of Daniel Wilson, Bishop of Calcutta*, pp. 266 and 232.
[2] See *Memoir of Rev. E. Bickersteth*, by Rev. T. R. Birks, i. 163 and *passim*.

metrópolis was no unimportant centre of the Evangelical party; we must pass on to other places.

Oxford, unlike its sister University, was never a stronghold of Evangelicalism. Of course there were Evangelicals there, as there were in all parts of the country, but there was no Simeon or Isaac Milner to lead them; they made no mark in the schools,[1] and there was no college with Evangelical traditions, except the humble little St. Edmund's Hall. The principal, Dr. Crouch, was decidedly Evangelical, and he attracted thither men of the same way of thinking; but the hall had no standing in the University. It rose a little when Daniel Wilson became assistant-tutor in 1804, and still more when he became vice-principal and sole tutor in 1809; and his successor, Mr. Hill, kept up the reputation of the place. Perhaps also, towards the close of our period, Wadham was beginning to be, to a certain extent, an Evangelical college, owing to the known sentiments of its sub-warden, Dr. Symonds; and the fact that Dr. Macbride, the principal, was highly respected by the Evangelicals, may have led them to think Magdalen Hall a safe place. But, after all, Evangelicalism took no real root in Oxford—the *genius loci* was against it; and it would be hardly too much to say that a man who went up with an Evangelical bias would probably lose it before long.

But the popular watering-places, inland and marine, were strongholds of the party. Cheltenham (where Simeon found "almost a heaven upon earth"[2]), Brighton, Bath, Hastings, Tunbridge Wells, were all great Evangelical centres. Many, again, of the best and ablest of the Evangelical clergy were to be found in the great centres of industry. Hull was particularly favoured; Thomas Dykes, John Scott, John King, and William Knight were stars of the first magnitude, and the traditions of Joseph Milner still hung about the place. Liverpool had its McNeile and Falloon; Manchester its Hugh Stowell; Halifax its Coulthurst and its Samuel Knight;

---

[1] Dr. Mozley, who was by no means prejudiced in favour of St. Edmund's Hall, says that it *had* a good reputation in the schools. But surely the class lists are the test of this, and it will be found that in them the names of St. Edmund's Hall men are conspicuous for their absence.

[2] Carus, p. 551.

Leeds its Miles Atkinson ; Colchester its William Marsh ; York its John Overton and its William Richardson ; Leicester its Thomas Robinson.

The party is said to have made not much way in country places ; but, at any rate, some of its most prominent leaders were country clergymen. There was, *e.g.*, Mr. Pugh, Rector of Rauceby, at a well-known clerical meeting in whose rectory was broached the very first idea which afterwards expanded into the conception of the Church Missionary Society.

Again, *Legh Richmond* (1772-1828) was a country clergyman all through his ministerial life—first in the Isle of Wight, where he had the charge of two villages near Ryde, Brading and Arreton ; and then at Turvey, in Bedfordshire, where he laboured with conspicuous success for more than twenty years (1805-1827). Legh Richmond, like many of the Evangelicals, must have been a man of a singularly lovable character. This appears not only from the testimony of his admiring biographer, who might be suspected of partiality, but from known facts, and from the spirit which breathes through all his writings. He was a man of varied accomplishments—a musician, a mineralogist, and, what was rare in his day, a keen appreciator of the beauties of nature. He seems to have been almost adored in his own family, and was (again like so many of the Evangelicals) a most entertaining companion. Dean Burgon, who could have had very little sympathy with his religious views, evidently conceived a most favourable impression of the *man* from what he had heard at Turvey Abbey, the home of "Charles Longuet Higgins, the Good Layman." The dean speaks of him as "an excellent specimen of the school" (Evangelical) ; as one who "could not fail to exert a powerful influence over the inmates of Turvey Abbey ; " as being "a very entertaining person, besides being a sincerely pious man."[1] Everything we read points to the same conclusion. Legh Richmond will come before us again in connection both with the literature and with the missionary work of the period. It will here suffice to say that the presence of such a man in a country neighbourhood must have tended to throw light all around him,

[1] *Lives of Twelve Good Men:* "C. L. Higgins," ii. 359, 360.

and also to commend strongly the Evangelical cause, to which he attached himself heart and soul.[1]

The same may be said of *Edward Bickersteth* (1786–1850), who in 1830 was presented to the country living of Watton, in Herts, by Mr. Abel Smith, M.P., a leading Evangelical layman, and one of Mr. Bickersteth's hearers at Wheler Chapel;[2] but as Mr. Bickersteth's life as a country clergyman only covers three out of the thirty-three years of our period, and as, like Mr. Legh Richmond, he will come before us again in connection both with missionary and with literary work, his holy and blameless life must not be dwelt upon here.

Several other country clergy might be named, but to the general reader they would be but like "the brave Gyas and the brave Cloanthus," names and nothing more; so it will be better to pass on to a class of men who, from their position at any rate, if for nothing else, require a word of notice.

The growing strength of the Evangelical cause showed itself, among other ways, in the sympathy which it began to call forth from the Episcopate. Till the close of the eighteenth century there was only one on the bench of bishops who at all sympathized with the Evangelicals, and he only in a very guarded and general way. Up to that time, and indeed for some years later, there was scarcely a bishop who did not feel bound to charge his clergy against the Methodists, taking care to make it plain that he included in that term those who would now be called Evangelicals as well as Methodists proper. But Dr. Beilby Porteus, Bishop of London, though cautious, went, in many points, heart and soul with the Evangelicals. He was one of their most cordial and effective supporters in their crusade against the Slave Trade, and an early patron of the Church Missionary Society and the Bible Society, which were crucial tests of Evangelicalism; he supported Hannah More in all her good works; laid great stress upon the observance of the Lord's day, patronized Sunday schools, and, in short, threw the weight of his influence into most of the schemes which the Evangelicals held dear. His sympathy was valuable, for, apart from his high station, he was deservedly respected as a good, consistent man.

---

[1] See Grimshaw's *Life of the Rev. Legh Richmond*, *passim*.
[2] See Birks' *Memoir of the Rev. E. Bickersteth*, *passim*.

He was the most amiable of beings, but he had also a vein of satirical humour, which on more than one occasion enabled him, in a telling way, to retaliate upon those who loved to make a joke against Methodism. It was a grievous loss to the Evangelicals when, upon his death in 1809, he was succeeded in the influential see of London by Dr. Randolph, Bishop of Oxford, who always had been, and still continued to be, an uncompromising opponent of "Methodism" in every shape and form.

Another prelate who gave a dignified and qualified support to the cause was the amiable and highly aristocratic Bishop of Durham, Dr. Shute Barrington. He, too, joined the Church Missionary Society and the Bible Society, and made himself generally agreeable to the Evangelicals; and they, in their turn, duly appreciated his condescension. Among other things, he took a deep interest in week-day and Sunday schools, and was a liberal supporter of both. None were more prominent in educational matters than the Evangelicals, and this furnished a point of contact between them and the Bishop of Durham. There is an interesting letter from Wilberforce to Hannah More which illustrates this so forcibly that it is worth quoting. It appears that Mrs. More had been invited to assist the bishop in his design of establishing schools in his diocese, and that she hesitated about leaving her work at Cheddar. So Wilberforce wrote, "Though no one can prize your services in Somerset more than myself, yet I believe it would be right for you to pay a visit to the prince-bishop. Go, then, to Auckland, and may the grace of God go with you. I am convinced that, on many accounts, you would be able to do far more than myself, or any other person living, with this primary planet, which is surrounded with satellites. It is more; it is a very sun, the centre of an entire system. I will meet you there, if possible. The bishop has often invited me and Mrs. Wilberforce."[1] It was another distinct loss to the Evangelicals when Bishop Barrington died, in 1826; for though his successor, Bishop Van Mildert, belonged to that nobler and more spiritual section of the High Churchmen, which was by no means inclined to condemn indiscriminately all the Evangelicals as

[1] *Life of William Wilberforce*, p. 194.

Methodists, he was of course far from being in sympathy with them.

Bishop Burgess, first of St. David's, then of Salisbury, was another prelate who greatly sympathized with many of the objects which were most dear to the Evangelical mind. He was, indeed, according to his biographer, "cavilled at as an exclusive patron of Evangelical clergy;"[1] but he does not appear to me to have completely identified himself with them.

In fact, upon none of these three good men could the Evangelicals quite reckon as their own; they respected all three, and always wrote and spoke of them in the high terms which they deserved. But it was not until the Hon. *Dudley Ryder* was promoted to the see of Gloucester, in 1815, that they could really feel that they were represented on the episcopal bench. Then, indeed, there was rejoicing in the Evangelical camp. His elevation was anticipated some time before the event. As Dean of Wells he had been a prominent man, and the Evangelicals watched him with great satisfaction as he became more and more sympathetic with them. "How delightful it is," exclaims Simeon, "to see dignitaries in our Church thus coming forward, and disciples springing up in Cæsar's household!"[2]—not at all a happy use of a text, for it would imply a resemblance between dignitaries of the Church and the heathen household of a heathen emperor. The good man did not, doubtless, mean this; but it was just one of those phrases which gave not unreasonable offence, and which are far too common in Evangelical writings. Wilberforce "highly prized and loved Bishop Ryder as a prelate after his own heart, who united to the zeal of an apostle the most amiable and endearing qualities, and the polished manners of the best society."[3]

The two brothers Sumner, the one Bishop of Winchester, the other of Chester (afterwards Archbishop of Canterbury), were both warmly welcomed by the Evangelicals. They both gave their preferments far more extensively than any other prelates had done to clergymen of Evangelical views. It was

---

[1] *Life of Thomas Burgess, Bishop of Salisbury*, by J. S. Harford, p. 341.
[2] Carus, p. 264.
[3] *Recollections of W. Wilberforce*, p. 68.

to the Bishop of Winchester that Dr. Dealtry owed the small dignities which were tardily conferred upon him. The same prelate was also the friend of Charles Jerram, and gave him the living of Witney; and the Bishop of Chester was at least as favourable to the Evangelical cause.

With the exception of the good men of Clapham, most of the Evangelicals who have been noticed were clergymen ; but it must not be supposed that there were not many leading Evangelicals among the laity besides the Claphamites. Hannah More herself was, of course, a tower of strength. She was a link both between the Evangelicals of the first and the second generation, and also between the latter and the world without. Of her eighteenth-century life I have written elsewhere ;[1] but she lived all through the first thirty-three years of the nineteenth century, and this was the happiest and most influential part of her life ; for then she began to see the battle against vice and ignorance which she had long been waging, if not single-handed, at any rate with the support of a very few, carried on by a large and formidable army in all parts of the country. The reputation which this estimable lady enjoyed for piety, talents, and, it may be added, agreeableness, was extraordinary, extending far beyond the Evangelical circle. Her house at Barley Wood, where she resided with her four sisters, all of whom were her helpmates in her benevolent schemes, was really a sort of Mecca, whither pilgrims of all sorts resorted.[2] We hear of Southey, Wordsworth, Alexander Knox, Bishop Jebb, and others, who certainly did not belong to the Evangelical school, visiting the sisters, and most of them coming away in raptures. But, of course, it was with the Evangelicals that she was most at home ; and their expressions of respect (one might say reverence) for her personally, even apart from her writings, are most striking. When her writings, which will be noticed in their proper place, are also taken into account, it is hardly too much to say that she was the most influential person—certainly the most influential lady—who lived at the time.[3]

[1] See *English Church in the Eighteenth Century.*
[2] See, *inter alia*, Mrs. Sherwood's *Autobiography*, p. 217.
[3] At Clifton she was called " The Queen of the Methodists."

Among other influential laymen who favoured the Evangelicals were Mr. Spencer Perceval, the Prime Minister, whose sad death in 1811 was a great blow to the cause; the Duke of Kent, "in whom," writes the Evangelical Mr. Grimshaw, "every religious and benevolent undertaking found a powerful friend and patron,"[1] and whose bias is shown by the fact that he made Mr. Legh Richmond his chaplain; the Earl of Harrowby, elder brother of Bishop Ryder; Sir T. A. Acland; Mr. Abel Smith, mentioned above; Sir T. Fowell Buxton; and Mr. Carus Wilson, for some time M.P. for Pontefract.[2] But without wearying the reader with a long list of names, it may be said generally that, during the first quarter of the present century, there was a rapid increase in the strength of the Evangelical party till it became, beyond all question, the dominant spiritual force in the Church. What Mr. Jerram tells us of one particular district is true, more or less, of the whole kingdom. Referring to the early years of the present century, he writes, "A report had been spread that a person who took a prominent lead among the sect called Evangelicals had been appointed to the livings of Chobham and Bisley, and a stronger feeling could scarcely have been excited if it had been published that a pestilence had visited those unhappy villages. There was only one clergyman who had the least claim to that distinction, or who would not have recoiled from the imputation."[3] Referring to a later period (1822), he says, "At the time at which my narrative has now arrived, a great change had taken place throughout the whole kingdom in the state of religion. Instead of here and there a few scattered clergymen who preached the doctrines of the Reformation, and who were almost everywhere looked upon with suspicion, and treated with neglect, if not with scorn, there were great numbers in every part of the kingdom, who advocated them with boldness, and were received with respect and affection."[4]

If the rise of the Evangelical party was rapid, equally so

---

[1] *Life of Legh Richmond*, p. 343.
[2] *i.e.* Carus Wilson the father; the best-known Carus Wilson, the son, was of course a clergyman, and belongs to a later period.
[3] *Memoir of the Rev. Charles Jerram*, p. 262.
[4] *Id.*, p. 295.

was what in one sense may be called its decline. It is very necessary to insert this qualifying clause, "in one sense," because in another sense there has never been a decline. So far as Evangelicalism means simply a revival of spiritual religion on distinctively Christian principles, it can never die out. For giving life to the dry bones of barren orthodoxy and cold morality, the Church of England is greatly indebted to the Evangelicals, and should never forget her obligation. But the form in which essential truths were presented and the accretions which grew around them are different matters; and the Church, having assimilated the essence, gradually threw off the accidents; and this is all that is meant by the decline of Evangelicalism. Moreover, the Church began to realize that there was another side of religion besides that presented by the Evangelicals—an objective as well as a subjective side.

Perhaps what is meant will be most vividly brought before us if we consider the attitude of the Evangelicals of our period to the Church and to the world. What is the Church? What is the world? The answers practically given by them to both these questions are answers which have been less and less generally accepted by members of the Church of England ever since the rise of the Oxford Movement, and not only by those who identified themselves with that movement.

There must always be to the Christian an antagonism between the Church and the world, but the Evangelical theory about both Church and world can hardly be regarded as a logical one. To take the last question first, What is the world? Now, one can quite understand the line taken by a St. Jerome in his cave, or a St. Simeon on his pillar, or a sour Puritan setting himself against all the amenities of life, in regard to the world. But the Evangelicals of whom we have been treating in this chapter took quite a different course from any of these. In all sincerity they strove to renounce the world; but their theory of what "the world" was, was surely a very arbitrary one. It consisted mainly of certain recreations, which, though liable—perhaps peculiarly liable— to abuse, seem to the ordinary mind to be in themselves absolutely indifferent. But, putting aside these recreations, the typical Evangelical managed to make life exceedingly comfortable; nobly, indeed, doing his duty towards his fellow-men, but leaving a wide margin for enjoying himself after his own fashion. Instead of living in a cave or on a pillar, he might live in a luxurious villa at Clapham or elsewhere. He might keep a most abundant table, and at that table might be found some of the best table-talk of the day. It is curious to observe how frequently *bonhomie* and conversational powers of a high order were predicated of the Evangelicals. Wilberforce was of "a most gay and playful disposition;" he "touched life at so many points;" lived "in perpetual sunshine, and shed its radiance all around him."[1] "The Dean" must have been perfectly delightful; few subjects would make a prettier picture than Isaac Milner laying himself out to amuse the young Macaulay, as the latter so graphically describes the scene.[2] Legh Richmond was "exceedingly good company."[3] Robinson of Leicester was "a capital conversationalist, very lively and bright."[4] This is the way in which two acute observers from the sister Isle describe the impressions made upon them by the English Evangelicals. "We have already," writes Bishop Jebb from London, in 1809, to a friend in Ireland, "met some of the religious world at the house of a Mr. Pearson,[5] where we were most hospitably entertained. Among the company were Mr. and Mrs. H. Thornton. You may have heard that he is a great friend of Mr. Wilberforce, and one of the party in the house whom they call 'the saints.' . . . We are pressed to dine with Mr. H. Thornton next week." Next comes a letter—written, probably, after the dinner-party at Mr. Thornton's—which describes his delight with Mr. Wilberforce and with "the saints" generally.[6] We have a similar account, some years earlier, from Alexander Knox. He, too, went from Ireland, and was introduced to the English Evangelicals. He "drinks

---

[1] *Life*, pp. 408, 417. See also *Life of Bishop Jebb*, ii. 164, where he gives an account of Wilberforce which more than bears out what is said about him in the text.

[2] See Morison's *Macaulay*.

[3] Burgon, *Lives of Twelve Good Men*, ii. 360.

[4] *Memoir of the Rev. Charles Jerram*, p. 148.

[5] A leading Evangelical clergyman, afterwards Dean of Salisbury.

[6] *Life and Correspondence of Bishop Jebb*, ii. 162-164.

coffee with Mrs. Hannah More," and finds that she "far exceeded his expectations in pleasant manners and interesting conversation." He pays her another visit, and writes, " At Mrs. More's we met a serious, well-bred, well-informed gentleman, an intimate friend of Mrs. More's and Mr. Wilberforce's—Mr. Pratt, with whom we dine to-morrow. You're not to suppose, when I use the word 'serious,' I mean disconsolate or gloomy. On the contrary, I have met with no people further from everything of the kind ;" and so forth.[1]

Now, there was absolutely nothing inconsistent with the Christian profession in this mode of life—this mild hospitality, this cheerfulness and agreeableness. On the contrary, it all adds a grace to their beautiful Christian characters. But it *does* seem difficult to see on what logical grounds men who were certainly in their way enjoying the good things of this life should condemn others who were only enjoying them in a slightly different manner.[2] Stated bluntly, it came to this. If a person was enjoying a well-spread feast at Clapham, with all the charms of the conversation of Wilberforce or Milner—which to many people would be infinitely more entertaining than most of the so-called entertainments provided by the "world"—he was doing right, and was, so far as outward surroundings went, on the way to heaven. But if he was reading one of Miss Austen's novels, which came out at this period,[3] or at a dance or a concert, or at a card-table (not necessarily gambling), or seeing one of Goldsmith's delightful plays acted, he was doing wrong, and, so far as outward surroundings went, in plain words, on the way to hell.

One of the worst features of this theory was, that it was like those prophecies which have a tendency to bring about their own fulfilment. When certain amusements are assumed

[1] *Remains of Alexander Knox*, iv. 64, 67, 68.
[2] The unconscious inconsistency is admirably pointed out by Mrs. Oliphant, in her *Literary History of England in the End of the Eighteenth and Beginning of the Nineteenth Century*, iii. 369–373 : " The Evangelicals."
[3] Admirers of Miss Austen—that is, all persons blessed with brains and culture —will remember how she complains in *Persuasion* of the stigma which was attached to novels. It is well known that T. B. Macaulay and his sister used to "cap quotations" with one another from Miss Austen's novels, and that they were inveterate novel-readers. " Zachary Macaulay disapproved of novel-reading ; but his family read more novels and remembered them better than any in the kingdom."—*Life and Letters of Lord Macaulay*, by Sir G. O. Trevelyan, i. 61.

to be fit only for the immoral and irreligious, those who provide them will be tempted to cater only for their own public. The supply will answer to the demand, and the providers will be inclined to retaliate upon the "unco' guid" by running into the other extreme, and pouring ridicule upon the good altogether. There can be no question that some of the novels and plays in fashion at the beginning of this century were quite unfit for the entertainment of Christian people. But let such people demand a pure article, and, depend upon it, they will be supplied. "Abusus non tollit usum" is a maxim which the Evangelicals of the time never succeeded in grasping.

Another evil arising from this indiscriminate condemnation of things in themselves indifferent was that it indirectly, but very really, led people into sin. In this way. If you at once forfeited your title to be accounted a Christian by countenancing any of these things,—well, to use a vulgar phrase, you might as well be hanged for stealing a sheep as a lamb, so you had better plunge at once into the grossest dissipation. Hence the fact, too patent to escape notice, that the children of Evangelical parents so frequently turned out ill. It was not merely that their good parents drew the rein so tightly that it snapped. It was also that a wider culture taught those who had been brought up in this school to doubt whether many things from which they had been debarred as wrong were really wrong; and when a man's standard of right and wrong becomes unsettled, he is very apt *in pejus ruere*. Sometimes, instead of going wrong, they highly distinguished themselves, but by pursuing a very different line of thought and action from that of their parents. It is only necessary to mention the names of Wilberforce, Macaulay, Neale, and Stephen as illustrations of this. But though the result was far more satisfactory, it equally illustrates the fact that these Evangelicals of the second generation[1] failed as a rule to keep their children within

---

[1] The failure does not appear in the Evangelicals of the first generation. *Their* children followed, as a rule, the course of their parents, only with a wider range of ideas and more *savoir faire*. See on this point some excellent remarks by Sir James Stephen, *Essays on Ecclesiastical Biography* : "The Clapham Sect," pp. 308, 309 ; also the *Autobiography of William Jay*, pp. 175-177. Mr. Jay knew personally the men of both generations. But perhaps the most

their own lines of thought. Indeed, the failure is even more striking than in those melancholy instances in which they went morally wrong: for in the one case it might be urged that they merely gave way to the depravity of human nature without thinking at all; in the other they certainly *did* think, and their thinking led them to an entirely different conclusion from what their fathers had drawn.[1]

In the answer to that other question, What is the Church? the Evangelicals of the second generation seem also to have taken up an illogical position. On the one hand, you may hold with the Liberals, and almost every sect of Dissenters, and, we may add, with many of the first generation of Evangelicals, that any society of Christians which professes a belief in Christ is a Church in itself; or, on the other hand, you may hold with the Greeks, the Romans, and the Anglicans, that there is one Holy Catholic Church, a visible, not an invisible one, and that when the expression "Churches" is used, it is used in a strictly geographical sense. But it is difficult with any consistency to blend the two theories, and this is what the Evangelicals virtually attempted to do. They were far stricter and more exclusive Churchmen than their fathers had been. They clung in all sincerity to the Church of England; they loved her Liturgy, they pinned their faith to her Articles, and yet, like their fathers, they manifestly agreed with the Dissenter's, not with the Anglican's, theory of the Church. This is admirably brought out by Dr. R. W. Dale, the Congregationalist (of all men in the world!). "Nor," he writes, "were the Evangelical clergy zealous supporters of Episcopacy; their imagination was not touched by that great—though, as we believe, false—conception of the Church which fired the passion of the leaders

interesting of all is the account given by one who was *grandson* of a leading Evangelical of the first generation, and *son* of a leader of the second. See sermon on the death of Josiah Pratt by H. Venn, appended to his *Retrospect and Prospect of the Operations of the Church Missionary Society*, 1865. Henry Venn the younger was a marked exception to the rule that the sons of Evangelical parents went off at a tangent, either spiritually, morally, or intellectually.

[1] Sir George Trevelyan remarks with perfect truth, "There could have been nothing vulgar, and little that was narrow, in a training which produced Samuel Wilberforce, J. Stephen, and Macaulay."—*Life of Lord Macaulay*, i. 63. Certainly not; but the writer will hardly contend that any of these eminent 'men were Evangelicals like their fathers.

H

of the Tractarian Revival. . . . The Evangelical Movement encouraged what is called an undenominational temper. It emphasized the vital importance of the Evangelical creed, but it regarded almost with indifference all forms of Church polity that were not in apparent and irreconcilable antagonism to that creed. It demanded as the basis of fellowship a common religious life and common religious beliefs, but was satisfied with fellowship of an accidental and precarious kind. It cared nothing for the idea of the Church as the august society of saints. It was the ally of individualism."[1] This is more glaringly true of the first generation of Evangelicals than it is of the second; but the latter put no intelligible theory in its place. So it is not in the least surprising that, coincident with the rise of Evangelicalism, there was a vast increase of all kinds of Dissent, which many of the Evangelicals themselves observed with dismay. But really one is inclined to say, "Tu l'as voulu, Georges Dandin;" for in point of fact the Evangelical was more in sympathy with the Dissenting than with the Church principle, except in the one single point of establishment, which is, after all, an accident, not of the essence of the matter. The Evangelicals loved their Prayer-book; but it was a hard matter indeed to reconcile, as some of the party gallantly endeavoured to do, their distinctive tenets with the plain teaching of that book. Some, indeed, instead of attempting the hopeless task, frankly owned that they tolerated it in lieu of something better. But as soon as men began to study the Prayer-book, and especially the history of the Prayer-book, more deeply, it was inevitable that the old Evangelical teaching should lose ground.

And this applies to the study of theology generally. Thoughtful Churchmen would naturally turn to the standard divines of their own Church as their best guides; and Hooker, Barrow, South, Jeremy Taylor, Bingham, Butler, Sherlock, and Waterland would teach them divinity, but not Evangelicalism, so far as it differed from the old-fashioned Church teaching.

Still more powerful in the same direction would be the influence of the general literature of the period. The early

[1] *The Old Evangelicalism and the New*, by R. W. Dale, LL.D., pp. 16, 17.

part of the nineteenth century witnessed an outburst of poetry which had not been equalled since the days of Queen Elizabeth; and though the two schools of poetry which then arose differed violently and diametrically from one another in almost every conceivable point, they agreed in this: they were both opposed, to a man, to the Evangelical system. Whether men read and admired Wordsworth, Coleridge, Southey, Scott, De Quincey, and Landor on the one side, or Byron, Shelley, and Keats on the other, they would in all cases be reading anti-Evangelical literature.

Another cause of the decline of Evangelicalism has been so frequently alleged, and upon such high authority, that one cannot with any modesty affirm that there was no force in it. It is said that the Evangelical party grievously degenerated in the years immediately preceding the Oxford Movement; but I feel bound in common justice to add that I can find no traces of this degeneracy in the lives of its leaders. In point of real goodness and spiritual activity, Simeon, Bickersteth, and Legh Richmond will bear comparison with Newton, Romaine, and Cecil. Henry Thornton, John Venn, and John Scott were not degenerate sons of John Thornton, Henry Venn, and Thomas Scott; and, in point of numbers, the later Evangelicals who attained more or less distinction were as ten to one compared with the earlier.[1] At the same time, one can well understand that when the Evangelical became the popular instead of the "calumniated" party (to use Hannah More's epithet) it might contain among its rank and file a much larger number of unworthy members. For it was extremely easy to catch the tone and phraseology of Evangelicalism. Its whole teaching was compressed within

[1] The following passage from the *Memoir of the Rev. Basil Woodd*, who was a link between the first and second generations of Evangelicals, and knew intimately the leaders of both, is worth quoting: "His general estimate from the comparison [between the two generations] was, that scriptural piety is not only far more widely diffused in the present day [1831] than it was forty years since; but that, with some unhappy exceptions which he bitterly lamented, the doctrinal views of that portion of the clergy with whom he was usually classed were more sound, sober, practical, and scriptural than those of some whom he had known in early life; that they were consistent Churchmen and useful parish priests, and were chiefly defective in those deep spiritual attainments, that fervent communion with God, and that 'blessed unction from above,' which characterized some of the fathers of his youth"—rather a grave defect.—Wilks' *Memoir*, p. 26.

a very narrow compass. The repeating of a very few shibboleths, the abstaining from a very few tabooed practices, the occasional attendance at the proper kind of church, the investment of a very small sum of money in support of the right sort of societies, was enough to stamp a man as "serious."

But, after all, the real weakness of Evangelicalism was not so much on its moral and spiritual as on its intellectual side. It produced many good men, but no really first-rate writers. It is most interesting and profitable to study the lives and characters of those who were trained under this system, but who ever thinks now of reading their books? Even in the department of biblical exegesis, in which one would have expected them most to shine, they produced nothing of really permanent value. They read the Bible devoutly, but they threw little or no light upon the meaning of that sacred book. Scott's Commentary is the one solitary treatise of which even the reputation has survived; and that Biblical student must be easily satisfied who is content with Scott's Commentary.[1] Even their preaching power, in which they were supposed especially to excel, has to be taken upon trust; for the very best of their printed sermons which have survived are but "as water unto wine" when compared with those of the really great preachers of the English Church.

And yet, in one sense, the Evangelicals were assuredly not deficient in intellectual capacity. Almost all the leading men who have been mentioned in this chapter were decidedly above the average in point of abilities and attainments. The defect lay, not in their mental powers, which have been too much depreciated, but in their way of looking at and treating religious and secular subjects, and the relationship between them. "The Evangelical school," writes Principal Tulloch most truly, "with all its merits, had conceived of Christianity rather as something superadded to the highest life of humanity, than as the perfect development of that life; as a scheme for human salvation authenticated by miracles, and, so to speak,

[1] I have not forgotten Hartwell Horne's *Introduction;* but (1) that book scarcely comes under the head of biblical exegesis; (2) there is nothing distinctively and exclusively Evangelical in it; (3) Hartwell Horne, though more attached to the Evangelical than to any other party in the Church, can hardly be reckoned as a pronounced Evangelical.

interpolated into human history, rather than a divine philosophy. Philosophy, literature, art, and science were conceived apart from religion. The world and the Church were severed portions of life divided by outward signs and badges ; and those who joined the one or the other were supposed to be clearly marked off."[1] This thoughtful writer illustrates what he means by instances from Newton and Romaine ; but it would be equally easy to find illustrations from the Evangelicals of the next generation. "There are persons," says the biographer of Isaac Milner, "who secretly, if not avowedly, associate the ideas of piety and imbecility ; and who, however illogical such a conclusion may be, do not hesitate to decide, that he who professes to be governed by Christian principles must be deficient in natural understanding."[2] This notion of the alienation of piety from intellect was a most mischievous one to go abroad, and it is not quite just to the Evangelicals to say that they were responsible for it. On the contrary, they could, and they did, point with pardonable pride to members of their body in whom piety was combined with great intellectual eminence. It was partly with this object that the sermons of Isaac Milner were published immediately after his death. "There have not been wanting," it is said in the preface, "men ready to assert that pure and vital godliness has not ranked among its advocates many who have been distinguished for the strength of their minds and their intellectual superiority. It seems, therefore, desirable, when a bright instance occurs to the contrary, that his religious sentiments should be handed down to posterity."[3] And yet it must be confessed that the Evangelicals did not quite go the right way about the task of disabusing men of this idea. They sought human knowledge "because of the present distress," not because they valued it. Claudius Buchanan, who was sent to Cambridge at the expense of Mr. Thornton, admits this with great *naïveté*. "They are desirous that we should *excel* in the studies of the place that we may (as it were) shed some lustre (in the eyes of men) on that gospel

---

[1] *Movements of Religious Thought in Britain during the Nineteenth Century*, p. 13.
[2] *Life of Isaac Milner*, by his niece, Mary Milner (1844), preface, p. iv.
[3] *Sermons by Isaac Milner* (2 vols., 1820), preface.

which the learned despise. The grand argument which we use against infidels, who deride the truth as being only professed by men of weak judgment, is to point out some learned Christian (if such can be found)."[1] In very much the same spirit Charles Jerram speaks of attending Simeon's meetings, "which," he says, "served to keep alive the spark of personal religion, which was in danger of being quenched by the uncongenial pursuit of mathematical subjects, or the impure mythology and profane poetry, which constitute the daily routine of study."[2] A still more memorable instance of the Evangelical tendency to regard the pursuit of knowledge as, at best, a necessary evil, may be found in the relations between Zachary Macaulay and his brilliant son. The father positively discouraged and disliked the successful efforts which the young Macaulay had, even in those early days, made to distinguish himself in literature; and it has always seemed to me that the markedly unspiritual tone which pervades Lord Macaulay's writings may be traced to the revulsion against the rigid school in which he had been brought up.[3]

What has been said of literature is equally true of the fine arts. Mrs. Cecil records with evident approval how her good husband, who had been an accomplished musician and an admirer of good pictures, "cut his violin-strings and never afterwards replaced them," and "determined never to frequent the exhibition" [of the Royal Academy?], because such tastes interfered with the one thing needful.[4] Edward Bickersteth's sole reflection, after he had seen Lincoln Cathedral, and calculated that it would cost £500,000 to build, was, "Well, the religious societies of England are doing far better than if they built such a cathedral every year, in raising that sum to scatter in every direction the light of

---

[1] *Memoir of the Life and Writings of the Rev. Claudius Buchanan*, by the Rev. Hugh Pearson, i. 67.

[2] *Memoir of Charles Jerram*, p. 84.

[3] See Morison's *Macaulay* (English Men of Letters Series) on this point, ch. i., especially p. 16. Sir George Trevelyan, however, tells us that though Zachary Macaulay was so distressed at his son's writing in *Knight's Quarterly Magazine* that the son promised to do so no more, yet he afterwards wrote with his father's approval. See *Life*, i. 115.

[4] See Memoir prefixed to Cecil's *Remains*, xcviii.

Divine truth. This will do far more for the honour of God our Saviour, and the salvation of our fellow-creatures."[1] Legh Richmond warned his daughters against reading, not only novels—that goes without saying—but poetry, and against all music except sacred music. Charlotte Elizabeth writes with bitter compunction of having been tempted to read Shakespeare, as if she had committed a deadly sin in so doing.[2]

It is curious to observe how very generally such views as these have been now discarded. Some of the severest critics of the Evangelicals of the past are to be found, not among High Churchmen, but among those to whom, one would have thought, their slender Churchmanship would be a recommendation rather than an offence. Two such critics have already been quoted;[3] let me finish the ungrateful but necessary task of pointing out the weaknesses of really good men, by quoting a third. Dr. Stoughton, whose desire to be fair all round is beyond praise, writes, "The defects of the early Evangelicals[4] are manifest. They were destitute generally of any great taste for literature and art, and used a somewhat peculiar religious dialect; intolerant of other men's opinions, questioning the religion of those pronounced unevangelical, and one-sided in their theological system; and they did not

[1] Birks' *Memoir of Edward Bickersteth*, ii. 53.
[2] "I was permitted to read . . . *The Merchant of Venice*. I drank a cup of intoxication under which my brain reeled for many a year. The character of Shylock burst upon me, even as Shakespeare had conceived it. I revelled in the terrible excitement that it gave rise to; page after page was stereotyped upon a most retentive memory without an effort, and during a sleepless night I feasted on the pernicious sweets thus hoarded in my brain. . . . Oh, how many wasted hours, how much of unprofitable labour, what wrong to my fellow-creatures, what robbery of God, must I refer to this ensnaring book [Shakespeare generally!] . . . But for this I might have early sought the consolations of the gospel. Parents know not what they do when they foster in a young girl what is called a poetical taste. Those things highly esteemed among men, are held in abomination with God; they thrust Him from His creature's thoughts, and enshrine a host of polluting idols in His place."—*Personal Recollections of Charlotte Elizabeth*, pp. 26, 27. After this, we are not surprised to find the good lady, after she had ceased to be "a young girl," writing, "I exclude from my book-shelves all the furniture of a worldly library."—*Id.*, p. 64.
[3] Principal Tulloch and Dr. R. W. Dale.
[4] That he means those of the second as well as of the first generation is evident from his reference to Bishop Herbert Marsh. Besides, his subject is, *Religion in England*, 1800-1850.

clearly distinguish between scientific theology and spiritual religion. The inferences of eminent divines amongst reformers, amongst Puritans, and even amongst themselves, were too often confounded with the teachings of Scripture. . . . They repudiated all authority but that of the Bible, yet they were powerfully influenced by their own favourite authors. . . . Perspective was neglected in their theological pictures, the relative proportions of certain doctrines being almost overlooked, and an undue importance attached to minor points in details of belief. Of course, it was not possible for them to anticipate the results of modern criticism. Perhaps they scarcely appreciated the value of what was being accomplished by Herbert Marsh and others. A dislike to the theology of such men interfered with a due estimate of their biblical researches." [1]

What gave the Evangelical party its vitality, in spite of these weaknesses, was—

1. The spiritual earnestness and activity of its leaders, including those of the second quite as much as those of the first generation. Their lives were "an epistle read of all men," who do not care now to read anything that they wrote.

2. The admirable organization of the party. The business talents of the men of Clapham and others were turned to good account in the management of their religious affairs. There was always plenty of money at the disposal of the Evangelical leaders, for they faithfully and very rightly impressed upon their wealthy followers the Christian duty of giving; and that money was not wasted. Large sums were spent by the Thorntons, Simeon, and others in purchasing the advowson of livings, the special ones selected being generally the great centres of activity, which formed effective *points d'appui* for the party; the patronage was vested in trustees, so that in "the multitude of counsellors" there might be "wisdom," and that all jobbery might be guarded against. Societies were founded at various places which furnished pecuniary assistance to young men, who were piously and evangelically disposed, but of straitened means, in their University course, after a searching examination into their circumstances, piety, and attainments by the ablest men of the party. The young

[1] *Religion in England*, 1800–1850, by John Stoughton, D.D., i. 113.

men thus helped were not left to their own devices at the University; they were placed under the careful supervision of such men as Simeon, Milner, Farish, Jowett, Crouch, or Daniel Wilson; their colleges were chosen for them—Magdalen or Queen's[1] at Cambridge (King's was, of course, not available), St. Edmund's Hall at Oxford; when they had qualified themselves for Holy Orders, curacies were found for them where their Evangelical training would still go on, or Indian chaplaincies for those who had a mind to go abroad. The missionary and other societies connected with the Evangelical party were well managed and very prosperous. The party presented a united front to the outer world; and, after the Calvinistic controversy had subsided, was not much torn by internal dissent. In short, everything that *could* be done *was* done, in the way of organization, to perpetuate and extend the system.

3. The real, practical work of Christian piety and charity, about the desirableness of which most good people, to whatever school they belonged, would agree, largely contributed to keep up the credit of the party. Men who cared little about abstract doctrine, could, at any rate, appreciate the merits of those who devoted themselves to the work of founding schools, establishing libraries, ameliorating prison-discipline, building churches, and, above all, abolishing the Slave Trade and ultimately emancipating the negro.

4. The Evangelicals reaped great advantages from the infatuation of their adversaries, many of whom played most effectively into their hands. Nothing could be more conducive to the spread of the system than the indiscriminate stigmatizing of everything which was really a part of spiritual religion as methodistical and unorthodox. There is a passage in one of the early numbers of the *British Critic* which so exactly expresses what is meant, that it had better be quoted. "The most discreet and orthodox Christian," says the writer, "shall not fail to be branded with the indiscriminate, opprobrious denomination of Methodist, merely for showing a becoming regularity as to sacred things, and

---

[1] To these may be added, at one time, Trinity Hall. When Isaac Milner was president of Queen's, and Joseph Jowett was tutor at Trinity Hall, and much under Milner's influence, Trinity Hall used to be called a fief of Queen's.

leading, in a word, a Christian life. We have more than once protested against this most shameful, yet most prevalent abuse of terms; and we intreat those who feel or affect a regard for the Church, not to pay it so ill a compliment as to place all persons in the class of sectaries who live as every Christian ought to live. It originates, doubtless, in a desire to countenance that general relaxation of manners which has long endangered our whole system of morality and religion."[1] Not altogether, I venture to think. There was a real confusion in the minds of some of the honest assailants of Evangelicalism; they mixed up two quite different classes of men, as is pointed out in a remarkably able and thoughtful volume or pamphlet (it comes between the two) which has been already quoted. "There exists," says the writer, "a distinction between those who are called Evangelical ministers; there are sober thinkers as well as enthusiasts, orderly clergymen as well as irregular ones, lovers of peace and union as well as litigious controversialists. Of this distinction it appears to be the endeavour of some writers to obliterate every mark by which it might be discovered. The character of the pious clergyman, devoted to the prosperity of the national Church and the welfare of his flock, cannot be greatly affected, among his parishioners, by this procedure. Those who 'know the man and his communication' will not confound his assiduity with the zeal of a proselyting sectary, . . . nor will they be persuaded so far to distrust their own senses as to believe that, on the affirmation of nobody knows who, in that place of worship which they constantly attend, there are means used to propagate anything different from what the Church of England requires of her members, if it be not really so."[2] Let any one apply these remarks to men like Legh Richmond or Josiah Pratt, and he will perceive how true they are; the abuse of such men by those who knew nothing about them would be sure to produce a strong feeling in their favour among those who knew them.

It was, no doubt, sufficiently provoking to men of real learning and goodness to be told, as they incessantly *were*

[1] Review of a *Sermon on the General Thanksgiving*, June 1, 1802, by Sir A. Gordon, in the *British Critic*, 1803.
[2] *Zeal without Innovation*, preface.

told, that they knew nothing of the real nature of Christianity; that "the gospel was not preached in the national pulpits," as the phrase went. We can well understand the indignation with which, in the early part of the century, bishops were wont to repudiate the imputation in their Charges;[1] and how it was made the special subject of two remarkably able and interesting courses of Bampton Lectures, in 1803 and 1812 respectively,[2] as well as of innumerable parochial sermons. But, after all, in spite of much crudity, the Evangelicals *did* meet a real want which their adversaries did not supply. It was quite against the spirit of the times to inveigh against all enthusiasm. The quiet, old-fashioned view of religion which had suited the eighteenth century was out of date in the nineteenth, when the spirit which had stirred up the French Revolution was rife, though happily in a different form, throughout England. The crowded and enthusiastic services and meetings so vividly described by Legh Richmond and Edward Bickersteth in their accounts of their missionary tours in all parts of England,[3] or at Carlisle Cathedral when Dean Milner preached,[4] or at Warton under the ministry of Daniel Wilson,[5] or at Cambridge under Simeon and Farish, or at Birmingham, where "crowds turned away from the doors," when the evangelical Dr. W. Marsh preached,[6] were indices of the popular feeling. It was in vain that sober divines declaimed against the love of excitement and the bane of fanaticism. The movement which the Methodists proper had raised among the lower classes was spreading upwards, and the Evangelicals were the only men who could satisfy the craving.

[1] See, *inter alia*, the Charges of the Bishop of Oxford (Dr. Randolph) in 1802 and 1805; Bishop Horsley's Charges, *passim*, especially his Charge to the diocese of Rochester in 1803; the Charge of the Bishop of Lincoln in 1804, etc.

[2] *Religious Enthusiasm considered*, the Bampton Lectures for 1803, by G. F. Nott; and *An Appeal to the Gospel*, etc., the Bampton Lectures for 1812, by Richard Mant.

[3] See Grimshaw's *Life of Legh Richmond*, pp. 234, 238, 243, 263; and Birks' *Memoir of Edward Bickersteth*, i. 220, 369.

[4] See *Life of Isaac Milner*, p. 360, etc.; and *Life of William Paley*, vol. i. p. 152, which shows that Milner's admiring biographer did not at all exaggerate the fact.

[5] See Bateman's *Life of Daniel Wilson*, p. 126.

[6] *Life of the Rev. William Marsh, D.D.*, by his daughter, p. 145.

(5) The very name "Evangelical" told greatly in their favour. Unlike that of "Methodist," it was not given as a term of reproach; it sprung up, we scarcely know when or how.[1] One of the bitterest and most frequent complaints against the party was that "they arrogated to themselves the title of Evangelical," and thus cast a tacit slur upon their Christian brethren, who, if not Evangelical, were hardly worthy of being termed Christians at all. The accusation was so far unjust, that the Evangelicals never formally, in so many words, gave themselves the exclusive title; on the contrary, they invariably disclaimed any such presumption.[2] But they *did* hold that the gospel consisted of a certain rigorous system, which they, and they alone, presented in its fulness; and therefore they certainly left it to be implied that they, and they alone, were truly Evangelical. And the fact that a name, to which every Christian ought to lay claim, was exclusively applied to *them*, had not a little to do with the prosperity of their cause.

To bring this long chapter to a conclusion. If it be thought that too much space has been devoted to the Evangelicals, the apology is, that they constituted by far the most prominent and spiritually active party during the greater part of the

[1] The following passage illustrates the feeling of earnest-minded laymen, who were not trained to appreciate the niceties of ecclesiastical distinctions, on this point: "To men thus orthodox in their principles, affectionate to the national Establishment, of unblemished morals, and exceptionally assiduous in the discharge of their pastoral duties, do a certain number of their clerical brethren apply the epithet of *Evangelical ministers* (in whatever way this application may have originated) as a term of reproach. Do these clergymen who thus endeavour to excite a prejudice against their brethren, to weaken their influence, and obstruct their success, wish the world to understand that they themselves are not Evangelical ministers; or, in other words, that they do not preach the gospel of Jesus Christ, which they received an express commission to teach at their ordination? Such an imputation would doubtless be repelled as calumnious; it would be resented as unjust and highly offensive; and with good reason, since no charge could be more serious against the Church of England than this, that her ministers in general are not Evangelical ministers. A great misunderstanding must exist somewhere" (*Life of William Hay*, by John Pearson, ii. 50). Yes! there must; but I am bound to say that the misunderstanding exists on the part of the good surgeon, Mr. Pearson, himself. The prejudice against the Evangelical clergy was not because they *were* Evangelical, but because they were supposed to have assumed the exclusive title.

[2] "The body of men called *Evangelical* clergymen (I do not say who gave them that name—*I* did not)," writes Thomas Scott.—*Life*, by his son, John Scott.

period before us. They were the salt of the earth in their day, and the Church owes a debt of gratitude to those holy men whose names have come before us in this chapter, which it will never forget so long as personal piety and the spiritual side of religion are valued at their proper worth.

CHAPTER IV.

THE LIBERALS.

IT is extremely difficult to find any positive bond of union which would connect together all those whom it is desired to bring before the reader in the present chapter, and which would at the same time differentiate them from the "Orthodox" on the one hand and the "Evangelicals" on the other. But, negatively, the term "Liberals" will answer the purpose; for they would all have considered both the Orthodox and the Evangelical platforms too narrow for them. They would not have agreed with the former in holding that there is but one visible, Catholic Church, the sole representative of which in this country is the Church of England; and they would not have agreed with the latter, as to the narrow limits within which they confined "the gospel." In short, they would have claimed to be more "liberal" than either party; but, when we have said this, we have said all that can be predicated of them in common. It has been suggested to me that "the distinctive, or a distinctive, feature of the Liberal theologians of 1800-33 was their Erastianism;" and I have been reminded that "it was this that excited Newman's alarm." This is quite true so far as the Liberals proper are concerned; but I doubt whether all those whom it is desired to include held the theory that the Church is a mere department of the State; for under the title of "Liberals," in default of a better, it is purposed to treat, first, of men who, without committing themselves to the distinguishing tenets of either High or Low Churchmen, were yet prominent thinkers or workers in the Church in their way; and, secondly, of a party which arose in the later part of our period, and which promised for a time, though only a very short time, to be the dominant party in the Church of England.

Among those who deserve special mention under the first head is *William Paley* (1743-1805). He retired, indeed, from active service with the beginning of the new century; but he lived on for five years, and during that time wrote perhaps the most valuable of all his works. His writings will be discussed in a future chapter.[1] Suffice it here to say that he was distinctly a Liberal, "adopting," his biographer tells us, "for his model Sherlock, Clarke, and Hoadley; the latter of whom he calls 'the excellent Hoadley.'" Sherlock would scarcely have felt it a compliment to be bracketed with the other two; but this by the way.[2]

With the name of William Paley one naturally associates that of *Samuel Parr* (1746-1824), because the two used frequently to be coupled together as glaring instances of the way in which merit was overlooked in the distribution of Church patronage.[3] Whether either Dr. Paley or Dr. Parr would have made quite an ideal bishop—at least, according to our modern ideas—may be open to question; but the Church of England certainly owes a debt to both for having contributed to keep up that high standard of learning which has ever been traditional in her. As Paley was the greatest theological writer, so Parr was the greatest scholar of his day. Dr. Parr was not, like Dr. Paley, a Liberal in the strict sense of the term. On the contrary, so far as his theological views

[1] See *infra*, chapter on "Church Literature."
[2] *Life of William Paley*, *D.D.*, prefixed to his *Works*. It does not appear whether William Sherlock the father, or Thomas Sherlock the son, is meant; but the remark in the text would apply to both, though more strongly to the son.
[3] "How painful," writes Sydney Smith of Dr. Parr, "to reflect that a truly devout and attentive minister, a strenuous defender of the Church Establishment, and by far the most learned man of his day, should be permitted to languish on a little paltry curacy in Warwickshire!" To which the following note is appended: "The courtly phrase was, that Dr. Parr was not a *producible* man. The same phrase was used for the neglect of Paley."—S. Smith's *Works*, i. 9. "Some dared to say," writes Dr. Parr's biographer, "that there were insuperable obstacles to his being promoted to the episcopal Bench, and Lord Grenville is said to have apologized for not raising to the Bench the greatest scholar of his age, who was also a man of the most unblemished character, on the plea that this divine was not popular among his brethren."—*Life*, prefixed to *Works*, p. 589. Paley was more than satisfied with the preferment he received. See his dedication of his *Natural Theology* to the Bishop of Durham (Dr. Shute Barrington).

appear at all, they were decidedly of a High Church cast;[1] but it has been thought best to refer to him in the present chapter, because his merits lay not in the domain of theology, to which he contributed little or nothing, but in his classical and metaphysical works, and in his conversational powers, which rivalled those of Dr. Johnson himself. By them he shed a lustre upon the Church of which he was a learned and consistent member; and he was appropriately indebted to one of the most learned and scholarly of our bishops, Dr. Lowth, for the only piece of ecclesiastical preferment of any value that he ever enjoyed, a prebend of St. Paul's.

There is no doubt about the Liberalism of another member of the cathedral body of St. Paul's, the *Rev. Sydney Smith* (1771-1845). Unlike Dr. Parr, he was a writer whose works will continue to be read so long as Englishmen retain any sense of humour; and they are all, more or less, connected with ecclesiastical, if not exactly theological, subjects. Sydney Smith had, after his own fashion, a very real sense of religion, and he did good service to the cause of toleration, which certainly required in those days a champion. The Church never has been, and never will be, in a really more prosperous or influential position by being hemmed round with privileges, which put others under an unfair disadvantage; she is quite strong enough to fight her own battles, and requires nothing more than a fair field and no favour. She need, therefore, owe no grudge to Sydney Smith because he took up the then anomalous position of a Liberal clergyman; he is never tired of advocating, in his own bright and piquant way, the repeal of all laws which bore hardly upon Roman Catholics on the one hand and Protestant Dissenters on the other; he laughed out of their prejudices men who could not be argued out of them; and the Church has been the stronger, not the weaker, for the removal of those so-called safeguards which no man had a greater share in abolishing than Sydney Smith. But, in another way, his liberality, like that of many other liberal divines, did not at all extend to those who disagreed with himself. The highest of High Churchmen was not more bitter than he was, in his youth and middle age, against "Methodism" in all its forms; and the lowest of Low Churchmen was not

[1] See *Life*, p. 827.

more bitter than he was, in his old age, against " Puseyism." Lady Holland tells us, in her biography of her father, that " he thought the highest duty of a clergyman was to calm religious hatred and spread religious peace and toleration ; and dreaded as the greatest of all evils that the golden chain reaching from earth to heaven should be injured either by fanaticism or scepticism."[1] Whether such choice expressions as "the nasty and numerous vermin of Methodism," "a canting, deluded, Methodistical populace,"[2] "the low mischief of the *Christian Observer*,"[3] "the odious vigour of the Evangelical Perceval,"[4] were altogether calculated to "calm religious hatred and spread peace," may be doubted. His equally violent denunciation of the Puseyites, of course, belongs to a much later date, and, therefore, happily does not come within our province.

Another leading Liberal of the day was *Henry Bathurst* (1744-1837), Bishop of Norwich. Unlike Sydney Smith, he recognized the good points in the Evangelicals,[5] "being convinced that their zeal and piety, when under due regulation, were productive of very great good."[6] But Sydney Smith was so delighted with his liberal views generally, that he wrote of him in the early part of his episcopate (1808) in wildly extravagant terms of praise : " The bishop is incomparable ! He should *touch* for bigotry and absurdity ! He does honour to the times in which he lives, and more good to Christianity than all the sermons of his brethren would do if they were to live a thousand years."[7] In politics Bishop Bathurst was, as he himself says, "a sincere Whig," and he carried his liberal ideas into the domain of theology. He was a consistent advocate of the claims both of Roman Catholics [8]

[1] *Memoir of the Rev. Sydney Smith*, by his daughter, Lady Holland, i. 29.
[2] Article on "Methodism," in the *Edinburgh Review*, 1809 ; reprinted in Sydney Smith's *Works*.
[3] Article on " Indian Missions," *Edinburgh Review*, 1808 ; also reprinted.
[4] " Peter Plymley's Letters," *Works*, vol. iii. p. 427.
[5] See his *First Charge to the Clergy of the Diocese of Norwich*, 1806.
[6] Letter to his son about Mr. Simeon's disciples, 1817.
[7] *Works*, vol. ii. p. 36. Letter to Dr. Reeve.
[8] The following story is told, much to his credit : " When the Ministry of the day were stiffly opposed to concessions to the Roman Catholics, and Dr. Bathurst was informed that, if he advocated them in Parliament, he would be left in that miserably poor see [Norwich], whereas his silence might facilitate a translation that must needs be for the better—a thing which his very large family rendered desirable enough—the intimation only increased his zeal ; he spoke most energeti-

I

and of Dissenters; one of the earliest and most ardent among the episcopal supporters of the Bible Society, which he calls "that most excellent of all human institutions;" and in the educational controversies of the day was alike the friend of Bell the Churchman, and Lancaster the Quaker. But he thought "the National Society would have been more useful, and have had a better right to be called *National*, had it received with open arms the children of all who acknowledged the Bible as the standard of faith and rule of practice."[1] His own theological views were so broad that he incurred, unjustly perhaps, the charge of Socinianism. In his later years he stood almost alone among his episcopal brethren as an advocate of the Reform Bill, and this gave him great popularity with the multitude.[2] But his general amiability rendered him far too lax in the administration of his diocese, and his long episcopate of thirty-two years was not a success.

Bishop Bathurst's successor at Norwich, *Edward Stanley*, (1779–1849), did not commence his episcopate until after the close of our period, but he was well known as a liberal and, it must be added, most earnest and energetic clergyman many years earlier. In fact, he became Rector of Alderley, a family living, in the very year that Dr. Bathurst was appointed to Norwich (1805). He there worked a moral revolution, presenting a marked contrast to the neighbouring clergy, of whom his son's account exactly tallies with what has been already said of the general lives of the clergy at the close of the last and the beginning of the present century. The name of Stanley, of course, carried great weight at Alderley and through Cheshire generally; both his parishioners and his brother-clergy would bear more from the reforming rector

cally in favour of the measure. The peer who sat next him said, 'I am happy to find the air of Norwich agrees so well with your lordship; you don't seem inclined to change it.' To which the bishop meekly replied, 'My lord, whatever I change, I trust I shall not change my principles.'"—*Personal Recollections*, by Charlotte Elizabeth, pp. 61, 62.

[1] *Charge*, 1820.

[2] The Rev. F. Trench gives an instance in a scene of which he was an eyewitness. "1831, November.—Meeting in Lincoln's Inn Fields to form a London political union. The Bishop of Norwich happened to pass through the crowd in the midst of the speeches. At first, simply as a bishop, he was violently hissed and hooted. Some one cried out, 'Bishop of Norwich, a Reform bishop!' Hootings at once converted into loud applause."—*A Few Notes from Past Life*, p. 266.

than they would have done from a stranger ; and, from his biographer's account, Edward Stanley succeeded in bringing about a great reform both at Alderley and among the neighbouring clergy. It is a bad habit, to which clergymen, like other mortals, are prone, for a new-comer to depreciate the work of his predecessor; tales of parishes neglected before the reformer appears on the scene, whether they occur in biographies or are told *vivâ voce*, should be regarded with grave suspicion and be sifted narrowly ; and all the more so when, as in the present case, the tale is that of an admiring son. But the biographer—himself a much more distinguished man than his subject—has wisely fortified his own testimony by quoting that of Chancellor Raikes, of Chester, a man well known and of high repute in his day, who says of the Rector of Alderley, " The rector did not do what other rectors did ; and though he never censured in public nor rebuked in private, his conduct testified to a difference of views, and some were dissatisfied with him because they became dissatisfied with themselves while seeing how he lived."[1] The same unimpeachable witness testifies to Edward Stanley's enlightened views and unselfish exertions in the matter of the education of the poor. On such burning questions as the Test Act, Roman Catholic relief, and Church Reform, Mr. Stanley, of course, took a different side from that taken by the vast majority of the clergy ; and it is impossible to help admiring the moral courage which he showed in adhering to what was then regarded a most unclerical position. There is a curious resemblance between the circumstances in which Edward Stanley and his friend Sydney Smith found themselves placed, though a more complete contrast than that which in other respects existed between the two men it would be difficult to conceive. Both received Holy Orders in deference to the wishes of their respective fathers, while both had a strong bias in favour of other professions ; both, when they became clergymen, threw themselves, to their credit be it said, into their work with energy and earnestness ; both lived for a great part of their lives in country places, where they found themselves entirely out of sympathy with the views of

[1] *Memoirs of Edward Stanley, Bishop of Norwich*, by Arthur Penrhyn Stanley, p. 19.

their clerical neighbours ; both held their own in this difficult position manfully and successfully ; and both combined very decided views on what may be termed the negative duties of Christianity—the duty of not persecuting others, not living immoral lives, and so forth—with very vague and indefinite views of dogmatic truth. Hence their influence negatively was good, but positively they made very little impression ; for, as far as one can gather, they had very little that was positive to impress.

Among others who would, more or less correctly, fall under the heading of this chapter may be reckoned the learned Dr. Croly, a fine, manly character, and much admired in his day, both as a preacher and a writer, but one who did not develop any particular views until the Tractarian Movement ranged him in strong opposition to it ;[1] Henry Hart Milman, who in the earlier part of the century was chiefly known as a poet, but before the close of our period startled the religious world by the publication of a work which verged upon what would now be called rationalism ; the two Hares, Julius and Augustus, both of whom, but especially Julius, were profoundly influenced by the philosophical rather than the theological side of S. T. Coleridge's later teaching ;[2] Richard Watson, Bishop of Llandaff, who was essentially a man of the eighteenth century, but who survived for some years into the nineteenth to be a connecting link with a past generation ; and Connop Thirlwall, a still abler man, who lived on to be a connecting link with a future generation ; Reginald Heber, who has been claimed both by High and Low Churchmen, but, on the whole, seems to me to find his more fitting place under the present heading. As the names will show, there were among them men of far more than the average talent and culture ; men who thought out great questions for themselves, and men who showed themselves most zealous and successful parish priests ; but they never combined to propagate their views, and so, as a body, their influence was unimportant.

[1] See *Personal Recollections of Dr. Croly*, by R. Herring, *passim*. Dr. Croly attempted the very unpromising task for a clergyman of writing a *Personal History of George IV.* (in 2 vols.), and executed it remarkably well.

[2] See *Memorials of a Quiet Life*, *passim*.

Meanwhile, however, there was arising what promised to be a very compact party indeed, and one which seemed likely to hold in its hands the Church of the future. It emanated from the same spot from which shortly afterwards arose "the Oxford School," that is, the common-room of Oriel. This was not a strange, but a very natural coincidence; for in the first quarter of this century Oriel was the centre of intellectual life in the University; and the same mental activity which made some " Noetics," made others " Tractarians." The term " Noetics " will not convey much meaning to the general public, but to students of Aristotle's " Ethics," as, of course, the Oriel men were, it conveyed a very definite meaning indeed: a Noetic was a man who exercised his highest faculties, as opposed to those who let them lie dormant; and the description certainly applied to those to whom the title was given. *Edward Copleston* (1776–1849), in virtue of his position as the very successful provost of the college and of his very high reputation as a scholar, was the natural head of the party, so far as he belonged to it at all, but that was only in a very limited sense. Mr. J. B. Mozley, indeed, who, if any man, ought to have known, tells us that in 1830 "a speculative liberalism had been the growing element for some time, even in Oxford and in Oriel, under the fostering patronage of Dr. Copleston, and Dr. Whately's vigorous and argumentative training;"[1] and Whately himself writes to Copleston (1846), " From you I have derived the main principles on which I have acted and speculated through life."[2] But Copleston himself declares, in a letter to his father in 1814, the year when he became provost of Oriel, that he was really more of a High Churchman than those who were then so called at Oxford.[3] And, on the other hand, Charles Simeon, of all people in the world, having dined with Copleston at Oxford in 1822, "and held most profitable conversation," says, " He accords more with my views of Scripture than almost any other person I am acquainted with."[4] Copleston, on his part, was evidently no less struck with

[1] J. B. Mozley, *Essays*, vol. ii. pp. 27, 28: "Dr. Arnold."
[2] See Principal Tulloch's *Movements of Religious Thought in Britain during the Nineteenth Century*, p. 45.
[3] *Memoir of Edward Copleston, Bishop of Llandaff*, by W. J. Copleston.
[4] Quoted by Mr. Moule, *Life of Simeon*, p. 236.

Simeon, to whom he writes the same year, " I consider it no slight proof that my services are likely to be of some use, when they obtain the approbation of one who has laboured so long and so ably in the same cause, and whose life has given the strongest evidence of disinterestedness and sincerity."[1] The fact is, it is impossible to label Copleston as belonging to any party, and it is only his friendship with the Noetics which his position at Oriel brought about that renders it necessary to mention him in this connection at all. When he left Oxford, on being raised to the see of Llandaff in 1827, he disappears from the scene.

Far different was it with *Richard Whately* (1787–1863), who calls himself the disciple of Copleston, but was in fact a man who thought out great questions for himself, and was really a disciple of nobody. His clear, cold, penetrating intellect, which was not tempered by any sympathy with an emotional religion of any kind, caused him to be more in his element when he was engaged in destructive than in constructive work; but it is a great mistake to regard him as an irreligious man. He had a very firm belief in the fundamental truths of Christianity, and rendered valuable service to the Church by his masterly confutations of unbelief in its various forms; but he could never be mistaken for a High Churchman or a Low Churchman; theologically as well as politically he was a Liberal of Liberals. And yet, strange to say, it was Whately who first gave Newman the true idea of the Church as a substantive body, and fixed in him " those anti-Erastian views of Church polity which constituted one of the most prominent features of the Tractarian Movement."[2] Here Whately's clearness of intellect came in; it was impossible for him to rest satisfied with the too prevalent idea of the Church as a mere creature of the State; if it was only that, it was not worth contending for; but he showed, in his " Letters on the Church,"[3] that he had thoroughly grasped the conception of the Church as a great spiritual society,

---

[1] Moule, *Life of Simeon*, pp. 207, 208.   [2] *Apologia pro Vitâ Suâ*, ch. i.
[3] *Letters on the Church by an Episcopalian*, 1826. Internal evidence, apart from the general opinion, and the fact that he never denied the authorship when taxed with it, is quite enough to show that "an Episcopalian" was none other than Whately himself. They were reviewed by Whately's friend Arnold in the *Edinburgh Review*, and referred to in Arnold's *Life*, p. 68.

which might or might not be connected with that other society, the State. This, however, does not imply that he had the slightest sympathy, except on this particular point, with the High Church party, either in its old form which was passing away, or in the new form which it was so soon about to assume. He had neither the respect for authority nor the eye for the beautiful which were two chief ingredients in the composition of the character of the typical High Churchman. But still less had he any fellow-feeling with the Evangelicals, except so far as the bond of a common Christianity must unite all believers to a certain extent together. He had a great—too great—contempt for their intellects. Perhaps he did not see the most favourable specimens of the class at Oxford; but if he had done so, his whole tone of mind was so totally different from theirs that there could never have been any real sympathy between them. It is one of those grotesque anomalies which the changes in men's mental histories sometimes present, that the chief barrier between him and Newman, when they were together at Oxford, was that Whately thought Newman leaned too much towards the Evangelicals. Whately was beyond a doubt the leading spirit of that rising party which never rose, but which for a short time appeared likely to do for the Church what Earl Grey and his friends did for the State. He was listened to as an oracle in the common-room at Oriel, and wherever else Church reformers mostly did congregate. The very oddity of his manners and habits, setting at defiance as he did all the conventionalities which had long been *de rigueur* at Oxford, increased rather than detracted from his influence. The old order was to change, giving place to new, and it was as well that even in things indifferent old prejudices should be set at nought, as Whately, tutor at Oriel, and still more, Whately, principal of St. Alban's Hall, took a delight in doing. Stories about his eccentric sayings and doings were plentiful as blackberries; and then, to the amazement of everybody, came the startling announcement, in 1831, that he had been made an archbishop! Was it a grim joke of the same premier who told the bishops in the House of Lords that they must set their house in order? Was it a *reductio ad absurdum* of the episcopate by an enemy of episcopacy?

Was it a deep-laid plot to ruin the poor, weak Church of Ireland? Or was it, as some few friends thought, the beginning of a better day—the firstfruits of a new and happier state of things for both countries? We need not now follow Whately across the water. Whether, if he had remained in England, he would have increased, or even retained, the influence he undoubtedly possessed in the days preceding the Oxford Movement, is very doubtful. He does not seem to me to have had anything sufficiently positive and definite to offer, in lieu of the Evangelicalism on the one side, which he did his best to upset, or the High Churchmanship on the other, from which he drifted further and further away. At the same time, it is surely a mistaken, not to say suicidal, policy of the defenders of Christianity to persist in regarding him as an enemy, and not as an ally, and a very effective ally, as far as he went. In the literature of the period, his works occupy a prominent place; and, as will be shown in a future chapter, they are all on the side of belief *versus* unbelief; and a time which was by no means rich in apologetic literature can ill afford to reject the sincerely proffered aid of one who possessed one of the most luminous and powerful intellects of the day.

Far inferior intellectually (as it seems to me), but far superior in moral weight, was Whately's friend, and in some respects one might almost say disciple, *Thomas Arnold* (1795–1842), who must be reckoned among the foremost of the old Oriel school. One who, like the present writer, was educated first at Laleham, under Dr. Arnold's brother-in-law, and then at Rugby, under his coadjutors and most devoted disciples, finds it difficult to deal dispassionately with the influence of that remarkable man. What is said here, therefore, should perhaps be taken *cum grano*. It is, however, said without any prejudice in favour of Dr. Arnold's peculiar opinions—indeed, with a strong conviction that many of his theories will not bear criticism for a moment. Take, for instance, his theory of the Church, as being most germane to the subject of this work. He held that Church and State were not two societies, but one—so far he had Hooker and other great divines with him; that it was an utter mistake to look upon the clergy as the Church—where, again, he would of course have all thinking persons with him; that, as the laity were a real and substantive portion of the Church, they ought to have their share in the administration of its affairs—and here, again, he will carry all sensible people with him. But then the question arises, What share? And in his answer to this question, many—indeed, all well-read Churchmen—would part company with him. For he would have had the laity admitted, not only into friendly conferences, but into clerical synods. He would have had them commissioned, not only to preach, but to administer the Holy Communion itself under certain circumstances and conditions, thus to all intents and purposes obliterating all distinctions between clergy and laity. He would have made the Church so wide as to admit within its pale Dissenters of all kinds—Roman Catholics, Quakers, and Unitarians excepted—without any compromise of principle on either side. How all this was to be brought about does not appear very clearly. But as he did not carry with him even his own friends—such men as Whately, Augustus Hare, Cornish, Thirlwall,[1] and Hawkins expressing their disapproval (the latter going so far as to hint that he was writing on subjects which he did not understand, and which were not within his proper province)—and as his scheme of making the Church a sort of theological omnibus never took any definite shape, it is not necessary to dwell upon it.

The fact is, it was not Arnold the writer, nor Arnold the thinker, but Arnold the man, who was the real power. He it was who more than any other man helped to bridge over the gulf which separated intellect from piety. It is a sad fact, admitted while it is deplored by the Evangelicals themselves, that piety had come to be associated in men's minds with intellectual weakness. The "union of religious earnestness with intellectual activity," which Dr. Arnold himself remarks as characteristic of the Oriel Noetics, was conspicuous in his own pupils, and the many who were influenced by them. It was the best part of the admirable work he did at Rugby, and though the full fruit of it was not reaped until after the time with which this volume is concerned—indeed, it is being

[1] See Thirlwall's letter to Bunsen, in *Letters Literary and Theological of Connop Thirlwall*, edited by Perowne and Stokes, p. 107.

reaped still—yet the seed was sown during our period. In the eloquent language of his biographer, himself a notable instance of the influence exercised by Dr. Arnold in moulding character, "pupils with characters most different from each other's and from his own—often with opinions diverging more and more widely from his as they advanced in life—looked upon him with love and reverence, which made his gratification one of the brightest rewards of their academical studies; his good or evil fame, a constant source of interest and anxiety to them; his approbation and censure, amongst their most practical motives of action; his example, one of their most habitual rules of life. To him they turned for advice in every emergency of life, not so much for the sake of the advice itself, as because they felt that no important step ought to be taken without consulting him. An additional zest was imparted to whatever work they were engaged in by a consciousness of the interest which he felt in the progress of their undertaking, and the importance which he attached to its result. . . . His very presence seemed to create a new spring of health and vigour within them, and to give to life an interest and an elevation which remained with them long after they had left him, and dwelt so habitually in their thoughts, as a living image, that, when death had taken him away, the bond appeared to be still unbroken, and the sense of separation almost lost in the still deeper sense of a life and a union indestructible."[1] To appreciate the extent of this influence, it should be remembered that those over whom it was exercised were, many of them, like Dean Stanley himself, no ordinary men, but great centres of influence in their turn. That higher and nobler idea of life, for which so many were indebted to Dr. Arnold, continued long after his presence was withdrawn, and communicated itself to others who had not come under his personal spell. We shall perhaps realize best what it was by studying his sermons. They have a sort of unconventional ring about them which differentiated them, in a way difficult to describe, from the general run of sermons in that day. Among other things, they helped many to realize the beauty, the attractiveness, the unique character, of Jesus Christ, who had been rather repelled by

[1] Stanley's *Life of Arnold*, p. 142.

the form in which many good men had been in the habit of presenting to their readers and hearers that unspeakably important subject. The intense earnestness of Arnold's own personal faith in, and love of, Jesus Christ prevented him from falling into that vague and colourless *soi-disant* Christianity which is the peculiar danger of those who are ready to sacrifice dogmatic truth for the sake of a shadowy unity. What further development his views would have undergone, if his valuable life had not been prematurely cut off, it is impossible to say. He lived long enough to see a serious divergence between himself and some of his Liberal friends ; for the separation of education from religion, which was one of their objects, was abhorrent to his highest feelings ; and other points of disagreement must have arisen. He could never have harmonized with the Evangelicals. Like his friend Whately, he had a very mean opinion of their intellectual calibre ; he thought their general tone of mind was cramped and narrow ; and they, on their part, cordially reciprocated the antipathy. But with neither Liberals nor Evangelicals was he so fundamentally at variance as with the rising Oxford school, with the leaders of which he had been personally on the friendliest terms. His article in the *Edinburgh Review*, under the significant title of "The Oxford Malignants," was too strong even for his most sympathizing friends, and perhaps he himself regretted afterwards that he had written it ; but it was characteristic of his eager, impulsive, and chivalrous temperament to rush into the fray without much consideration.[1] It is fair to remember that he only knew "Tractarianism" (so-called) in its earlier and cruder stage ; but he could never have been in sympathy with the movement, except by a *volte de face*, which he was the last man in the world likely to execute. But it is no use speculating what Dr. Arnold *might* have done. What he *did* do was to effect on a much larger scale throughout the country what he aimed at in the little world of Rugby, where "the fruit which he above all things longed for was moral thoughtfulness—the inquiring love of truth going along with the devoted love of goodness."[2] No amount of disagreement

---

[1] See the admirable article on Dr. Arnold in Professor J. B. Mozley's *Essays*.
[2] Stanley, p. 103.

with his theological views ought to make us forget the good he did in this direction.

Other members of the old Oriel school were R. D. Hampden, a name which a year or two later became exceedingly notorious in connection with Church matters, but was as yet only known beyond the walls of his own college by his Bampton Lectures on "The Scholastic Philosophy considered in its Relation to Christian Theology" (1832), preceded by two or three articles on similar subjects;[1] Blanco White, who gave a further impetus in the Liberal direction to men already sufficiently inclined to Liberalism; and John Davison, a Noetic, but one who in no way identified himself with the Liberals except in so far as he was personally friendly with them. One speaks of these as a "school" for want of a better name; but they never became what is popularly termed "a school of thought."

Indeed, it is very difficult to construct any coherent and definite system which could at all be said to represent the views of the Liberals generally at any time during our period. There *was* no Liberal *party*. There were, no doubt, many estimable clergymen, and more laymen, who agreed negatively in holding aloof alike from High Churchmen and Low Churchmen; but when we inquire what were the positive opinions which differentiated them from the others, and bound them to one another, the answer is not forthcoming. The Oriel Noetics, as a party, soon vanished into thin air. Copleston subsided into a worthy but rather tame bishop in the wilds of Wales; Whately went off to Dublin, and threw himself into Irish affairs; Arnold's real work was done at Rugby, and the minds he formed there did not come to maturity till a later day; Davison, having enriched theological literature by his great work on "Prophecy," never again came to the front; poor Blanco White passed through various phases of belief and unbelief, and quite ceased to be a power as a Liberal Churchman.

In fact, the whole history of Liberal Churchmen during our period is simply a history of individuals, most of them men of great talents and culture, whose works will form a conspicuous feature in another chapter, but who never formed

---

[1] See Mozley's *Reminiscences*, vol. i. ch. lvi. pp. 354, 355.

a united body. Had they done so, there was assuredly a great opportunity for the exercise of their force. For Liberalism was in the air. The swing of the pendulum had gone back from the violent reaction against all innovation which the horrors of the French Revolution had caused during the early years of the century. The same spirit which in the domain of politico-ecclesiastical questions brought about the abolition of the Corporation and Test Acts, the emancipation of the Roman Catholics, and the Reform Bill, existed also in reference to theology and to innovations within the Church. But among Liberal Churchmen there was no united action; indeed, there could not be, for there was no united theory which could lead to action.

There *was* a party of Liberals who had very definite opinions indeed on theological matters; but this would be a source of embarrassment rather than encouragement to Liberal Churchmen. It was the party of which Jeremy Bentham and the two Mills were the extreme representatives. It sought to reform the nation by a system from which all dogmatic theology was carefully eliminated. The *Westminster Review*, founded in 1824, was its organ in the press to propagate its views among the more intellectual classes; the *Penny Magazine*, to suit the masses. The Society for the Diffusion of Useful Knowledge, the London University, and the first Mechanics' Institutes were some of the results of its activity. If this were a general history of the time, or a history of religious thought during the time, it would be necessary to dwell longer upon this phase of Liberalism; but as this work is confined to the Church of England, and as, to use the mildest term, the efforts of the party were not founded on a Church basis, it would be wandering away from our proper subject to dwell upon them further.

Nor does it quite come within our limits to touch upon that group of Liberal Churchmen which was growing up at Cambridge, chiefly under the inspiration of Julius Hare and Connop Thirlwall, during the later part of our period. The most noted of these, such as F. D. Maurice, John Sterling, and Charles Kingsley, were still *in statu pupillari;* and therefore whatever is said about the movement will come in better in connection with University life than with the general life of the Church. But, turning from Cambridge to Oxford, are we to place the great name of E. B. Pusey in his early days among the Liberals? He was a Liberal in politics, and in the domain of theology he certainly opposed one of the chief champions of orthodoxy; an objection was alleged against his appointment to the Hebrew Professorship in 1828 on the ground that his orthodoxy was doubtful, and he withdrew from circulation the work which caused him to be suspected. But, in spite of all this, it is doubtful whether to group him with the Liberals would not be to mistake his position. That position will best be understood by those who are best acquainted with the state of religion, in Germany and in England respectively, in the eighteenth and early nineteenth centuries. Pusey had studied, on the spot and as few Englishmen had done, the rise of Rationalism in Germany; and he had come to the conclusion that it had arisen from a reaction, on the one hand against an overstrained pietism, and, on the other, against a narrow and barren orthodoxy which he termed "orthodoxism." He thought he saw traces of the same causes at work in England; and when Mr. H. J. Rose published his "*Discourses on the State of the Protestant Religion in Germany*," he wrote in reply, "*An Historical Enquiry into the Rational Character of German Theology*," which delighted the Germans and the English Liberals more than the Orthodox. He thought Rose had misunderstood, or not quite done justice to, some of the German writers; and while stating his points strongly, he ran, as young men are apt to do, into an opposite direction, and advanced statements which it would be difficult to justify on Church principles. But he differed from Rose on the *causes* rather than on the *dangers* of Rationalism, to which he was a foe, not a friend; and when the tendency of some of his remarks was brought home to him, he suppressed his work, and ever expressed a deep regret that he had published it. Hence he must be regarded as, at most, only an unconscious, not a conscious, Liberal.[1]

---

[1] See Canon Liddon's *Life of Dr. Pusey*, i. 72-177. May I also refer to an account of German theology in *The English Church in the Eighteenth Century*, vol. i. pp. 244-268, published in 1878, which shows my views fifteen years before I had the privilege of reading Canon Liddon's work?

CHAPTER V.

CHURCH SERVICES AND CHURCH FABRICS.

THE readers of the foregoing pages will be prepared for a somewhat depressing account of the Church services and their adjuncts during our period; but he will also be prepared to find a slow but steady improvement in this, as in other matters, as the years rolled on.

In treating of the Church services, we must, of course, begin with the highest of all, the Holy Eucharist.

"Four celebrations in the year are the very fewest that ought to be allowed in the very smallest parishes. It were to be wished that it were in all more frequent." In these words the ablest prelate of the day, a distinct High Churchman in the best sense of the term, addresses the clergy of one of the most populous and central dioceses in the kingdom at the dawn of the new century.[1] As bishops in their Charges naturally take a high standard which they hardly hope will be reached by all, it must be confessed that the prospect is not very promising; and to judge from a letter written towards the close of our period, matters do not seem to have improved as to the frequency of celebrations in country churches. "In many country villages," writes a correspondent to the *British Critic* in 1832, "the sacrament of the Lord's Supper is administered four times a year—Easter, Whitsunday, Michaelmas, and Christmas. I would suggest at each of these seasons the sacrament may be administered twice—Christmas Day and the Sunday after, Palm Sunday and Easter Sunday, Whitsunday and Trinity Sunday, and on Sundays before and after Michaelmas Day. By this arrange-

[1] Second Charge of the Bishop of Rochester (Dr. Horsley) in 1800.

ment the husband and wife of every family may be able, *if they please*, to attend at least four times in the year." To which the editor appends a note: "This is the habit at many country places. In one large village, known to the editor, there is an early sacrament at eight o'clock, as well as at the usual hour, on the great festivals."

On the other hand, Edward Bickersteth, when a young man in London in 1806, had the opportunity 'of communicating every week, and used to avail himself of it.[1] At Turvey, not a very large village, Legh Richmond had a monthly celebration from 1805 onwards, preceded by a monthly communicant class on the Saturday evening; and he exercised a very strict discipline in the admission to that holy ordinance.[2]

The number of communicants was more satisfactory, at least in many places. At St. John's, Bedford Row, under its successive incumbents; at the parish church, Islington, under Daniel Wilson'; and at Whitechapel, under Bickersteth, the numbers were very large. Simeon notes with special thankfulness the vast increase in the number of communicants at Trinity Church, Cambridge, since the time when, in his early manhood, he communicated there with only three others;[3] and there is a most remarkable account of the number of communicants at Stretton, a country village in Suffolk, which tells of there being already 153, with a hope that they may be raised to 244, in a population of 610. The clergyman of this wonderful parish was the Rev. J. S. Sawbridge, a friend of Joshua Watson and Thomas Sikes, and the incumbent who gave H. H. Norris his title to Holy Orders,—in short, to all intents and purposes a member of the Hackney phalanx. It was natural that among such men the Holy Sacrament should hold the highest possible place; but, strange as it may sound, it is certainly true that, next to them, the Evangelicals laid the greatest stress on the Holy Communion in those days. One is really quite startled sometimes at their expressions on the subject. "I will lead my child to the altar of our Eucharistic Sacrifice." "Blessed Lord, I am now about to

---

[1] *Memoir of the Rev. E. Bickersteth*, i. 34.
[2] See *Life of the Rev. Legh Richmond*, p. 131.
[3] Carus, p. 554.

partake of Thy Body as broken, and Thy Blood as shed for me. Oh, enable me to resign myself to Thee! At Thy Altar may I renew my dedication." These are not the words of a Thomas Sikes, but of an Evangelical of Evangelicals, Daniel Wilson.[1] The Evangelicals made a great point of communicating, and drew together a large number of communicants. It was the large number, no doubt, which led to the objectionable practice of "communicating rails full"—a practice which was very prevalent in large towns until the influence of the Oxford Movement made itself felt.[2] The followers, also, of John Wesley added largely to the numbers of communicants. The counsels, or rather the commands, of their great leader had not yet lost their force; good Methodists still made a point of communicating at their parish church, as they still made a point of holding no services of their own during Church hours.[3] In fact, the duty of communicating was very much more generally recognized then than it is now ; but it was too often put on a low footing. It was sometimes regarded more as a legal obligation than as a blessed privilege—a view which the existence of the Test and Corporation Acts would foster. A man could not be a sound "Church and State" man unless he was at least an occasional communicant. Others regarded it as merely a commemorative act—a higher and more religious view than the former, but still a miserably inadequate one. It was this view, no doubt, which led to the survival all through our period of the notion which had been rife throughout the eighteenth century, that of all days the day on which a celebration was most appropriate was Good Friday. This is not, as it may seem, inconsistent with what has been said above about the four times a year, of which Good Friday was not one. The Christmas, Easter, Whitsuntide, and Michaelmas celebrations were regarded as the legal ones, the Good Friday one as a counsel of piety.

With regard to the other Church services, it is to be feared that they were too often performed in a very slovenly and irregular manner. Some clergy had even the audacity to

[1] See Bateman's *Life of Daniel Wilson*, pp. 157 and 284.
[2] See *Remains of Bishop Copleston*, with Reminiscences by R. Whately.
[3] See *Report from the Clergy of a District in the Diocese of Lincoln, etc.*

K

mutilate the Liturgy. In 1814, Bishop Law, of Chester, in an otherwise rosy-coloured picture of the state of his diocese, speaks sternly on this point: "The whole of the Liturgy must be read without alteration, substitution, or omission." In 1818, Mr. (afterwards Bishop) Blomfield added some notes to a sermon he preached at Saffron Walden at a visitation of Bishop Howley—an occasion on which a man would naturally be careful not to make random statements; and in these notes he reprobates "the irregular practice which prevails amongst some of the clergy, who embrace the peculiar tenets of Calvin, of curtailing and mutilating the service of Baptism, so as to bring it somewhat nearer to their own notions of regeneration."[2] Another pretext for curtailing the Liturgy was the exigency of time. When a clergyman had to serve several churches on the same day, he was obliged, not only to hurry over, but to cut short the service. Stories of the indecent haste with which an officiating minister would rush off from one church to another are too numerous and well authenticated to admit of any doubt. One, which came under the writer's own personal knowledge, may be given as a specimen. A clergyman served three churches at a considerable distance from each other, living at a central point between the three. As one Sunday service was considered sufficient, there was no difficulty about giving a morning and an evening service alternately at the two outsiders; but the middle church had to be content with a sort of sandwich service, interpolated in the long ride between the two others, at midday. The bishop at last insisted that this middle church should also have an alternate morning and evening service, which looked like a death-blow to the happy arrangement. But the ingenious divine was equal to the occasion; he had only to arrive at church one Sunday at five minutes before twelve and take the morning service, and the next at five minutes past twelve and take the evening service—and the thing was done!

In the country all sorts of irregularities were tolerated. A very common one was the reading of the ante-Communion

---

[1] Charge to the clergy of Chester, by Bishop Henry Law, at his Primary Visitation in 1814.

[2] See *Memoir of Bishop Blomfield*, i. 64.

Service at the prayer-desk—a practice which the wretched state of many chancels made convenient. Even so good a Churchman as Richard Mant, when he was a young curate at Buriton, was guilty of it, until he was shamed out of it by a parishioner with whom he was remonstrating for encouraging cricket on Sunday evening. "The old gentleman, while acknowledging his error, retorted on the curate for a breach of rubrical conformity. He had followed a custom, very common at that time [1804] in country churches in England, particularly when there was a long chancel, of reading the Communion Service from the reading-desk instead of the Lord's Table; and when Mr. B—— pointed out to him the irregularity of so doing, he at once acknowledged his mistake, and corrected his practice ever after."[1]

Another bad habit was that of the whole congregation sitting down during the singing. Bishop Mant's remarks on this point, and indeed on psalmody generally, disclose a state of things which it is difficult to realize at the present day.[2] In the first place, he seems almost to despair of congregational singing. "Amongst a variety of people," he writes, "part of them with bad ears, and most of them with untaught voices, there will be some who had better totally abstain; only attending to the sense, as well as the sound of what is uttered by the rest." He then makes some suggestions which can scarcely be thought unreasonable: "If we will not employ our lips in the service, we may still fix our minds upon it; at least we should not hinder others from doing either. And particularly we should abstain from giving the bad example and the offence of indecently holding conversation at that time, for which there cannot surely be so pressing an occasion but that it may very safely be deferred till after church, if not altogether omitted." The only thing that can be said against this excellent advice is that it is too gentle; it is shocking to think there should have been any need of it at all. "In the singing of psalms," the writer goes on, "different persons use different postures. The prose psalms, so far as we know,

---

[1] *Memoir of Bishop Richard Mant*, p. 65.
[2] As Bishop Mant was an Irish bishop, it may be necessary to state that he is not referring to the Irish Church especially in these remarks, which occur in his notes on the *Book of Common Prayer*.

are and ever have been repeated by all persons everywhere standing. In the verse psalms we all stand at the Doxology." And then he proceeds to show that it ought to be the posture all through, but adds a passage which shows that, so far from this being the case, it would attract attention, and that allowance should be made for those who shrank from doing so. "Were it more uncommon than it is, it would be far from a dishonourable singularity. But still, as very many in most congregations have by long habit been prejudiced in favour of sitting, or, though they disapprove the custom, feel a difficulty of quitting it unless every one did, they should not be censured for a practice by which they mean nothing amiss, but kindly encouraged to an alteration in this point, which we may thus hope will gradually become general."[1] We hear of one clergyman using an amusingly effectual method for inducing his congregation to stand up during the singing. After speaking of "the irreverent posture of sitting down," he added, "For the aged, the diseased, and the infirm, in retaining their seats every apology is to be offered;" and at the next psalm all who did not desire to be classified under any of those categories stood up.[2]

Whether we consider the words or the music, psalmody was generally in a very unsatisfactory state. As to the words, the ill-educated parish clerk was left to make his own selection from the meagre stores of Tate and Brady. There was a strong prejudice against hymns as being Methodistical. Even so enlightened a prelate as Dr. Herbert Marsh inveighed strongly against them in his Charges, actually using the same argument which William Romaine had been so mercilessly ridiculed for using in the University pulpit half a century before, viz. that it was exchanging the Word of God for the word of man. No doubt there was something to be said for his prejudice, inasmuch as some hymns used were highly objectionable; but there were also many that were not.[3] If he had deigned to look at the hymns of the Wesleys,

[1] Bishop Mant's edition of the *Book of Common Prayer*, abridged from his larger edition, 1824, vol. i. pp. 133, 134: "On Psalmody."

[2] Review of Dr. E. Barry's *Works* in the *British Critic*, vol. xxviii., July to December, 1806.

[3] See Charge of the Bishop of Peterborough at his Primary Visitation, 1820, especially the Appendix. Also his Charge in 1823.

he would have found many, not only free from bad taste, but also of a far more distinctly Church tone than the lucubrations of Tate and Brady. Even so moderate a man as Reginald Heber, after he had compiled a hymn-book for the use of Hodnet Church, "felt," he says, "some High Church scruples about using it."[1] Nothing shows more strongly the prejudice which the "orthodox" had against hymns, than the fact that though this collection was made on distinctly Church lines, being "intended to be appropriate to the Sundays and principal holidays of the year," Heber applied in vain in 1820 to the Archbishop of Canterbury (Dr. Manners-Sutton) and the Bishop of London (Dr. Howley), both more or less High Churchmen, for an authorization of its use. He dwelt with great force and reasonableness on "the powerful engine which hymns were among the Dissenters, and on the irregular use of them in the Church, which it was impossible to suppress and better to regulate;"[2] but, being a loyal Churchman, he would not publish them without being authorized, and it was not until after his death that they appeared. The introduction of hymns into Church was chiefly the work of the Evangelicals. The accomplished writer of the article on "Church of England Hymnody" in Mr. Julian's "Dictionary of Hymnology" speaks of our period as one of the most prolific in hymns; and an examination of the names of the compilers and editors will show that the majority of them were well-known Evangelicals. In fact, the introduction of this attractive feature into public worship was one of the auxiliary causes of the life and vigour of Evangelicalism. How popular it became may be judged by the fact that the sale of Edward Bickersteth's "Christian Psalmody" (1833) soon reached a hundred and fifty thousand copies. The attempts to stop hymn-singing was one of the many vain attempts by which their opponents really played into the hands of the Evangelicals.

Turning from the words to the music, we find here too a general testimony that an unsatisfactory state of things prevailed, as a rule, in town and country alike. Bishop Beilby Porteus, who in many respects was in advance of his age,

[1] Taylor's *Life of Bishop Heber*, p. 90. This was in 1819.
[2] See Julian's *Dictionary of Hymnology*, p. 503.

complained of it bitterly before the nineteenth century began, and justly reprobated an effort to improve it in London, which was a glaring instance of the way how *not* to do it. "Of all the services of the Church," he writes, "none had sunk to so low an ebb as our parochial psalmody; especially as Dr. Burney, in his 'History of Music,' had very injudiciously taken great pains to ridicule and discredit the use of psalmody in our churches, and to introduce in the room of it cathedral music. In consequence of this, many churches and chapels in London had already adopted his ideas; and at their charity sermons professional singers, both male and female, were brought from various places of public entertainment to sing hymns and anthems for the benefit of the children. Nay, in one or two churches there had been musical entertainments upon Sunday evenings without even prayers or a sermon. I thought it highly necessary, in order to prevent our places of public worship from being converted into concert-rooms, to endeavour to check this musical madness, and, if possible, to bring back our psalmody to its ancient purity and simplicity."[1] Even professional music does not appear to have been attractive, for the author of "*Zeal without Innovation*" tells us, in 1808, that "with numerous attendance of ministers, and the finest specimens of Church music by professionals, the seats of St. Paul's were seldom half filled." As late as 1827, a writer in the *British Critic* complains that "with all the facilities for excellent psalmody—powerful organs, numerous congregations, and often a multitude of charity children—some of the London churches contrive to convert this joyous spiritual exercise into a positive infliction." He then mentions some honourable exceptions, "especially the present Bishop of Chester at St. Botolph's, Bishopsgate, the psalmody of which is known to be an object of his lordship's anxious and constant attention"—which would have been highly creditable to his lordship, did one not feel that "his lordship's anxious and constant attention"[2] ought to have been concentrated on a large sphere of labour two hundred miles away from St. Botolph's, Bishopsgate.

In the country the psalmody was a very great difficulty,

---

[1] Hodgson's *Life of Bishop Beilby Porteus*, pp. 108, 109.
[2] *British Critic* for April, 1827; Art. x., "Ecclesiastical Discipline."

even to those who had everything in their favour, when trying to reform it. No one, for instance, would presumably have a better chance of success than Reginald Heber at Hodnet. Son of the lord of the manor and patron of the living, of an old family which had been long connected with the place, with a name which would carry weight, a most attractive personality, and a high University reputation (which counts for more even in a village than is generally supposed), one would have thought he could have done anything he wished. And yet his biographer tells us that "he made several vigorous efforts to reform the psalmody in his parish, but had the mortification to find that they were almost entirely ineffectual."[1] Local musicians are a stubborn race, and they would not easily forego the privilege of bringing into the gallery their violins, bassoons, hautboys, or whatever their favourite instruments might be, and using them with a will. Some of the country clergy cut the Gordian knot by having no singing at all—a convenient arrangement for those with whom time was an object because they had to rush off to take another service elsewhere. Archdeacon Bailey, in his Charge to the clergy of the archdeaconry of Stow (which takes in a fair slice of Lincolnshire), in 1826, implies that the absence of singing was common. "Sacred music," he says, "is an essential part of the Liturgy; it is the very life and soul of every new method of Dissenting worship. Why, then, is it so rarely invited to impart a solemn interest to our parochial services? Does it not argue a want of taste, or rather a want of zeal, among us, that, whilst every conventicle is made to resound with hallelujahs, the courts of the temple alone should ever fail to repeat the strains of the sweet Psalmist of Israel?[2] that whilst all creation, everything that hath breath, is summoned by the voice of nature and of inspiration to sing praises unto the Lord, we only, the favoured sons of the Church, should at any time seem to maintain an ungracious and indolent silence?" To the same effect an anonymous writer in 1832: "I believe it to be a matter of regret general among my

---

[1] Taylor's *Life of Bishop Heber*, p. 50.
[2] Archdeacon Bailey was a High Churchman, a friend of Joshua Watson and the rest of the "Clapton sect;" hence he contemplates only the singing of psalms, and ignores hymns.

clerical brethren, that while almost every Dissenting congregation cultivates sacred music as a part of their public worship, it is altogether neglected in so many of our country churches."[1]

Perhaps some country clergymen might think that no music at all was better than such as is amusingly described by Ambrose Serle in his "*Christian Remembrancer.*"[2] "I cannot," he writes, "but shake my head when I hear an officer of the Church calling upon people to sing to the praise and glory of God, and immediately half a dozen merry men, in a high place, shall take up the matter, and most loudly shout it away to the praise and glory of themselves. The tune, perhaps, shall be too difficult for the greater part of the congregation, who have no leisure for crotchets and quavers; and so the most delightful part of all our public worship shall be wrested from them, and the praises of God taken out of their mouths."[3]

One finds, however, here and there, glimpses of light among the darkness. Sydney Smith, for instance, who, in spite of his buoyant light-heartedness, generally takes the gloomiest view of everything connected with the Church, is yet "very glad to find we are calling in more and more the aid of music to our service. In London, where it can be commanded, good music has a prodigious effect in filling a church; organs have been put up in various churches in the country, and, as I have been informed, with the best possible effect."[4] Legh Richmond, on one of his missionary tours in 1812, describes the singing at Manchester Collegiate Church as "magnificent, almost beyond precedent. There was the 'Hallelujah Chorus' to conclude with. Hallelujahs rang in reiterated peals from every part of the immense congregation. The organ was finely played; an excellent trumpet was in the band, and added much to the brilliancy of the effect." At Bolton, in 1815, he found the "singing grand and impressive in the highest degree. Anthems and choruses were sung, and accompanied

---

[1] *British Magazine* for 1832, vol. i.
[2] Not to be confounded with the periodical of that name.
[3] See selections from the writings of Ambrose Serle by the Rev. E. Bickersteth, *The Christian Remembrancer*, chap. xx.
[4] See Lady Holland's *Memoir of the Rev. Sydney Smith*, p. 87.

by trumpets, horns, etc., in a very fine style indeed."[1] The testimony is the more valuable because Mr. Richmond himself was a musical man. But it is exceptional. The general evidence is that the music was a weak point in the services of the Church. It was something, however, that the weakness was recognized, for that was the first step towards an improvement. Among other suggestions, Alexander Knox made one which was a sort of adaptation of his favourite theory of the *via media* to psalmody. "In psalmody," he writes (1823), "a few persons who might be found capable and willing, should be taught to accompany, or perhaps rather supersede, the clerk. I am no admirer of the whole congregation making an effort to sing, *indocti doctique*. But the drawling of a solitary clerk is, if possible, a worse extreme. The medium of a few taught in some measure to sing, and the rest listening, appears to me to be in the appropriate spirit of the Church of England, as akin to choir singing; while the congeniality of congregational singing, *rebus sic stantibus*, is at least disputable. ... *Festina lentè* is a capital maxim."[2]

Church-people could scarcely complain that they had too many sermons inflicted upon them. In those days the clergy, as a rule, were not very attentive to the rubrics; but there was one rubric which many of them religiously observed, the one which prescribes a sermon in the morning and makes no allusion to any other sermon. In those country churches where there was only one service, there could of course be only one sermon, morning or afternoon, at whichever time the service might be; but where there was a double service, the second one frequently consisted of Evensong without sermon. Many of the bishops in their Charges urged a double sermon, and not without effect; for the afternoon sermon, or catechizing, or exposition, became more and more the rule as the years rolled on.

Sermons have been from time immemorial regarded in some quarters as a legitimate subject of abuse. It would, therefore, be most unfair simply to make a collection (for which the materials are only too abundant) of the various

---

[1] Grimshaw's *Life of the Rev. Legh Richmond*, pp. 243, 263.
[2] *Thirty Years' Correspondence between Bishop Jebb and Alexander Knox*, ii. 475.

complaints against the sermons of the period, and to estimate their quality by that standard.

Equally unfair would it be to take the printed sermons of the time as a true measure of pulpit eloquence. Everybody knows how a sermon which is most effective when delivered orally may be very flat and disappointing when read in cold blood. This is especially the case with sermons chiefly addressed to the feelings, as those of the Evangelicals mostly were. It is not, therefore, among the famous Evangelical preachers of the day, the Gisbornes, the Milners, and the Daniel Wilsons, but among men like Hugh James Rose, William Van Mildert, and John Jebb, all of whose sermons read admirably, that we must look for the best specimens of the preaching of the day.

It has been seen that much indignation was expressed against the Evangelicals for their supposed assumption that the gospel was not preached in the "national pulpits" except by themselves. But we do not find that the chief complaints against the preaching of the day come from the Evangelical leaders, who are remarkably reticent on the subject in their writings, but from men of quite a different bias. Thus it is Southey, the High Churchman of the old type, who complains that "bad sermons are among the many causes which have combined to weaken the Church of England," with much more to the same effect.[1] It is Alexander Knox, the High Churchman of the new type, who affirms that "the clergy have lost the art of preaching," and so forth.[2] It is Sydney Smith, the Broad Churchman, who, descanting upon "the low state of pulpit eloquence," says, " Preaching has become a byword for long and dull conversation of any kind ; and whoever wishes to imply, in any piece of writing, the absence of everything agreeable and inviting, calls it a sermon."[3] And again, "The great object of modern sermons is to hazard nothing ; their characteristic is decent debility ; which alike guards their authors from ludicrous errors, and precludes them from striking beauties. Every man of sense, in taking up an English sermon, expects to

---

[1] See *Life and Correspondence of Robert Southey*, vii. 90.
[2] *Remains of Alexander Knox*, iv. 105, *et seq.*
[3] See Lady Holland's *Memoir of the Rev. Sydney Smith*, p. 81.

find it a tedious essay, full of commonplace morality."[1] It is dangerous to assert a negative, but it certainly would be difficult to find such severe strictures on sermons in the writings of those who were accused of maligning the Church by maintaining that the gospel was not preached in it.

Turning from the matter to the manner of preaching, we find the same Sydney Smith repeating a complaint which was at least as old as the days of Queen Anne,[2] and pouring forth the vials of his wrath and of his wit against the apathetic delivery of sermons, which was especially affected at this time by the orthodox clergy to distinguish them from the excited and exciting Methodist. "Is it," he asks, "wonder that every semi-delirious sectary who pours forth his animated nonsense with the genuine look and voice of passion should gesticulate away the congregation of the most profound and learned divine of the Established Church, and in two Sundays preach him bare to the very sexton? Why call in the aid of paralysis to piety? Is sin to be taken from men, as Eve was from Adam, by casting them into a deep slumber? Or from what possible perversion of common sense are we all to look like field-preachers in Zembla, holy lumps of ice, numbed into quiescence and stagnation and mumbling? It is theatrical to use action, and it is methodistical to use action? But we have cherished contempt for sectaries, and persevered in dignified tameness so long, that while we are freezing common sense for large salaries in stately churches, amidst whole acres and furlongs of empty pews, the crowd are feasting on ungrammatical fervour and illiterate animation in the crumbling hovels of Methodists."[3]

The same witty writer took a very decided line on the vexed question between written and unwritten sermons—and not quite the line one would have expected from him; for it was one of the distinctions between the "Orthodox" and the "Methodist," that the former, as a rule, preferred the manuscript, while the latter did not. "Pulpit discourses," he says,

---

[1] Article on "Dr. Rennell" in the *Edinburgh Review*, 1802; reprinted in Sydney Smith's *Works*, vol. i. p. 10.
[2] See *Spectator*.
[3] Lady Holland's *Memoir*, p. 85.

"have insensibly dwindled from speaking to reading—a practice of itself sufficient to stifle every germ of eloquence. What can be more ludicrous than an orator delivering stale indignation, and fervour of a week old; turning over whole pages of violent passions, written out in German text; reading the tropes and apostrophes into which he is hurried by the ardour of his mind, and so affected at a preconcerted line that he is unable to proceed any further?"[1] But there were men who not only practised but defended the habit of preaching from manuscript. No less a personage than the Christian advocate at Cambridge in 1805 (W. Cockburn) boldly argued that any other kind of preaching was actually immoral. "I now enter my protest," he says, "against all extempore preaching. Many, indeed, of our communion adopt this custom; but I humbly conceive that it must be wrong, because it is deceitful. We know by experience that the common people, the major part of every congregation, consider the power of preaching without any assistance to be an especial gift of God. This opinion of theirs is absurd; but still it is their opinion. You know, and are convinced, my Christian brethren, who preach extempore, that these people follow you and attend to you because they believe this talent to be a plain proof that God's Spirit resides in you and speaks from your mouth. Unless, then, you take pains to convince them that your fluency of speech is the consequence only of human exertion (which yourselves know to be the fact), you acquire a spiritual dominion over them by deceit."[2] The *British Critic* highly approves of these sentiments.[3] Reginald Heber, in a letter to a young clergyman in 1819, advises him to "avoid singularities," and specifies among them "the High Churchman who shuffles in a pompous tone through his nose, and the Evangelical minister who preaches extempore."[4]

---

[1] Sydney Smith's *Works*, i. 12.

[2] *Address to Methodists*, etc. The course recommended in the last sentence was actually adopted by an old clergyman whom I knew well in my boyhood. "I love to hear you preach without the book, sir," said a parishioner to him, "for then I feel you have the gift of the Spirit." "My good woman," he replied, "you quite mistake the matter; it is not the gift of the Spirit, it's the gift of the gab!"

[3] Vol. xxvi., July to December, 1805.

[4] *Life of Bishop Heber*, by his widow, i. 552.

As a general rule, sermons in parish churches were read from manuscript, and the majority of congregations seem to have preferred that they should be so.

But, whether written or unwritten, and in spite of many complaints, there is little doubt that the sermon, in those days when there was little to attract in the mode of conducting divine service, and when the sacramental system was most imperfectly understood, was the chief attraction to the church-goer; and it would have been wise on the part of the Church to give the people their sermon, as the Methodists did, at the time when it was most convenient to them. That time was the evening. A change had come over the habits of the nation in the matters of rising and going to bed. Both were later than they had been in the eighteenth century, and the consequence was that *something* was required to fill up the long Sunday evenings. The question of Sunday evening services was much agitated during the early years of the present century. The clergy were, as a rule, against them, partly because they considered them an imitation of Methodism, partly on the more rational ground that they encouraged young people to be abroad in the dark to the detriment of morality, and partly from a general dislike of all innovation. The *British Critic*, in 1802, curtly dismisses a work which earnestly advocated Sunday evening lectures in the parish churches of large towns,[1] with the single remark that it is "a serious and temperate plea for Sunday evening lectures, which, however, neither enumerates many of the objections against them, nor satisfactorily answers those which are enumerated." It was, however, useless to resist the spirit of the times, and Sunday evening services in large towns became more and more common. The Evangelicals, as usual, led the way. In the closing years of the eighteenth century, Simeon had evening service at Trinity Church, Cambridge, and "the novelty," he tells us, "attracted some attention. In the college chapels it was no novelty; but in a parish church it conveyed the notion that it must be established for the establishment of true religion, or what the world would call

[1] "A Summary View of the Nature and Tendency of Sunday Evening Lectures in the Parish Churches of Large Towns," etc. See the *British Critic* for 1802.

Methodism"[1]—another instance, by the way, of this good man using an expression which was calculated to cause unnecessary offence. In Marylebone, about 1807, Lord Teignmouth, who was a strong Evangelical, but a stiff Churchman, persuaded the rector, Archdeacon Heslop, who consulted him much about parochial matters, to introduce evening services into the different churches of that extensive parish;[2] and by 1824 the prejudices had been so far overcome that "in many large towns, and in London itself, the practice had been adopted with very general success."[3]

It will be noticed that the Sunday services have been spoken of as if there were no others. This was, of course, not literally the case, but it was painfully near to being so. Even in London week-day services were dropping out of use. There is a sad contrast between the ample supply of such services enumerated by Mr. Paterson in his "*Pietas Londinensis*" in 1714, and the meagre list given in a similar publication in 1824. When daily service was held, it was evidently rather a survival of the past than an instance of present energy. A delightful story is told by the biographer of Joshua Watson, commencing with the ominous words, "Daily prayers in some London churches was *not yet* [about 1800] discontinued"—which evidently implies that it soon *was* discontinued—"and he [Joshua Watson] was a constant attendant at St. Vedast, Foster Lane." He met there Mr. Sikes one day, when there was no other congregation, and said, as they went out, "Never mind; if you will not tell of me, I will not tell of you."[4] There was just this excuse for the discontinuance—that people absolutely declined to frequent them. It became so much a matter of course that there should be none, that in 1832 an excellent Church periodical, the *British Magazine*, gravely urged the following plea in favour of cathedrals: "Is it nothing that cathedrals are the only Protestant churches in England which preserve the *daily* offering of supplication and thanksgiving?"—as if it were a thing unheard of that it should be found elsewhere.

---

[1] Quoted by Carus, p. 69.
[2] *Memoir of Life, etc., of John, Lord Teignmouth*, by his son, ii. 153.
[3] *Quarterly Review*, No. lxi., December, 1824; Art. xiv., "New Churches."
[4] Churton's *Memoir of Joshua Watson*, i. 30.

Indeed, it would appear, from Bishop Horsley's Charge to the diocese of Rochester in 1800, that even the most marked days in the Church's year were in danger of being ignored. "The festivals and fasts of the Church," he says, "are, I fear, not without some connivance of the clergy, gone too much into oblivion and neglect. There can be no excuse for the neglect of the Feast of our Lord's Nativity, and the stated fasts of Ash Wednesday and Good Friday, even in the smallest country parishes ; but in towns and the more populous villages the church ought certainly to be opened for worship on the forenoon at least of every day in the Passion Week, of the Mondays and Tuesdays of Easter Week and Whitsuntide, on the Epiphany, and on some, if not all, of the other festivals."

The undoubted revival of religious earnestness which arose about the beginning of the century found its expression in private prayer-meetings rather than in the more regular services of the Church. The clergy had not much encouragement to establish week-day services, for there was little demand for them. When Richard Mant became Vicar of Great Coggeshall, in 1810, he was frequently invited "to go to extemporaneous prayer-meetings." He always declined, but "offered to have prayers according to the Liturgy more frequently in church if the parishioners desired it."[1] It does not, however, appear that the parishioners accepted his offer. This preference of prayer-meetings to regular services was attributed to the influence of the Evangelicals. "By their preaching," says the thoughtful writer of "*Zeal without Innovation*," "while they revived an attention to some neglected truths of the first importance to mankind, they brought on a mean opinion of the form of religion. To this, as one cause, we may perhaps ascribe the almost entire desertion of our churches on prayer-days, though more to the increased disregard of all religion." It is, however, only fair to add, that when one *does* find week-day services established, it is almost always in places where there was an Evangelical clergyman. There is a significant silence about them in the biographies of several non-Evangelical clergymen when their admiring biographers are enumerating the good works their

[1] *Memoirs of Bishop R. Mant*, p. 70.

heroes did in their respective parishes. But of Legh Richmond we *do* read that when he was at Brading he established daily services in Holy Week; and that when he went to Turvey, in 1805, he had on every Friday evening "a lecture in church, the prayers for Evening Service being previously read."[1] The only prelate who leaned towards the Evangelicals in their early trials (Bishop Porteus) was also the only prelate who really exerted himself to any effectual purpose to bring about a better observance of the neglected season of Lent. His Friday evening lectures at St. James's, Piccadilly, begun in 1798 and continued for four successive Lents, created quite a *furore*, attracting crowds, and among them many of the most fashionable people in that fashionable neighbourhood.[2] It is observable that the bishop set up this service, not only for the benefit of the congregation who attended it, but " hoping it might be the means of drawing a little more attention to that holy but too much neglected season [of Lent]."[3] The effort, we are told, " produced the most eminent, substantial, and salutary advantages."[4] When Daniel Wilson became Vicar of Islington, in 1824, he at once set himself to increase the number of Church services on week-days as well as Sundays, and that in a perfectly right direction. By 1828 he had established " three full services in the church on Sundays and great festival days, and one in the week, besides morning prayers on Wednesdays and Fridays, and on saints' days."[5] The Evangelicals were, after all, better Churchmen than the *laissez-faire* clergy and laity, who were continually opposing them in the name of the Church.

Turning from the Church services to the fabrics in which those services were conducted, the first thing that strikes us is the glaring insufficiency of accommodation for worshippers which they afforded. Figures are dry reading, but the mention of a few statistics is the only way to give the

[1] Grimshaw's *Life of Legh Richmond*, pp. 73, 114.
[2] " The Bishop of London," writes W. Wilberforce in 1798, "preaching every Friday in Lent. Crowds to hear him; fine people and gentlemen standing all the time." See *Life of W. Wilberforce*, by his son, the Bishop of Oxford, p. 187.
[3] See Hodgson's *Life of Bishop Beilby Porteus*, pp. 133, 134.
[4] Review in the *British Critic* for 1802 of the " Lectures on the Gospel of St. Matthew " in St. James's, Westminster, in 1798-1801, by the Bishop of London.
[5] Bateman's *Life of Daniel Wilson, Bishop of Calcutta*, p. 264.

reader an adequate idea of the dearth that prevailed. In the Parliamentary debates of 1818—that is, when a Royal Commission had been appointed to inquire into the deficiency of churches—we find the Chancellor of the Exchequer giving the following startling facts. Liverpool, with a population of 94,376, could only accommodate 21,000; Manchester, with a population of 79,459, only 10,950; while in London and the vicinity there was a population of 1,129,451, of whom churches and Episcopal chapels could only contain 151,536, leaving an excess of 977,915.[1] Even this must have been better than it was a few years earlier, if we may judge by one parish. For in 1818 the Chancellor of the Exchequer specifies Marylebone as having a population of 75,624, with church accommodation for 8700; whereas a letter addressed to Mr. Perceval in 1811 (just before his death) declares that "the parish of Marylebone is said to contain 60,000 inhabitants, while its church will not accommodate more than 900;[2] and St. Pancras is in the same predicament."[3] The last clause is more than borne out by Dr. Middleton, who, when he became vicar in 1812, found St. Pancras in an even worse predicament. "He found himself," says his biographer, "in his new cure, the spiritual guardian of nearly 50,000 persons. The church was an ancient edifice capable of accommodating about 200. At Kentish Town there was a chapel of ease which contained about the same number."[4] John Bowdler the elder, in a letter to the Bishop of London in 1814, declares that "not a *tenth* part of the Church of England population in the west and east parts of the metropolis, and in populous parts of the county of Middlesex, can be accommodated in our churches and chapels."[5] In a famous pamphlet, of which more will be said presently,[6] we are told that in London 953,000 souls were left without the possibility of parochial worship. And we can easily believe it, if it be true that, in

---

[1] That is, excluding the City, where there was an excess of churches.
[2] Proprietary chapels do not seem to be included, but something will be said of these presently.
[3] Letter quoted in the *Quarterly Review*, May, 1811; Article, "State of the Established Church."
[4] Le Bas' *Life of Bishop T. F. Middleton*, i. pp. 25, 26.
[5] See *Memoir of the late John Bowdler, Esq.*
[6] *The Church in Danger*, by the Rev. Richard Yates, 1815.

spite of the vast increase of population, "during the long period from the commencement of the reign of George III. almost to its close, there were not (including St. Alphege and St. Mary's, Whitechapel) six churches erected in the metropolis."[1] And yet we are told that the want of church accommodation was more noticeable in other parts of the kingdom than in the metropolis![2]

But, appalling as are the figures quoted above, they do not cover the full extent of the evil; for even the scanty accommodation which they denote was by no means all available for the general worshipper. The pew system was flourishing almost universally, and, worst of all, the system of faculty pews. "When," says a thoughtful writer in 1824, "alterations in the church, by no means of an extensive nature, might add materially to the general comfort and accommodation, it is inconceivable how great difficulties are thrown in the way of the clergy by old prescriptive rights and faculties granted by the injudicious facility of the ecclesiastical courts whenever the fees are to be raised. A large portion of the area is secured perhaps by enclosure, and jealously preserved for the temporary accommodation of some family not always resident in the parish; but the right is maintained with a strictness which neither conciliation, argument, nor the duty of sacrificing personal convenience to the general good, can induce the owner to abandon."[3] Evidences of the evils of the pew system are only too numerous. "The people," writes Charles Simeon about 1784, "almost universally put locks on their pews [at Trinity Church, Cambridge], and would neither come to church themselves, nor suffer others; and multitudes from time to time were forced to go out of church for want of necessary accommodation." And five years later, "The greater part of the pews still continued shut."[4] Bishop Sumner, in his Primary Charge to the clergy of Winchester diocese in 1829, descants

---

[1] Charles Knight's *History of London*, v. 202.
[2] See *A Letter on Toleration and the Establishment addressed to the Right Hon. Spencer Perceval*, 1808.
[3] *Quarterly Review* for December, 1824, No. lxi.; Art. xiv., "New Churches —Progress of Dissent."
[4] Carus' *Memoirs of the Life of Charles Simeon*, pp. 39, 54.

upon "the flagrant abuses which prevail with respect to pews," and complains that "a system of sale and hire has become inveterate in many places." Thomas Gisborne, though the Evangelicals as a rule were not prominent in any crusade against the pew system, strongly inveighs against "the distinction of churches into pews." "This custom," he says, "of comparatively modern prevalence, goes at once in its very nature to the exclusion of the poor. . . . I could point to a village in my own neighbourhood [Needwood Forest] in which the church, were it still in open seats, as it was within the memory of some of its present inhabitants, would be amply sufficient for the accommodation of the parish."[1] And the anonymous writer of the letter to Mr. Perceval (1808), already quoted, says, "The pews in parish churches being usually appropriated to the higher and middle ranks, and reserved at all times for them, whether they attend or not, the churches afford but little accommodation to the lower ranks."

If this was the case with parish churches, much more was it so with proprietary chapels, the accommodation afforded by which is presumably included in the statistics quoted above. When proprietary chapels were managed as St. Mary's, Brighton, was managed by Mr. Venn Elliott they were an unmixed blessing ; but it is to be feared that all proprietors and incumbents were not Venn Elliotts ; and the temptations to less high-minded men were very great. The evils of the system are well stated by Mr. Yates in his "Church in Danger." "The chapel system," he writes, "as it is at present permitted to operate, though it supplies the means of public worship to many rich people, does harm to the church ; indirectly, by the appearance of supplying in some measure the defect which would otherwise impress itself more strongly upon public notice ; and directly, by withdrawing from ecclesiastical uses into private and secular channels those resources which might be used for supplying proper ministers. The chapels are built and conducted wholly as pecuniary and commercial speculations. The first object of the proprietor is to get the highest rent for pews ; and the poor are excluded." Proprietary chapels were, as a

[1] Note on a passage in a sermon on "Christian Patriotism illustrated by the Character of Nehemiah," in Gisborne's *Sermons*, vol. iii., 1810.

rule, strongholds of the Evangelicals, and it must have been like a bolt from the blue to some of these good men when they found the system condemned by their own special organ in the press; nevertheless, so it was. "The proprietary chapel system," says the *Christian Observer* in 1829, when the plan had been tried for some time and found wanting, "is utterly at variance with clerical efficiency and parochial instruction," with much more to the same effect.[1]

If the "*broad-bottom chapels*," which Archdeacon Daubeny describes in his "*Guide to the Church*" as "a sort of extra-parochial, extra-episcopal congregations intended to do away every distinct idea of Church communion," ever flourished to any appreciable extent, and if the accommodation *they* afforded is taken into account in the figures cited, this would make matters still worse; but as the archdeacon speaks of them rather as a scheme in the air than as actually existing,[2] and as I can find no trace of them elsewhere, let us hope that they need not be reckoned with.

It would be unfair to blame either the Church or the State—at any rate, the Church or the State of the nineteenth century—for all this spiritual destitution. On the contrary, great credit is due to both for the vigorous exertions which they made to remedy it when the opportunity occurred. But how was it that it was allowed to grow to so gigantic a height before the remedy was applied? The answer to this question is an illustration in detail of what was said generally in the opening chapter about the state of the country during the early part of the century. The war allowed neither attention nor money to be devoted to church-building. There was an enormous increase of commercial prosperity, which, to use the words of the Bishop of London (Dr. Howley) "caused a transference of large masses from districts well planted with churches to places altogether without means of public worship."[3] But men's eyes were fixed, not

---

[1] See a review of the Bishop of Winchester's (Sumner's) Charge in the *Christian Observer* for 1829.

[2] "I understand that the plan from which the greatest success is expected against the Establishment, is that of setting up what are called *broad-bottom* chapels,".etc.—Daubeny's *Guide to the Church*, ii. 438.

[3] *Charge to the Clergy of London*, by Bishop Howley, 1818.

on the teeming populations of London, Liverpool, Manchester, Nottingham, Leeds, Sheffield, etc., but of the brave soldiers in the Peninsula, or the brave sailors on the wide ocean. When war-ships had to be built, there was nothing left for building churches; when soldiers had to be maintained, there was nothing left for the maintenance of additional clergy. Indeed, it would have been difficult to find additional clergy; for, as Bishop Kaye said, "in consequence of opportunities of employment in the army and navy afforded to young men during the war, the number of candidates for Holy Orders was not equal to the demand for curates. During the first ten years of this century, the number of young men who annually graduated as B.A. in January at Cambridge averaged little more than a hundred; it now [1852] averages more than three hundred."[1] Men might reasonably argue, What is the use of building churches when there is no one to serve them? Not that the matter ever reached this stage. It was tacitly admitted that every halfpenny was wanted for the war, and there was an end of it.

It should be remembered, too, that the war was considered by many as essentially a holy war. Churchmen took the deepest interest in it, not only as patriots, but as Christians. It was not merely a question whether French rulers should dominate over English bodies, but whether French principles, which were identified with atheistical principles, should dominate over English minds. It is true that many scorned and bitterly resented this view of the case;[2] but these were not Churchmen. If the question of church-building on any extensive scale had been raised, the answer would in effect have been, "Why build churches when the Gaul is at the gates? If the gates are stormed, the country will be ruined, and Christianity itself will fall amid the ruins." Here is a specimen of the sort of language which was used, and which expressed the feelings of thousands. Speaking of Buonaparte and France, an eloquent preacher

---

[1] Charge of the Bishop of Lincoln in 1852. See *Nine Charges to the Clergy of Lincoln, and some other Works*, by J. Kaye, late Bishop of Lincoln, edited by his son, Archdeacon Kaye, 1854.

[2] See, for instance, *The Black Book*, p. 273; and S. T. Coleridge's early prose writings, *passim*.

said, "This prodigy is gazed at by every eye. It dwells on every tongue. It equally interests and agitates the rulers and the people. Shall there be none among us to view it with the eyes of a Christian?"[1]

Simultaneously with the cessation of the war, the current in favour of church-building at once set in, increasing in volume as it went on, and carrying all before it; so that the last seventeen or eighteen years of our period will, in this respect, compare favourably with any similar period in the long history of the Church of England. The war, as we all know, ended in 1815; and in 1815 the trumpet was sounded by an obscure clergyman, the Rev. Richard Yates, chaplain of Chelsea Hospital, in the form of a letter to Lord Liverpool, bearing the title of the old, old war-cry, "The Church in Danger." This pamphlet at once awakened an activity in the Church and nation that never flagged until it had to a great extent wiped out the stigma which was attached to both Church and nation of neglecting adequately to supply men's spiritual needs in their National Church. Funds were provided from two different sources. Mainly through the efforts of the Prime Minister, Lord Liverpool, to whom Mr. Yates had addressed his "Letter," and who was a good friend of the Church, a Parliamentary grant of a million pounds was voted for church-building. On January 27, 1818, the subject was mentioned in the Speech from the Throne; and on March 16 the Chancellor of the Exchequer, Mr. Vansittart, moved that one million sterling, to be raised by the issue of exchequer bills, should be applied to the erection of additional churches in the metropolis, and in other large towns in which the population greatly exceeded the church accommodation provided. This was followed by another grant of half a million in 1824. A remission of duty on materials employed in building the churches further helped on the work. All this was, of course, inadequate to what was required; but it was a great aid, and would have been a greater if it had been judiciously employed. It was, in fact, far more than has ever been done by Parliament either before or since.

[1] *The Ways of God vindicated by the Word of God*: a sermon preached by Dr. O'Beirne, Bishop of Meath, in 1804.

But, side by side with these State efforts, another effort was being made by purely voluntary exertions. This was done through the *Church Building Society*, which was also founded soon after the Peace. The society, like so many other good works, seems to have originated with that little band of High Churchmen of whom Joshua Watson was the most prominent. But the project had been agitated for some time before it took a definite shape. As early as 1814, four laymen—Sir J. Allan Park, John Bowdler, C. H. Turner, and W. Davis—had written a stirring letter to the Bishop of London (Dr. Howley) on the subject. "We," they said, "who travel much about the country, are thoroughly convinced that the great majority of the people of this land are, notwithstanding all that has been said to the contrary, strongly attached to the Church of England, and that one great cause of the apparent defection from the Church, and of the increase of sectarism and Methodism, is the want of places of worship upon the Establishment. We are now rejoicing at the end of the war. Let us show our thanks by immediately dedicating to God's honour a number of free churches and chapels, sufficient to supply the wants of all God's faithful worshippers in the Established Church of England."[1] The good men were a little premature in assuming that the war was at an end; they shared the general impression that when Napoleon had retired to Elba, and the allies had entered Paris, all was over. But in 1815, when the war was really ended, they returned to the charge. A memorial was presented to the Earl of Liverpool, framed by John Bowdler and signed by about one hundred and twenty laymen, expressing "extreme alarm at the danger to which the constitution of the country, both in Church and State, is exposed from want of places of worship, particularly for persons of the middle and lower classes." They then referred to the "noble efforts made by the National Society," and expressed an opinion that these labours would be lost if churches were not provided; and then they quoted statistics similar to those which have been given above. This probably helped to bring on the proposal of the

[1] The letter, signed J. A. Park, J. Bowdler, C. H. Turner, and W. Davis, is quoted in the *Memoir of John Bowdler, Esq.*, published 1825.

Parliamentary grant. But those who were anxious about church-building were not content with applying to Parliament. In 1817 various meetings were held, in which Joshua Watson, John Bowdler, Sir T. D. Acland, William Cotton, and others took part, to talk the matter over; and the result was that at a meeting held at the Freemasons' Tavern on February 6, 1818, with the Archbishop of Canterbury (Dr. Manners-Sutton) in the chair, the Church Building Society was founded. Joshua Watson, aided by the counsel of his relative, Archdeacon Daubeny, seems to have been mainly instrumental in drawing up its original regulations.

One great benefit conferred by this voluntary society, besides the very essential one of raising funds, was that it helped to dispel the foolish notion that an Established Church must do everything through the State. It is difficult now to realize the undoubted fact that it was once considered beneath the dignity of the National Church, and worthy only of Methodists and other fanatics, to raise money by voluntary contributions,[1] and that such a course would tend to place the Church on the level with Dissent. And the State encouraged such ideas by passing Acts of Parliament for objects for which it would not now be thought at all necessary to do so. Thus, when a spire was erected in 1807 at St. Nicholas' Church, Yarmouth, an Act was first obtained for the purpose; when the obviously necessary work of erecting a new church for the overgrown parish of St. Pancras, London, was projected, a Bill was first prepared, introduced into Parliament, and, after some delay, passed. And a most dismal failure it was; for even when armed with this indisputable authority (as it was thought), the good and able vicar could not carry out his object.[2] The Parliamentary briefs for such purposes had been so unsuccessful, and even in some cases so shamefully abused, that they were on the point of being abolished. Then the Church Building Society stepped in, and showed what could be done without such adventitious aid, or rather such vexatious hampering. Its success was very marked.

---

[1] As late as 1818, Sir William Scott argued in the House of Lords that "it was unworthy in the Church to depend on private funds for its increase and support." See Hansard's *Debates*, April 30, 1818.

[2] See *Life of Bishop Thomas Fanshaw Middleton*, i. 25, 26.

It would be cruel to inflict upon the reader another list of figures. Let it suffice to say that, roughly speaking, in the first fourteen years of its existence, it raised and spent about as much money as the Parliamentary grants.[1] So that we have a total of at least three millions; and this must be, perhaps, nearly doubled; though on this point it is impossible to speak at all accurately, because the spirit of church-building which had been raised found a vent in numberless acts of private benevolence, which no statistics of Parliaments or voluntary societies account for.[2] A sum of at least six millions may fairly be supposed to have been spent on church-building during the last fifteen years of our period; that is, infinitely more than had been spent during the whole of the hundred years immediately preceding.

The result was all the more remarkable because there were difficulties to be contended with which have now to a great extent disappeared. The old *laissez-faire* feeling which had been dominant for a century did not die out without a struggle. "The principle generally inculcated," says a contemporary writer, "was—Let things alone. I have frequently heard this maxim delivered with an oracular gravity, a nod of the head intended to silence all schemes of improvement."[3] When the oracle was also the obstructive incumbent, what could be done? Intrenched within his impregnable fortress of freehold rights, he can defy everybody. There he is, and there he will remain. Like Æolus—

"Sedet æternumque sedebit."

Opposition, however, came more frequently from recalcitrant parishioners than from recalcitrant incumbents. A sad instance has already been noticed in the parish of St. Pancras. The vicar was most anxious to supply the crying want of church accommodation, and he had "the cordial support of many of the most honoured and respected names in the parish;" but an opposition was raised which for the time was

[1] By the expression "raised" I mean to include the money raised by private subscriptions to meet the grant from the society.

[2] For example, Archdeacon Daubeny must have spent nearly £10,000 on his churches. Thomas Dykes spent or raised thousands at Hull for church-building. Dr. Christopher Wordsworth did the same at Lambeth.

[3] *Christian Remembrancer* for 1841; Article, "Prospects of the Church of England."

fatal.¹ Archdeacon Daubeny found the same difficulty at North Bradley, and many more instances might be given.

Another difficulty arose from the painful fact that opposers could argue with some plausibility, "You are too late; the ground is occupied." The almost insuperable obstacles which had stood in the way of church-building in the first fifteen years of the century did not exist to the same extent in the case of Dissenters. And that, for many reasons. In the first place, they were, as a body, opposed to the war. They were hampered, therefore, by no scruples about diverting money from the patriotic and, as most Churchmen thought, truly Christian object of repelling infidel assailants. Nor did any foolish feeling of dignity make them hesitate to procure money where they could. And, again, to run up a cheap meeting-house was a far less formidable task than to erect a costly church. And, lastly, they had no prescriptive rights, either of obstructive incumbents or of selfish pew-owners, to contend with. Man's religious instinct must be satisfied somewhere; and if it cannot find satisfaction in one place, it will seek it in another. Hence the projector of a Dissenting place of worship had the double advantage of knowing that he could combine a pious Christian work with a promising commercial speculation; for it was often a more profitable adventure to build a chapel than to build a house.

And it must be confessed that some, though by no means all, of the most prominent party in the Church played into his hands. "I am not at all particular as to the place of worship you attend, so as it may be under a serious preacher, and so as you attend regularly." "I do not much heed to what place of worship you go, so as you are but a serious and regular attendant." Thus wrote Henry Kirke White, when he was preparing for the ministry of the Church; and though it may be said that the opinions of a mere boy do not count for much, yet it must be remembered that he was a phenomenal boy, and that he was under the direct influence of leading Evangelicals at the time, and would presumably reflect their sentiments.² "Some of the most lively and pious

---

[1] *Life of Bishop Middleton*, i. 26.
[2] See the *Remains of Henry Kirke White*, with an account of his life by R. Southey, *passim*.

Christians I know," writes Edward Bickersteth in 1810, "do not hesitate to go wherever they can get benefit."[1] Well might Bishop Jebb write to his friend Knox in 1815, "As to the religious world, it would seem that Churches are more and more assuming a Dissenting tendency"![2]

Once more, it might be argued, and *was* argued with terrible force, " You are asking us to build new churches, but are the existing churches filled?" There is only too much evidence that they were not. The very first chapter in that striking work, "Zeal without Innovation," bears the ominous title, "On the Visible Decline of Attendance on Public Worship;" the contents may be guessed. And the title of the next chapter, " On the Increase of Dissent," suggests one cause. Sydney Smith is full of complaints about the emptiness of churches, some of which have been already quoted.[3] One of the objections raised several times in Parliament against the million grant was that the present churches were not filled.[4]

That in spite of all these difficulties and objections so much could be done in the way of church-building, is a very remarkable and creditable fact; but whether the money was always spent in the best way, is quite another question. The fact is, that while from the practical point of view this church-building era came too late, many of the sheep whom it was desired to pen having strayed into other pastures, from an architectural point of view it came too early. They built their churches first, and began to study the principles of church architecture afterwards. There are probably no churches which are more of a puzzle and a despair to architects and clergymen than the churches built in the early part of the nineteenth century. Unmitigated ugliness and hopeless inconvenience are their chief characteristics.[5] The last great

[1] Birks' *Memoir of E. Bickersteth*, i. 160.
[2] *Thirty Years' Correspondence between Bishop Jebb and A. Knox*, ii. 282.
[3] See *supra*, p. 139.
[4] See Hansard's *Parliamentary Debates*.
[5] When it was too late, people began to realize with dismay the ugliness of the structures they had erected. In the debate in the House of Commons on the new churches in 1824, Mr. Grey Bennet "asked the name of the architect who built the new church in Langham Place. Everybody who saw it shrugged up his shoulders, and asked who invented such a monstrosity." Others took up the same strain of abuse, and no one had a word to say in favour of the building.

era of church-building, that which extended from the Fire of London to the death of Queen Anne, did at least produce a distinctive style of its own. Sir Christopher Wren and his disciples are surely to be admired. Many—the present writer among the number—see with a pang any obliteration of their work. But who could even affect to raise a sigh of regret at the demolition or transformation of churches built during the period before us? Specimens are only too numerous in every part of the country. They have not even the merit of originality in their ugliness; they are either absolutely nondescript or sham Gothic. Still less have they the merit of cheapness; they were very expensive indeed. Dr. Stoughton calculates that, between 1801 and 1831, five hundred churches were built at a cost of three millions; that would mean £6000 on an average for each church. This costly estimate is more than borne out by other evidences. Bishop Sumner, in his Primary Charge to the diocese of Winchester in 1829, while bearing grateful testimony to the good work done by the Parliamentary grants and the Church Building Society, tells us that "in one parish of Surrey more than £94,000 have been expended within the last ten years in the erection of five additional places of worship," and that "in another parish in Hants two new churches, containing four thousand sittings, had been recently built at an expense of nearly £30,000." This would imply that these seven churches would cost on an average nearly £18,000. In Daniel Wilson's time Islington was "enriched with three large and noble churches, which had in reality cost £30000."[1] We learn from Dean Burgon that the sister of Dr. Routh, Mrs. Sheppard, built at Thrale a church which cost £26,000, including the parsonage house.[2]

We have only to look at St. Pancras, finished in 1822, to form an idea of how the money was spent; and we can well understand the reasonableness of the complaint made about its neighbour St. Marylebone.[3] "If," says an anonymous writer to the Bishop of London in 1818, "new churches are

---

[1] See *Life of Bishop Daniel Wilson*, p. 266.
[2] *Lives of Twelve Good Men*: "Master Joseph Routh," i. 53.
[3] It seems almost incredible, but I believe it is true, that the cost of the two churches actually amounted to more than £150,000.

to be erected on the costly and perverted plan of the new one in Marylebone, if the solemnity and sobriety of ecclesiastical architecture are to be converted into the flaunting and theatrical character of that, very few can be built."[1] More *were* built than the writer anticipated ; but that was because far more money was raised than the most sanguine could have hoped.[2]

Another objection to the expenditure of the money was that the poor were not properly provided for. "Only about one-third of the sittings in the churches erected out of the Parliamentary grants were free. The rented pews were three feet from back to back, and the free seats only two feet four inches."[3]

To Archdeacon Daubeny belongs the credit of erecting the first absolutely free church in England. As this marks an epoch, and as the example was happily by degrees followed by many others, the account of it is worth quoting. "For several years Mr. Daubeny was anxiously engaged in promoting a plan, which originated with himself, to erect a *free church* in Bath, where accommodation for the lower classes was grievously wanted. The first stone was laid in 1795, and in 1798 a handsome building, containing free sittings for 1360, exclusive of the galleries, was consecrated by Dr. Moss, Bishop of Bath and Wells, and called Christ Church. It was the first free church that ever was erected in this country ; he officiated in it for fifteen years. The example was followed in many parts owing to its success."[4]

[1] Letter to the Bishop of London (Dr. Howley) on the Society for Church Building, 1818.

[2] The lavish expenditure of money arose from a right feeling that God's house ought to be handsomely built. In a debate in the House of Lords, May 20, 1818, on the clauses of the Bill which limited the powers of the Commissioners "to building churches so as to afford the greatest possible accommodation to the largest number of persons," Lord Grenville said very properly that, " while he deprecated all useless splendour in building of churches, he thought it of importance that that mode should be adopted which was best calculated to inspire devotion, and which was characteristic of the Established Church, and that there should be a decent decoration." The Earls of Liverpool and Harrowby spoke to the same effect. See Hansard.

[3] *Church Quarterly Review* for January, 1885 ; Art. iv., " The Church in East London," an article which is full of most interesting and accurate information.

[4] *Life of Charles Daubeny, Archdeacon of Sarum*, prefixed to the third edition of the *Guide to the Church*, 1830.

Among others who were much impressed with the success of Christ Church, Bath, was John Bowdler, one of the chief founders of the Church Building Society; he also thought "it set an example in style—simple, chaste, free from all useless or expensive decoration; yet such that no passer-by can mistake its character." His biographer adds that "he looked to the Church Building Society to correct a vicious taste, and encourage a plainer and less expensive method."[1]

What has hitherto been said applies chiefly to the great centres of population. It was, perhaps, on the whole a happy thing that men's minds were so much taken up with providing accommodation for the teeming masses in large towns that they did not meddle much with the old country churches. One trembles to think what would have been the result of a rage for the "improvement" of these old Gothic edifices if it had arisen before the study of Gothic architecture had been revived. Looking at the matter from an artistic point of view, we may certainly be thankful that the later part of our period was a period of church *building*, not of church *restoration*. What might have been expected may be gathered from the following ludicrous account written in 1841: "The last rector of the parish in which we write was as kind-hearted, good a man as ever lived; but he knew no more of architecture than he did of Sanscrit, and had no more taste in church matters than his old coach-horse; the consequence was that, having resolved, one fine morning, to beautify his church, he cut up an old ornamental chancel-screen, and fronted his pew with the tracery; half of the little stained glass that remained in the windows he gave to a neighbouring peer, who was decorating his paternal mansion; an ancient doorway, on the north side of the church, surmounted with a bas-relief of St. Michael, he destroyed, and put an abominable modern window in its place; pulled down a splendid altar-tomb of the fourteenth century, clapped the sides round the chancel, and set the recumbent figures upright, building them into the window. The churchwardens made no objection."[2] Similar handiwork may be found in other places, suggesting that after all King Log was better than King Stork.

[1] *Memoir of the late John Bowdler, Esq.*, 1825.
[2] *Christian Remembrancer*, vol. ii., July to December, 1841.

SQUALOR OF COUNTRY CHURCHES. 159

Nevertheless the reign of King Log was very grievous, and it is lamentable to reflect what the state of our country churches, as a rule, was. From what the elders among us will themselves remember, they will easily believe that there is no exaggeration in the following passage, written in 1827 : " Let any one make a circuit of the villages throughout a considerable portion of these realms, and what is the spectacle which in too many instances will salute his eyes on entering the churchyard? On looking at the exterior of the church, he will often find it half buried beneath the mould, which has been suffered to accumulate round it for ages, and to spread a gradual decay throughout the walls and foundations. On entering it, he will find that everything answers faithfully to the promise without ; and that the external provision for perpetuating dampness and discomfort within has succeeded to admiration. The walls will appear decorated with hangings of green ; a carpeting of the same pattern often partially covers the floor ; and the very first and last thoughts which are excited by the whole appearance of the building are those of ague, catarrh, and rheumatism."[1]

Another writer, a few years later, puts the matter in a very striking and original way. " The traveller," he writes, " through these islands, whose lot it was to have before his eyes the evidence of the gradual substitution of Christianity in the place of Druidical superstition, or Roman, Saxon, or Danish idolatry, could hardly perhaps have found among the decaying fanes of Jupiter or Woden, scenes of more dismal ruin and dank desolation than are to be seen at the present moment in some of the houses of God in our rural districts ; and the reason why so little is said about it, seems to be that we are so accustomed to see our churches generally in a dilapidated condition, that we have altogether ceased to find anything remarkable in it. But if dirt and damp, if crumbling rafters and tottering walls, if systematic neglect and wanton mutilation, were to be found in the one case, most assuredly they are in the other ; the owls and the bats have been permitted to dwell in both ; and at the very porch, the long rank grass (itself well-nigh choked with hemlock and nettles) has testified in both that the paths of entrance

[1] *British Critic* for April, 1827 ; Art. x., " Ecclesiastical Discipline."

are no longer thronged by daily worshippers, and that either the power or the will is wanting that maintained them in their ancient honours. . . . Many of the churches in small parishes of the rural districts are more like monuments of some effete and almost forgotten superstition, lingering only in the prejudices of a rude and ignorant peasantry, than edifices meet for the service of the most high God."[1]

Specific accounts amply bear out these general strictures. Bishop Copleston complains in 1827 that in his diocese of Llandaff "the churches are, many of them, in a state of squalid neglect."[2] When Venn Elliott, in 1813, made a pious pilgrimage to Yelling, the living of his famous grandfather, Henry Venn, he found the church almost in ruins, and the steeple taken down by the vicar's order. "The church walls were overgrown, as well as the churchyard, with weeds and nettles, and the inside presented a picture that asked in piercing accents, 'Could this have been the loved and frequented house of God not twenty years ago?'"[3] Richard Cecil, looking upon such churches with an artist's eye, seems rather to like the squalor; but his testimony is to the same effect. "The very damp," he says, "that trickles down the walls, and the unsightly green that moulders upon the pillars, are far more pleasing to me from their associations than the trim, finished, classic, heathen piles of the present fashion."[4] But really there is no need to multiply details; for there are many now living who have seen for themselves, or whose fathers have told them, of the abject condition of the generality of country churches before the Oxford Movement; or perhaps, in this connection, it would be more correct to say the Cambridge Movement, for it was at Cambridge, not Oxford, that the revived interest in church architecture had its origin.

The following verses, kindly sent to me by the Rev. R. H. Whitworth, strikingly illustrate what has been said

[1] *Christian Remembrancer*, July to December, 1841; Article on "Churches and Churchwardens."
[2] See *Memoir of Edward Copleston, Bishop of Llandaff*, by W. J. Copleston, p. 132.
[3] *Life of the Rev. H. V. Elliott*, p. 31.
[4] Memoir of R. Cecil, prefixed to his *Remains*, p. civ.

above about the Church services. The writer was the Rev. W. Goodacre.

A CLERGYMAN'S WORK, A.D. 1825.

1.

This journal of the eighth of May,
    In eighteen hundred twenty-five,
Is penned to show that after all
    The night is come and I'm alive.

2.

My breakfast done, at half-past eight
    I left my home and took my way
Towards Mansfield Woodhouse, where began
    The labours of this toilsome day.

3.

The Sunday schools, to teach the young
    Their duty both to God and man,
I first inspected, and approved
    The faithful labourers and their plan.

4.

At half-past ten to church I went,
    Said prayers and preached, four pairs did ask,
A woman churched, and half-past twelve
    Completed saw my morning task.

5.

I mounted steed, to Skegby rode,
    Imparted to a female ill
The Holy Eucharist, as before
    She had to me expressed her will.

6.

At this place, too, I prayed and preached,
    And set the congregation free ;
Then mounting steed to Sutton hied,
    And reached the church just after three.

7.

Two children here I first baptized,
    Then prayed and preached as heretofore ;
Seven couples published when the hour
    Exceeded somewhat half-past four.

8.

Two children more I christened then;
   Ten minutes, too, in vestry stayed
Among the teachers of the school,
   To hear some plans that they had made.

9.

Again to Mansfield Woodhouse went;
   A corpse in waiting there I found:
The last sad rites, 'mid weeping friends,
   I read,—and dust gave to the ground.

10.

A fourth time then I prayed and preached,
   And, this performed, the hour drew nigh
Whereof the kirk-hammer 'gainst the bell
   Eight hours would sound to passers-by.

11.

Two children more I then did name,
   In private manner as allowed
By Holy Church—tho' not approved—
   But 'tis the humour of the crowd.

12.

A person sick who wished my prayers
   I called to see, as I was bound;
And after giving some advice,
   My duty done with joy I found.

13.

Bestowed with welcome by a friend,
   Some food I ate with eager zest,
Which, dinner or my supper call,
   Or any name that you like best.

14.

I sat awhile as loth to move;
   But, knowing I was not at home,
I sallied forth, and safe arrived
   Beneath my humble, peaceful dome.

15.

This scrawl complete, the hour of "twelve"
   Brings my day's labours to a close.
The past fatigue secures my rest;
   To you I wish a sound repose.

CHAPTER VI.

CHURCH LITERATURE.

THE early part of the nineteenth century witnessed a great revival of interest in theological questions, but it was not an age of great theological writers. This is all the more strange, because in some other departments of literature it was the greatest age since

"The spacious days of Queen Elizabeth."

But the Church of England still kept up the traditions of a learned Church; and if she produced no theological giants, she yet produced some whose stature was above the average, and whose writings may be read with pleasure and profit at this day and in all days.

Perhaps her two greatest divines were survivals of the eighteenth century, who just lived on to see the dawn of the nineteenth. The first of these is *Samuel Horsley* (1733-1806). He had demolished Priestley, and preached most of his grand sermons, before the new century began; but his later Charges, as bishop, first of Rochester and then of St. Asaph, belong to our period. He was a very powerful writer, but not a voluminous one; and it is much to the credit of the new generation that it showed its appreciation of intellectual power, though not lavishly exercised, by warmly recognizing the merits of the veteran. He is "our ablest modern prelate,"[1] "the one red leaf, the last of its clan, with relation to the learned teachers of our Church,"[2] "the first episcopal authority (if learning, wisdom, and knowledge of the Scrip-

---

[1] So Bishop Jebb called him in 1818. See Forster's *Life of Jebb*, p. 408.
[2] S. T. Coleridge. See introduction to *Essays on his own Times*. In his early Radical days, Coleridge had a violent antipathy against Horsley.

tures be any foundation for authority),"[1] "the light and glory of the Established Church."[2] Horsley, however, was essentially an eighteenth-century man, and we cannot in this volume claim him as our own.

The other veteran was *William Paley* (1743-1805), the close of whose active life exactly coincided with the close of the eighteenth century. But though his bodily weakness prevented him from taking any active part in Church work, his mind was as vigorous as ever; and it was in the nineteenth century that he wrote what his biographer rightly terms "his last, but the most original and entertaining of his works"—his "*Natural Theology*" (1802). The vastness of the subject, which this chapter very imperfectly attempts to cover, renders a subdivision necessary ; and, both in point of date as well as, in some respects, of merit, Paley's " Natural Theology " claims the first place under our first head.

EVIDENTIAL WRITINGS.

The history of Paley's " Natural Theology " is interesting, and cannot be better told than in the writer's own words in his grateful dedication of the work to his patron and diocesan, the Bishop of Durham (Dr. Shute Barrington), who gave him the living of Bishop Wearmouth. "A weak," he says, "and, of late, a painful state of health, deprived me of the power of discharging the duties of my station in a manner at all suitable, either to my sense of those duties, or to my anxious wishes concerning them. My inability for the public functions of my profession left me much at leisure. That leisure was not to be lost. It was only in my study that I could repair my deficiencies in the Church ; it was only through the press that I could speak. These circumstances entitled your lordship in particular to call upon me for the only species of exertion of which I was capable, and disposed me without hesitation to obey the call in the best manner that

---

[1] Isaac Milner in his later life (see *Life*, p. 212)—a very unexceptionable testimony, for Horsley had no sympathy with the Evangelicals.

[2] John Milner's *End of Controversy*, prefatory address—another unexceptionable testimony, for Horsley had as little sympathy with Roman Catholics as with Evangelicals.

I could." What the parishioners of Bishop Wearmouth thought of this arrangement we are not told; but people were not so particular about parochial activity in those days as they are now; and the Church at large was certainly a gainer from the fact that the rector of the large parish of Bishop Wearmouth was disabled for parish work. The plan of the "Natural Theology" was a continuation, or rather a carrying back, of earlier works. The writer says (again to quote from the dedication), "The following discussion alone was wanted to make up my works into a system; in which works, such as they are, the public have now before them the evidences of Natural Religion, the evidences of Revealed Religion, and an account of the duties that result from both. It is of small importance that they have been written in an order the very reverse of that in which they ought to be read."

It is rather too much the tendency of the present day to depreciate Paley—a tendency which has probably been increased rather than lessened by the fact that he still is a text-book in his own University for the humblest yet most indispensable of her examinations. But the "Natural Theology," with which alone the present volume is concerned, still appears to me to be, within its limits and from its writer's point of view, a most lucid, powerful, and unanswerable defence of Divine truth. The whole book is an illustration and amplification of the famous simile of the watch, with which it commences, and which, by the way, was by no means an original idea of Paley's. A watch is found. The machine demonstrates, by its construction, contrivance and design. Contrivance must have had a contriver; design, a designer. But every indication of contrivance, every manifestation of design, which existed in the watch, exists in the works of nature; with the difference, on the side of nature, of being greater, and that in a degree which exceeds all computation. This is the gist of the whole book; but it is worked out with a wonderful wealth of illustration, and with great ingenuity. Mr. Leslie Stephen, who of course does not agree with Paley, is yet candid enough to own that the work is " a marvel of skilful statement."[1]

[1] See *English Thought in the Eighteenth Century*, i. 403.

Paley lived before the days of Darwin, and therefore we cannot be surprised that he does not grapple with the theory of evolution. He probably knew nothing about German metaphysics, which were then just beginning to exercise an influence upon English thought. He was simply a plain, common-sense Englishman, not at all likely to commend himself to the mystical mind of a man like S. T. Coleridge, fresh from the study of the great German writers. "The watchmaker's scheme of prudence" seemed to Coleridge grovelling and inadequate. The majority of Englishmen, however, were not Coleridges, but plain, commonplace people, and the arguments which Paley uses are just of the sort that would come home to them; and his plain, downright, lucid style, without any rhapsody or superfluous ornament, is just the style to suit them. Of course, if any one stops short at the "Natural Theology," he gains a very poor conception of the whole field of religious truth; but it is his own fault if he does so, not the writer's, who fairly tells him what a very little way he is carrying him.

Books on the evidences are numerous during our period, as antidotes to the unbelief introduced into England through the French Revolution. But all that can be attempted here is to select a few of those which seem to be most notable. Among them a high place must be given to a little anonymous *brochure* which appeared in 1819, and which in its way was a singularly effective contribution to evidential literature. It was entitled "*Historic Doubts Relative to Napoleon Buonaparte*," and was so popular that in thirty years it passed through nine editions—a large number considering the nature of the work. The writer was Archbishop Whately, then a young Fellow of Oriel, and his object was to show that the same doubts which were alleged against the Scripture might be applied to the history of one whose name had been in everybody's mouth, and in whose existence they had had only too good reason to believe; for Napoleon Buonaparte had been the plague of Europe, and of no part of it more so than of England. Whately's cool, unimpassioned, logical mind enabled him to treat his *bizarre* subject more effectively than perhaps any man living could have done. He applies to it very cleverly the arguments used by Hume in his

"Essay on Miracles." "We entertain," argues Hume, "a suspicion concerning any matter of fact, when the witnesses *contradict* each other; when they are of a *suspicious* character; when they have an *interest* in what they affirm." Whately shows that the newspapers, from which nine-tenths of the people derive all they know about Napoleon, are liable to all these objections. The newspapers "fail in *all* the most essential points on which their credibility depends. (1) We have no assurance that they have correct information; (2) they have an apparent interest in propagating falsehood; (3) they palpably contradict each other in the most important points." Hume argued that it was contrary to experience that miracles should be true. Whately shows that Napoleon's rapid victories were quite contrary to experience. He puts the emperor's career very cleverly into scriptural phraseology—"And it came to pass, etc.,"—and then asks, "Now, if a free-thinking philosopher were to meet such a tissue of absurdities as this in an old Jewish record, would he not reject it at once as too palpable an imposture to deserve even any inquiry into its evidence?" The value and influence of this little book were out of all proportion to its bulk.

Another work of an evidential nature, very different from the one last mentioned, but very able and effective in its way, was Thomas Rennell's "*Remarks on Scepticism, especially as it is connected with Organization and Life.*" The writer was son of another Thomas Rennell, Dean of Winchester and Master of the Temple, who survived him for many years. His "Remarks" were published in 1819, and quickly passed through six editions. He wrote them because he saw "medical science made the handmaid of irreligion, the doctrine of materialism paving the way for infidelity and atheism;" and his object was "to reconcile the views of the philosopher and the Christian." In his capacity of Christian Advocate at Cambridge, he also published another evidential work, entitled "Proofs of Inspiration, or Grounds of Distinction between the New Testament and the Apocryphal Volume; occasioned by the recent publication of the Apocryphal New Testament by Hone," 1822. Rennell won early a very high reputation for learning and ability, and his premature death in 1824 was a great loss to the Church, which sorely needed at that time men of his calibre.[1]

Among his numerous avocations, Daniel Wilson found time to publish a work on "*The Evidences of Christianity stated in a Popular and Practical Manner*" (2 vols.). They were "a course of lectures delivered in the parish church of St. Mary's, Islington, in the years 1827-30." The lectures were an amplification of some previous lectures which he had delivered in 1819, when he was minister of St. John's, Bedford Row; and, as was natural, having been addressed to a congregation, they aimed at combining the two objects of instruction and edification. The writer very properly considered that "*evidences* of Christianity included internal as well as external evidences," and that a work on the subject which excluded either would be incomplete. He did not underrate the difficulties of the task, as an amusing letter to Hannah More shows; "but seriously," he says, "I have a notion in my head that something of argument and practice might be conjoined;" and he manfully set himself to conjoin them. It was not only a hard thing "to combine close reasoning on the evidences with strong appeals to the conscience," but, when done, there was the dilemma which is thus pointedly put by his biographer: "Those who need the evidences will disregard the appeals, and those who value the appeals will not need the evidences."[2] However, considering its difficulties, the work was well done, and it remained for some time very popular with the Evangelical school, the special teaching of which is strongly brought out in it.

[1] Among those who highly appreciated his intellectual powers was Dr. Samuel Parr, an excellent judge in such matters. In defending Dr. Rennell, Dean of Winchester, against Dr. Milner, the author of *The End of Religious Controversy*, he remarks in dignified terms, "He has a son not quite unworthy of such an illustrious father; not quite unable to wield the choicest weapons of lawful warfare, when confronted by so sturdy and well-disciplined a champion as yourself. My authority is good, Dr. Milner, not only from common fame, but from the general consent of scholars, and my own personal observations, when I say with equal confidence to Protestants and Romanists, that by profound erudition, by various and extensive knowledge, etc., the son of the Dean of Winchester stands among the brightest luminaries of our national literature or national Church." —*Works of Dr. Samuel Parr*, edited by J. Johnstone, vol. iii. p. 461. Letter to Dr. Milner on his *End of Religious Controversy*, June, 1819.

[2] Bateman's *Life of D. Wilson*, p. 168.

Two more works of a directly evidential nature require special notice, viz.: William Van Mildert's Boyle Lectures (1802-1805), "*On the Rise and Progress of Infidelity*," and John Bird Sumner's "*Evidence of Christianity*" (1825). It is a striking instance of the general apathy which pervaded the Church of the eighteenth century, that when the former work appeared, no Boyle Lectures had been printed for more than twenty years, and that for many years before that time they had been published very irregularly. When Van Mildert wrote his Boyle Lectures he was a young man, and had not reached that maturity of style and thought which he afterwards showed in his Bamptons and his "Life of Waterland." They consist of twenty-four long sermons, twelve in each volume. The first volume is virtually a proof of the fulfilment of the prophecy, "Thou shalt bruise his heel," which the writer explains, "Thou shalt be the cause of bitter sufferings to the Redeemer Himself, and to His faithful followers." He illustrates his point by giving "a detail of the most remarkable instances in which the hostility to the gracious design of man's redemption has been manifested." He shows this historically, referring to Jewish history before Christ; to pagan theology before Christ; to the opposition of the Jews to the first propagation of the gospel; to that of the heathens, first up to the reign of Constantine, and thence to the end of the sixth century; to the rise and progress of Mahometanism; to infidelity during the Middle Ages and at the Protestant Reformation; to the origin and progress of deism, to the French philosophy at the time of the Revolution; and finally to the infidelity of his own time. This, which it will be seen covers a wide ground, fills the first volume. The second is occupied with a defence of revealed religion, of the usual type.

The full title of Dr. Sumner's work is, "*The Evidence of Christianity derived from its Nature and Reception.*" The writer argues that a religion like Christianity could never have existed unless it had been introduced by Divine authority. "It could not have been invented; it would not have been received." He dwells on the originality of the doctrines introduced by its Author; their originality both in His own nation and in the world, while at the same time "they received confirmation from many singular facts, singular enactments, and minute prophecies contained in the Jewish Scriptures;" he points out the "internal evidence of the Christian writings to be drawn from their language, their anticipation of conduct subsequently developed, and their general wisdom;" he calls attention to "the peculiar character formed under the influence of Christianity, its excellence in individuals, its beneficial effects upon mankind, its suitableness to their condition as dependent and corrupt beings;" he points out the rapidity of the spread of Christianity, and other phenomena, which (he argues) nothing except the truth of the religion can adequately explain. The whole work is written in a very lucid, scholarly style, and deserves to rank high among the evidential works of the period.

It may seem strange to place under the category of evidential literature a book popularly known as "Bishop Middleton on the Greek Article." It would appear to belong rather to that class of purely scholastic works which appeared from the pens of dignitaries in the age of "the Greek-play bishops." But, as the full title of the book is, "*The Doctrine of the Greek Article applied to the Criticism and Illustration of the New Testament*" (1808), the reader will readily perceive that such a work might touch some vital points of Christianity. And so, indeed, it did; and most opportunely. Mr. Gilbert Wakefield had published some years before a new translation of the New Testament, in which, whenever the definite article was not prefixed to such terms as υἱὸς Θεοῦ and Πνεῦμα Ἅγιον, he translated them, "*a* son of God," "*a* holy spirit;" implying, according to his avowed principles, that the blessed Saviour was only one out of many sons of God, and the Holy Spirit only one out of many holy spirits. On the other hand, Mr. Granville Sharp had propounded, and on the whole made good, a most valuable principle, which, stated shortly, was that when two substantives were coupled together, and the definite article preceded only the first, those two substantives always referred to one and the same subject. Thus ὁ Θεὸς καὶ Σωτήρ must mean, "He who is our God and Saviour;" τοῦ Χριστοῦ καὶ Θεοῦ, "of Him who is Christ and God," ὤν and ὄντος being in each case understood. Gilbert Wakefield and Granville Sharp were both good general scholars, but they were not specialists. Middleton was far superior in scholarship to both; and he came in as a crushing adversary of the former, and a valuable but discriminating supporter of the latter, who also received most important aid from Christopher Wordsworth, afterwards Master of Trinity. A passage from Bishop Middleton's preface (p. xli.) will illustrate the latter point, and also explain the object and gist of his work. " The subject has of late acquired additional interest from the controversy occasioned by a work of Mr. Granville Sharp. . . . The interpretation maintained by Mr. Sharp became the more probable from being sanctioned by the excellent editor of *Dawes's Miscellanea Critica*, the present *Bishop of St. David's*. The same interpretation was also powerfully confirmed by the elaborate researches of Mr. *Wordsworth*, who has proved that most of the disputed texts were so understood by the Fathers. If anything remained to be done, it was to show that the same form of expression in the classical writers required a similar explanation, and also to investigate the principle of the canon, and to ascertain its limitations : this I have attempted in some of the following pages." Middleton divides his work into two parts. Part I. proves by innumerable instances the various principles on which the article was used by classical authors, and vindicates successfully the application of rules founded on classical usage to the diction of the sacred writers. Part II. consists of " Notes on the New Testament," in which the writer applies his principles in detail to every book, from the beginning of St. Matthew to the end of the Revelation of St. John the Divine. Incidentally, this second part is a valuable commentary on the New Testament, and, in this light, comes also under the head of biblical literature, to be noticed presently; but its main object was evidential, and, therefore, it is more fitly treated under the present heading. The work was stamped with the approval of another excellent Greek scholar, Hugh James Rose, who put out a new edition of it in 1833,[1]

---

[1] Dean Burgon says, "It belongs (according to Miller) to the year 1831" (*Lives of Twelve Good Men*, i. 145); but I can find no traces, either in the 1833 edition or elsewhere, of any earlier edition put forth by Hugh James Rose. Nor did the dean himself, for he adds, "The only editions with which I am acquainted bear the dates of 1833 and 1841."

nine years after the bishop's death, with some valuable "Preliminary Observations" of his own.

Are we to include *Hannah More* among the evidence writers of the period? If the object of evidential works is to convince people of the truth of Christianity, there is a general consensus of testimony that Hannah More *did* effect that object in a very remarkable degree. Many of the writings against Christianity, which were, directly or indirectly, the product of the French Revolution, were addressed, not *ad clerum*, but *ad populum*. This was notably the case with the writings of Thomas Paine, who, as Bishop Porteus said with characteristic quaintness, "rendered irreligion easy to the meanest capacity." To such works answers which flew above the heads of the people would be no answers at all; and it is the peculiar merit of Mrs. H. More that she succeeded in catching the ear of the people, while she more than satisfied the requirements of the learned. Such titles as "Village Politics by Will Chip," "Cheap Repository Tracts," "The Shepherd of Salisbury Plain," and so forth, do not carry with them the idea of great evidential works; but in such a case we must judge by results, and there is no doubt that they produced an amount of conviction which the most learned and elaborate treatises would have failed to do. And the appreciation of them by men of culture is very striking. Bishop Porteus, for instance, is not a man whose opinion is to be lightly passed over; and his estimate of Mrs. More's writings is extraordinarily high. "I look upon Mr. Chip," he said, "to be one of the finest writers of the age."[1] When she published anonymously "An Estimate of the Religion of the Fashionable World," in answer to a pamphlet by the Duke of Grafton, the bishop's remark about the unknown author was, "Aut Morus aut Angelus." When he read her ballad, "Turn the Carpet," "Here," he said, "you have Bishop Butler's 'Analogy' all for a halfpenny!" And he not only gave praise, but substantial coin, to promote the admired writer's circulation.[2] Legh Richmond, who was no ignoramus, wrote to his sister on her marriage, "Let me beg of you to buy the

---

[1] Hodgson's *Life of Bishop Beilby Porteus*, p. 126.

[2] See *Hannah More*, by C. M. Yonge, in the Eminent Women Series, edited by J. H. Ingram, pp. 88, 89, 109, 111, 115, etc.

new edition of Hannah More's Works [1802], and invariably read them once a year."[1] An anonymous writer in 1815, quoted by Mr. Colquhoun, attributes the great religious improvement he had witnessed in twenty years to two causes— Mr. Raikes' Sunday schools, and the writings of Hannah More.[2] Sydney Smith, in his sarcastic apology for venturing to treat her as an uninspired being, implies that in some quarters she was regarded as a writer almost above criticism.[3] And finally, Bishop Jebb, who would certainly not agree with Mrs. More on every point, writes to Miss Jebb in 1805, "Get by all means 'Hints for a Young Princess.' It is by far the best book which has, for a considerable time, issued from the press. The Bishop of Exeter (preceptor to the Princess Charlotte, for whose use it has been written) declares that he has derived more information from it, on the important subject next to his thoughts, than from all his reading; and he is both a learned and a good man."[4] But though Mrs. More may, in one sense, justly claim a place in the very first rank of evidential writers, she belongs more properly to our next head.

PRACTICAL AND DEVOTIONAL WORKS.

Among these there can be no doubt about placing the works of *Hannah More*. And those of them which belong to the nineteenth century are, in point of style, a great improvement upon those which belong to the eighteenth. When she began to write for the multitude, she had sense enough to see that she must write simply. Hence with "Village Politics" she ceases to write Johnsonese and begins to write English. The sale of her works was enormous. Two millions of the "Cheap Repository Tracts" were sold in a year. The first edition of " Cœlebs in Search of a Wife," published in 1805, was sold off in a day, and thirty more editions before the close of the author's life, twenty-four years later.[5]

[1] Grimshaw's *Life of Legh Richmond*, p. 56.
[2] See *William Wilberforce, his Friends and his Times*, by J. C. Colquhoun: "Hannah More."
[3] See *Edinburgh Review*.
[4] *Life of Bishop Jebb*, vol. ii. (Correspondence), p. 55.
[5] See *Hannah More*, by C. M. Yonge, pp. 121 and 154.

Her "Practical Piety" (1811) and her "Christian Morals" (1813), if not so extraordinarily successful, were yet very popular. It would be wearisome to the reader to give even the titles of all her works; suffice it to say that they may all be found in a new edition, published in eleven volumes, in 1830. Perhaps the boldest experiment she made was to publish, not only a novel—if novel it can be called—but even a volume of "Sacred Dramas." When we remember in what abhorrence both the novel and the drama were held by the school to which Hannah More was supposed to belong, we may realize how great the weight of her name must have been to have allowed even the faintest approach to such objectionable ground. At the same time, one can well understand how delightful a thing it must have been to "the religious world," to whom all light literature was strictly tabooed, to find a writer with whom it was not only an allowable, but even a creditable, thing to be entertained. The greatest credit is due to Hannah More, as the first among the Evangelicals who dared to enlist the novel and the drama on the side of virtue and religion; and she reaped the due reward of her hardihood in the almost unparalleled popularity she achieved, and, what would be much more highly valued by so good a woman, in the widespread influence for good which her writings exercised.

As a popular tract-writer, *Legh Richmond* will bear comparison even with Hannah More. The "Annals of the Poor" generally were as successful as the "Cheap Repository Tracts," and "The Dairyman's Daughter" and "Jam, the Young Cottager," in particular, as "The Shepherd of Salisbury Plain." Four million copies of "The Dairyman's Daughter" are said to have been circulated in the nineteen languages into which it was translated.[1] Legh Richmond is a very pleasing writer; his style is plain and pure, and he commends himself to the reader by his appreciative way of describing natural scenery—a somewhat rare gift in his day—which he may have partly acquired through his residence in the beautiful Isle of Wight. When he undertook a more ambitious work than the "Annals of the Poor," consisting of voluminous extracts from the Reformers, whom he terms the *Fathers of*

[1] See *Life of Legh Richmond*, p. 319.

the Church, he was not so successful; and we may really be thankful that he was not, for the title, and of course also the work itself, encouraged the popular but utterly untenable theory that the Church of England only dated from the sixteenth century—a theory from which we are now happily, but very slowly, becoming emancipated.

Edward Bickersteth was a more strictly devotional writer than either of the two last noticed. Some of his works, especially those of a controversial nature, belong to a later period, after he had settled down at Watton, and after the rise of the Oxford Movement had stirred him to take up his parable in defence of the Evangelical school. But several of his devotional works, such as "A Treatise on Prayer" (1818), "Scripture Help" (1819), and others,[1] come within our limits. They found so ready a demand that the sale of them materially assisted him to educate his young family; and their great popularity, like that of Hannah More's and Legh Richmond's works, is partly an illustration of the dominancy of the Evangelical school, and partly helped to keep up that dominancy. Henry Blunt, Josiah Pratt, William Jowett, Basil Woodd,[2] in fact, almost all the leaders of the Evangelical party, were writers of devotional works, which have shared the inevitable fate of the vast majority of such works, and, having served their purpose in their day, passed into oblivion.

But the instability of fame is most markedly illustrated by the fate of the works of *Thomas Gisborne*, which at one time seemed destined for immortality. They mostly consist of sermons, though they were largely used as devotional works. Their general object is to promote morality from the Evangelical point of view. "Of late years," says the writer in the preface to his first volume (1802), "it has been loudly asserted that, among clergymen who have showed themselves very earnest in doctrinal points, adequate regard has not been evinced to moral instruction." Mr. Gisborne thinks that, though the defect had been greatly exaggerated, there was

---

[1] e.g. *A Treatise on the Lord's Supper; Christian Truth, a Family Guide to the Chief Truths of the Gospel.*

[2] Basil Woodd's *Brief Explanation of the Church Catechism* passed through forty-six editions; and his *Tractate on Confirmation*, thirty-six—apparently in the writer's lifetime. See Wilks' *Memoir, sub finem.*

some real ground for the charge. Hence the tendency of his own writings, which have already been touched on in the chapter on the Evangelicals; it is only necessary to add here that they have suffered from the inevitable reaction against the absurdly overrated value which was once attached to them.

Something of the same kind may be said of another very popular devotional writer in his day, *Ambrose Serle*, (1742–1812), a pious layman, whose "Horæ Solitariæ" (2 vols.) were once quite a classic in Evangelical circles. His other books, viz. "The Church of God," "The Christian Remembrancer," "Christian Husbandry," "The Christian Parent," "Charis, or Reflections on the Office of the Holy Spirit," and "Secret Thoughts," written in the last year of his life, were not quite so well known, but were still much admired. As an instance of the esteem in which the writer was held, it may be mentioned that when the living of Turvey became vacant by the death of Erasmus Middleton in 1805, the patroness, "Mrs. Fuller, an eminently pious lady," wrote to Mr. Serle, saying that she was much indebted to his writings, and would present to Turvey any clergyman of similar sentiments with himself whom he could recommend. Mr. Serle was a constant worshipper at the Lock Chapel, where Mr. Legh Richmond was then officiating as an assistant to the chaplain, Mr. Fry, and he immediately fixed on Mr. Richmond as the proper man. Ambrose Serle's works seemed to have died a natural death, until they were galvanized into a sort of fresh life by the publication of "Selections" from them in 1833 by Edward Bickersteth, whose name was sufficient to call attention for a time to their merits.

From devotional works generally we pass by an easy transition to a particular class, the highest of all, in which the devotional element was blended with the didactic. It is the class which may be grouped under the head of

BIBLICAL LITERATURE.

In regard to this most important department of theology, the century opened in the midst of a storm. Herbert Marsh was one of the very few Englishmen of the day who had any acquaintance with the great writers and thinkers of

Germany. He had studied at Leipsic under J. D. Michaelis, and corresponded with Griesbach on the text of the New Testament; and in 1793 he startled English theologians by publishing the first volume of a translation of Michaelis' "Introduction to the New Testament," with notes and dissertations of his own. Three more volumes followed in succession, the last in 1801. This appears as a separate work, under the title of "*The Origin and Composition of the Three First Canonical Gospels.*" Marsh was at once attacked, among others by *Dr. Randolph*, Bishop of Oxford, who in 1802 published anonymously "*Remarks on Michaelis and his Commentator,*" in which he stigmatized Marsh's work as "derogating from the character of the Sacred Books, and injurious to Christianity, as fostering a spirit of scepticism." Marsh, who enjoyed controversy, and was an adept in it, was not slow to reply; and a lively war of pamphlets ensued. The reader will find the whole matter in one volume of Dr. Marsh's works, in which five tracts are bound up, the titles of which tell their own tales.[1] It seemed as if Marsh was about to anticipate the impetus given to the study of German theology a few years later by Julius Hare and Connop Thirlwall; but this was not the case. I am inclined to think that the tendency of Marsh's work was misunderstood, and that it was in reality a valuable contribution to biblical criticism; as also were his lectures delivered as Lady Margaret Professor of Divinity, to which office he was appointed in 1807. The titles of these sufficiently indicate their contents.[2]

Considering the supreme importance which the Evangelicals, then by far the most active party in the Church, attached to Holy Scripture, it might have been expected that our period would have been peculiarly rich in works of

[1] *Letters to Author of "Remarks on Michaelis and his Commentator,"* 1802; Randolph's *"Remarks on Michaelis' Introduction to the New Testament,"* 1802; *Illustration of the Hypothesis proposed in the Dissertation on the Origin, etc., of our Three First Gospels,* 1803; *Randolph's Supplement to "Remarks on Michaelis' Introduction,"* 1804; *Defence of the "Illustration, etc.,"* 1804.

[2] *The History of Sacred Criticism,* 1809; *The Criticism of the Greek Testament,* 1810; *The Interpretation of the Bible,* 1813; *The Interpretation of Prophecy,* 1816 (all published in 1 vol. in 1828); *The Authenticity of the New Testament,* 1820; *The Credibility of the New Testament,* 1822; *The Authority of the Old Testament,* 1823.

biblical exegesis; but this assuredly was not the case. The most important work on the subject, and that not a very important one, emanated, not from the Evangelical, but from the Orthodox school. This was "*D'Oyly and Mant's Family Bible*," published by the Society for Promoting Christian Knowledge in 1817. Archdeacon Churton tells us that as early as 1811 some such work was projected by Joshua Watson, Christopher Wordsworth, William Van Mildert, and Richard Mant, and that it was afterwards committed by the Archbishop of Canterbury, Dr. Manners-Sutton, to his two chaplains, Dr. D'Oyly and Mr. Mant.[1] A fuller, and rather different, but not inconsistent, account is given by the biographer of Bishop Mant. "At a meeting," he writes, "of the S.P.C.K. in 1813, March 16, a report was presented by Van Mildert relative to the society's adoption of a Bible with notes and commentaries, collected from the writings of divines of the Church of England. The report arose out of a communication from the Coventry District Committee, that many persons were found taking in Bibles published in numbers, with notes and explanations by Dissenting teachers; some from want of an authorized edition of the Bible in a similar form, others thinking the notes were by Churchmen. So they suggested that the society should afford their patronage to some convenient-sized edition, in numbers, and at a moderate expense, with familiar notes, etc., by divines of the Church of England, to meet the increased demands among the middle classes for publications of that description."[2]

A *Family Bible* was recommended. Then at a committee meeting Mr. Norris communicated a letter from Mr. Mant, expressing his readiness to undertake the selection of notes and commentaries. A committee was formed for the revision of the notes, consisting of Archdeacons Pott, Cambridge, Middleton, and Van Mildert, and H. H. Norris; and a request was made to the Bishops of London (Dr. Randolph) and Lincoln (Dr. Tomline) "to permit the revised portions of the projected edition of the Bible to be submitted to their inspection before publication." It is a question whether

---

[1] *Memoir of Joshua Watson*, i. 126-129.
[2] See *Life of Bishop Richard Mant*, by Archdeacon Walter Mant, p. 100, etc.

there were not too many hands at work. There does not appear to have been any subdivision of labour—one divine undertaking one book, and another, another. All seem to have given their opinions on the work generally, and the result was certainly a disappointment. From the first there were few who were really satisfied with "D'Oyly and Mant." At the same time, it seems to me a distinct improvement upon previous commentaries. Neither Thomas Scott's nor Matthew Henry's, the most popular commentaries then in use, can be regarded as an adequate guide to Churchmen. Of course, also, it must be remembered that the "Family Bible" was meant to be an essentially popular work; no attempt whatever was made at originality, and it was intended at least as much for edification as instruction.

In respect to instruction, it is certainly inferior to another contribution to biblical literature made during our period— Thomas Hartwell Horne's "*Introduction to the Critical Study of Holy Scripture.*" It was published in 1818, when the writer was yet a layman; but in consequence of its publication he was ordained by Bishop Howley, who wrote to him thus about his book: "It contains, I believe, more than any other work in our language on the subject, with much information drawn from sources not accessible to ordinary scholars."[1] This is high praise from one who always measured his words, and who was, though he wrote little himself, a remarkably competent judge of literary work, particularly in the domain of theology. And it was not undeserved. Horne's "Introduction" still holds a high place among works of its kind; but it is very lengthy, filling four stout octavo volumes, and rather heavy reading. It is certainly creditable to the public that it should have rapidly passed through several editions, for it owes its success to sound, sterling merit, not to any attractiveness of style.

Far otherwise is it with another work which deserves special notice under our present head, viz. Dr. Van Mildert's Bampton Lectures for 1814, "*An Inquiry into the General Principles of Scriptural Interpretation.*" Since the death of Bishop Horsley there had been no divine of the calibre of Van Mildert, and it may be doubted whether there was his

[1] See *Reminiscences of T. Hartwell Horne*, p. 31.

equal during the whole of our period. Unlike some of the Bamptons, Dr. Van Mildert's lectures are eminently readable by others than specialists. Written in a clear, pure, and scholarly style, they lay down principles of scriptural interpretation of a markedly Church character; and they would well repay perusal even at the present day, when a flood of light is supposed to have been shed upon the subject.

The sister University of Cambridge also produced a contribution to biblical literature which was as valuable in its way, and far more popular than Van Mildert's Bampton Lectures. In 1828 appeared the first of a series of volumes by J. J. Blunt, in which he extended the argument from undesigned coincidences applied by Paley to the Epistles of St. Paul, to establish the veracity of all the historical books of the Bible. It was entitled "The Veracity of the Gospels and Acts of the Apostles argued from the Undesigned Coincidences to be found in them when compared (1) with each other, and (2) with Josephus." It was the substance of a course of sermons preached at Cambridge in 1827. In 1830 came another volume, also the substance of University sermons, entitled "The Veracity of the Five Books of Moses argued from the Undesigned Coincidences to be found in them when compared in their Several Parts;" then, in 1832, the Hulsean Lectures for the year 1831, "The Veracity of the Historical Books of the Old Testament, from the Conclusion of the Pentateuch to the Opening of the Prophets, argued from the Undesigned Coincidences to be found in them when compared in their Several Parts," etc.; and finally, in 1833, the Hulsean Lectures for the year 1832, "Principles for the Proper Understanding of the Mosaic Writings stated and applied, together with an Incidental Argument for the Truth of the Resurrection of our Lord." It was not till 1847 that the substance of all the volumes appeared in one, as the "Undesigned Coincidences" we all know so well.[1]

If profundity of subject were a test of merit, something would have to be said about the profound studies, or rather conjectures, into which some of the weaker vessels among the Evangelicals plunged in connection with unfulfilled pro-

---

[1] See Memoir of J. J. Blunt prefixed to *Two Introductory Lectures on the Study of the Early Fathers*, and the article on J. J. Blunt in the *Dictionary of National Biography*.

phecy, especially in its relation to the restoration of the Jews to their own land, the millennium, and Christ's personal reign which was to precede it. (It may be noted, by the way, that, metaphorically speaking, the weaker the vessel, the deeper and vaster the sea in which it loves to embark.) The Evangelical *leaders* were far too sensible men to encourage such crude speculations, against which we find Edward Bickersteth,[1] Thomas Scott,[2] and, above all, Charles Simeon,[3] lifting up their voices. It was rather in the pulpit than in the press that these interpreters of prophecy in the first instance aired their views; but they were often persuaded by admiring and injudicious hearers to give the world at large the benefit of their speculations in print. It is almost needless to say that this class of literature was absolutely worthless; but it seems to have given occasion for the publication of one of the most valuable works on the subject of prophecy in the English language.

John Davison (1777-1834) was a great name at Oriel in Oriel's palmiest days. He had been the highly respected tutor of some of her most brilliant sons; but he did nothing with his pen to justify his high reputation, until his appointment as Warburtonian lecturer, when his twelve sermons,

[1] He writes in 1829, "I find the prophetical spirit doing injury to some. Men get full of their own views, and press them as all-essential, and speak as positively as if futurity were as open to them as the past" (see *Life*, i. 437); and in 1831, "Things are most dead and cold here [the Midland Counties]; the good men are all afloat on prophesying, and the immediate work of the Lord is disregarded for the uncertain future."—*Id.*, ii. 45.

[2] "So you are become a dabbler in prophecy, as almost every one is in these days."—Letter to Rev. J. Mayor in 1821. See *Life*, p. 511.

[3] "You speak of your having now got views of prophecy relating to the Second Advent; and you tell us that you are unfolding them to your hearers. But I wish you to remember what was the exclusive subject of St. Paul's ministry—not Jesus Christ *reigning* upon earth, but Jesus Christ and Him *crucified*, etc., etc."—Letter to a clergyman in 1829. See Carus, p. 440.

To a friend who asked him to attack the work of a clergyman who denied the restoration of the Jews to their own land, hoping that he would "answer him and knock him down,"—" I have neither taste nor talent for controversy; nor do I on the whole envy those by whom such tastes are possessed. . . This is a day of trifling; all these things are *about* religion, but they are very little to do with religion itself."—Carus, p. 445.

1830.—On the study of prophecy. To Miss E. E.: "Men are led aside from Christ crucified to Christ glorified personally upon earth; from a doctrine which is both the power of God and the wisdom of God to a doctrine which is neither the one nor the other"—with much more to the same effect.—Carus, p. 460.

preached in the chapel of Lincoln's Inn, formed the substance of the well-known "*Discourses on Prophecy*," in which are considered its structure, use, and inspiration. The writer possessed all those qualities in which the many dabblers in prophecy who favoured the public with their views were conspicuously deficient—modesty, scholarship, general culture, and intercourse with the most highly trained intellects of the time. "*Davison on Prophecy*" is worth all the sermons on the subject, which were so plentiful during our period, put together. In fact, we must cross the Irish Channel to find any treatise on prophecy that can for a moment be compared with it. In 1808 *Dr. William Hales* published the "*Dissertations on Prophecy, expressing the Divine and Human Character of our Lord Jesus Christ.*" As the titles indicate, the two works do not interfere with one another, and Dr. Hales' learned work still retains a special value of its own. The subject of his next work, however, he made more exclusively his own. In 1809 appeared the first volume of his "*Analysis of Chronology*," and in 1811 and 1813 the second and third volumes respectively. The Irish divine's writings made him many friends on this side the Channel, including Bishops Burgess and Middleton, Mr. Perceval, Lord Ellenborough, Archdeacons Daubeny and Churton, Dr. Kennicott, and Mr. Hartwell Horne—all men whose praise was worth having.

Judging merely by the title, it would seem strangely out of place to group such a work as *Milman's* "*History of the Jews*" under the head of biblical literature. But, after much doubt and deliberation, it appears to me on the whole most correct to describe it in this connection; for it was, to all intents and purposes, a new reading of, or comment upon, the Old Testament. Henry Hart Milman had long been known as a scholar and a poet before he startled the English world by his new work. In point of composition and research, the "History of the Jews," which appeared in 1828, was quite worthy of the high reputation already achieved by its author; but we can hardly be surprised that it created alarm. There was an evident tendency to reduce everything in the history of the chosen people that could be so reduced to the level of reason, and to explain away, when it was at all possible to do so, the supernatural element in it. Men were shocked to find Abraham treated as an ordinary Arab sheik, and the appearance of the manna and the quails attributed to natural causes. The book came out as one of a series called "The Family Library," and caused such dismay that the series was stopped. The learned writer was probably a little misunderstood. In the interests of truth and reality, it was desirable for some one to bring out the human side of the history of the most remarkable people the world has ever seen; and Dr. Milman's later career, which was even more brilliant from a literary point of view than his earlier, seems to indicate that he had really no desire to depreciate the Bible. He lived quite long enough to regain his character for orthodoxy, and perhaps also to show men that his "History of the Jews" was not quite what people thought it. But taking the work simply by itself, there is certainly some reason for regarding it as a precursor of a class of works with which in our day we are very familiar, but which were then unknown—that is, works in derogation of revelation from the Christian side.

A new field of biblical criticism was opened to the English in 1825 by the publication of a translation of Schleiermacher's "Essay on St. Luke," with a remarkable introduction, by *Connop Thirlwall*, largely aided by his friend, *Julius Hare*.[1] With the exception of S. T. Coleridge (whose reading, though extensive, was very desultory), Thirlwall and Hare were at that time probably the only Englishmen who had made a real study of the literature of Germany.[2] Judging by after results, it may be thought a questionable benefit to have introduced into England German speculation, and especially the speculations of Schleiermacher. For Schleiermacher was the spiritual and intellectual father of Strauss, and the orthodox Christian may well hold that English Christianity was not furthered by Strauss's "Leben Jesu" and other works, nor, indeed, by the writings of Schleiermacher himself. At the same time, they were eminently thoughtful and suggestive.

[1] "Of the Schleiermacher," writes Thirlwall to Hare in 1824, "nobody has so good a right to dispose as yourself, to whom I am indebted for the knowledge of the book itself, and for almost all the materials of my Introduction."—*Letters Literary and Theological of Connop Thirlwall*, edited by Perowne and Stokes, pp. 74, 75.

[2] It was in the same year, 1825, that Dr. Pusey was persuaded by Dr. Lloyd to go to Gottingen "to study at once the German and the theology."—*Life*, i. 72.

What may be called "the ostrich policy" is never a wholesome one ; and if such speculations as those of the German professors were going on, it was as well that they should be known and answered. The particular work in question did not give rise to nearly so much controversy as another German work, introduced by the same two friends, Thirlwall and Hare, two years later. This was their translation of Niebuhr's "History of Rome," the first instalment of which appeared in 1827. It was severely handled in the *Quarterly Review*, on the ground that the application of the principles of Niebuhr to biblical criticism would undermine men's belief in the literal truth of the early Bible history. Hare defended what he had done in a pamphlet entitled "A Vindication of Niebuhr" (1829); and Thirlwall annexed a postscript, signed "C. T.," in which he declares that "there was nothing inconsistent with their profession in giving publicity to an historical work containing two or three speculations not sanctioned by the most approved commentators on the first ten chapters of Genesis."[1] The two friends were not deterred by hostile criticism from continuing their labours, and the whole translation was accomplished in 1832.

Liturgical Literature.

Next to his Bible, the Churchman values his Prayer-book ; but the tone of thought during the early part of the nineteenth century was not of a nature likely to produce much on this important subject. By far the most valuable work in this department was done by *William* (afterwards Sir William) *Palmer*, in his "*Origines Liturgicæ*." The history of this great work, as given partly by the writer himself, is interesting. The idea was suggested to him by the course of study prescribed when he was a candidate for Holy Orders under Bishop Jebb at Limerick. Mr. Palmer came from Trinity College, Dublin, to Worcester College, Oxford, because he thought Oxford was a suitable place in which to pursue his favourite studies; but he there found that the Bishop of Oxford, who was also Regius Professor of Divinity (Dr. Lloyd), was engaged in a similar work ; so he abandoned

[1] See *Letters, etc., of Thirlwall, ut supra*, p. 90.

his design. But, on the premature death of Bishop Lloyd in 1829, he was requested by Dr. Burton, the bishop's successor in the divinity chair, to resume his work, and to incorporate with it the results of Bishop Lloyd's labours. Mr. Palmer accordingly did so, and in 1832 his book was published by the University Press. It was warmly praised by the learned Dr. Routh, who could speak with authority on such a subject. It certainly marked an era in the Church, being one of the chief factors in the preparation for the Oxford Movement. Being, as the title implies, an inquiry into the sources from which the Prayer-book is derived, it gave Churchmen quite a different idea of the book from that which had been ordinarily taken; and it also led them to make further inquiries for themselves, "of which the Church is reaping the beneficial results at the present hour."[1]

The only other liturgical work which seems to require any special notice is Dr. Mant's "*Prayer-Book*," which began to come out in numbers in 1819, and which, when completed, filled two thick octavo volumes. It may be regarded as a sort of companion to the "Family Bible." Like that work, it aimed at combining edification with instruction; and, like that work, it did not profess to be original. Much of its information is taken *verbatim* from Wheatley, Comber, and others; while the notes on the Psalms seem to be transferred bodily from the pages of Bishop Horne.

THE CALVINISTIC CONTROVERSY.

This controversy, an unhappy legacy from the eighteenth century, produced a certain amount of *soi-disant* theological literature, but the greater part of it has no permanent interest. Oddly enough, it is almost all on one side; for, very unlike their predecessors in the seventeenth and eighteenth centuries, the so-called Calvinists expressly deprecate any controversy on the subject, and explain away that part of their teaching which raised the most opposition. According to their enemies, the Calvinists were rampant everywhere. "Here in England," writes Southey in 1806, "Calvinism is the popular faith."[2]

[1] Burgon's *Lives of Twelve Good Men* : "Hugh James Rose," i. 160.
[2] *Life and Correspondence of Robert Southey*, iii. 18.

The *British Critic*, in reviewing the work of a Calvinist, remarks, "That his doctrine is indeed popular, we have long known and deeply regretted."[1] "Is it not wonderful," asks Alexander Knox in 1806, "that the strongest Calvinists now in England should be the serious clergy?"[2] And the same assumption runs through all the anti-Calvinistic writings. But when we turn to the writings of the leading Evangelicals (who were all called Calvinists), we find a very different story. "Let me speak the truth before God," writes Simeon. "Though I am no Arminian, I do think that the refinements of Calvin have done great harm in the Church; they have driven multitudes from the plain and popular way of speaking used by the inspired writers, and have made them unreasonably and unscripturally squeamish in their expressions."[3] And in a singularly beautiful passage in the preface to his "Horæ Homileticæ," "he [the author] bitterly regrets that men will range themselves under human banners and leaders, and employ themselves in converting the inspired writers into friends and partisans of their peculiar principles. . . . One thing he knows, viz. that pious men both of the Calvinistic and Arminian persuasion approximate very nearly when they are upon their knees before God in prayer; the devout Arminian then acknowledging his total dependence upon God as strongly as the most confirmed Calvinist, and the Calvinist acknowledging his responsibility to God, and his obligation to exertion, in terms as decisive as the most determined Arminian. And that which both these individuals are upon their knees, it is the wish of the author to become in his writings."[4] Edward Bickersteth, an Evangelical of Evangelicals, writes in 1825 respecting a pamphlet which had appeared against him: "I have been charged with being an enemy to the free, sovereign, and everlasting grace of God, and that the principle I maintain is man co-operating as in joint free partnership with God, to do good."[5] A similar charge was made against Hannah More's "Practical Piety"

---

[1] Review of "Plain Truths; or, The Presbyter's Reply to all his Anti-Calvinistic Opponents," in the *British Critic*, vol. xxvii., July to December, 1805.
[2] *Remains of Alexander Knox*, iii. 182.
[3] Carus, p. 218. [4] *Id.*, p. 369. [5] *Life*, i. 405.

(1811).[1] William Wilberforce, the lay leader of the Evangelicals, declares over and over again in his letters that he is no Calvinist;[2] and Bishop Porteus, the first prelate who favoured the Evangelicals, "would never admit the Calvinistic interpretation of the Articles to be the true one."[8]

It would really seem from all this that the writers against Calvinism were fighting with an imaginary foe. But the great names of those who were leaders of the fray forbid such a supposition. Bishop Herbert Marsh, of Peterborough, for instance, was one of the ablest prelates of his day, and not at all the sort of man to fight with shadows. Yet he was so alarmed at the progress of Calvinism, that in 1822 he framed eighty-seven questions for his ordination candidates, on purpose to exclude those who held Calvinistic views. It is fair to add that when the matter came before the House of Lords, the bishop declared that this was not his object; but the official correspondence between the bishop and the rector of Blatherwycke, and the Rev. J. Green, who desired to be ordained to the curacy, leaves us in little doubt that if this was not the object, it was the practical result. Bishop Tomline, who was a very clear-headed man, with a large experience of the clergy, distinctly implies in his "Refutation of Calvinism" that its tenets were very generally held; and the same conviction runs through all the writings of Alexander Knox, Bishop Mant, Archdeacon Daubeny, and others whose competency to judge it is impossible to deny.

The explanation of the apparent discrepancy is indicated in the charges against Bickersteth and Hannah More which have been quoted above. While the *leaders* of the Evangelicals either held Calvinistic views in a very modified form, or so guarded them that they were not liable to abuse, the rank and file of the party expressed them in a much more unguarded and extravagant fashion.

But one at least, who from his abilities and character deserved to be a leader, had no scruple about avowing his Calvinistic opinions in the most outspoken fashion, and, more

[1] See *Hannah More*, by C. M. Yonge, p. 159.
[2] See, *inter alia*, *Life of Bishop S. Wilberforce*, vol. i., note by Canon Ashwell, p. 38; also *Life of William Wilberforce*, p. 210 and *passim*.
[3] See Hodgson's *Life*.

than that, declared point-blank that those were no true Churchmen who did not do so. This was *John Overton*, Vicar of St. Crux and St. Margaret's, York, who in 1801 published a work entitled "*The True Churchman ascertained; or, An Apology for those of the Regular Clergy of the Establishment, who are sometimes called Evangelical Ministers: occasioned by the publications of Drs. Paley, Hey, Croft; Messrs. Daubeny, Ludlam, Polwhele, Fellowes, the Reviewers, etc.*" The alternative title shows that the writer was prepared to meet opponents from all quarters; and he was not disappointed. His book, which is, beyond all question, a most able, honest, and manly work, but exceedingly combative, created a great sensation and called forth many answers. He boldly carried the war into the enemy's country, and instead of assuming an apologetic tone, and deprecating opposition to his views, he claimed for those views the credit of alone properly representing the Church of England. "We, then," he concludes, "are the *true Churchmen*, and, in a very fundamental and important sense, Mr. Daubeny and his associates are *Dissenters*."[1]

Mr. Daubeny was not at all the kind of man to sit still under such a challenge, and there very quickly appeared his "*Vindiciæ Ecclesiæ Anglicanæ*" (1803), a direct reply to Mr. Overton. It was a sort of sequel to his more famous "Guide to the Church," published in 1798, the appendix to which was directed against another Calvinist, Sir Richard Hill, brother of the preacher, Rowland Hill. Mr. Overton, however, though less known,[2] was a far more able writer than Sir R. Hill; and he and Mr. Daubeny were well matched. The latter dwells especially on Mr. Overton's argument that Calvinism was not only a permissible but a necessary doctrine for all true Churchmen; and affirms with perfect truth that "neither Calvinism nor anti-Calvinism, abstractedly considered, constitutes the precise standard by which true Christian characters ought definitively to be ascertained; because most conscientious and exemplary Christians have

---

[1] *True Churchman ascertained*, p. 397.
[2] That is, less known *now*. From a number of private letters now before the writer, it is evident that Mr. Overton's book was widely known and highly appreciated when it first came out.

been, and doubtless still are to be, found under each description. It is only when Calvinism, as seems to be attempted in the present day, is made the criterion by which sound divinity is to be ascertained, that we complain. This is, as it were, to throw down the gauntlet of public challenge; and there never will be wanting, among the faithful sons of our Church, those who will feel themselves called upon to take it up. But all controversies on this subject are to be deprecated; as they tend, generally speaking, more to diminish charity than to increase knowledge." The sentiment of the last sentence is most laudable; but unfortunately, from the early days of Whitefield and Wesley, sixty years before, good men on both sides were constantly expressing such sentiments, and then plunging into the hopeless and interminable controversy with renewed vigour.

Mr. Daubeny found a very powerful champion in Dr. Tomline, Bishop of Lincoln (soon afterwards of Winchester), whose "*Refutation of Calvinism*" was partly intended, it would appear, as a contribution to the Daubeny and Overton controversy.[1] What is now the first chapter, "On Universal Redemption," was originally the Charge delivered by the bishop to the clergy of his diocese in 1803. He went on with the subject in his Triennial Charges in 1806 and 1809, but deferred publishing them until the whole was completed, that is, until 1811. Tomline's " Refutation of Calvinism " was unquestionably an able work, and it was also a popular one, as is shown by the fact that it had reached an eighth edition by 1823. It paints the effects of Calvinistic teaching in the very darkest colours. For example : " Men who fancy they have received this second birth consider themselves full of Divine grace, are too often regardless of the laws both of God and man, affect to govern themselves by some secret rules in their own breasts, urge the suggestions of the Spirit upon the most trifling occasions, and pretend the most positive assurance of their salvation, while perhaps they are guilty of the grossest immoralities " (p. 94). " Those who listen to the enthusiasts of the present day, too often

[1] At least, he refers pointedly to the *True Churchman ascertained*, and takes up the cudgels for Mr. Daubeny, who was quite strong enough to fight his own battles.

suppose themselves the chosen vessels of God, and are persuaded that no conduct atrocious, however unchristian, can finally deprive them of eternal felicity" (p. 171). "They not only delude their unlearned congregations, and encourage vice and immorality among their followers, but they really delude themselves, and fall into opinions and assertions totally inconsistent with the spirit of our holy religion" (p. 177). All this seems more applicable to the teaching of some "Trusty Tomkins" in the seventeenth century than to that of a Simeon, a Venn, or a Legh Richmond in the nineteenth, and we are not surprised to find that an answer appeared from the pen of that veteran Evangelical, *Thomas Scott*, who published in 1817, "*Remarks on the Bishop of Lincoln's 'Refutation of Calvinism.'*" The significance of Scott's reply is emphasized by the fact that his own sermons show that he was fully alive to the dangers of ultra-Calvinism; in fact, the burden of many of them is a warning against these dangers. But the old man had known too much of the saintly lives of many who would be classed as Calvinists, to allow so sweeping an attack upon the whole system to pass unchallenged.

The controversy about Baptismal Regeneration, which produced a certain amount of literature, such as it was, is really a part of the Calvinistic controversy. For the Calvinists held that no man was in a justified state until he had a conscious sense of pardon and peace with God. The "Orthodox," on the other hand, held that all baptized Christians were in a justified state, and that there was no such thing as a second birth after that which took place in the Sacrament of Holy Baptism; they made, of course, a marked distinction between regeneration and conversion, and laid stress upon the daily renewal by God's Holy Spirit which most Christians in their present imperfect state required.[1]

The question of Baptismal Regeneration came to the front mainly in consequence of Mr. (afterwards Bishop) Mant's Bampton Lectures in 1811, the sixth and seventh of which were devoted to the subject of regeneration and

[1] "Grant that we, being regenerate and made Thy children by adoption and grace, may daily be renewed by Thy Holy Spirit."—Collect for Christmas Day.

conversion. The writer, of course, strongly advocates the doctrine of Baptismal Regeneration, adding, "This doctrine is virtually at least, if not actually, denied by some ministers of our Church; and it is denied in terms which charge the maintainers of it with blindness and ignorance; with innovating on evangelical truth; with being opposers of the doctrines of the gospel, and patrons of a heathenish superstition." The lectures made a great sensation; and the Salop Committee of the S.P.C.K. passed a resolution "that it would materially serve the interests of genuine religion and of the Church of England if the Rev. R. Mant could be induced to print the two excellent sermons of his Bampton Lectures, viz. the sixth and seventh, on Regeneration and Conversion, in a form calculated for circulation amongst the community." The result was that the sermons were published by the S.P.C.K., under the title of "*Two Tracts on Regeneration and Conversion.*" But Low Churchmen as well as High Churchmen belonged to the S.P.C.K.; and it is not surprising that the former looked with dismay on the publication of the two tracts, which contained a direct attack upon their party. John Scott, of Hull, the son of the commentator, and T. J. Biddulph, of Bristol, both leading Evangelicals, had written pamphlets in reply to Mr. Mant's strictures before the S.P.C.K. had committed itself to his views. When the tracts were put on the list of the society, Daniel Wilson published a pamphlet entitled "*A Respectful Address to the Society on certain Inconsistencies and Contradictions which have lately appeared in some of their Books and Tracts.*" The High Churchmen were not slow to reply. Among others, Dr. Christopher Wordsworth defended the society in print. Excited meetings were held, at one of which the Archbishop of Canterbury (Dr. Manners-Sutton) and the Bishop of London (Dr. Howley) were present, and threw all the weight of their authority into the High Church scale.[1] A committee was appointed to examine the matter

---

[1] Daniel Wilson writes: "February 10, 1816.—The meeting of S.P.C.K. took place last Tuesday,—all the world there." And of the next meeting: "We expected nothing. But what do you think? There was the Archbishop of Canterbury in the chair, and by him the Bishop of London. Mr. Dealtry presented his letter. It was read twice. The archbishop followed, and condemned it

thoroughly and to report upon the society's works; and the somewhat feeble conclusion was that a new edition of Mant's tracts was published, in which the most obnoxious expressions were expunged or modified. One of the ablest writers on the High Church side in this controversy was *Alexander Knox*, who in 1810 published a treatise on "Justification," addressed to his friend Mr. Parkin, editor of the *Eclectic Review*, who would of course hold very different views. Mr. Knox's trumpet gave no uncertain sound. "In the judgment," he says, "of the Church—ancient and Anglican alike—every one baptized in infancy commences life in a justified state." In 1820 he published a more elaborate work, entitled "*The Doctrine respecting Baptism held by the Church of England*," in which he contends that "all infants who are baptized infallibly participate in the inward and spiritual grace which the Sacrament of Baptism is intended to convey."

BIOGRAPHY.

Under this head we have, in the first place, the lives of the early Evangelical leaders, which naturally came out during our period. One of the best executed and most interesting of these is the "*Life of Thomas Scott*," by his son, John Scott (1822). It is written in excellent taste, with filial appreciation, but without any undue filial partiality. The "*Life of John Newton*" was also written well, as, indeed, goes without saying, when we remember that the writer was his old friend Richard Cecil, the most refined and cultured of all the early Evangelicals. The "Life" is prefixed to the first volume of Newton's works, published in six volumes, in 1808. Cecil's own life was briefly but gracefully written by his widow, and prefixed to the "Remains," edited by his friend Josiah Pratt in 1810. There is a singularly pathetic interest attached to the "*Life of Joseph Milner*," written by his brother Isaac, and published in 1814. Isaac felt that he owed everything in life to his brother, who was prematurely cut off in his prime, and he throws his whole heart—which

---

strongly as self-willed."—*Life of D. Wilson*, p. 143. Archbishop Manners-Sutton admired Mant's Bampton Lectures greatly, and is said to have made the writer his domestic chaplain in consequence. See *Life of Bishop R. Mant*, pp. 97, *et seq.*

was a very large one—into his work. The strong man was bowed down by his loss, and he takes the public into his confidence. Henry Venn, Thomas Robinson of Leicester, Claudius Buchanan, and other leading Evangelicals were also the subjects of biographies, more or less interesting, written during our period. But there is yet another—are we to call him an Evangelical leader or not?—who furnished material for a "Life" of far wider and more enduring interest than any yet named. In 1820 appeared *Southey's "Life of Wesley,"* one of the few κτήματα ἐς ἀεὶ which the biographical art has given to the world. In spite of the innumerable works on the same subject, some of which are much fuller and more accurate, while some give far truer estimates of the aims and personal character of the great reformer, Southey's "Life" has never yet been really superseded. In point of literary finish, the only biographical work of our period that can at all compare with it is *Bishop Van Mildert's "Life of Daniel Waterland,"* prefixed to the bishop's admirable edition of Waterland's works, in six volumes, 1823. Whatever Van Mildert's pen touched, it adorned; but he is especially in his element when writing about a great divine and scholar, and his book is a model of biographical skill. Another great English divine was also brought before the public by another bishop. Reginald Heber published a *"Life of Jeremy Taylor,"* in 1822, and an edition of his works; but neither life nor edition was a model of its kind. Lives or memoirs of Granville Sharp (1827), John Bowdler (1825), Bishop Middleton (1831), Thomas Rennell (1824), Charles Daubeny (1830), all have an interest of their own; and more amusing, if not more edifying, is the sort of autobiography of Bishop Watson, published by his son in 1818, under the title of *"Anecdotes of my own Life."* There were also two works which, as partaking of the nature of biography, come under our present head—*Dr. Christopher Wordsworth's "Ecclesiastical Biography,"* and the *Rev. Erasmus Middleton's "Biographia Evangelica."* The former is a sort of hagiology of the Orthodox, the latter of the Evangelical, school. Both authors were well qualified for their task, and both were themselves worthy representatives of the schools about which they respectively wrote. But as Mr. Middleton (who was the

O

predecessor of Legh Richmond in the living of Turvey) died in 1804, his " Biographia " has the drawback of not including many of the most brilliant specimens of the Evangelical party, which did not reach its zenith until after that date. Dr. Wordsworth, as the exponent of the old historical Church school, had the advantage of having his greatest heroes in the far past. His biography is a collection of lives not written by himself, but "arranged in chronological order from the Reformation to the Revolution, the authors having been contemporaries of their subjects." The work was a most seasonable one at the time when it appeared, for this reason: piety and Evangelicalism were then almost convertible terms; and Dr. Wordsworth drew attention to the fact that there had been men, whose piety none could doubt, but who were of a very different type from the modern Evangelicals. It is a curious illustration of the way in which "establishment" was then considered as almost an essential of the Church, that Dr. Wordsworth does not include a single Nonjuror among his subjects; though it would be difficult to find men more suitable for his obvious purpose than Thomas Ken, John Kettlewell, Robert Nelson, or William Law.

CHURCH HISTORY.

The best known, if not the most valuable, work on this subject which appeared during our period, is *Southey's* "*Book of the Church*" (1824). The work was well received. The Bishop of London, among others, wrote to thank the author for it; and, as has been hinted before, there were few men whose praise was better worth having on theological literature than Bishop Howley's. Southey writes from the point of view of a high and dry Churchman of the old-fashioned type, and his sentiments were all the more stiff and unbending owing to the violent reaction which followed in his case, as in that of many others, from the wildly extravagant liberalism, not to say scepticism, which he had imbibed in his youth from his sympathy with the French Revolutionists. The charm of his literary style and the substantial soundness of his views combine to make his book still a classic; but there are few competent people in the present day who would be thoroughly satisfied with his conclusions. The horizon has become widened on all sides; and while the number of those who, like Southey, are enthusiastic admirers of the Church of England has been immensely increased, the vast majority of them take a broader and truer view of the functions and position of that Church. No one can read Southey's "Book of the Church" without pleasure and profit, but most people will feel that it wants supplementing and modifying in many respects before it can at all satisfy the larger intelligence of the present day. It is, however, only fair to remember the humble object which Southey had in view. He never intended his "Book of the Church" to be a full and satisfactory account for advanced students. It grew upon his hands, and is now sometimes cited for purposes for which it was never meant. This will appear from the writer's own description of the origin of the work. "Upon the first institution," he tells us, "of the National Society for Promoting the Education of the Poor in the Principles of the Established Church, and after the initiatory books which are used in its schools had been prepared, my excellent friend, Dr. Bell, asked me to compose a summary view of Church history for the elder pupils. I easily promised what, for the moment, I thought might be presently done. But, upon considering the matter, I soon perceived that it would be both easier and of more utility to extend the design, and compose such a compendium as might be a fit manual for our English youth; that is, for those (still, happily, the great majority) whose good fortune it is to be bred up in the principles of our twofold constitution."[1] "The 'Book of the Church' was avowedly composed for the youth of this kingdom, that they might be trained up in the way they should go, and made in time to understand from what corruptions and evils the Reformation delivered their fathers, and how dearly the blessed deliverance was purchased."[2] It is absurd to measure a book, written under such circumstances and for such purposes, by the standard of an exhaustive history.

---

[1] *Vindiciæ Ecclesiæ Anglicanæ.* Letters to Charles Butler, Esq., comprising Essays on the Romish Religion and vindicating the "Book of the Church."—Introduction.

[2] *Id.*, p. 43.

Southey's "*Book of the Church*" was soon followed by two similar works, viz. "*A History of the Church of England to the Revolution*," by the Rev. J. B. S. Carwithen, in three volumes, which came out at intervals from 1829 to 1833; and another work, in two volumes, with exactly the same title, by the Rev. T. Vowler Short, afterwards Bishop of St. Asaph, in 1832. Bishop Short's book became by far the more popular—in fact, it still holds its ground as a text-book; but, in my opinion, Mr. Carwithen's is the better book of the two. The writer is a sounder Churchman, and he writes in a stronger and better style. But an obscure country clergyman had hardly a chance against a tutor at the largest and most famous college at Oxford and an embryo bishop. Bishop Short, though accurate enough in detail, falls into the fatal error of giving the reader the general impression that a new Church was set up in the reign of Henry VIII. Such expressions as, "the Church of England dated from the divorce" (p. 86), are an upsettal of all history. He also entirely ignores all that was done for the conversion of England by the Scottish mission under St. Aidan and his successors. In fact, he fosters the old, old fallacy that the Church was Roman Catholic before the Reformation, and Protestant after. No history written on such a principle can be trustworthy, and Short's "*History of the Church of England*" is fast becoming one of the authorities that have been. *Troja fuit.* But all three writers deserve the gratitude of Churchmen for opening out a field which had been untouched since the days of Thomas Carte and Jeremy Collier. They, at any rate, awakened a desire in English Churchmen to know something about their own Church, if they did not altogether satisfy that desire. As dealing with a part of the same subject, we may also mention here *Professor J. J. Blunt's* deservedly popular "*Sketch of the Reformation in England*," which appeared in 1832, as one of the volumes of Murray's " Family Library," and which has since passed through a vast number of editions.

A much more ambitious essay in the sphere of Church history was undertaken by the Rev. George Waddington, afterwards Dean of Durham; but at the time a resident Fellow of Trinity College, Cambridge. *Waddington's*

"*Church History*," which appeared in 1833, undertakes the gigantic task of giving the history of the Church of Christ in all parts of the world for fifteen centuries; that is, from the time of the Apostles to the Reformation. To complete such a work adequately would take up many, many volumes; but the future dean did it in one! It is true, it is a very bulky volume indeed; but, even so, the information had to be so closely condensed that it is very heavy reading. The work had the doubtful advantage of coming out under the auspices of the Society for the Diffusion of Useful Knowledge; and considering the avowed object of its sponsor, it is wonderful how little there is in it to which a Churchman can object. It remains master of the field, for the simple reason that no other human being ever has, or is ever likely to embrace so vast a subject in anything like so small a compass.

Strictly speaking, Milner's "History of the Church of Christ," in its finished form, belongs to our period; but this book has been already described in a work dealing with the century in which it first appeared.[1]

Works of a very different type from those hitherto mentioned, but in their way most valuable contributions towards the knowledge of Church history, were published during our period by two very learned divines, *Bishop Kaye* and *Dr. Routh*. In 1826 Dr. John Kaye, then Bishop of Bristol, published the first of his valuable patristic works, under the title of "*The Ecclesiastical History of the Second and Third Centuries, illustrated from the Writings of Tertullian;*" and in 1829, "*An Account of the Writings and Opinions of Justin Martyr.*" There was a seasonableness about these publications which enhanced their intrinsic merits, great as these were. It was high time that, amid the confusion and strife of tongues which the late religious movements had caused, the attention of Churchmen should be turned to long-neglected studies, which after all were indispensable to sound theology. To Bishop Kaye, above all other men, the credit is due for having aroused a revival of interest in the study of the ancient Fathers, which was never

[1] See *The English Church in the Eighteenth Century*, vol. ii. ch. ii. pp. 209-213.

more needed than in the early days of the present century. His later works in the same direction do not come within our limits. The first instalment of Dr. Routh's long and learned labours in the same direction came out in two volumes, in 1814, under the title of "*Reliquiæ Sacræ: sive Auctorum ferè jam perditorum secundi tertiique sæculi post Christum natum, quæ supersunt.*"[1] To the very few who then took an interest in the theology of the second and third centuries, Dr. Routh's labours were invaluable; but they were "*caviare* to the general." Even the majority of what was called "the religious world" knew little and cared less for the "sacred reliques of authors" *not* "nearly lost" belonging to those bygone ages; so, of course, they would not be vitally interested in the rescue from oblivion of "reliques" which *were* "nearly lost." As a living influence upon the Church of his day, Dr. Routh's effort may not count for such; but as a work of permanent value, and as a monument of the tradition of learning which had not quite died out in the learned Church of England, it deserves special notice. Like Bishop Kaye, Dr. Routh extended his labours, and gave the results of them to the world for many years after our period closes, though he had nearly reached the age of fourscore when the Oxford Movement began.

THE ROMAN CONTROVERSY.

Though in one way this was the most prominent and bitter of all the religious controversies of our period, yet the form it took was not of a kind to produce much theological literature. It turned not so much upon doctrinal questions as upon the very practical one, whether the Roman Catholics were to be relieved of their civil disabilities. This question produced abundance of printed matter; but it was in the form of sermons and pamphlets, which could be quickly and easily read, and were only of an ephemeral interest, not in that of formal, elaborate treatises. Two works, however, appeared on the Roman side, which required and received more extended answers. The one was *Bishop Milner's "End of Religious Controversy"* (1824), which

[1] "Oxford University Reform," by Goldwin Smith, in *Oxford Essays*, 1858.

attacked the position of bare Protestantism with telling effect. "It is an absurdity," argues the writer, "to talk of the *Church* or *Society* of *Protestants*, for the term PROTESTANT expresses *nothing positive*, much less any union or association of persons : it barely signifies one who *protests*, or declares against some other person or persons, thing or things ; and in the present instance it signifies those who *protest against the Catholic Church*. Hence there may be, and there are, numberless sects of Protestants divided from each other in everything except in opposing their true mother, the Catholic Church. St. Augustine reckons up ninety heresies which had protested against the Church before his time" (p. 124). In days when, as Thomas Sikes complains, few men had any definite notion what they meant when they said, "I believe in the Holy Catholic Church," such arguments were difficult to answer. The bishop seems to have had an inkling that the Church of England had something more to say for itself than that it was "protestant," for he adds, "I grant that your Communion [the Church of England] has better pretensions to the marks of the Church than any other Protestant Society has" (p. 125). The other book was by a layman, Mr. Charles Butler, and was entitled "*The Book of the Roman Catholic Church.*"

Among the answers to both, one was written by that doughty champion *Dr. Henry Phillpotts*, afterwards Bishop of Exeter, in a volume entitled "*Letters to Charles Butler, Esq., on the Theological Parts of his 'Book of the Roman Catholic Church.'*" Though it professes to deal only with Mr. Butler, it also grapples with many of the arguments used by Bishop Milner, to whom the able writer frequently refers by name. But long before Dr. Milner's or Mr. Butler's books appeared, the watchful eye of Archdeacon Daubeny detected rocks ahead in the direction of Rome. In his Charges from 1813 onwards he dwells much upon Romanism, and it is needless to say that he defends his own Church on positive grounds, not on the negative ones of mere Protestantism. In his Charge of 1819 he intimates that he is becoming more and more alarmed. "Time was, and not very long since, when any cry of alarm on the score of popery in this country would have been considered too ridiculous to have merited the attention of a thinking man. But I have lived to see a wonderful change of public opinion on this subject." In 1824 he wrote an anti-Roman treatise, entitled "*The Protestant's Companion*," for which he was warmly thanked by the Bishops of London and Winchester. There were also, of course, many other writers on the subject; but it was not one which from a theological point of view was very prominent during our period, and it need not, therefore, be dwelt upon further.

Religious Periodicals.

The rise of religious periodicals was a notable feature in the history of the Church at the beginning of the nineteenth century. Before that century began they had hardly existed at all, except among the Methodists; but with the commencement of the century both the two great parties in the Church provided themselves with an organ in the press.

The *British Critic* was one of the results of the formation of a short-lived "Society for the Reformation of Principles," originating among that little group of High Churchmen whose centre was Nayland Vicarage. It was preceded by a publication entitled *The Scholar Armed*, which consisted of an exceedingly well-selected number of extracts from the works of standard divines. This was an extremely useful work; but, from the nature of it, it soon came to an end—sooner, indeed, than it might with advantage have done. But on its ruins arose and throve the *British Critic*, which lasted for many years. One generally hears Mr. Jones of Nayland called its originator, but this is only so far true that the seeds from which it sprang were sown at his house, and by his friends, or rather disciples. But he never was the editor, and never wrote a single word in it. In fact, he was marked for death by the time that the first number appeared. At first it was conducted on distinctly High Church lines; then, for a time, under the editorship of Archdeacon Nares, its principles were not so distinctive; but about the year 1812 it was purchased by Joshua Watson and Henry Handley Norris, for the express purpose of restoring it to its original intention. It had some of the ablest divines of the day for its editors, including William Van Mildert (for a very short time), Thomas Fanshawe Middleton, and Thomas Rennell; and, as any one can see who turns to its pages, it commanded a staff of extremely competent writers. In 1824 it was changed from a monthly into a quarterly. As it survived our period for several years, the story of its extinction does not fall within our limits.

The *Christian Observer* was almost coeval with the *British Critic*, and continued for many years to be the monthly organ of the Evangelical party. As early as 1798 we find an entry in Wilberforce's diary: "Much occupied with a plan for setting up a religious publication." A little more than two years later the plan took a definite shape in the *Christian Observer*, the first number of which is dated "January, 1801." Oddly enough, a similar error has prevailed about its editorship as about that of the *British Critic*. The first editor was not, as is often said, Zachary Macaulay, but Josiah Pratt, who may really almost be called the projector as well as the editor.[1] But Josiah Pratt had not sufficient time at his command; moreover, he was a remarkably retiring man, and that is not a virtue which is useful for the floating of a new periodical. So he withdrew almost immediately in favour of Zachary Macaulay, who was the ideal man for the post. He held it for nearly sixteen years, and the success of the *Christian Observer* was largely due to his efforts. To enumerate its early contributors would be to enumerate almost all the Evangelical leaders of the second generation. William Wilberforce, Hannah More, Henry Thornton, Thomas Scott, John Venn, Legh Richmond, Thomas Gisborne, William Farish, Henry Martyn, Claudius Buchanan, Josiah Pratt, Charles Simeon, Lord Teignmouth, John Overton, John Scott, and, outside the strictly Evangelical circle,

---

[1] The biographer of William Hey claims for his hero a large share in the introduction of the *Christian Observer*. "In 1800 and 1801, Mr. Hey reflected on the advantages of a monthly publication, to oppose the inroads of infidelity and heresy, support the doctrines and discipline of the Church of England, and promote piety. He commenced a correspondence with persons in different parts; promised his own assistance, and best efforts to procure aid of learned and pious men; and it is to be ascribed, in a great measure, to his zeal and activity that the *Christian Observer* was introduced to the world."—Pearson's *Life of William Hey*, i. 198.

Bishop Heber, Bishop Burgess, and John Bowdler the younger, all wrote for it. It passed through none of the vicissitudes which, as we have seen, overtook its rival, but, on the other hand, it never reached the high intellectual level of the *British Critic* in its best days.

Weekly newspapers hardly come within our province; otherwise we should have to notice the appearance of the first religious newspaper, the *Record*, in 1828—a paper which still exists, but which has happily improved as much in ability as in Christian charity. But there are two periodicals, both emanating from the High Church party, which should be mentioned.

It is generally supposed that the *Christian Remembrancer* rose on the ruins of the *British Critic*. But, in point of fact, there was an earlier *Christian Remembrancer*, which was started, mainly through the efforts of Joshua Watson and H. H. Norris, not so much to advocate Church principles as to stimulate the clergy to take a livelier interest in theological studies generally. "The country clergy," said Norris, "are constant readers of the *Gentleman's Magazine*, deep in the antiquities of the signs of inns, speculations as to what becomes of swallows in winter, and whether hedgehogs or other urchins are most justly accused of sucking milch-cows dry at night." Feeling that they should be raised to higher interests, he persuaded the Rev. F. Iremonger to start the *Christian Remembrancer*, the first number of which appeared in January, 1819, and was issued quarterly for eleven years. Van Mildert, a very competent counsellor, advised the editor to give "succinct and careful abridgments of standard theological works by the best English and foreign divines;"[1] and a glance at the earlier numbers of the *Christian Remembrancer* will show that an effort was made to follow this advice. Though its main object was to encourage theological study generally, there is no doubt about the standpoint from which it desired the study to be conducted, as the following sentence in the introduction to the first number will show: "We seek not to conceal our alliance with those who see little or no prospect of extending the influence of Christianity except through the instrumentality of the Church."

[1] See *Memoir of Joshua Watson*, i. 277.

In almost all the early numbers there is an article bearing more or less on Calvinism and Antinomianism, against which it waged internecine war.

Another periodical arose under distinctly High Church auspices in March, 1832, with the title of *The British Magazine*. The *British Critic* had by this time become a Quarterly, and the *Christian Remembrancer* (also a Quarterly) was not exactly extinct, but in a state of suspended animation. It was thought that a monthly paper consisting, not of long essays and reviews, but of short articles, poetry, and general intelligence, was a desideratum. No periodical could have been started with a fairer promise. Its originator and first editor was Hugh James Rose, then by far the most brilliant and prominent man among the High Church party. Among its contributors were Keble, Newman, and Isaac Williams, who first published in it the exquisite hymns which afterwards appeared in the "Lyra Apostolica." Its second editor, Dr. Samuel Maitland, if a less brilliant, was quite as able, and certainly a more learned man than the first. And yet it was very short-lived, being swept away, probably, in the excitement caused by the Oxford Movement.

RELIGIOUS POETRY.

With one marked exception, the age before us was singularly weak in what may strictly be termed religious poetry; and yet it was the great poets of the day who tended more than any other writers to affect men's attitude towards religion. For the first quarter of the century there were religious men who wrote poetry of a higher order than any that had appeared since the days of Milton, but there was no religious poetry of any real mark, with the exception of hymns for public worship. To explain this apparent paradox it is necessary to enter into details. The last great religious poet, William Cowper, died with the old century, and left no successor behind him. The two religious poets of the next generation who are best known were Bowles and Heber; but posterity has not at all confirmed the contemporary verdict upon their poetry. Bowles was rather a religious man who wrote poetry than a religious poet. Reginald Heber is a name still fresh in the hearts of his countrymen; but it is not for his "*Palestine*," or for any of his writings, except one or two hymns, but for his personality and his career. In the words of a thoughtful writer, "men gazed delightedly on so fine a combination of the scholar, the gentleman, and the Christian, and gladly seized on circumstances which half warranted them in adding, the martyr."[1] Henry Hart Milman at one time seemed likely to be the rising poet of the day; but he soon devoted himself to prose, and his prose has lived, while his poetry is well-nigh forgotten. George Crabbe was another clergyman who wrote poetry which *has* lived, but it cannot be called religious poetry. In fact, from the death of Cowper in 1800 till the year 1827, there is no one who can properly be called a religious poet of any real mark. But in 1827 *John Keble* published "*The Christian Year*," and the effect is rightly described in words which have now become classical : " When the general tone of religious literature was so powerless and impotent as it was at that time, Keble struck an original note, and woke up in the hearts of thousands a new music, the music of a school long unknown in England."[2]

Keble's "*Christian Year*" was partly the cause, but partly also the index, of a change of feeling which had been going on for some time; and among the chief producers of that change were four great writers, all of them poets, though perhaps only one of the four can be said to have made his poetry the chief organ of the influence which he exercised. These four were Sir Walter Scott, S. T. Coleridge, William Wordsworth, and Robert Southey.

Let us take the most popular and voluminous of them all first. Of the early life of Sir Walter Scott, we read the old, old story, repeated a thousand times during our period, of a strong reaction against a narrow and over-strict religious training. Happily, in Sir Walter's case, this reaction did not lead, as it did in the case of many others, to scepticism, irreligion, or immorality. Retaining the kernel of the

---

[1] *Christian Remembrancer*, vol. i., January to June, 1841; Article, "The Religious Poets of the Day."
[2] Newman's *Apologia pro Vitâ Suâ*, p. 77.

religion he had been taught, and only throwing away the husk, he found a congenial home in a religious system which appealed alike to his love of antiquity, to his refined literary taste, to his sense of the beautiful, and to his calm, equable temperament. The more he saw of the Anglican Church, the more he liked it; but the narrowness and gloominess of the system in which he had been brought up repelled him from the first, and he never shook off that feeling. He always seems to have taken an interest in theological questions, and once actually perpetrated a volume of sermons—which was about as incongruous a performance as "The Christian Hero" of poor Sir Richard Steele. But, in his way, he was the most effective preacher of his day, and his preaching was all in favour of the old faith and the old system of the Church of England. He possessed the priceless advantage of catching the public ear. Thousands upon thousands eagerly drank in his words; and when a new tale from his pen appeared, it made all other books a drug in the market. But while his countless readers were charmed with the humour of Andrew Fairservice, or the powerful description of Balfour of Burley, they were, all unconsciously, imbibing sentiments which tended to undermine the predominant theology. The Evangelicals knew their enemy, and suspected him from the first. It is true that they were not directly concerned in his representation of the Covenanters, which called forth the wrath of some of his compatriots; for they would probably sympathize with the Cavaliers rather than with the Roundheads. But none the less is it true that *his* way of looking at things was not *their* way. To begin with, he broke down once and for all their assumption that novel-reading was essentially evil. So long as "Tom Jones" and "Humphry Clinker," or even "Pamela" and "The Castle of Otranto," were regarded as the type of novels generally, there was something to be said for the view that novel-reading could not possibly tend to edification; but unprejudiced persons revolted from the idea that "Waverley" and "The Heart of Mid-Lothian" were demoralizing. Sir Walter's inimitable biographer claims for his hero, with perfect justice, the credit of having taught Christian morality in a most captivating form; and no one can gainsay him when he dwells upon the healthy, manly tone of the great novelist's writings. Bishop Van Mildert was no flatterer when he told Scott that "he could reflect upon the labours of a long literary life, with the consciousness that everything he had written tended to the practice of virtue, and to the improvement of the human race." Perhaps Scott was thinking of the bishop's words when he said a little before his death, "I am drawing near to the close of my career; I am fast shuffling off the stage. I have been perhaps the most voluminous author of the day; and it *is* a comfort to me to think that I have tried to unsettle no man's faith, to corrupt no man's principle." His satisfaction was well grounded, if we understand by "faith" the broad, general views of Christian truth; but if we understand by it the popular theology as held by "the serious," the case is different. The High Churchmen of the generation that was coming on saw clearly enough that he had been preparing the way for them. The long essay which John Keble wrote upon him for the *British Critic*, evidently *con amore*, is a witness of this; and as it would be impossible to express what is meant in better language, an extract from that very remarkable essay may be permitted. "It is not perhaps too much to say that never did a single writer exert a greater influence on his age. No slight benefit was the substitution of his manly realities for the flimsy, enervating literature which peopled the shelves of those who read chiefly for amusement. In verse he had noble coadjutors, but the reformation of the novel was exclusively his own work. . . . But it was for far more than an improvement in such things for which this generation is indebted to him. Whatever of good feeling and salutary prejudice exists in favour of ancient institutions . . . is it not in a good measure attributable to the chivalrous tone which his writings have diffused over the studies and tastes of those now in the prime of manhood? His rod, like that of a beneficent enchanter, has touched and guarded hundreds, who would else have been *reforming* enthusiasts. His writings are all against the cold, supercilious tone of the age, and the great temptations to utilitarian views. . . . What if these generous feelings had been allowed to ripen into that of which they are undoubtedly the germ and rudiment? What if this gifted writer had become the poet of the Church, in as eminent a sense as he was the poet of the Border and Highland chivalry?" If it were not too presumptuous, I should certainly be inclined to answer these questions in a different way from that in which the writer intends them to be answered. Sir Walter Scott seems to me to have done his part better by writing as he did, than he would have done if he had attempted to do, as a poet, the work which Mr. Keble himself and Mr. Isaac Williams did, or, as a tale-writer, that which was so well done by Mr. Paget and Mr. Gresley. But instead of venturing to demur to Mr. Keble, it will be better to fall back on an authority equal to his own. Dr. Newman, referring to his famous article in the *British Critic* in 1839, when he touches upon the causes which led to the movement of 1883, writes : " First I mentioned the literary influence of Walter Scott, who turned men's minds to the direction of the Middle Ages. The general need of something deeper and more attractive than what had offered itself elsewhere, may be considered to have led to his popularity; and by means of his popularity he reacted on his readers, stimulating their mental thirst, feeding their hopes, setting before them visions which, when once seen, are not easily forgotten, and silently indoctrinating them with nobler ideas, which might afterwards be appealed to as first principles."[1] That was Sir Walter's proper work ; he was a most effective pioneer, but he would have been only an indifferent teacher of what followed.

We next come to the Lake poets—Coleridge, Wordsworth, and Southey. Far more than any professed theologians of their age, these three, or at any rate the two first of them, seem to me to have influenced the public mind, though perhaps slowly and indirectly, in its attitude towards religion. All three, in their early years, sympathized with the vague but generous aspirations after liberty and truth awakened by the French Revolution; all three suffered the same rude shock of bitter disappointment when liberty degenerated into licence, and the most cruel tyranny took the place of the glorious freedom they had dreamed of; all three, by a violent reaction, became, instead of democrats and sceptics, the staunchest supporters of the British constitution in Church

[1] See Newman's *Apologia pro Vitâ Suâ* ; also Canon Liddon's *Life of Dr Pusey*, i. 254.

and State. But in the case of Wordsworth the change was not so marked as in the other two, because he had never drifted away, as they had done, from the faith, but had confined his liberalism to politics.

But let us begin with that one of the three whose own character was the most imperfect, whose writings were the least voluminous and the least complete, but who, strange to say, had the most influence of them all—*Samuel Taylor Coleridge* (1772-1834). From his earliest years his mind was constantly running in the direction of theology. As a mere schoolboy he had revolted against the hard, dry, utilitarian view of religion prevalent in the eighteenth century. He does not seem in early life to have come into contact with the then rising Evangelicalism; but when he did, it did not at all commend itself to him. His experience at college (Jesus, Cambridge) only confirmed the impressions he had formed at school (Christ's Hospital). He passed rapidly through the downward steps—from orthodoxy to Socinianism; from Socinianism, through a vague sort of Pantheism, to Unitarianism; from Unitarianism to something very like downright scepticism, not to say atheism. He then passed through exactly the same stages upwards, and finally found his permanent home in the Church of his baptism, a most firm believer in all the doctrines of the Church, and a most ardent admirer of our great divines, especially those of the seventeenth century. From first to last he was thoroughly in earnest, and, one may even say, spiritually minded. But his downward and also his upward progress is perfectly intelligible and perfectly consistent. His mental history is simply the history of a truly pious soul painfully groping its way until it at last found the right way, from which it henceforth never swerved for one moment. Before he had found the light, he describes his case in his own exquisite language—

> "Thrice holy faith! Whatever thorns I meet,
> As on I totter with unpractis'd feet,
> Still let me stretch my arms and cling to Thee,
> Meek nurse of souls through their long infancy." [1]

It is no part of the present work to discuss his frailties, the

[1] "To an Infant." Written in 1794. Quoted by Mr. Abbey in *The English Church in the Eighteenth Century*, ii. 346.

root of which lay in physical rather than moral or intellectual sources. It was latent disease which caused him to be a confirmed opium-eater, culpably negligent in providing for his family, and morbidly averse from any sustained intellectual exertion. His heart was always in the right place, and his weaknesses should move pity rather than blame. But it is a fair subject of inquiry, How is it that this indolent, desultory man, who in his religious views almost boxed the theological compass, whose life stands out as a warning rather than an example, whose writings consist more of beautiful fragments than of any great consecutive work, who glaringly contradicts in his later life what he had written with vehemence, not to say violence, in his earlier, who did not earn enough by his pen to maintain himself, much less his family, yet exercised an influence which few other men did over the minds of his countrymen? Was it the magical power of genius, which turns everything it touches, however slightly, into gold? This, no doubt, may account for much, but not for all. Coleridge was a true *prophet* as well as a true *poet*. He had the courage of his convictions, and his convictions were far in advance of his age. It quite startles one to observe how at one time he exactly lays his finger upon the weak point of a position, how at another he hits the very centre of the bull's-eye. Just one fragmentary remark of his is sometimes more fertile in suggestion than whole chapters and whole volumes of other writers. Those who are fond of historical parallels might find an interesting subject for speculation in comparing S. T. Coleridge with Alexander Knox. Both were recluses more or less; both quitted the world without leaving any *magnum opus* behind them; both acted as a sort of ζύμη (and at very nearly the same time), which spread and spread till it leavened a large mass; both were admirable conversationalists; and both were sought out in their respective retreats by men of thought and culture who came to hear the oracle speak.

The very truth of Coleridge's sayings in prose and verse renders it difficult to appreciate their originality. They have proved *so* true that they sound like truisms; and only those who have thoroughly saturated themselves with the mind of England in the early part of the present century can realize

P

how powerful a solvent they are of deeply rooted ideas and prejudices. To give instances would be like presenting a brick as a specimen of a building. A man must go through a course of Coleridge before he can realize what his teaching was.[1] Let it suffice to quote the testimony of one of his most distinguished disciples on the point. "Of all recent writers," says Julius Hare, "the one whose sanction I have chiefly desired is the great religious philosopher to whom the mind of our generation in England owes more than to any other man, and whose aim it was to spiritualize not only our philosophy, but our theology; to raise them both above the empiricism into which they had fallen, and to free them from the technical trammels of logical systems."

But Coleridge does not stand alone; he must be taken closely in connection with Wordsworth; for the one was the complement of the other.

"Every great poet is a teacher; I desire to be considered either as a teacher, or nothing." So said *William Wordsworth* (1770–1850) when reviewers were scoffing at, and the world was ignoring, his immortal verse. But he had his desire. By slow degrees men began to see, what his friends had seen all along, that a great poet, and therefore a great teacher, had been among them, and they knew it not. There is something truly heroic in Wordsworth's dogged determination to fulfil his mission, in spite of ridicule and in spite of neglect. Without attacking, as his friend Coleridge attacked, popular beliefs or prejudices, he quietly, and perhaps unconsciously, undermined them by pointing out what he considered the better way. It was not new teaching, but a return to the old, though it seemed new to a generation which had quite lost sight of the old. One can quite understand the enthusiastic admiration which John Keble felt for Wordsworth; but Keble was a mystic, and mysticism was an unintelligible jargon, not only to the survivors of the prosaic eighteenth century, but also alike to the popular pietists and to the utilitarian reformers of the nineteenth. The blending of religion and philosophy, the

---

[1] If any reader happens to have read an article in a leading periodical on "The Religious Opinions of S. T. Coleridge," and observes here any repetition of the sentiments there expressed, he will perhaps guess the reason.

sacredness of nature as the outward expression of God, the sacredness of childhood, the sacredness of common, homely life,—these were the truths he had to teach to those who had eyes to see and ears to hear. His teaching led some in the direction in which Keble and Newman and Isaac Williams carried them further ; it led others in a different direction, in which they were guided onward by such men as the two Hares and F. D. Maurice. But to the Evangelicals, on the one hand, and the Whig reformers on the other, it all seemed worse than nonsense. Lord Jeffrey's now historical exclamation, " This will never do ! " is perfectly intelligible. No! it would never do for men who felt that their business in life was to make war against Corporation and Test Acts, game laws and steel traps and spring guns, Lord Eldon and the Court of Chancery, to have held out to them as an ideal one who felt

> " A sense sublime
> Of something far more deeply interfused,
> Whose dwelling is the light of setting suns,
> And the round ocean, and the living air,
> And the blue sky, and in the mind of man ; "

one whose

> " Daily teachers had been clouds and hills,
> The silence that is in the starry sky,
> The sleep that is among the lonely hills;

one whose

> " Soul was like a star, and dwelt apart."

The Evangelical found, not poetry, but flat heresy, in such lines as—

> " Our birth is but a sleep and a forgetting :
> The soul that rises with us, our life's star,
> Hath had elsewhere its setting,
> And cometh from afar :
> Not in entire forgetfulness,
> And not in utter nakedness,
> But trailing clouds of glory, do we come
> From God, who is our home."

Wordsworth and Coleridge, as has been said, must be taken together. Let me conclude the notice of these two great men by quoting the testimony to their influence of two very thoughtful writers, the one an outsider, the other belonging to the esoteric school. "If," writes Mr. Walter Bagehot, "all cultivated men speak differently because of the existence of Wordsworth and Coleridge ; if not a thoughtful English book has appeared for forty years without some trace for good or evil of their influence ; if sermon-writers subsist upon their thoughts ; if 'sacred poets' thrive by translating their weaker portions into the speech of women ; if, when all this is over, some sufficient feast of their writing will ever be fitting food for wild musing and solitary meditation ; surely this is because they possessed the inner nature—'an intense and glowing mind,' 'the vision and the faculty divine.'"[1] Julius Hare, in his dedication of "*Guesses at Truth*" to William Wordsworth, writes, "You and he [Coleridge] came forward together in a shallow, hard, and worldly age—an age alien and almost averse from the higher and more strenuous exercises of imagination and thought—as the purifiers and regenerators of poetry and philosophy. It was a great aim, and greatly have you both wrought for its accomplishment. Many, among those who are now England's best hope and stay, will respond to my thankful acknowledgment of the benefits my heart and mind have received from you both."[2]

All this is strong language, but not too strong for the facts of the case. Wordsworth and Coleridge have exercised a deeper and a stronger influence—an influence that is increasing rather than decaying—upon the more thoughtful part of their countrymen than any other writers who have come under our notice in this volume ; and, what is more to the point, the Church of the future was largely being moulded, not at Lambeth and Bishopthorpe, but at Rydal Mount and Highgate, by men who little dreamed that they were doing anything of the kind.

---

[1] *Literary Studies*, i. 28 : "The First Edinburgh Reviewers." This was written in 1855. It illustrates, by the way, another great change which has taken place in the estimate of another poet, who was in one sense a disciple of Wordsworth. In the clause about "sacred poets thriving by translating the weaker portions of Wordsworth's poetry into the speech of women," the writer refers especially to John Keble, as another passage in his very able *Studies* shows beyond a doubt. Would any writer in 1892, of equal calibre, now write of Keble as Mr. Bagehot wrote in 1855?

[2] *Guesses at Truth*, 2nd edit., 1st series, 1838.

The influence of the third member of the great triumvirate upon the Church was far more simple and direct, but far less potent in the long run. Unlike Wordsworth and Coleridge, *Robert Southey* (1774-1843) was essentially a man of his own time. There is nothing complicated either about his character or his writings. When he had once settled down, after his early escapades, into a steady, old-fashioned orthodoxy, he simply expressed the sentiments of hundreds and thousands (only in much better language than they could have used), in fact, one might almost say, the sentiments of the majority of his countrymen. For, though its enemies were blatant and noisy, I believe the Church of England, after all, reflected the feelings of the nation of England. Southey's poetry counts for little, at any rate in this connection, but his prose was excellent—in fact, in its way, the best that was then written; and it was always on the side of Church and State. Perhaps he went a little too much in one rut, and could appreciate no good outside it. There was some truth in the reproof which he received on the publication of his " Life of Wesley "—" Thou hast nothing to draw with, and the well is deep." Coleridge, by the way, who admired his friend's book enthusiastically, was quite alive to this weakness. But it was no slight advantage to the Church, always to have on her side, as a warm and conscientious defender, one of the most charming and industrious writers of the day; while his own spotless and nobly unselfish life would have been a real credit to any religious community to which he might attach himself.

Before quitting the great writers in general literature who made the first thirty years of the nineteenth century one of the most brilliant of all eras in literary annals, special notice should be taken of a point to which attention is drawn by a thoughtful writer in 1841. It is what he calls "the increasing tendency of true poets among us to the Christian religion." "To detect this," he proceeds, "we need not have recourse to works professedly religious. With the exception of Byron, Shelley, and Keats, no poet of any consideration has appeared in England this century whose works, taken as a whole, have a tendency to alienate men from the faith. . . . Their poetry is on the side of God and of good, not of the devil and evil."[1] Not only is this perfectly true, but the importance of the exceptions all melts away when we look into their history. Byron, Shelley, and Keats all died young. The longest-lived of them, Byron, only reached the age of thirty-six, Shelley only thirty, Keats hardly twenty-six. Why, at that age, Coleridge was prophesying that "the age of priesthood would soon be no more, and the torch of superstition be extinguished for ever;" railing at "the dear-bought grace of cathedrals," and "the supple dulness which loses half its shame by wearing a mitre where reason would have placed a fool's cap!" Southey's religious views were in a vague and unsettled state. Writing of the latter at the age of thirty-two, his son and biographer has a passage which is worth quoting, as it bears upon others besides Southey. "His religious views during middle life were settling down into a more definite shape, and were drawing year after year nearer to a conformity with the doctrines of the Church of England. . . . Many whose mental and social qualifications he most admired were unsettled in their faith, though almost without exception in later life they sought and found the only sure resting-place for their hopes and fears."[2] Now, this is just what none of the three great poets before us had a chance of doing, for they never reached that "later life;" but to one of them, at least, Southey himself anticipated that the change would come. "Here," he writes to his friend Grosvenor Bedford in 1812, "is a man at Keswick who acts upon me as my own ghost would do. His name is Shelley. . . . At present he has got to the Pantheistic stage of philosophy, and in the course of a week I expect he will be a Berkeleyan, for I have put him on a course of Berkeley. I tell him that all the difference between us is that he is nineteen and I am thirty-seven."[3] Scott anticipated a similar change in Byron. "Our sentiments," he writes to Moore, "agreed a good deal

---

[1] *Christian Remembrancer*, vol. i., January to June, 1841, No. ii., Article, "The Religious Poets of the Day," p. 159.
[2] *Life, etc., of Robert Southey*, iii. 6.
[3] *Life*, iii. 325, 326. Mrs. Oliphant remarks on this: "Excellent Southey! He did not suspect how absolutely out of all possibility of resemblance were his own well-ordered conservative character and this wild spirit."—*Lit. Hist. of England*, iii. 47, 48. But, as will appear below, a brother-poet (Robert Browning) thought differently.

except upon the subjects of religion and politics, upon neither of which I was inclined to believe that Lord Byron entertained very fixed opinions. I remember saying to him that I really thought that, if he lived a few years, he would alter his sentiments. He answered rather sharply, ' I suppose you are one of those who prophesy I shall turn Methodist?' I replied, 'No; I don't expect your conversion to be of such an ordinary kind. I would look to see you retreat upon the Catholic faith, and distinguish yourself by the austerity of your penances.'"[1] Robert Browning was of opinion that, had Shelley lived, he would have ranged himself finally with the Christians.[2] It is, of course, impossible to say how far such anticipations might have been verified; but it is also impossible to attach any importance to the opinions on religious subjects of men even of the greatest genius, who had manifestly not studied those subjects with any real, serious application. A poet may be born, not made; but a theologian is made, not born. With respect to Keats, it is doubtful how far he is to be classed among unbelievers. In the words of Professor Masson: "In religious belief, he had no wish to disturb existing opinions and institutions, partly because he had really no such quarrel with them as Shelley had, partly because he had no confidence in his ability to dogmatize on such points."[3] And a very wise diffidence it was. It is really absurd to spend time in discussing what the religious views of a youth of twenty-five, who had never made any special study of the subject, may have been. "Religion," writes another biographer, "unless in certain pictorial aspects, took little hold of him;" and this being so, we may apply to his religion with tenfold force what the same writer most truly remarks about the whole man: "It is madness to speak as though Keats had found his highest life or expression. To be as we find him at twenty-five years of age is mystery enough. God did not give him 'the years that bring the philosophic mind.'"[4]

[1] Lockhart's *Life*, i. 325.
[2] See Professor David Masson's interesting volume, *Wordsworth, Shelley, Keats, and other Essays*: "Shelley," p. 118.
[3] See Masson, *ut supra*, p. 170.
[4] Introductory sketch by John Hogben to the 1885 edition of *The Poetical Works of John Keats*, pp. 32, 33.

One direct outcome of the teaching of Coleridge and Wordsworth was the singularly thoughtful work of the two brothers, *Julius and Augustus Hare*, entitled "*Guesses at Truth*," which first appeared in 1827. Augustus died young, but Julius followed up this early effort (he was only thirty-one when it appeared) by a number of other works which do not come within our period. It was "the more spiritual theology and philosophy" (to use their own words), derived from Coleridge and Wordsworth, which distinguished the writings of the Hares from those of the rising Liberal school to which, broadly speaking, they belonged. It has been noticed in a former chapter how, during the ten or twelve years immediately preceding the Oxford Movement, this seemed likely to become the predominant party in the Church. It was exceedingly active among other ways, in literary work, which was generally of an able, and sometimes of a rather startling, character. *Richard Whately*, after having won his spurs as a defender of Christianity by his "Historic Doubts" already noticed, was chosen Bampton Lecturer in 1822, and, very characteristically, created a flutter in the ecclesiastical dove-cot by taking as his subject "*The Use and Abuse of Party Feeling in Matters of Religion*," and treating it in a way which certainly would not commend itself either to High Churchmen or to Evangelicals. This he followed up in 1825 by a work "*On Some of the Peculiarities of the Christian Religion*," which his old-fashioned readers would, no doubt, consider very peculiar indeed; and this in 1828 by another, "*On Some of the Difficulties in the Writings of St. Paul*," which directly traversed the Evangelical interpretation of St. Paul's Epistles. In 1827 the then comparatively unknown *R. D. Hampden* published his first work, entitled "*The Philosophical Evidence of Christianity*," the true aim of which was not perhaps fully realized until the publication of his Bampton Lectures for 1832, on "*Scholastic Philosophy and Christian Theology;*" his general purport in both seems to have been to show that the theology grew up under the influence of the philosophy—a theory not likely to find acceptance with either High or Low Churchmen. Then came, in 1829, *H. H. Milman's* "*History of the Jews*," about which, as it has been already noticed, it need only be added here that it so far harmonized with the other writings we are now considering, that it was calculated to raise alarm in Orthodox and Evangelical breasts. How far Dr. Pusey's first publication, "*An Historical Enquiry into the Rational Character of German Theology*," can be fairly said to belong to the same category, has already been discussed in an earlier chapter. Dr. Arnold had published the first volume of his admirable "*Sermons preached at Rugby School*" before our period closes, in which only those who can read between the lines will detect anything to which either High or Low Churchmen could object ; and his pamphlet on "*Church Reform*," which to many minds seems adapted to reform the Church from off the face of the earth, just comes within our purview, being the very last work of any mark on a theological subject before the Oxford Movement began.

To sum up this long chapter. When Bishop Hobart visited England in 1823-4, he "spoke" to Thomas Sikes "with much admiration of the varied acquirements, learning, and science of the English clergy ; but he complained that they were too often defective in the peculiar science of their profession—he found very few accomplished theologians."[1] The keen-sighted American undoubtedly hit a blot. Churchmen, lay and clerical alike, were as a body highly accomplished men in many subjects, but not, unfortunately, in theology. One reason of this may undoubtedly be found in the fact that the circumstances of the age did not call forth the exercise of the highest intellectual powers in the service of theology. There was abundance of infidelity to grapple with, but it was flippant and shallow, and its confutation was better adapted for the pen of a "Will Chip" than for that of a Butler or a Waterland. Evangelicalism was a moral and spiritual rather than an intellectual force. The Roman controversy turned rather upon the question as to whether Roman Catholics were to have a vote at elections than as to whether their doctrines were true. If Church literature did not reach a high mark, anti-Church literature certainly reached a still lower one. Cultured men turned their attention to scholarship rather than theology ; it was the age of the Greek-play bishops.

Still, the rapid sketch which has been given will, it is hoped, show that the land was not quite so barren as it has

[1] See Churton's *Memoir of Joshua Watson*, i. 245.

been represented. If there were few really great theologians, there were at least many pious and cultured men who kept up the tradition of the Church of England as a learned Church. It was not an empty boast, but a real truth, which Alexander Knox uttered, when he wrote in 1825, " It is in the Church of England, in which due and proportioned provision is made for both understanding and imagination, that the closest and most unreserved and most cordial union has existed between minds of the first order and the Christian religion."

CHAPTER VII.

THE CHURCH AND EDUCATION.

IN no department of her work was the increased energy of the Church more conspicuous than in that of education in all its branches, from the highest to the lowest. Let us begin with the highest.

UNIVERSITIES AND COLLEGES.

It need scarcely be said that during the whole of our period the two great national Universities were exclusively connected with the national Church. What was done in them, therefore, may be regarded as part of the work of the Church in the most literal sense.

Oxford had reached her nadir in the eighteenth century. Professors who never lectured, tutors who never taught, students who never studied, were the rule rather than the exception. Very eminent men were still to be found among her sons; some were pious and hardy enough to defend their Alma Mater; others indignantly complained of her neglect of her children. The few defences and the many complaints need not be specified, for they do not belong to our period. But an Oxford man must own with shame that, with some honourable exceptions, his University was no credit to the nation during the eighteenth century. But the very commencement of the new century gave a promise of better things. In 1800 examinations began to be made public; by the new examination statute of 1801, honours were to be awarded to those who offered themselves for a stricter examination than the ordinary one; and the first class-list appeared in 1802. The examinations for degrees had degenerated into the merest farce; they had been conducted in private, and the most ludicrous stories (not worth quoting) are told about them.[1] The changes were regarded with suspicion and dislike: the "old *régime* thought it the era of an alarming revolution."[2] But the new system was soon well taken up, as is shown by the mere fact that in 1802 only two men took honours, and in 1832 one hundred and seventy-three. Everybody who has had anything to do with the training of young men knows that at a place like Oxford idleness means mischief; so that if Oxford had done nothing more than offer fresh incentives to study, it would have incalculably raised the moral tone of the place. The colleges followed the lead of the University; indeed, at least in two cases, they gave the lead. Oriel and Balliol had already made college work a reality before the University examinations had become realities; and to the heads of these two colleges, Dr. Eveleigh, Provost of Oriel, and Dr. Parsons, Master of Balliol, in conjunction with the Dean of Christ Church (Dr. Cyril Jackson), belongs the chief credit of giving the stimulus to the University.

We have evidence, both positive and negative, of the improvement which took place. In 1817 Bishop Jebb paid a visit to Oxford, and was so impressed with what he saw, that he wrote to Mr. Butterworth, "The Oxford system of education has certainly received great improvement of late years; to religious instruction, both in the separate colleges and in the public University education, considerable attention is paid. Studious habits are the fashion; scarcely a young man is to be seen in the streets or in the squares of the colleges before two o'clock each day"—with much more

---

[1] Mr. G. V. Cox, writing of the year 1799, after having referred to the farce of examinations at that time, says, "Well might such a state of things expire with the expiring century. The 'New Examination Statute' was already on the anvil, and being worked into shape; Dean Cyril Jackson, Dr. Eveleigh, and Dr. Parsons were labouring hard for the revival of scholarship and the credit of our Alma Mater. Nothing was talked of but the forthcoming statute."—*Recollections of Oxford*, by G. V. Cox, p. 37.

[2] *Memoir of Bishop Copleston*, p. 110. Copleston was a warm supporter of the reform, but he most ably defended the Oxford system of a classical education against the attacks of the *Edinburgh Review*.

to the same effect.[1] Henry Handley Norris wrote to Bishop Hobart in 1820, "Our Universities, Oxford especially, have been repairing the decay of discipline, and of the requisite knowledge for their degrees; and a competent knowledge of the evidences and principles of Christianity is made indispensable to every one."[2] The glimpses we have in the lives of Arnold, Keble, Ward, Newman, and many others, give a wholly different impression of the University from a study of earlier lives.

It is only, however, in comparison with its low condition in the eighteenth century that Oxford can be regarded as in at all a hopeful state in the early part of the nineteenth. It was not yet to any adequate extent availing itself of its unique opportunities as an educator, and least of all as a religious educator, of the flower of the English nation. A vast amount of bigotry and obstructiveness which had been dispelled elsewhere still lingered in its cloisters. A vehement attachment to the Church as it was, was not incompatible with a low standard of religious life. It is to be feared that there is too much truth in Copleston's description of it in 1814 (the year of his election to the Provostship of Oriel): "This place is the head-quarters of what is falsely called High Church principle. . . . But the leading partisans appear to me only occupied with the thought of converting the property of the Church to their private advantage, leaving the duties of it to be performed how they can."[3] Bishop Charles Wordsworth, writing of the Oxford of 1826, says that "religious worship and instruction, however it might wear a fair appearance of formal routine, was essentially deficient, and in no respect satisfactory."[4] A very sad tone runs through all the famous sermons of John Miller, of Worcester College, published in 1830; and though they are not exclusively confined to the state of things at Oxford, it is obvious that he had his own University especially in view. The bad old habits of intemperance had not been rooted out.

[1] See Forster's *Life of Bishop Jebb and Letters*, ii. 302.
[2] *Life of Bishop Hobart*, by John M'Vicar, D.D., p. 492.
[3] Letter to his father, quoted in *Memoir of Bishop Copleston*, by W. J. Copleston.
[4] *Annals of my Early Life*, 1806-1846.

Evangelicalism had produced very little effect at Oxford, and there really was no definite system of faith which at all laid hold of the mind of the University generally. Its religion was a political religion. It could lash itself into a fury when any of the outworks of the Church appeared to be in danger, as it did when Lord Grenville was elected Chancellor in 1814 against Lord Eldon, who had almost all the residents on his side; or when it turned out Peel in 1829 for his conduct in regard to Roman Catholic Emancipation; but of spiritual activity it had very little.

Perhaps, on the whole, Cambridge was not in such crying need of reform as Oxford was; the mere fact that she had begun to make her examinations a reality, and to offer inducements to study in the shape of honours some time before Oxford did, is an indication of this. But, after all, there was not very much to choose between these two Universities in the eighteenth century. The melancholy tale of Gray the poet is taken up by his brother-poet, William Cowper, and then by Mr. Gunning, and then by Professor Pryme;[1] and Simeon's early experiences confirm the impression they all leave, that Cambridge was almost as hopeless an Augean stable as Oxford. The history of our period at Cambridge, no less than at Oxford, is the history of an attempt to cleanse it.

It was partly an advantage, partly a very great disadvantage to Cambridge, that from the first it was a great centre of Evangelicalism, which Oxford never was. On the one hand, it could not but be beneficial to any place, and most of all to a place whose very *raison d'être* was to foster Christian piety as well as sound learning, to have in its midst, and indeed among its leaders, men of such true religious earnestness as Dean Milner, Charles Simeon, Professors Farish, Jowett, Dealtry, and Scholefield. On the other hand, just in proportion to the very goodness of these men and their followers, was the extent of the mischief that was

---

[1] Among other things, Professor Pryme says, "When I first went to Cambridge [about 1800] the habit of hard drinking was almost as prevalent there as it was in country society" (*Autobiographic Recollections*, p. 49); and two pages later, "There was throughout their parties an endeavour to make each other drunk."

done by the violent prejudice raised against them.[1] But this point has been fully explained in the chapter on the Evangelicals.

It must not, however, be supposed that the Evangelicals monopolized all the religion of Cambridge during our period. There were two other religious movements which, while they had much in common with one another, were both quite out of sympathy with Evangelicalism. One was that of the old High Church party, which had no more died out at Cambridge than it had anywhere else. In the earlier part of the century the ablest leader of this party was Herbert Marsh, afterwards Bishop of Peterborough. As Margaret Professor of Divinity, he used the influence which his position gave him against the Evangelicals; he was, beyond all comparison, their most formidable opponent, but his opposition was not of that blind, unreasoning sort, which vaguely stigmatized all spiritual religion as Methodism. His work was eminently *con*structive as well as *des*tructive; he strove, not altogether in vain, to bring his University back into the old paths in which the great Anglican divines of the seventeenth century walked. He was the one man who roused that slumbering lion, Dean Milner, from his repose. The Dean hated controversy much, but he loved the Evangelicals more; and he felt it necessary to draw his sword to meet an adversary well worthy of his steel. Marsh was a man of real learning, a clear writer, and an adroit disputant. He was also a man whose personal character was calculated to commend his opinions. Professor Pryme, having told us that he differed from him in politics and theology, adds, " But his amiability and benevolence in private life attracted the admiration of all who had opportunities of observing him;" and, as an illustration of the reputation and influence which he had at Cambridge, he continues, "When he was elected Lady Margaret Professor of Divinity, so many persons were desirous of hearing his early lectures, that he obtained leave

---

[1] "A young man," writes Charlotte Elizabeth, "could not with impunity be a Christian at either of the Universities."—*Personal Recollections*, p. 57. The biographer of Henry Venn the younger writes concerning the Cambridge of 1814, "The distinction between a 'religious man' and one who was not was in those days very sharply marked, the former being commonly known as Simeonites."— *Memoir of Henry Venn, Prebendary of St. Paul's, etc.*, by W. Knight, p. 21.

to give them from the pulpit of Great St. Mary's, and his audience, including some ladies, nearly filled the church."[1]

During the later years of our period, we have Christopher Wordsworth, Master of Trinity, J. J. Blunt, W. Le Bas, and, above all, Hugh James Rose, among the most prominent of those who were keeping up, or rather spreading, the traditions of the High Church party, which, until the rise of the Tract Movement, was perhaps stronger at Cambridge than it was at Oxford.

The other movement may be directly traced to the influence of S. T. Coleridge and W. Wordsworth, who were among the many distinguished men who left Cambridge without any distinction. The leading spirit of this movement was Julius Charles Hare, who was resident as tutor at Trinity from 1822 to 1832. Among those who were more or less affected by it at Cambridge were W. Whewell, R. C. Trench, and F. D. Maurice. It was not a large body, but it numbered some of the most thoughtful young men at the University.

These special religious movements would not much affect, at least directly, the great mass of the students, but they are significant as indications of the stirring of the dry bones which was going on.

At both Oxford and Cambridge, however, there was much greater reality in the work both of professors and tutors in the early part of the nineteenth than there had been in the eighteenth century, and much more intellectual activity on the part of the undergraduates. Among other symptoms of the latter was the foundation of the "Unions," or debating societies, at both Universities during our period; in these, as a rule, the ablest, and afterwards most distinguished students took the most prominent part. Again, scholarships and fellowships began to be given by merit rather than by favour; and though the "close foundations" were still undisturbed, yet when fairness of selection was exercised within the prescribed limits, competent men could generally be found. Indeed, the evils of the close system seem to me to have affected the country generally more than the Universities themselves. At Oxford, as one of its most distinguished sons has observed, "Middlesex was almost excluded, while

[1] *Autobiographic Recollections of Professor George Pryme*, p. 155.

Lincolnshire was gorged."[1] This was hard upon Middlesex, but not so hard upon Oxford as might have been expected. It is astonishing how many good men were found even in the English Bœotia when (though it must in fairness be admitted that this was not always the case) merit was really made the sole qualification.

The weakest part of the Church's work at both the Universities, as, indeed, throughout the country, was her public services. There were, of course, the show services, as they may be called, at Magdalen and New, Oxford, and at King's, Cambridge; but I can find no attempt whatever to make the ordinary services in the college chapels at either University attractive or effective.[2] This seems all the more strange because compulsory attendance was rigorously enforced; and one would have thought that the church, with her revived life, would not have neglected so powerful an instrument for good. At Cambridge the more piously disposed undergraduates appear to have found their spiritual sustenance at the parish churches rather than at the college chapels.

Besides our two great Universities, several institutions for the religious education of those who were past school age, date from our period. Good Bishop Burgess during his incumbency of the see of St. David's (1803-1825) founded a college at Lampeter for the education of the future clergy of Wales—an institution which happily still exists and thrives. The establishment of the London University, from which all distinctive religious teaching was to be excluded, led to the foundation of King's College in 1828. It is said to have been first suggested in a letter to Mr. (Sir Robert) Peel on the subject of the London University by Dr. D'Oyly, and was

---

[1] Goldwin Smith, *Oxford Essays*.

[2] With regard to Cambridge, Connop Thirlwall writes in 1834, "With an immense majority of our congregation it [College Chapel] is not a religious service at all, and to the remaining few it is the least impressive and edifying that can well be conceived."—Letter to the Rev. Thomas Turton, D.D., on the admission of Dissenters to Cambridge, quoted in *Letters Literary and Theological of Connop Thirlwall*, edited by Perowne and Stokes, pp. 114, 115. But his brother-tutor at Trinity, W. Whewell, demurred to this statement; and the master, Dr. Wordsworth, was so annoyed at the "Letter," that he requested Thirlwall to resign his assistant-tutorship.

intended to supply the Church element which was lacking in that institution. In 1825 the Islington College for the training of missionaries was founded by the Church Missionary Society; and towards the close of our period, a scheme which "had been elaborated by the provident wisdom and munificence of William Van Mildert,"[1] for the education, especially of the future clergy, in a new University at Durham, took definite shape. It is impossible here to enter into a detailed account of these institutions, but they are mentioned as a proof that the higher religious education was a subject that engaged the attention of Churchmen.

PUBLIC SCHOOLS.

The dissatisfaction with things as they were, and the eager desire for reform, which were the ever-growing tendencies during the whole of our period, were nowhere more conspicuous than in the feelings towards our public schools. These great institutions were represented as nurseries of vice, where, beyond a little Latin and Greek, the youth of our upper classes learnt nothing but evil. The deterioration of our public schools seems to me to have been grossly exaggerated, especially on the intellectual side. The fact remains that a very large proportion of the most highly cultured men who flourished during the first half of the present century, received their education at these much-abused institutions. We think of the Cannings, and H. H. Milman, and J. T. Coleridge, and E. C. Hawtrey, and W. M. Praed, and Arthur Hallam, and G. C. Lewis, and W. E. Gladstone at Eton; of Byron, and Peel, and Palmerston, and the Drurys at Harrow; of S. T. Coleridge, and C. Lamb, and T. F. Middleton at Christ's Hospital; of Page Wood, and G. Moberly, and the Wordsworths at Winchester; of Butler and his brilliant scholars at Shrewsbury; of R. Southey at Westminster; of Thirlwall, and Julius Hare, and Grote, and the Waddingtons at Charterhouse; and of countless others; and we feel at once the absurdity of supposing that no education worthy of the name was given at our public schools. The curriculum was undoubtedly much narrower

[1] Burgon's *Lives of Twelve Good Men:* "Hugh James Rose," i. 181.

than it is now; but it is a great question whether it did not gain in depth what it wanted in breadth, and whether a thorough knowledge of a few subjects is not a better mental training than a smattering of many. The life was undoubtedly rougher than it is now, both among the boys themselves and in the relationship of the masters to them; flogging was universal, and was at least as often applied for the correction of intellectual as of moral offences; so essential to discipline was it thought, that Southey was expelled from Westminster because he called it, in print, an invention of the devil. But life was rougher in every department, not in schools only; and this rough training produced some wonderfully good results. The weakest part of the public-school system was its directly religious training. Evidences of this are only too strong and numerous. "It seems incredible," writes Mr. Maxwell Lyte in his "History of Eton College," "that there should ever have been an entire absence of religious teaching at the greatest school in Christian England; yet such, from all accounts, must have been the case at Eton until about fifty years ago."[1] This was written in 1875. The present Dean of Ely, Dr. Merivale, gives an equally unsatisfactory report of the religious state of Harrow from 1818 to 1825, and adds, "Let me contend, however, for the undoubted fact that the low state of feeling at Harrow in my time was shared by the public schools generally throughout the land."[2] Harrow ought to have been in better case; for at the very time of which the dean begins to write (1818), Mr. Cunningham, a leading Evangelical, became vicar of the parish, and was soon afterwards appointed a governor of the school; and at least two other good Evangelicals, Mr. Batten and Mr. Phelps, were popular housemasters. Indeed, Harrow was in consequence the only public school against which the Evangelicals did not steadily set their faces—at least, for a time; but about 1825, Harrow, which had been very prosperous at the beginning of the century, began to decline, one of the reasons given being that "the religious world, as represented by Mr. Wilberforce

[1] *A History of Eton College*, 1440–1875, by H. C. Maxwell Lyte, p. 370.
[2] See *Harrow School and its Surroundings*, by Percy M. Thornton, pp. 241–243.

and his associates, had declared against the prevailing system."[1]

So many dreary details have been given in a former chapter of the unsatisfactory state of public worship generally, that it is not necessary to inflict upon the reader a fresh list in connection with public schools. Just one testimony may be quoted, to which it may be added most truly—*ex uno disce omnes*. The writer is referring to a period a few years later than that with which this work is concerned, but what he says applies *à fortiori* to the earlier period,[2] for matters certainly had grown better, rather than worse, in his day. "Words cannot describe," writes Mr. Beresford Hope respecting Harrow in the thirties, "the dreariness of the worship offered to us in my days. One rustic, battered gallery filled up the west end of the rear of Harrow parish church, and served for the upper boys; another stifling and cavernous gallery was hitched into the north aisle for the lower boys. The worship took no account of the needs and peculiarities of schoolboys, but was merely the parish worship of which they were casual spectators. The worship, too, was conducted under pronounced Low Church influence, and was far from attractive."[3]

This want of what may be called "the plant" was the rule, not the exception. When Dr. Arnold went to Rugby in 1828, it is mentioned, as an exceptional case, that he found not only "commodious buildings, but (what was not then usual) a chapel."[4] The other religious provisions were of a piece with the provisions for public worship. We are told on all hands that religious instruction was not only infrequent, but of the driest and dullest description when given; and the complaint is fully borne out by a glance at the few

---

[1] *Harrow School and its Surroundings*, p. 248.

[2] In fact, an even worse account is given by the Dean of Ely in the passage referred to in the preceding note.

[3] Letter to the writer inserted in the *Life of Bishop Christopher Wordsworth* (1st edit.), p. 84.

[4] Article on Dr. Arnold in *Dictionary of National Biography*. Mr. Percy Thornton dwells on the disadvantage which Dr. Joseph Drury, a really good man, who exercised great influence over his pupils at Harrow, laboured under, from having "no pulpit of his own from whence to deliver the teaching which experience bade him impart."—*Harrow School and its Surroundings*, p. 206.

school-books dealing with divinity which still remain, of the date of the late eighteenth or early nineteenth century. A little before our period, S. T. Coleridge's master at Christ's Hospital (Dr. Boyer) could devise no better expedient for dealing with his pupil's precocious infidelity than to flog it out of him ; and Coleridge declares, not at all ironically, that it was the only just flogging he ever received. The method was a thoroughly characteristic one up to the time of the revolution wrought by Arnold. It was no part of a boy's duty to think for himself; he was simply to follow in the beaten track, and if he diverged from it, why, of course, he was to be flogged, and there was an end of it. With the same unreasoning obedience, he was to go through the prescribed course of the Established Church, but there was no need of any special preparation. The late Bishop of St. Andrew's (Dr. C. Wordsworth) tells us that when he was confirmed at Harrow, in 1824, he had had " no preparation." " All that my tutor did for me was to ask whether I knew my Catechism. In no case," he adds, "so far as I can remember, was Confirmation followed up by the reception of the Holy Communion ; in short, as regards the school, it was, I fear, a thing unknown."[1] An opposite, but quite as objectionable an arrangement appears to have prevailed at Winchester, as we learn from a curious letter from the Master of Trinity to his son, Christopher Wordsworth, which implies that the elder boys were expected to communicate at the rare celebrations, whether they were confirmed or not. " Till you have been confirmed," he writes in 1823, "it is more correct that you should not receive the sacrament ; and I have written, therefore, to Dr. Gabell, to beg him, if it be not wholly inconsistent with the rules of the school, that he will dispense with your attendance."[2] For other instances of the unsatisfactory state of religion at our public schools, the reader must be referred to the professed histories of those institutions.

It is surely not the mere partiality of an old Rugbeian which places in the very forefront of the reformers of our public schools the name of Thomas Arnold. His claims to

[1] *Annals of my Early Years*, by Bishop Charles Wordsworth, p. 21.
[2] See *Life of Christopher Wordsworth, Bishop of Lincoln*, p. 23 (1st edit.).

this pre-eminence are so manifest that it is quite unnecessary to exalt him, as has been sometimes done, at the expense of others. We can well understand, for instance, Mr. Gladstone, with his recollection of what Dr. Hawtrey had done at Eton, writing, "The popular supposition is, that Eton (from 1830 onwards) was swept along by a tide of renovation due to the fame and contagious example of Dr. Arnold. But this, in my opinion, is an error. Eton was in a singularly small degree open to influence from other public schools."[1] And Bishop Charles Wordsworth: "As Stanley's 'Life of Arnold' is widely read, I must qualify the impression which Moberly's letter conveys in justice to other school reformers, and not least to Moberly himself. The truth is, there was a general awakening, which in many instances, as with us at Winchester, *partook decidedly of a Church character*, such as Arnold's teaching and example did not."[2] But without drawing any invidious comparisons, let us see what Arnold's work was. When he was a candidate for the head-mastership of Rugby in 1827, his friend, Dr. Hawkins, prophesied of him in his testimonial that if he were elected, he would "change the face of education all through the public schools of England;" and it was mainly on the strength of this prophecy that he was, though very late in the field, elected. This fact is significant, as showing how the need for a change was recognized. In fact, Arnold was not only the right man in the right place, but also the right man at the right time. The fields were ripe and ready for harvest, and it only remained for the proper sort of reaper to enter in and gather the harvest. Reform was in the air; let the reformer come, and he would be met half-way. The place, too, as well as the time, was suitable. Rugby was already a sufficiently important school to allow him ample scope for his experiment; but it had the advantage of not being hampered by ancient traditions which it is exceedingly difficult to break through, while there was no other authority strong enough to thwart him. We have only to compare Dr. Arnold's efforts at Rugby with those of Dr. Hawtrey at Eton while Dr. Goodall was provost, to perceive

---

[1] Quoted by the Rev. F. St. John Thackeray in the *Dictionary of National Biography*, under "Hawtrey, Edward Craven."

[2] *Annals of my Early Life*, by Bishop Charles Wordsworth, p. 278.

the difference. A biographical notice of Dr. Arnold by one of his most distinguished pupils remarks on the simplicity of Arnold's method.[1] But simplicity is often a mark of genius ; and, simple as it seems, it was a stroke of genius to show, as Arnold began by showing, confidence in the boys, and to utilize the system of monitors, or, as they are called at Rugby, præpostors, and turn the elder boys from the natural enemies into the most valuable friends of the masters. But Arnold could never have afforded to place implicit confidence in the boys unless he had won *their* confidence. The transparent honesty and reality of the man, his ardent piety without a tincture of cant in it, his thorough knowledge of boy-nature, his happy combination of strictness and tenderness, impressed them, and they came to regard him with a feeling almost akin to worship. It has been asserted that the Arnold of Dean Stanley was an ideal Arnold, not the real man ; but such an idea could only have come from those who knew him as a friend or acquaintance, not from a pupil. Quite apart from the glamour which his most fascinating biographer has thrown over him, we have only to consider his own words and deeds, and the testimony—nay, the very *existence*—of such men as his many distinguished pupils became, to realize the power of the man. Arnold in the common-room at Oriel, and Arnold in the big school, or the school-chapel, or the school-house, or above all, in the sixth-form schoolroom at Rugby, were different men. Dr. Arnold's work must not be limited to his own pupils ; he was not only a trainer of boys, but a trainer of their trainers. If Rugby did not affect so much the older foundations like Eton and Westminster, it was certainly the mother of many younger institutions which have become almost as large and as important as their parent. At Marlborough, Clifton, Haileybury, and many other schools, the influence of Arnold at second-hand might be distinctly traced. And it is difficult to exaggerate the importance of that influence. It was, as it were, purifying the life of the nation at its source. The public-school system, in spite of its detractors, has too firm a hold upon Englishmen ever to be displaced. The public-school boys of one generation are the leading men of the next. And as the Duke of Wellington said the Battle

[1] Mr. Theodore Walrond, in *Dict. Nat. Biog.*: "Arnold, Thomas."

of Waterloo was won in the playing-fields of Eton, so the great battle of life is fought, and won or lost, by those whose character is formed, for good or evil, at our public schools.

The grammar schools, and private adventure schools, which supplied the education of the great middle-class, from the lesser gentry—a race that has almost died out—to the small tradesmen, were more closely connected with the Church than they are now. The head-masters of the vast majority of the endowed grammar schools, and in many cases the "ushers" also, were *ex-officio* clergymen; and the masters of a great number of the private adventure schools were either the incumbents or the curates-in-charge of the parishes in which they dwelt. The Vicar of Doncaster—which was even then a considerable town—kept a very flourishing academy during the later part of our period, and long after. The restoration of our churches has swept away an interesting relic of the connection between the grammar school or the private academy with the church; but many are old enough to remember how in old-fashioned churches there used often to be a square space marked off, different from the ordinary pews, and seated with forms, for the boys of the grammar or other schools of the place. The Holydays of the Church were often the whole holidays of the school; whether the modern arrangement of giving a holiday in honour of a mayor, or some local celebrity, instead of an Apostle be an improvement, need not here be discussed. Both the grammar schools and the private schools were relatively far more important than they are now; the centripetal force which railways have naturally brought into action has affected no institutions more than these schools.

Elementary Education.

The first really systematic attempts to educate the children of the poor only date from the early years of the nineteenth century. There had, indeed, been many laudable efforts long before that time. The Charity Schools, almost all founded by Churchmen, and conducted on strictly Church lines, had flourished all through the eighteenth century, though, like most Church work, more vigorously in the earlier than in the later years of that period ; catechetical instruction in Church, and, later on, Sunday schools, had in some slight degree supplied the want; individual clergymen, either personally or by deputy, had educated their poorer parishioners to a far greater extent than is commonly supposed ; nor should we quite ignore the humble dames' schools, which furnished some sort of mental pabulum in most towns and villages throughout the land. But it is no derogation to these various sporadic efforts to say that they did not, and could not, all put together, effect what was required. .It was, indeed, a gigantic task to do so ; and our forefathers in the eighteenth century were not exactly the men to set their hands to gigantic tasks of this kind.

Probably the revived energy of the Church would have led her under any circumstances to make some special effort in what has from time immemorial been recognized by her as her duty, the Christian education of the poor. But just about the beginning of the century special circumstances arose which both forced, as it were, her hand, and also greatly facilitated her task. These circumstances arose out of the once famous "Bell and Lancaster controversy," which it is necessary to describe at some length. In 1787 Dr. Andrew Bell went out to India as an army chaplain at Madras. He there offered his gratuitous services as superintendent of the education of the boys at the Military Orphan Asylum at Egmore, near the city of Madras. He had so many boys under his charge that he did not know how to deal with them. On one of his morning rides he happened to pass by a Malabar school, where he saw a number of children seated on the ground writing with their fingers on the sand. He went home and told the usher of the lowest class in his own school to teach the alphabet in the same way. The man neglected to do so ; and then the happy thought occurred to the doctor to employ one of the elder scholars to teach the younger in this fashion. The plan was so successful, that he thought what had been done with the alphabet might be done throughout the school. The first boy, John Friskin—his name deserves to be immortalized as the first of the goodly company of pupil-teachers—had been chosen for his aptitude both to teach and to learn, and also for his good character; and the others were selected on the same principles. The effects were rapid and marvellous. Not only was there a great improvement in the instruction, but the moral tone of the school rose; for the pupil-teachers, being invested with a sort of authority, and being chosen for their goodness as well as their cleverness, exercised a wholesome influence out of school, and prevented bullying and immorality. In short, as Dr. Bell's biographer puts it, "the boys managed the school under Dr. Bell's superintendence, who made it the great business and pleasure of his life."[1] The masters did not at once enter into the scheme. One resigned. Another said Dr. Bell was "a very odd kind of gentleman, and very fond of abusing and quarrelling with the teachers." However, the school prospered in spite of recalcitrant masters and its irascible superintendent. It had only been opened in 1789; boy-teachers were introduced in 1791; and in 1792 Dr. Bell wrote to an old college-friend, Dr. Adamson of St. Andrew's, "The conduct of the school, which is entirely in my own hands, is particular. Every boy is either a master, or scholar, or both. He teaches one boy, while another teaches him. The success has been rapid." We have not to take the latter assertion merely on Dr. Bell's own word. In 1796 ill health obliged the doctor to return to England; and the authorities of the asylum resolved, "That under the immediate care and superintendence of Dr. Bell, and the wise and judicious regulations which he has established for the education of the boys, this institution has been brought to a degree of perfection and promising utility, far succeeding what the most sanguine hopes could have suggested at the time of its establishment"—and then follows a vote of thanks. All friction with the masters, too, seems to have been smoothed down; for they wrote, "We, the masters of the asylum, who have had the honour of being under your direction during the time we have been employed as teachers, being apprised of the loss we must shortly sustain by your declining the arduous task of the tuition of this school, which you have so long upheld by your indefatigable attention in establishing the gentle and pious order which now subsists throughout the whole"—another vote of thanks.

[1] Southey's *Life of Dr. Bell*, vol. i.

Immediately on his arrival in England, Dr. Bell published in 1797 an account of what he had done in Madras. "I have printed my essay," he wrote to General Floyd, "on the mode of teaching at the Male Asylum, and have now a design of publishing it. By the end of the next century I hope it will be generally practised in Europe; but it is probable that others will fall upon the same scheme before this be much attended to." To the printer he wrote, "You will mark me for an enthusiast; but if you and I live a thousand years, we shall see this system of education spread over the world." He sent copies of his "Report" to influential persons, and "members of societies for promoting Christianity," and was soon engaged in superintending schools on what was long known as the *Madras System*, in various parts. One of the first thus organized was at St. Botolph's, Aldgate, which was said to be "the oldest Protestant parochial school in London." Then followed the schools in Whitechapel, Gower's Walk, the schools of industry at Kendal, and in 1807 the Royal Military Asylum at Chelsea. In 1811 regimental schools were established by general orders of the Government, on the Madras System, "after the experience" (it is said in the orders) "of its most complete success at Chelsea." The Barrington School at Auckland, founded and munificently endowed by the Bishop of Durham, and many others adopted the system; and nowhere was it more successful than in Dr. Bell's own parish. In 1801 he received the rectory of Swanage from a private patron, Mr. Calcraft, and, after some difficulties, he established the Madras System there. "Enthusiastic as I am," he writes to a friend in 1806, "I am astonished at the event. . . . It is like magic; order and regularity started up all at once. In half an hour more was learned and far better than had been done the whole day before."

This was all very smooth and delightful; but, *surgit amari aliquid.* Dr. Bell's prophecy that "others would fall upon the same scheme before his was much attended to," was fulfilled. In 1798 a poor Quaker lad, barely twenty years of age, named Joseph Lancaster, obtained from his father the use of a room in the Borough Road in the city of London, in which he might keep a cheap school for the poor in the neighbourhood. Scholars came in abundance, but money did not. He could not afford to pay an assistant. "This *compelled* him to make use of the services of his pupils to teach each other as monitors; and this practice, the sheer offspring of necessity, ended in the demonstration and definition of the power of one master to teach hundreds."[1] This, it will be seen, was some years after Dr. Bell had hit upon the same plan—indeed, after he had published in England an account of his experiment in Madras; but there is not the slightest reason for supposing that Lancaster borrowed the main idea from Bell. He *did* borrow several hints from Dr. Bell's account, as he himself gratefully owns. A most friendly intercourse arose between the two educational reformers. In 1804 Lancaster wrote to Bell asking advice, and received a reply which he characterized to Dr. Bell as "thy most acceptable letter." He then went to Swanage to have a personal interview with the doctor; and said to the first person he met there, "I would go to Madras to see him." The next year Dr. Bell published a second edition of the Madras Report of 1797, and sent Mr. Lancaster fifty copies of it; whereupon Mr. Lancaster "sent a deputation of his scholars to wait on him and return him thanks."[2]

But this was the last of the friendly relations between Bell and Lancaster. The apple of discord between them was thrown in this very year (1805) by Mrs. Trimmer. She wrote to tell Dr. Bell what she was going to do, and then appeared a work whose title tells its own tale: "A Comparative View of the New Plan of Education promulgated by Mr. Joseph Lancaster in his Tracts concerning the Instruction of the Children of the Labouring Part of the Community; and of the System of Christian Education founded by our Pious Forefathers for the Initiation of the Young Members of the Established Church in the Principles of the Reformed Religion, by Mrs. Trimmer, 1805." Mrs. Trimmer, it should be remembered, was an educational authority. She was editor of the *Guardian of Education*, and probably knew

[1] *Epitome of Some of the Chief Events and Transactions in the Life of Joseph Lancaster, containing an account of the rise and progress of the Lancasterian System of Education, and the author's future prospects of usefulness to mankind; written by himself, and published to promote the education of his family*, 1833.

[2] Southey's *Life of Dr. Bell.*

very much more about the subject generally than either Bell or Lancaster did. It is not in the least surprising that she should have objected to the Lancasterian System on some points of vital importance; and if she objected it was her bounden duty to make a public protest. For Mr. Lancaster's system was raising a greater sensation than Dr. Bell's. As early as 1803 his institution in the Borough Road had "become a place for strangers to visit as one of London's wonders."[1] In 1805 King George III. and the Royal Family took him under their patronage, and his schools were called "The Royal Free Schools, Borough Road." The powerful *Edinburgh Review* supported him, and he was mentioned in Parliament. Some very eminent clergy, such as the Dean of Westminster (Dr. Vincent), the Bishop of Norwich (Dr. Bathurst), and Archdeacon Wrangham patronized him. The Lancasterian system was introduced into parish schools with the sanction of the clergy—at Hodnet, for instance, by Reginald Heber. Now, it was of the essence of Joseph Lancaster's system that distinctive religious teaching was to be excluded from his schools. "Above all things," he writes, "education ought not to be made subservient to the propagation of the peculiar tenets of any sect beyond its own number." It was not to be irreligious, but it was to be strictly undenominational. This was quite contrary to the views of Churchmen, and Mrs. Trimmer sounded the warning note. Lancaster said she was "a bigot, and having set up to herself that golden image, the Church, she wanted every knee to bow down to it." This really was the question at issue between Dr. Bell and Mr. Lancaster, though it often went off at a tangent into side issues. It is not of any real importance to know how far Lancaster borrowed from Bell, or how far Bell was stimulated by Lancaster; and it is quite unnecessary to awaken the echoes of a bygone controversy which has long ceased to have any interest. But it is a matter of living interest as to whether education is to be conducted on the basis of a definite faith, or whether it is not. As a matter of history, what Mr. Lancaster thought to be the weakness of Dr. Bell's plan, proved to be its strength. "My hat," he writes, "would not

[1] *Epitome, etc., ut supra.*

hinder my entering any house or any nation; but Dr. Bell is tied down to a burden beyond his strength. He is compelled to push a massive old church before him, and to drag a mighty old steeple after him." But it was the massiveness of the old church and the mightiness of the old steeple which were towers of strength to Dr. Bell's designs; and, on the other hand, it was the happy discovery of Dr. Bell which enabled the massive old Church to see its way to doing, on a large scale and in a systematic fashion, that which it had long been attempting to do spasmodically and unsystematically. Lancaster's efforts resulted in the formation of *The British and Foreign School Society*, Bell's in *The National Society*. The former was first in the field,[1] but the latter very soon followed. Churchmen were no doubt stimulated to action by the progress of the British Schools. They would not have been true to their principles if they had not been. For it should be carefully remembered that Mr. Lancaster's system was quite different from that now in use; it did not leave religious instruction optional; it was on a distinctly religious basis, and it was of its essence to inculcate upon the children that different forms of Christianity stood upon the same footing. The Church Catechism, the authorized formula for the instruction of young Churchpeople in the rudiments of the faith, was *absolutely* excluded from the Lancasterian schools.[2] It was no unworthy spirit of jealousy, but simply the logical result of their most elementary principles, which led Churchmen to institute, not so much a rival system, as a system which would at least allow them to teach what they believed to be essential to a proper education. The pupil-teacher arrangement was not the only new feature of the Madras System, but it was the most distinctive, and the one which, above all others, tended

---

[1] That is in fact, though not in name. "The Royal Lancasterian Society" was the name of the first society founded for the spread of schools on Lancaster's system; this was practically the same as that now called "The British and Foreign School Society." The following dates will make the matter clear to the reader:—
1808. Royal Lancasterian Society founded.
1811. National Society founded.
1814. British and Foreign School Society founded.

[2] See *Instructions for forming and conducting a Society for the Education of the Poor according to the General Principles of the Lancasterian or British Plan*, 1810.

to simplify the task. Language hardly seemed strong enough to express the value which was attached to it. It "gives to the master the hundred eyes of Argus, the hundred hands of Briareus, and the wings of Mercury;" it is "the lever of Archimedes transformed from matter to mind;" it is "the steam-engine of the moral world."

We may now dismiss the once famous controversy, about which it was said that "as much ink had been shed in the wars between Bell and Lancaster, as blood was shed in the civil wars between the Houses of York and Lancaster,"[1] and turn at once to the foundation of the *National Society*. And, first, a word must be said about the name. In 1808 Dr. Bell published a work entitled "A Sketch of a *National* Institution for training up the Children of the Poor." On June 13, 1811, Dr. Herbert Marsh, then Margaret Professor of Divinity at Cambridge, preached a sermon at the meeting of Charity School children at St. Paul's, which he entitled "The National Religion the Foundation of National Education." There is a singular interest in this sermon, apart from its intrinsic merits (which are great), partly because it forms a sort of link between the old ideas of education and the new—for it was preached for the *Charity Schools* (the old system), and just on the eve of the foundation of the *National Schools* (the new); and partly because the title was taken up as the watchword of the new society. In the very first Report of the National Society the principle is set forth "that the national religion should be made the groundwork of national education." Some desired to make the work a department of the S.P.C.K.; others showed a nervous apprehension of the name "national," on the highly characteristic ground that it might be supposed to be borrowed from the odious French nomenclature; but happily the counsels of neither prevailed. There is, indeed, one objection to the name; it might lead—in fact, *has* led —to misconception. "The word 'national,'" it has been argued, "implies that the schools belong to the whole nation, not to the Church, which is certainly not, as a matter of fact, though you may think it ought to be, coextensive with the nation." This idea is not altogether exploded even yet.

[1] See *Epitome, etc., ut supra*.

The National Society traces back its origin to a meeting of three friends, Joshua Watson, Henry Handley Norris, and John Bowles, at the house of Mr. Watson in London. After much correspondence, a preliminary meeting was held, October 16, 1811, with the Archbishop of Canterbury (Dr. Manners-Sutton) in the chair. The Prince Regent and one at least of the Royal Dukes had promised their patronage—a matter of great importance in those days, when the Church thought she could do nothing without the help of the State. Another meeting was held on October 21, at which the archbishop again presided, and the rules by which the new society was to be governed were framed. The archbishop then issued a circular to those who were elected on the committee. Joshua Watson was the first treasurer, Henry Handley Norris the first secretary; but when the society was organized, the latter resigned in favour of the Rev. T. T. Walmsley.

The most prominent names among the founders of the society were just those which are familiar to the reader of the second chapter of this work—John Bowdler, Christopher Wordsworth, Archdeacons Cambridge and Watson, Sir John Richardson, Sir James Allan Park. All the bishops were to be *ex-officio* vice-presidents and members of the committee. A very great share in the success of the undertaking is to be attributed to Archbishop Manners-Sutton. He was much more than a mere figure-head, who would look well on the prow of the good ship; he in many respects acted rather as an able and judicious pilot, who guided it safely through rocks ahead which it met with in its course. His services, though now forgotten, were warmly recognized at the time. The biographer of Joshua Watson, in speaking of the markedly Church character which was impressed upon the institution from the very first, adds, "It may be that the personal dignity and authority of the then archbishop made it easier for him to do this than it would have been for another in the same position."[1] Archdeacon Cambridge, writing of a painful dispute which had arisen at a meeting, the details of which do not appear, adds, " The manly, firm, and judicious manner in which our president spoke will perhaps prove a sort of

[1] *Memoir of Joshua Watson*, i. 112.

rallying-point among us ;"[1] and Dr. Bell himself ascribed "the extraordinary prosperity of the institution to the steady and uniform support of the late primate" (Dr. Manners-Sutton).[2] This "extraordinary prosperity" will be illustrated by the following figures. Bishop Howley, in his Charge to the clergy of London in 1818, tells us that at the first annual meeting of the National Society in June, 1812, there were 52 schools, containing 8000 children in union with it— a goodly number considering that the society had then existed for little more than half a year; in 1813 there were 240 schools with 40,000 children; in 1818, 1249 schools with 180,000 children. "This," he adds, "does not include schools not formally *united* to the society, but following its principles, and, in most, its mechanical practices, the number in such schools exceeding 50,000." Six years later we find no less than 3054 schools in connection with the society, and 400,000 children instructed in them; while there were no less than 800,000 educated through the medium of the Church of England.[3] In other words, in one year the work of the society increased five-fold, within the next five years five-fold again, and within twenty years from its foundation not very much less than a hundred-fold—indeed, including its indirect work, quite a hundred-fold. Such wonderfully rapid development it would be hard to parallel in the annals of any institution. All this while, it must be remembered, the national schools had received no help whatever from the State, for it was not till 1833 that the Government doled out its first small grant.

The efforts of Churchmen to promote education thoroughly deserved the success they met with. They were well represented at both Universities. At Cambridge Professor Herbert Marsh, one of the ablest writers then resident, was indefatigable. His position gave him access to many whom others could not reach; and he "most effectually recommended the design to the bishops and leading divines of his own University by letters and personal applications."[4] At Oxford, it is interest-

[1] *Memoir of Joshua Watson*, i. 119.
[2] See *British Magazine* for 1832; Article, " Church Reform.'
[3] See a most amusing and instructive paper in the *British Magazine* for 1832, vol. i., entitled " The Idle Church."
[4] *Memoir of Joshua Watson*, i. 106.

ing to note that the two men who, above all others, were instrumental in rendering the highest branch of education efficient, were also the two who, above all others, threw themselves heart and soul into the improvement of its most elementary department. These were Dr. Eveleigh, Provost of Oriel, and Dr. Parsons, Master of Balliol. They both corresponded with the Bishop of London (Dr. Randolph), and were supplied by him with the latest intelligence about the scheme; and Dr. Parsons is said to have framed, conjointly with Joshua Watson, the terms of union for district committees and the trustees of provincial schools.[1] The Hackney phalanx, it is almost needless to say, presented a united front, and fought most manfully and effectively for education, religious and secular, conducted on Church principles. Some of the greatest celebrities of that extraordinarily brilliant period of literature used the magic of their pens on its behalf. Southey wrote it up in the *Quarterly Review* and elsewhere; Coleridge almost deified Dr. Bell; and though Wordsworth, with his eye for the picturesque in humble life, mourned over the displacement of the cottage dame by the trim but rather prosaic figure of what he called " Dr. Bell's teacher in petticoats," he was (as the devoted brother of the Master of Trinity could hardly fail to be) thoroughly on the side of religious education. Dr. Bell himself took an active part in founding and superintending schools. At a meeting of the general committee of the National Society in St. Martin's Library, January 22, 1822, it was resolved "that Dr. Bell be requested to act under the direction of this society as superintendent in the formation and conduct of the central and other schools, to be established by this society, in the metropolis and its vicinity " etc. But, after all, the real secret of the success of the effort was the quiet, unobtrusive help of the parochial clergy in their respective parishes. We have abundant evidence of this, both generally and in detail. We hear of Richard Mant, when he was Vicar of Great Coggeshall, being "active in the superintendence of daily schools, whose efficiency he greatly promoted by establishing them upon the Madras System, then lately introduced by

---

[1] *Memoir of Joshua Watson*, i. 119.

Dr. Bell and adopted by the National Society;"[1] of Edward Stanley being equally active at Alderley,[2] and Reginald Heber at Hodnet.[3] The bishops did their best to impress this duty upon the parochial clergy, and, in one instance at least, set them an excellent example. The Bishop of Carlisle (Dr. Samuel Goodenough) "did not content himself with merely establishing the Carlisle Diocesan School. He rode over from Rose Castle for the purpose of attending the school every Thursday and Saturday. . . . He conscientiously paid to the school most sedulous attention ; giving it his personal superintendence, and spending in it several hours every week."[4] Joshua Watson, whose long and intimate connection with the National Society from the very first enabled him to speak with more authority than most men on such a point, wrote in 1828, "I had seen how deeply the cause of national education was indebted to the parochial clergy."[5] But perhaps the most striking testimony of all is that of Mr. (afterwards Lord) Brougham. He had been one of the warmest and ablest supporters of Lancaster *versus* Bell, the articles in the *Edinburgh Review* on that subject being doubtless from his pen. Hence he was the last person in the world to regard with a favourable eye the efforts of the clergy, who were, of course, as a body, for Bell *versus* Lancaster. But in 1818–19 he was chairman of the Education Committee, and in that capacity was put in correspondence with the whole body of the clergy, and had to investigate closely the state of elementary education throughout the country. The result was that he was converted—temporarily—from an indifferent, if not actually hostile, attitude to one of the most enthusiastic admiration. Those who know what he was before, and what he was after, can only gasp with amazement when they read the language which he used in Parliament in the debate on the education of the poor, June 28, 1820. But there it stands, in black and white, in the pages of Hansard : " Before he proceeded further, he felt it his duty to return his

[1] *Memoir of Bishop Richard Mant.*
[2] *Memoir of Edward Stanley, Bishop of Norwich,* p. 10.
[3] Taylor's *Life of Bishop Heber,* p. 45, etc.
[4] *Life of Isaac Milner, Dean of Carlisle, etc.,* by Mary Milner, p. 285.
[5] *Memoir of Joshua Watson,* i. 296.

most cordial thanks to those reverend gentlemen, without whose assistance they [the committee] could not have advanced a single step towards that part of their labours at which they had arrived—he meant the whole of the clergy of the Established Church. It was, however, quite impossible that any words of his could do justice to the zeal, the honesty, and the ability with which they had lent their assistance towards the attainment of the great object which had been proposed as the result of their inquiries. . . . Another proof of the good will to the cause which he was embarked in was this—that if any one would look through the digest he would find that in many cases a foundation was supported entirely by the charity and exertions of the incumbent himself. When he said this, he spoke of the working parish priests—of those meritorious individuals who, to their great honour, devoted to this laudable purpose a portion of their money and their time. He did not speak of the more dignified prelate, who could not, of course, be expected to reside upon the one particular spot; nor of the pluralist, who could not, if he would, reside there; but he meant the working parish minister—the true and effective labourer in the vineyard. In making this remark he meant no compliment to those reverend gentlemen. It was merely an act of justice towards them. He said thus much in order to make out his case for entrusting the clergymen of the Establishment with the execution of the proposed plan rather than any other body of men in the kingdom." [1]

It will be seen that, like other converts, Mr. Brougham retains some of the old Adam after his conversion—he cannot resist a gibe at the dignitaries and pluralists; and, a little later, an inconveniently accurate gentleman pointed out to him that many of these dignitaries and pluralists, whom he excepts from his panegyric, were, in fact, among the most liberal and powerful supporters of the educational cause.[2] But this is a detail. The broad fact remains that Mr. Brougham's investigations showed him that, after all, the clergy were the best friends of elementary education, and he had the honesty to own it. "That was the most unkindest cut of all" to his

[1] *Parliamentary Debates* in Hansard, June 28, 1820: "Education of the Poor."
[2] See *A Letter to H. Brougham, Esq., on his Durham Speech, and Three Articles in the last "Edinburgh Review" on the Subject of the Clergy*, 1823.

Dissenting friends, with whom he had acted in the Bell and Lancaster controversy; they succeeded in throwing out his bill, but they could not obliterate his words.[1]

At the commencement of the nineteenth century, the Sunday school had become a part of the regular organization of almost every well-worked parish. It was then a far more serious affair than it is now; for, where there was no weekday school, it supplied secular as well as religious instruction to the children. In fact, the Sunday school took up a considerable part of the day. "I should think," writes Bishop Porteus towards the close of the eighteenth century, and his remarks would apply equally to at least the first twelve years of the nineteenth, "that four, or at the most five, hours would be confinement fully sufficient for children engaged during the week in trade or manufacture. In villages, where they are of course more in the open air during the whole week, a little more time may be taken for instruction in the morning and evening." This accounts for a fact that might puzzle the uninitiated. The *generosity* of those who provided Sunday schools at their own cost is a frequent subject of praise. To institute a Sunday school, according to our modern idea of it, does not seem to involve a very ruinous outlay. But when it meant tuition for five, six, or even seven hours in the day, it would naturally cost money; for volunteer teachers could not be expected to devote all that time during their day of rest. In the early part of the nineteenth century, however, it began to be a question whether this combination of secular with religious instruction in the Sunday school should be continued. One of the pioneers of the educational movement was John Poole, a Fellow of Oriel and cousin of Thomas Poole whose name is so closely connected with Coleridge and Wordsworth. In 1803 John Poole took the living of Enmore, in Somersetshire, and at once set himself to the work of elementary education. "He had," we are told, "everything to do himself; and he seems to have begun with

[1] Full details of the early work of the National Society will be found in *Schools for the People*, by George C. T. Barclay (see especially pp. 52-54). The reader is referred to this work rather than to many others which were written from a distinctly Church point of view, because its writer cannot be suspected of any undue partiality to the Church, his sympathies apparently lying in a different direction.

a Sunday school only, where children were taught, not only to read, but even to write and reckon—such as had already existed for some years at Over and Nether Stowey." He began his day school in 1810; that is, more than a year before the National Society was instituted. But in a most interesting work, entitled "The Village School Improved," he still defends the practice of teaching children to write and reckon in the Sunday school—evidently implying that the custom had been impugned. And he does so on grounds which are only explicable by the fact that the Sunday school lasted very much longer than it does now. "It is not possible," he writes, "and, if possible, would not be wise, to confine a child's attention through the whole day to the subject of religion. To preserve his mind alert and active, and in a disposition to profit by instruction, there must be variety in his occupations."[1] The present writer, when he first took a country living in 1860, found several old persons still alive who had received their only education, secular as well as religious, in the Sunday school, where they had been taught by a hired teacher.

The Bell and Lancaster controversy exasperated a dispute which had existed long before their times. The dispute was, whether the children of different religious sects should be educated in one school with Church children, and be conducted thence to their separate places of worship. In 1791 we find the Bishop of Norwich (Dr. Horne) protesting against the practice in weighty words. "How can you," he asks, "bring them all up in a catholic way unless you have one catholic, that is, universal, general, common religion in which to bring them up? To be of a catholic spirit is to unite in that one religion, not to jumble together the errors, inconsistencies, and heresies of all. This must end in indifference. It may bring the people of the Church nearer to the sects;

---

[1] *Thomas Poole and his Friends*, by Mrs. Henry Sandford, vol. ii. p. 127 —an admirably written book, full of the most interesting information, not only about Wordsworth and Coleridge—especially poor Coleridge—but also about village life generally at the close of the eighteenth and the beginning of the nineteenth century. We find in this book an illustration of what has been said about the expense of keeping up a Sunday school in those early days. Thomas Poole writes to Dr. Majendie, Rector of Over Stowey, thanking him for the great and unprecedented liberality he had shown.

but the present times do not give us any hope that it will bring the sects nearer to the Church." His successor took a different view twenty-two years later (1813). "No inconvenience whatever," says Bishop Bathurst, "can (as it strikes me) possibly arise to our Establishment from the mixture in those schools of the children of Churchmen with those of Dissenters, if proper care be taken that *all* children indiscriminately are obliged to attend some place of religious worship approved by their parents or guardians." A most interesting discussion, conducted in a very courteous, Christian spirit, took place in the previous year (1812) between the Bishop and the Dean of Carlisle, the bishop (Dr. Goodenough) maintaining that the children ought to go to church, the dean (Dr. Isaac Milner) contending that they should be allowed to go to the place of worship which their parents preferred.[1] The controversy on the point had by this time reached its acute stage, as it formed one of the chief questions at issue between the advocates of the Lancasterian and those of the Madras System. Mr. Lancaster had made the most elaborate arrangements for settling this matter in his own way. "On being admitted into the school the children of Churchmen should be registered as such, and the children of Dissenters as such. On Sundays they should assemble at the school in the morning and afternoon, previous to the hour for Divine service, and the children of each denomination should be conducted from thence to their respective places of worship." It was part of the rules that "they are to attend places of worship, and two inspectors are to attend every Sunday, morning and afternoon, to see they do."[2]

An alarm was raised about Sunday schools, which one would have been inclined to set down as a mere bugbear, had it not been that one of the ablest and coolest divines of the period evidently thought there was some ground for it. Bishop Horsley was the last man in the world to speak without the book, and we cannot dismiss his distinct assertion that they were in danger of being made nurseries of Jacobinism as a mere groundless alarm. In his Charge of 1800

---

[1] See *Life of Isaac Milner*, p. 278.
[2] *Instructions for forming and conducting a Society for the Education of the Poor according to the General Principles of the Lancasterian or British Plan.*

he says, " In many parts of the kingdom new conventicles have been opened in great numbers, and congregations formed of one knows not what denomination. The pastor is often, in appearance at least, an illiterate peasant or mechanic. The congregation is visited occasionally by preachers from a distance. Sunday schools are opened in connection with these conventicles, and there is much reason to suspect that the expenses of these schools and conventicles are defrayed by associations formed in different places. . . . It is very remarkable that these new congregations of non-descripts have been mostly formed since the Jacobins have been laid under restraint of two most salutary statutes known by the names of the Sedition and Treason Bill; a circumstance which gives much ground for suspicion that sedition and atheism are the real objects of these institutions, rather than religion. Indeed, in some places this is known to be the case." Looking down with lofty contempt upon these poor sectaries from the serene heights of the Episcopate, the great prelate may have been inclined to exaggerate the danger; but that he wholly invented it I cannot for a moment believe. Sunday schools might easily be made a convenient pretext for inculcating principles which could not have been safely proclaimed in more suspected quarters. But the best way of meeting the danger was by furnishing counter-attractions. This the bishop felt, and so he urges his clergy "by all means in their power to promote the establishment of Sunday schools in their respective parishes." He indignantly denies that he had, as had been reported, " spoken in the House of Lords with disapprobation of all these institutions." " I spoke of them on that occasion as I have always spoken, and always shall speak, as institutions that may be very beneficial or very pernicious, according as they are well or ill regulated, and placed in proper or improper hands." This was a great relief to the friends of Church Sunday schools, for Bishop Horsley's was a great name. "Have you," writes Mrs. Trimmer (one of the ablest and most energetic workers in the Sunday school, as well as the week-day school field) to William Kirby, the excellent Vicar of Barham,[1] "read the Bishop of Rochester's Charge? It gave me particular pleasure

---

[1] See *supra*.

to find that he had been misrepresented in respect to his enmity to Sunday schools."[1] Bishop Horsley did not stand alone in his apprehensions. Even Bishop Porteus, who was justly regarded as the great patron of Sunday schools, was cautious about joining the movement. " He did not," writes his biographer, "give it his public approbation till time and experience and more accurate inquiry had enabled him to form a more decided judgment of its real value and probable effects."[2] The alarm, however, about Sunday schools fostering Jacobinism or any kind of disloyalty, soon passed away. They were regarded, at any rate, as harmless, though some still doubted whether they provided the best means of doing the Church's duty towards the young.

It would be invidious to select any individual Sunday schools for special comment; but there was one of so exceptional a character that it may be noticed without casting any slur upon the rest. This was the famous Jesus Lane Sunday school at Cambridge, founded in 1826 or 1827, the speciality of which was that it was entirely managed and supported by undergraduates, who elected a committee and a superintendent out of their own body. ·This school gave an impetus to the cause which extended far beyond the limits of Cambridge. It formed, in fact, a sort of voluntary training college for clerical teachers. The undergraduates who took part in it became, almost to a man, clergymen in due course, and so went forth to their various parishes thoroughly *au fait* in one most important branch of clerical work; in many a town and village throughout the length and breadth of the land the influence of the Jesus Lane Sunday school was felt. The history of its rise cannot be given better than in the language of its historian, the Rev. C. A. Jones.[3] "In 1827 a small party of undergraduates, chiefly members of Queen's College, used to attend the Sunday and Thursday evening

---

[1] *Life of the Rev. William Kirby*, by John Frewen, p. 212.
[2] *Life of Bishop Beilby Porteus*, by the Rev. R. Hodgson, prefixed to a new edition of the bishop's works (6 vols.), p. 93.
[3] *A History of the Jesus Lane Sunday School, Cambridge*, by C. A. Jones, 1864. A new edition was published in 1877, with revisions and additions by the Rev. R. Appleton, Fellow, Senior Dean and Tutor of Trinity, and the Rev. E. Leeke, now Chancellor of Lincoln Cathedral (son of W. Leeke, one of the original founders).

services at Trinity Church, and they often returned together to the rooms of one of their number to talk over Mr. Simeon's sermon. . . . One bright Sunday morning in spring, Wright and five others were in a summer-house at the back of 7, Tennis Court Road, where Wright lodged, and he remarked, ' It seems a pity that we do not spend some part of our time in Sunday school teaching;' and he put it to the others whether there was any parish in the town where teachers were required. One replied in the negative, adding he had gone round to all the churches, offering his services, but they had been declined. It was then remarked, 'Barnwell is a sadly neglected place, and near enough ; why not try to do something there ?'" It was then determined that a school should be held in Cambridge, and the Barnwell children invited to attend. A meeting-house belonging to the Society of Friends in Jesus Lane was mentioned as a suitable place if it could be obtained. One of the original teachers writes of the parish which the school was intended to benefit, " It was in a most neglected state ; there were no schools whatever, except, I believe, a very small one in connection with the Methodist chapel in Wellington Row." A number of zealous undergraduates, several of whom were more than usually advanced in life, occasionally heard of and visited cases of unheeded sickness and distress. The heathenish and dissolute state of the parish was thus forced upon their notice. The young men went out, two and two, to canvass Barnwell for scholars. The University was canvassed for teachers, and the school commenced with two hundred and thirty-two children ; the number of teachers soon increased to thirty-two, the majority being supplied by Queen's College. The first superintendent was James Wright, of Queen's, who, according to the foregoing account, originated the idea. It is doubtful, however, whether that honour does not belong to William Leeke, who, in a letter inserted in the history by Mr. Jones, claims the first idea of establishing a gownsman's Sunday school. It is always difficult to settle a question of priority in such a case, but at any rate we shall be safe in attributing the institution of the school chiefly to Wright, Leeke, J. M. and Abner Brown, Carr, Harden, Colley, and C. L. Higgins. Permission was obtained from Professors Scholefield and Farish for the children to attend their churches, St. Michael's and St. Peter's; and it is worth noticing that there never seems to have been any collision with the clergy. This is illustrated by the fact that the introduction to the history of the school was written by the Rev. J. H. Titcomb, who became Incumbent of St. Andrew the Less, the proper name for the parish commonly known as Barnwell, and that he writes in the highest terms of the good work that was done by the school. It may be added that though the school obviously arose from the Evangelical party, the originators being, as we have seen, "Simeonites," and the college which supplied the lion's share of the teaching staff being that stronghold of Evangelicalism under the rule of Milner, Queen's, the teachers were by no means confined to that school of thought. One of the early superintendents (1834) was Spencer Thornton, a Rugby disciple of Dr. Arnold; and many names will be found among the later teachers which do not belong to the Evangelical school. Dean Burgon, in his delightful account of "Charles Longuet Higgins," shows that the school really began in 1826, and that "the good layman" was one of the original founders. We learn also that the founders "took counsel with dear old Mr. Simeon," and other colleges as well as Queen's were well represented.[1]

Before quitting the subject of elementary education, mention must be made of its extension at both ends of the scale, in the form of training schools for teachers, and infant schools for those who were too young to enter into the regular curriculum. The training of masters and mistresses formed part of the original scheme of the National Society; the adoption of the Madras System rendered this work peculiarly necessary; for pupil-teachers, unlike poets, are made, not born; and the teachers have the making of them. Up to 1816, the teachers in connection with the National Society were trained at the central school in Baldwin Gardens, the proportion of masters to mistresses being about four to one. These central or model schools were established in the larger provincial towns

[1] J. W. Harden belonged to St. John's, C. L. Higgins to Trinity, James Colley to St. John's. See Dean Burgon's *Lives of Twelve Good Men*: "Charles Longuet Higgins," ii. 369–372 (1st edit., 1888).

on the principles of the central school in London.[1] Infant schools began to be established in England about the year 1818, and by the close of our period had become very general and efficient. They took up by degrees the work which had before been done in the dames' schools. They were the only part of the new educational plans which met with the full approval of Bishop Jebb. He took a great interest in them, and so did John Davison, the tutor at Oriel in its palmiest days, who thus became acquainted with education in its most advanced and its most rudimentary stage.[2] Finally, it may be noticed that our period just extended long enough to commencement of State aid, the first education grant— a very modest one of £20,000, " to encourage the building of school-houses "—being made in 1833.[3]

[1] See *The Schools for the People*, by George C. T. Barclay, p. 440. "Infant Schools and Dame Schools," p. 401.

[2] See Forster's *Life and Correspondence of Bishop Jebb*, i. p. 256. Bishop Jebb wrote to his friend, Mr. J. H. Butterworth, in 1818, "For the lowest class of life, we have everywhere established those Lancasterian and national schools; admirably constructed in material discipline, but, it is to be feared, quite destitute of that discipline which is mental."—*Id.*, ii. 315.

[3] See *History of England from the Conclusion of the Great War in* 1815, by Spencer Walpole, iii. 485.

CHAPTER VIII.

CHURCH SOCIETIES.

FOREIGN MISSIONS.

IT was said at the beginning of the last chapter that the revival of Church energy was in no department more conspicuous than in that of education; but the advance was almost as marked in the department of mission-work.

The Society for the Propagation of the Gospel in Foreign Parts had gone bravely on, through all the discouragements of the eighteenth century, doing what she could; and, considering how she was thwarted on all sides in that time of spiritual torpor, it is wonderful how much she did effect. Without derogating from the work done by other agencies, it ought in common fairness to be noted that, from the nature of the case, she has a claim upon the gratitude of Churchmen which later agencies cannot have. For it was she who kept alive the flame amid the darkness, when there was no other light burning.[1] It is surely a popular error to suppose that her work was intended to be confined to British colonists; it is true that the first object referred to in the charter of the society is "the providing of learned and orthodox ministers for the administration of God's Word and Sacraments among the king's loving subjects in the plantations, colonies, and

---

[1] Some of the Evangelicals themselves felt this, though of course their warmest sympathies were with the Church Missionary Society. Thus we are told that the Rev. Basil Woodd "ever spoke with the greatest veneration of those two institutions (the S.P.G. and the S.P.C.K.), as the oldest of our religious societies, and as honourably engaged in promoting the work of Christian philanthropy while all was darkness and coldness around."—Wilks' *Memoir of the Rev. Basil Woodd*, p. 43. Josiah Pratt seems to have felt the same.

factories beyond the seas belonging to the kingdom of England;" but it is added, "and the making such other provision as may be necessary for the propagation of the gospel in those parts." And this has always been understood by the society itself to cover the propagation of the gospel among the heathen.[1]

It might have been anticipated that the foundation of a new Church society for the conversion of the heathen would affect injuriously the older institution; but the very reverse was the case. The progress made by the S.P.G. during the first thirty-two years of the nineteenth century was marvellous and unprecedented. In 1800 there were 197 subscribers; the annual subscriptions were £457 16s.; altogether, the income of the society, including legacies, interest of money in the funds, etc., amounted to £4983 2s. 8d.; it maintained forty-three missionaries and thirty-two catechists and schoolmasters. In 1832 the society raised seventeen times as much money, had thirty-seven times as many subscribers, and employed four times as many missionaries as it did in 1800.[2] In the same year (1832), Dr. Croly, a cool observer, in preaching on behalf of the S.P.G. at Northfleet, called attention to the fact that "within a single generation the number of the society's missionaries, catechists, and schoolmasters had been increased tenfold." Its work in India alone was enormous; but that had better be noticed separately, because it worked there in conjunction with other agencies. But one point should be noticed, which applies with especial force to India, though it also extends generally to all mission-work. The even then venerable society rendered, perhaps unconsciously, a service to the cause of Christian missions which it is difficult to put into words, but which was of the very last importance. It was this. The cuckoo cry of Methodism was raised with considerable effect against the increased efforts made from the commencement of the nineteenth century for the conversion of the heathen. The S.P.G. alone was above suspicion on this score. It was impossible

---

[1] This point is well brought out in the Rev. J. S. M. Anderson's *History of the Colonial Church*, vol. iii. p. 27, etc. (2nd edit., 1856).

[2] See a striking article in the *British Magazine* for 1832, vol. i., entitled "The Idle Church."

for the keenest scent to detect in it any traces of that hated thing, Methodism; so when the society threw the ægis of its protection upon the new efforts, it stamped them, as it were, with the mark of respectability. The enemy might say that the workers were enthusiasts, but could not deny that they were Churchmen; whereas the Churchmanship of those who were connected with other agencies was in the eyes of many a very doubtful quantity.

What has been said about the wonderful progress of the S.P.G., which was essentially a High Church society, as high Churchmanship was then understood, may appear inconsistent with the assertion of an honoured veteran in the field of literature, whose authority it would be indeed presumption to dispute. "The young," writes Miss C. M. Yonge, respecting the period now under consideration, "will hardly believe how, in spite of the existence of the S.P.G. and the periodical Royal Letter for it, any real active interest in missions to the heathen seemed to be confined to the Evangelical party."[1] Perhaps the discrepancy may be in part explained by the fact that the Evangelicals were not unfriendly to the old society, though of course their chief interest was centred in the new society, which arose with the beginning of the new century under their auspices.

The Church Missionary Society was the outcome of an agitation that had been going on for some time. The idea of making fresh exertions for the conversion of the heathen had been, in various ways and places, a subject of discussion before it took definite shape in the formation of a new Missionary Society. In 1783 the Eclectic Society was formed in London "for religious intercourse and improvement," and it made a special exception to its strict rule against the admission of visitors in favour of missionaries. In 1786 it proposed the following question: "What is the best method of planting and propagating the gospel in Botany Bay? With a view to the Rev. R. Johnson [a missionary with strong Evangelical views in New South Wales] whose company is desired for the next meeting." In 1789, February 6, the discussion was, "What is the best method of propagating the

[1] *Musings on " The Christian Year" and " Lyra Innocentium "* (1871), introd. p. xl.

gospel in the East Indies?" In 1791, October 14 and November 7, "What is the best method of propagating the gospel in Africa?" the Rev. Melville Horne, chaplain at Sierra Leone, being present as a visitor. In 1795 the London Missionary Society was formed, in which the Evangelical clergy joined with Dissenters; but the union was not altogether satisfactory, the clergy holding that "their missionary operations ought to be carried on in direct connection with, and under the sanction of, the Church to which they belonged." In the same year (1795, May 6 and 7) an important advance was made at a clerical meeting held at Rauceby, in Lincolnshire, the incumbent of which, Mr. Pugh, was a leading Evangelical. Three pillars of the Evangelical cause, Thomas Robinson of Leicester, Samuel Knight of Halifax, and Charles Simeon of Cambridge, were present. Mr. Pugh announced that a sum of £4000 had been left to him by a clergyman of the name of Jane, "to be laid out by him to the best advantage to the interests of religion," and the opinion of the meeting was asked, whether the money might be most advantageously given to any scheme already in progress, or to any new object at home or abroad? If to the last, "the thing desirable seems to be, to send out missionaries." The question was adjourned to the next meeting, September 30 and October 1, 1795, when it was fully discussed in different shapes. One who was present at the first of the Rauceby meetings tells us that it was agreed that Simeon and Robinson should consult leading laymen such as Wilberforce and Grant, and he adds, what has been repeated by many, that "the first idea of forming a Church Missionary Society was suggested at Rauceby."[1] This is so far true that from that time the subject began to take a more tangible form; but, on the one hand, the idea of making fresh efforts for the conversion of the heathen had, as we have seen, been broached some years before; and, on the other, nothing definite was decided at

---

[1] See *Memoirs of the Rev. Charles Jerram*, p. 147. It is evidently the spring, not the autumn meeting at Rauceby, to which Mr. Jerram refers, because he says that Mr. Robinson was present; and Mr. Henry Venn the younger expressly states that Mr. Robinson was *not* present at the autumn meeting, and that he *was* at the spring one. See appendix to *Funeral Sermon on the Rev. Josiah Pratt*, which gives a most clear, full, and concise account of the origin of the Church Missionary Society.

CHURCH MISSIONARY SOCIETY.

Rauceby. On February 8, 1796, the subject was again brought before the Eclectic Society by Mr. Simeon; a discussion arose, and, according to Mr. Basil Woodd, who took notes of what occurred, "this conversation proved the foundation of the Church Missionary Society." But it was really not until April 12, 1799, that the society was actually formed. The matter had been carefully gone into at the meetings of the Eclectic (February 18, March 18, and April 1, 1799), and then "on the 12th of April a meeting was held at the Castle and Falcon Inn, Aldersgate Street, 'for the purpose of instituting a society amongst the members of the Established Church for sending missionaries among the heathen.' The Rev. John Venn was in the chair, and detailed the object of the meeting. Sixteen clergymen (nine of them belonged to the Eclectic Society) and nine laymen composed the meeting."[1]

From what has been said in a former chapter, the reader will see that no man could be fitter to preside on such an occasion than John Venn. To him more than to any one else the rules on which the society was worked are due. He had submitted them all to the important meeting of the Eclectic Society on March 18; and, as is gratefully acknowledged in the Jubilee volume of the Church Missionary Society, he was "a man of such wisdom and comprehension of mind, that on that memorable occasion he laid down before a small company of fellow-helpers those principles and regulations which have formed the basis of the society." He suggested, among other things, that it should be "conducted on the *Church principle*, but not on the *High Church* principle," thus differentiating it from the London Missionary Society on the one hand, and the S.P.G. on the other, though it was not intended to come into collision with either. Application was then made to the Archbishop of Canterbury (Dr. Moore), who declined to identify himself with the society, but promised "to watch its proceedings with candour." The Bishop of London (Dr. Beilby Porteus) was also cautious, but he went a step further than the primate, promising to ordain young men from the Elland and other societies who were recommended to him, for missionary work; and this

[1] Rev. H. Venn, appendix, *ut supra*.

S

was perhaps as much as could be expected, even from a prelate with Evangelical proclivities, in those days.

Although the formation of a new society was agreed to in 1799, the society itself was not actually established until the spring of 1801 ; and even then it limited its functions to one quarter, and was called simply "The African Institution," or "The Society for Missions in Africa and the East." The wider title, "Church Missionary Society," was not given to it until 1812. The first secretary was Thomas Scott, who also preached the first anniversary sermon, and is justly regarded as one of the fathers of the society. But shortly afterwards he left London, and the secretaryship devolved upon Josiah Pratt. Here, again, the reader of a former chapter need not be told that Mr. Pratt was emphatically the right man in the right place. He had the full confidence of the Evangelical party ; his piety was unquestioned ; he had a clear, calm head, and would do nothing rashly ; he was a man of culture, had wide sympathies and a conciliatory tone, and, what was of the utmost importance for the post, was an excellent man of business, having been trained in his youth for mercantile pursuits. The society owed not a little of its success to this combination of qualities in Josiah Pratt, who was its secretary for no less than twenty-two of the most critical years of its existence. He was well supported by his assistant, Edward Bickersteth, who became his successor in 1824.

The lay element was always strong in the Church Missionary Society, and from the very first it received invaluable aid from William Wilberforce, Henry Thornton, Zachary Macaulay, James Stephen, Thomas Babington, Granville Sharp, the three Grants, and other prominent Evangelical laymen. They had a peculiar interest in it, because it just fitted in with their own favourite project, the abolition of the Slave Trade. For the purpose of providing for those liberated slaves, who, by the law of our land, gained freedom when they touched the British shore, and who were rather an embarrassment to their friends,[1] a colony had been established at Sierra Leone, chiefly through the efforts of Henry Thornton, whose work is thus described by one who

[1] See on this point Sir G. O. Trevelyan's *Life and Letters of Lord Macaulay*, i. 11, 12.

had an intimate acquaintance with the Evangelical leaders of the time: "During the long struggle [against slavery], while he reflected calmly on the best mode of civilizing Africa, he selected colonization as the most effective instrument. He hoped, by the contact of industrious settlers, to stimulate the native mind; and by opening channels of legitimate trade to withdraw the natives gradually from the traffic in human flesh. Thus rose the colony of *Sierra Leone.* In this labour Thornton had the assistance of Wilberforce, Babington, Granville Sharp, Z. Macaulay, and others; but *he* devised the plan, formed the company, collected the capital, and arranged the constitution, etc."[1] "Of Granville Sharp's countless schemes of benevolence," writes one who also knew the mind of the man from personal acquaintance, "that which he loved best was the settlement at *Sierra Leone* of a free colony, to serve as a *point d'appui* in the future campaigns against the Slave Trade."[2] We can thus well understand how Sierra Leone was selected as the first field for the operations of the new society. It was not, however, until 1804 that a mission was commenced there by sending out two Lutherans, English clergymen apparently not being available; and for some years this was the only mission of the society. The close connection—indeed, the identity—of the abolitionists with the principal supporters of the Church Missionary Society rendered the choice of Sierra Leone a desirable one for some reasons; but for others it was an unhappy one. The climate was so unhealthy that few Europeans could bear it, and it was called "The White Man's Grave;" and the material upon which the missionaries had to work was singularly unpromising. On these points it will be well to quote the testimony of a true friend to the society. "Nearly twelve years had elapsed since the society had sent its first missionaries to the shores of Africa. These years had been a season of trial and disappointment. Many labourers had fallen victims to the deadly climate, and no remarkable success attended the efforts of those who were

[1] *William Wilberforce, his Friends and his Times,* by J. C. Colquhoun (1866), p. 286.
[2] Sir James Stephen, *Essays on Ecclesiastical Biography :* "The Evangelical Succession," p. 317 (2nd edit., 1850).

left. The natives, whose only intercourse with Europeans had been through the medium of the Slave Trade, were completely debased by its pernicious influence. They desired nothing but gain and traffic from the missionaries who came to offer them instruction. These discouragements had so disheartened them, that they had almost given up preaching to adults, and confined their attention to the schools in the settlement."[1] Then Mr. Bickersteth went out in 1816 to inspect the mission, and infused so much new life into the work, that "the scenes in West Africa recalled the primitive days of Christianity."[2]

The next mission-field of the society was New Zealand, which was occupied in 1809. The reason why this field was chosen was that a devoted Evangelical, Samuel Marsden, held the appointment of chaplain in New South Wales. Then began the work in India; but that must be considered separately, because it was a work in which both the great Church Societies, and other agencies outside both, had a share.

The Church had always recognized her duty both to supply the means of grace to the British residents in India, and also to evangelize the native races; but in both departments she had been checked by causes over which she had no control. The early years of the nineteenth century witnessed a marked change in public opinion as to both duties; and the credit of bringing about the change is greatly due to the Evangelical party, though at the same time it was precisely because Churchmen of a different type took the matter up that the changed feeling towards mission-work in India became permanent and widely influential. This apparent paradox will be best explained by a statement of facts.

In 1786 a Cambridge graduate named David Brown went to Bengal as a chaplain under the East India Company. He was at once placed in charge of a large orphan house at Calcutta, was appointed chaplain to the Brigade at Fort William, and had the care of the mission church; and in 1794 he was made presidency chaplain. In these various spheres he acquired great influence at Calcutta and the

[1] *Life of Edward Bickersteth*, i. 274, 275. [2] *Id.*, p. 311.

neighbourhood, which was enhanced by the respect felt for his personal character. He had been from his boyhood trained by the rising Evangelical school, having been educated first at the Grammar School, Hull, under Joseph Milner, and then at Magdalen College, Cambridge, a stronghold of Evangelicalism. He was deeply influenced at Cambridge by Charles Simeon, but it does not appear that Simeon was the means of his obtaining the Indian chaplaincy. But just about the time when Brown went out, Simeon *did* begin to exercise a great, almost a paramount, influence in the appointment of East India chaplains. A strong Evangelical element began to be infused into the directorate of the East India Company. This was chiefly due to the Grants, one of whom is said by Lord Macaulay to have afterwards "ruled India from Leadenhall Street." In 1787 an address was sent to Simeon, signed by David Brown, Charles Grant, and two others, asking him to become "the agent at home" for a projected mission to the East Indies. The scheme fell through, but from that time forward the appointment of East India chaplains was virtually in the hands of Simeon for several years; and the Evangelical element in India was still further strengthened when Sir John Shore, afterwards Lord Teignmouth, succeeded Lord Cornwallis as Governor-General. Chaplains suited Simeon's purpose better than avowed missionaries, for missionaries were in some quarters looked upon with suspicion, and had no such definite status as chaplains in the East India Company's service enjoyed. Meanwhile, William Wilberforce was doing *his* part at home in his own sphere. In 1793 he succeeded in passing through the House of Commons a resolution "that it is the peculiar and bounden duty of the Legislature to promote by all just and prudent means the interest and happiness of the British dominions in India; and for these ends such measures ought to be adopted as may gradually tend to their advancement in useful knowledge, and their religious and moral improvement;" also that "sufficient means of religious worship and instruction be provided for all persons of the Protestant communion in the service and under the protection of the East India Company in Asia, proper ministers being from time to time sent out from Great Britain for these purposes." But this resolution remained nugatory, the Company successfully opposing any practical effort to carry it out. However, in 1797, the Court of Directors issued an order for building churches in the Presidency of Bengal; but this, too, lay dormant for twenty years.[1] Before the beginning of the nineteenth century, Lord Wellesley had founded a college at Fort William, intended, according to Dr. Buchanan, "to enlighten the Oriental world." "Our hope," writes the doctor to the Archbishop of Canterbury in 1805, "of evangelizing India was once founded on the college of Fort William." Of this college David Brown was made provost and C. Buchanan vice-provost in 1800. The East India Company had made some little provision for supplying the spiritual wants of their European servants by the establishment of a few chaplains at each of the three Presidencies;[2] and these chaplaincies had, as we have seen, fallen to a great extent into the hands of Simeon. In the mission-work in India a very important place must be assigned to the memorable "five chaplains" in Bengal—David Brown, Claudius Buchanan, Henry Martyn, Daniel Corrie, and Thomas Thomason. All were avowed Simeonites, and all but the first owed their appointment directly to Simeon. David Brown was like a father to the rest, receiving each into his house when he first came out to Calcutta, and guiding him as to his future work. Of Claudius Buchanan more will be said presently; of Daniel Corrie it may suffice here to say that in a quiet, unpretentious way he was, according to a shrewd and competent observer, "perhaps the most useful man of the Established Church who ever set foot in India."[3] The same writer thinks that "his character was one which the Christian world never thoroughly appreciated as it really deserved;" but this was written when Corrie was still an obscure chaplain. He afterwards came into far greater prominence. Three times he was placed in the trying position of having to take, as far as he could, a bishop's place when he was not yet a bishop; and he was afterwards most deservedly appointed first Bishop of Madras.

[1] See *Memoir of John, Lord Teignmouth*, by his son (1843), vol. ii. pp. 109-112; also Moule's *Simeon*, p. 114.
[2] *Memoir of Claudius Buchanan*, by Hugh Pearson, i. 310.
[3] Mrs. Sherwood. See her *Life* (*chiefly Autobiographical*), *edited by her daughter, Sophia Kelly* (1854), p. 382.

Thomas Thomason was one of the most intimate, trusted, and beloved of all Simeon's friends; and his work in India, in which he was nobly aided by his devoted wife, fully justified the high expectations which his patron and quondam vicar at Cambridge had raised concerning it. Henry Martyn requires a longer notice. He has been termed "the one heroic name which adorns the annals of the Church of England from the days of Elizabeth to our own."[1] This was written more than forty years ago, since which time the Church can claim many heroic names. But even then it depends upon what we mean by "heroic" whether the sweeping assertion is in any sense true. If we mean simply a brave Christian, there had been many such. But if we mean by it a man whose character and career strike the imagination like a hero of romance, then, if not the *one*, his is perhaps the *most* heroic name which the hagiology of the Church can produce. His actual services to the Church in foreign lands consisted chiefly of his very valuable work in translations of the Holy Scriptures; for he was called to his rest before he reached his prime, and before he had time to make much progress in the way of evangelization. But there is a dramatic interest about his whole life which at once arrests attention, and which has done more than almost any other life has done to stimulate missionary zeal in others. Leaving the prospect of a brilliant career at home—for he was Senior Wrangler, First Smith's Prizeman, writer of the Latin Prize Essay, and Fellow of St. John's College, Cambridge; leaving also the prospect of domestic happiness—for his romantic love of Lydia Grenfell was not the least conspicuous feature in his life—he went forth, fired with an ardour which was then comparatively rare, and with a full conviction that the time had come when the earth should be filled with the knowledge of the Lord as the waters cover the seas. Mrs. Sherwood, the popular authoress, was introduced to him at Dinapore when he first went out to India; and he produced a different impression upon her in some respects from that which his own somewhat gloomy journal, and, still more, that of Lydia Grenfell, would convey. Those journals quite harmonize with what

[1] *Essays on Ecclesiastical Biography*, by Sir James Stephen: "The Evangelical Succession," p. 336.

Mrs. Sherwood writes in the following passages: "The conversion of the natives and the building up of the kingdom of Christ were the great objects for which alone that child of God seemed to exist then, and, in fact, for which he died. . . . Henry Martyn was one of the very few persons I ever met who appeared never to be drawn away from one leading and prevailing object of interest, and that object was the promotion of religion. He did not appear like one who felt the necessity of contending with the world and denying himself its delights, but rather as one who was unconscious of the existence of any attractions in the world, or of any delights which were worthy of his notice." But then she goes on: "When he relaxed from his labours in the presence of his friends, it was to play and laugh like an innocent, happy child, more especially if children were present to play and laugh with him. . . . Mr. Martyn is one of the most pleasing, mild, and heavenly-minded men, walking in this turbulent world with peace in his mind and charity in his heart."[1] He is the fascinating gentleman as well as the saint. He presents that curious combination which we have noticed in many others among the Evangelicals. Look at him from one side, and he appears to be "hampered by a narrow and gloomy spirit, made morbid by incessant self-introspection and a dread of everything bright and cheerful."[2] Look at him from another, and he seems to have a bright, sunny nature, tempered and mellowed rather than obscured by his creed. His aspirations were high and his hopes sanguine. He thought that the threefold translation of the Bible into Persian, Arabic, and Hindustani would be "the downfall of Mohammedanism," if properly done; and it was to the Mohammedans especially that he desired to make the gospel known, having more hope of them than of the Hindus. He set himself to the work of translation; completed the Hindustani New Testament in 1810, lived to add to it the Arabic and Persian versions, and made such progress in the Hindustani Old Testament that his work has proved helpful to later translators; all this was done in five or six years, in the midst of incessant active

---

[1] See the *Life of Mrs. Sherwood* (*chiefly Autobiographical*), *by her daughter, Sophia Kelly*, pp. 339-341.
[2] See *Under His Banner*, by H. W. Tucker, p. 24.

work, and when the seeds of the illness which proved fatal to him were already sown. He was, in the strictest sense of the word, a martyr to his work, for it was with a view to perfecting himself in the language that he went to Persia on his way home in 1811. There, "at Tocat, on the 16th of October, 1812, either falling a sacrifice to the plague, which then raged there, or sinking under that disorder which, when he penned his last words, had so greatly reduced him, Henry Martyn surrendered his soul into the hands of his Redeemer."[1] The dramatic element which is seen all through Martyn's life is visible also in the last scene. He died in absolute solitude spiritually. "Where he sank into his grave, men were strangers to him and to his God;" but it had not always been so. For Tocat is the ancient Comana, near to which St. Chrysostom died and was buried fourteen hundred years before, and where Basil and his saintly sister, Macrina, were brought up, and where they were both buried. The brief and romantic career of the saint and scholar—we may almost add martyr—made Martyn's a name to conjure with more than that of many who did a greater actual work for the mission cause in India; more, for example, than that of the last of the five famous chaplains, Claudius Buchanan, who of all others stirred most the public mind on the subject of Christianity in India.

Claudius Buchanan was sent to Queen's College, Cambridge, at the expense of Henry Thornton, having been previously "brought to the feet of Christ by a sermon of John Newton's, preached in St. Mary Woolnoth."[2] At Cambridge he of course joined the Simeon party, and went out to India as one of "Simeon's chaplains" in 1796. He became vice-provost of the college at Fort William; and in 1803 he conceived the idea of proposing "certain subjects for prize competition, connected with the civilization and moral improvement of India, to the universities of the United Kingdom." He carefully avoided mentioning the name of Christianity, and certainly seems to have acted with caution

---

[1] Notice of Martyn's death, quoted in an extremely interesting sermon on *Martyn translating the Scriptures*, preached by Canon Edmunds in Truro Cathedral on October 16, 1890.

[2] *Charles Simeon*, by H. C. G. Moule, p. 146.

as well as liberality (the sum he offered was £1600), for he consulted the Governor-General of India (Lord Wellesley) and the Episcopal Bench at home. The Bishop of London (Dr. Beilby Porteus) took a warm interest in the matter, and at his suggestion Dr. Buchanan wrote a "*Memoir of the Expediency of an Ecclesiastical Establishment for British India*"—a book which created a great sensation and raised a violent opposition. He was encouraged, however, not only by the Bishop of London, but also "by subsequent communications with the Marquis Wellesley," to call the attention of the nation to this subject. The book was published in England in the autumn of 1805. Meanwhile his offer of prizes, though declined by Oxford on a point of form, was accepted by Cambridge and some of the public schools; and in 1805 another offer of £500 was accepted both by Oxford and Cambridge. The plan drew out the energies of men who afterwards became eminent; among others, Thomas Rennell, Charles Grant, Francis Wrangham, John William Cunningham, all of whom have been already mentioned in this work, and Hugh Pearson, afterwards Dean of Salisbury and the donor's biographer. Buchanan's letter to the Archbishop of Canterbury, in 1805, is worth quoting. "It is," he writes, "the opinion of intelligent men in India that the formation of an extensive ecclesiastical establishment is a measure which, during the present revolutions of Europe, will tend greatly to confirm our dominion. . . . The toleration of all religions, and the zealous extension of our own, is the way to rule and preserve a conquered kingdom. It is certain that men are ruled virtually by the Church, though ostensibly by the State, in every country. The seeds of moral obedience and social order are all in the Church. . . . One observation I would make on the proposed ecclesiastical establishment. A partial or half-measure would have no useful effect. A few additional chaplains could do nothing towards the attainment of the great object in view. An archbishop is wanted for India; a sacred and exalted character, surrounded by his bishops, of ample revenue and extensive sway; a venerable personage whose name shall be greater than that of the transitory governor of the land; and whose fame for piety, and for the will and power to do good, may pass throughout every region. We want something royal, in a spiritual and temporal sense, for the abject subjects of this great Eastern empire to look up to." [1]

In 1806 Buchanan visited a colony of Syrian Christians— the Christians of St. Thomas, a body which had existed in Travancore, in South India, for nearly fifteen centuries—and this visit confirmed his most sanguine anticipations.

Unfortunately, during the same year (1806) a mutiny had broken out among the natives at Vellore, and their disaffection was attributed, by men who had been hostile enough to the evangelizing plan before, to their fears lest they were going to be Christianized by force.

In 1807 appeared a "*Letter to the Chairman of the East India Company, on the Danger of interfering in the Religious Opinions of the Natives of India, and on the Views of the British and Foreign Bible Society as directed to India.*" The pamphlet certainly contained a view of the case which was not to be lightly set aside. "A convulsion," it argued, "from religious sources no human efforts may be able to subdue. The natives think as much of their religion as we of our constitution. As long as we continue to govern India in the mild and tolerant spirit of Christianity, we may govern it with ease ; but if ever the fatal day shall arise when religious innovations shall set foot in that country, indignation will spread from one end of Hindostan to the other, and fifty millions will drive us away." The first edition of the pamphlet was anonymous ; but the second, which was called for within a year, came out under the name of " Thomas Twining, late senior merchant of the Company's Bengal Establishment." The pamphlet was immediately answered by Mr. Owen, secretary of the Bible Society, and by Bishop Porteus, who replied with great effect in that vein of irony, instances of which have already been given.[2]

---

[1] Quoted by the Rev. Hugh Pearson, in his *Memoirs of the Life and Writings of the Rev. Claudius Buchanan* (i. 377), from which much of the information in the preceding and following pages is derived.

[2] Bishop Porteus' work was published anonymously, under the title of *A Few Cursory Remarks on Mr. Twining's " Letter to the Chairman of the East India Company," by a member of the Bible Society ;* Mr. Owen's was entitled, *Address to the Chairman of the East India Company, occasioned by Mr. Twining's " Letter,"* by J. Owen.

Mr. Twining was followed by Major Scott Waring, who attacked Dr. Buchanan and his friends still more fiercely in two pamphlets, entitled respectively "*A Vindication of the Hindoos from the Expressions of Dr. Claudius Buchanan; with a Refutation of his Arguments for an Ecclesiastical Establishment in British India : by a Bengal officer;*" and "*Observations on the Present State of the East India Company; with Prefatory Remarks on the alarming intelligence lately received from Madras as to the general disaffection prevailing amongst the natives of every rank, from an opinion that it is the intention of the British Government to compel them to embrace Christianity: by Major Scott Waring.*" The latter speedily passed through four editions. It boldly recommended a clean sweep. "If," says the writer in his preface, "India is worth preserving, we should endeavour to regain the confidence of the people by the immediate recall of every English missionary, and by prohibiting every person of the Company's service from taking a part in circulating the translations of the Scriptures in Hindostan." Dr. Buchanan and Mr. Brown in Bengal, and Dr. Kerr in Madras, were the chief objects of the writer's attack. "These three gentlemen are clergymen of the Church of England, but classed under that description of our clergy who are termed *Evangelical.*" "*Subsequent,*" he says, " to the religious meeting at Vellore, I can affirm, from undoubted authority, that in every quarter of Hindostan the increase of English missionaries, and the gratuitous circulation of such parts of the Scriptures as are already translated, have caused the greatest alarm." He strongly reprobated Dr. Buchanan's visit to the Syrian Christians in Travancore, declaring that "the time chosen for visiting them was most impolitic and inopportune —soon after the religious meeting at Vellore ; and as if we were determined to increase the alarm of the people of India as to our future designs, Dr. Kerr, a Madras clergyman, was sent upon a mission to the same district." All this is in the preface. In the pamphlet itself he attacks Dr. Buchanan's proposal of " an ecclesiastical establishment, to consist of an archbishop, three bishops, and an indefinite number of clergy." "The British subjects in India," he says, "are only thirty thousand; so two clergy at each capital, and twelve chaplains for the army, the present establishment, are quite enough; but his object is to convert fifty millions to Christianity. He thinks that if his plan were adopted, India would conclude that, if they could not be reasoned out of the religion of their forefathers, they would be compelled to embrace Christianity. If the natives were to see a number of clergymen spread over Hindostan, paid and encouraged by the British Government, they would feel the most serious alarm." And then he has recourse to the *argumentum ad crumenam*. " The expense would amount to £200,000 a year. The archbishop would be next in rank to the Governor-General, with a salary double that of his Grace of Canterbury; the bishops could not have less than £15,000 a year each; and the inferior clergy could not be expected to leave England at less than £1600 a year."

This pamphlet has been quoted at some length, because it represents the views held by many. It is astonishing how soon a reaction arose; but in 1808 Major Scott Waring was a representative man, and required answering. He *was* answered, very effectively, by Lord Teignmouth, who, as an ex-Governor-General, could of course write with authority on the subject. Lord Teignmouth's "*Considerations on communicating the Knowledge of Christianity to the Natives of India*" is not the work of a visionary enthusiast, but a very sensible, moderate, and well-written work, calculated to carry conviction to reasonable minds. "I was not," he says in his Advertisement, "surprised, after perusing it [the 'Observations,' etc.], to find that it had made a considerable, though different, impression on the feelings of various readers. But I was astonished and concerned afterwards to learn that his recommendation for recalling every English missionary, and for prohibiting the circulation of the Scriptures in India, had become the subject of serious public consideration." In the body of the pamphlet, he wisely grasps his nettle. The sting of the indictment undoubtedly lay in the Vellore incident. "It appears," he writes, "by a proclamation of the Madras Government in December, 1806, that many of the native troops under its authority had given credit to malicious reports, circulated by disaffected persons, that it was the wish of the British Government to convert them by forcible means to Christianity. The object of the proclamation was to compose an existing ferment, which in the preceding month of July had exploded in a meeting at Vellore." But he affirms later on that "in all the inquiries made at Fort St. George into the causes of the mutiny at Vellore, in the course of which great numbers of the native troops were examined, the increase of missionaries, and the circulation of the Scriptures, religious tracts, and pamphlets, were never once mentioned by any of them." One more passage from this valuable pamphlet may be quoted, as showing the reasonableness of the writer as well as his ability. "If," he argues with convincing force, "Major Scott Waring's representation of the case could be made out, it would prove that we have been guilty of this act of violation, ever since we possessed the dominion of India, by tolerating missionaries and the circulation of the Scriptures, both which we had the power to prevent." And then he admits, "Anxious as I am that the natives of India should become Christians, from a regard for their temporal and eternal welfare, I know that this is not to be effected by violence, nor by undue influence; and although I consider this country bound by the strongest obligations of duty and interest, which will ever be found inseparable, to afford them the means of moral and religious instruction, I have no wish to limit that toleration, which has hitherto been observed with respect to their religion, laws, and customs. On the contrary, I hold a perseverance in the system of toleration not only as just in itself, but as essentially necessary to facilitate the means used for their conversion; and those means should be conciliatory under the guidance of prudence and discretion. But I should consider a prohibition of our Holy Scriptures and the recall of the missionaries most fatal prognostics with respect to the permanency of the British dominion in India." Lord Teignmouth acted throughout in this moderate spirit. Though he was heartily in favour of Dr. Buchanan's views, he did not approve of the methods the impulsive doctor took for carrying them out. His extensive knowledge of India made him doubt the practical wisdom of provoking public discussion. He advised Mr. Pearson to omit from his prize essay an intended recommendation to institute a college similar to that afterwards founded by Bishop Middleton, on the ground that the public mind was not then (1805) ripe for such an institution, and he wrote to Mr. Owen, secretary of the Bible Society, expressing his regret that the conversion of the natives of India had been put forward so conspicuously. "That Christianity may be introduced into India, and that the attempt may be safely made, I doubt not; but to tell the natives that we wish to convert them, is not the way to proceed."[1] On the side of the opponents of Indian missions was the powerful *Edinburgh Review*, in which Sydney Smith wrote a violent article when the controversy was at its height, in 1808.

After that date, the subject seemed to be dying out of the public notice, though there is no doubt that the efforts of Dr. Buchanan, Lord Teignmouth, and others had made an impression. In 1812 the approaching renewal of the Charter of the East India Company seemed to offer a favourable opportunity for renewing the efforts for an "ecclesiastical establishment" (to use the language of the day) in India. Great pressure was brought to bear upon Parliament from the outside; nine hundred addresses from all parts of the kingdom, imploring the interference of the legislature in behalf of the moral and religious interests of India, were presented. The indefatigable Dr. Buchanan was very busy with his pen. He published a work entitled "*Colonial Ecclesiastical Establishment : being a Brief View of the State of the Colonies of Great Britain, and of her Asiatic Empire, in respect to religions : prefaced by some considerations on the national duty of affording it.*" This was extensively circulated, particularly among members of both Houses of Parliament, and made a strong and general impression throughout the country. Later in the same year (1813) appeared from the same pen "*An Apology for promoting Christianity in India : containing Two Letters addressed to the Honourable East India Company concerning the Idol Juggernaut, and a Memorial presented to the Bengal Government in 1807, in Defence of Christian Missions in India. Printed by Order of the House of Commons.*" By this time, as may be inferred from the title-page, the battle

[1] *Life of Lord Teignmouth*, p. 131.

had been won. There was a long debate in the House of Commons, in which William Wilberforce spoke with his usual eloquence, and J. Stephen and W. Smith with their usual business talent; and the upshot of it all was that the Act which renewed the Charter of the Company (1813) erected their territories into one vast diocese, with an Archdeacon to be resident at each of the three Presidencies—Calcutta, Madras, and Bombay. It was a miserably inadequate provision; but the wonder is that any provision should have been made at all, for the majority of Anglo-Indians, whose voice in such a matter would of course have great weight, were probably against it. When the letters patent were granted, Parliament seemed almost ashamed of what it had done. Dr. Thomas Fanshawe Middleton was consecrated first Bishop of Calcutta, May 8, 1814; but the consecration took place in private, and the consecration sermon was not allowed to be printed.

Perhaps, however, it was this very timidity which brought about in one respect a singularly happy result. It has been seen that one strong objection to the work of Christian missions in India generally, and the establishment of an Indian episcopate in particular, was that the projects originated with "a narrow and ignorant party" in the Church; that they were, in short, a part of that hated thing called "Methodism." It was probably on this account that the first bishop was one whose "orthodoxy" and scholarship were beyond suspicion. Thomas Fanshawe Middleton had, as we have seen, thoroughly identified himself with the "Hackney phalanx;" figuratively speaking, he hailed from Clapton, not from Clapham. His character was irreproachable; he had been a most active parish priest, and he was one of the first scholars of the day. In short, he was just the man to make the movement respectable. The Evangelicals themselves saw this, and bore with a Christian spirit what must, one would have thought, have been rather a disappointment to them. Bishop Middleton was the last man in the world to be afraid of showing his colours. "He went out to India," writes his biographer, "as he entered the Church of England, with the profound conviction that episcopacy is, not merely one of many convenient forms of governing the Church of Christ, but that it is *the* form which was originally instituted by the Apostles, and which without interruption or question had been continued from generation to generation, from the apostolic times to the days of Calvin;" and therefore he would make no concession on this point.[1] One can hardly help reading between the lines of this account. All who believe in Christ are naturally drawn closer together when they are surrounded on all sides by those who do *not* believe in Him; and in India, men who had nothing to do with episcopacy were deservedly held by all Christians in the highest esteem, as the successful pioneers and first workers in the mission-field. Mr. Simeon's chaplains, with their many excellences, were not exactly the men to put forward that view of the Church which Mr. Le Bas describes; in fact, they would not hold it themselves. But one of them, Daniel Corrie, probably expressed the feelings of all when he rejoiced at the appointment of Bishop Middleton. " He thought," writes his biographer, "that the bishop gave mission-work exactly that kind of sanction it required. To labour for the moral improvement and conversion of our heathen fellow-subjects used to be regarded as characterizing a party in the Church, and as proceeding from a kind of fanaticism that would endanger the stability of our Oriental empire. But the interest which Bishop Middleton had taken in the missionary cause gave reason to believe that official dignity, combined with a high reputation for sound judgment and secular learning, were not incompatible with the conviction that our rule in India had everything to hope for from the spread of Christianity."[2] Of course, the esteem of the marked Evangelical for the marked High Churchman was a little qualified; he thought the new bishop "in some respects a valuable man;" but, on the whole, he was quite satisfied. So also were the Evangelicals at home, if William Wilberforce may be regarded as their spokesman. " The Bishop of Calcutta," he writes in his journal for 1814, " Teignmouth, and C. Grant dined with me. Long and highly interesting talk with Bishop Middleton. He seems very earnest, and pondering

[1] See Le Bas' *Life of Bishop Middleton,* ii. 335.
[2] *Memoirs of Daniel Corrie, First Bishop of Madras,* by his brother, p. 344.

T

to do good; hopes for Churches in different parts of India; favourable to schools and a public library, and a college with discipline."[1]

The bishop, on his part, was not slow to recognize the merits of such men as Corrie. In fact, none of the difficulties which might have been anticipated from placing a High Church bishop over a set of Low Church clergy appear to have occurred.

It has not, so far as I am aware, been observed elsewhere, but it seems to me that one of the causes of this happy result was the wide and varied experiences of men of different lines of thought through which the bishop had passed. It is a curious omission on the part of his excellent biographer, Mr. Le Bas, that he does not notice Middleton's friendship with S. T. Coleridge in the early stage of that extraordinary man's mental history. The two were schoolfellows together at Christ's Hospital. Many years later, Coleridge wrote of Middleton as "my schoolfellow, who had been my patron and protector, the truly learned and every way excellent Bishop of Calcutta."[2] Mr. Gillmore, who knew Coleridge in his later years better than any man did, says that "Middleton was to him, while at school and college, what the polar star is to the mariner on a wide sea without compass—his guide, and his influential friend and companion."[3] Like Coleridge, Middleton seems to have passed through a phase of theological liberalism,[4] and, like Coleridge, he found his spiritual and intellectual home in a very different quarter from that into which he appeared to be drifting; but his early experience may have stood him in good stead when he had to deal with men who did not take precisely the same views with himself; he would naturally have wider sympathies than if his thoughts had always run in the same channel.

Be this as it may, he proved an admirable bishop. His very presence in India gave a new stimulus to mission-work.

[1] *Life of William Wilberforce*, by his son, the Bishop of Oxford, p. 352.
[2] *Biographia Literaria*.
[3] *Life of S. T. Coleridge*, p. 56.
[4] Professor Brandl says that Middleton wrote a favourable review of Priestley, the famous Unitarian, for the *British Critic*. See *Samuel Taylor Coleridge and the English Romantic School* (Eng. edit.), by Lady Eastlake, pp. 50–56.

In 1815, the year after his appointment, the C.M.S. began its mission in Calcutta, and in 1818 the S.P.G. did the same. The bishop saw the need of good vernacular schools, and the S.P.G. established three circles of mission schools in the immediate neighbourhood of Calcutta. In 1820 he laid the foundation-stone of Bishop's College, Calcutta, in the first instance "for instructing both Mussulmans and Hindoos in every branch of useful knowledge, and for educating native and European Christians in the doctrines of the Church, and for the reception of such ministers as might be sent from England before they were appointed to their stations,"[1] but with the ultimate object of being the nursery of a native clergy.[2] The real originator of Bishop's College was undoubtedly Bishop Middleton; he started the idea; he drew up all the plans himself; gave four thousand rupees from his own private income, and induced the great societies to help most liberally. But he did not live to see its completion; his anxiety about it is thought to have hastened his end; he died suddenly, after a few days' illness, in 1822, being in his last hours, at his own request, ministered to by Daniel Corrie.

The amiable and accomplished Reginald Heber, who succeeded Bishop Middleton, had shown great interest in mission-work. The most popular, perhaps, of all missionary hymns, "From Greenland's icy mountains," was composed by him for an S.P.G. service at Wrexham, in 1819; the year before, he had attempted to effect a union between the C.M.S. and the S.P.G.; and his high reputation as a literary man generally, as well as an excellent clergyman, pointed him out as a proper man for the bishopric. Of course, his appointment was warmly welcomed by the Evangelical clergy, who were still dominant in India; for though he certainly did not identify himself with the Evangelical party, he sympathized with them in many points. D. Corrie hit the mark when he said, "Our bishop is the most free from party views of any man I ever met with."[3] A little later he reports, "You will have heard of the favour the bishop shows generally to the

---

[1] T. Taylor's *Life of Bishop Heber*, p. 166.
[2] *Under His Banner*, by Rev. H. W. Tucker, p. 28.
[3] *Life of Bishop Corrie*, p. 362.

righteous cause. Of the natural amiability of the man, it is impossible to convey an adequate idea;" and a little later still, "The Church is advancing. In our bishop we have all we can have in one man to unite us, and to help our work by its various instruments."[1] The friends of Bishop Middleton do not seem to have been quite so pleased with his successor.[2] They thought his antecedents were not quite those of a man likely to fill so responsible a position, and perhaps also they were not so convinced of his firm Churchmanship. But Heber, though a moderate, was not a colourless man. He took a decided line of his own, and his amiability did not prevent him from being firm on occasion, as the two following instances in different directions will show. He very properly insisted that the missionaries sent out by the C.M.S. should be as much under his jurisdiction as those sent out by other Church societies, and he succeeded in carrying his point, though the rule was not formally recognized by the society. Perhaps this very proper insistence upon his power led some who were hostile to the Evangelicals to hope that he might be induced to exercise it *im*properly. He was known to be a strong Arminian, and a vain attempt was made to induce him to exclude Calvinists. He was a very active bishop. He took up heartily Bishop Middleton's project of Bishop's College, and brought it to a successful completion in 1824. He made a visitation which ranged through Bengal, Bombay, and Ceylon, the not unnatural result being that he was prostrated by fever. Nothing daunted, he began a second visitation in Madras; but, on April 3, 1826, he was found dead in his bath at Trichinopoly. His tragic end, following his devoted life, threw a halo of romance over his whole career which impressed the imagination; and, better still, contributed to the practical result of bringing about a subdivision of his unwieldy diocese.

There seems little doubt that the first two bishops of Calcutta were practically killed by overwork. In the graceful language of the biographer of the first, "the dust of two English bishops, we might almost say two English martyrs, has now mixed itself with the soil of Hindostan. Let us

[1] *Life of Bishop Corrie*, pp. 369, 376.
[2] See *Memoir of Joshua Watson*, i. 240, etc.

hope that their remains have given a sort of consecration to that vast territory, and marked it out, in sight of men and angels, as a portion of the Redeemer's inheritance."[1] They were certainly two very remarkable men, though of a different type. In 1827, during the interregnum after Bishop Heber's death, Bishop Blomfield preached a sermon on the state of the Church in India, in which he said, with perfect truth, "It was the peculiar felicity of that Church, rather, I should say, it was of God's providential appointment, that its first rulers were two men singularly gifted and qualified for the work which it fell to their lot to perform." After two such men had sacrificed their lives to overwork, one would have thought that, for very shame, a further provision would have been made to avert another such catastrophe. But it was not. It is positively shocking to think that, within six years, two more valuable lives were sacrificed in the attempt to manage the hopelessly unwieldy diocese. In 1829 Bishop Heber's successor, Dr. James, "the much-respected Bishop of Calcutta," fell "a victim to the labours and anxieties of a diocese that ought to be divided into four;"[2] and in 1832 *his* successor, Dr. Turner, died in the prime of life (æt. 45), "worn down with the anxious responsibilities of his office, and the fatigues of his late laborious visitation of his diocese."[3] A memorial had been presented by the S.P.C.K. to the Court of Directors, after the death of Bishop Heber, praying for the appointment of more bishops; but it was not complied with until some years after our period, when Corrie, the Archdeacon of Madras, was most deservedly made its first bishop. In 1832 Daniel Wilson was appointed to Calcutta, and held the see for twenty-six years.

There can be no doubt that the establishment of the episcopate in India gave an enormous impetus to mission-

---

[1] Le Bas' *Life of Bishop Middleton*, i. 353.
[2] *Christian Observer*, 1829.
[3] *Brief Notice of Dr. John M. Turner, late Bishop of Calcutta*, by the Rev. S. C. Wilks. He is described as a man of "exemplary piety." He was educated at Christ Church, Oxford, where he was a favourite of the dean, Dr. Cyril Jackson. He was afterwards successively Vicar of Abingdon and Vicar of Wilmslow. He was examining chaplain to the Bishop of Chester. He was recommended by Lord Ellenborough for the bishopric of Calcutta, and many instances are given of his zeal in that capacity.

work. New centres were formed in all parts, and far more way was made, especially in Madras, than in any previous corresponding period.

S.P.C.K.

This oldest of Church societies, like its first offshoot the S.P.G., also made wonderful progress during our period. In 1832 it had seven times as many subscribers, and nearly seven times as much money subscribed, as it had in 1800; while it distributed thirty-three times as many Bibles and Prayer-books.

The general impetus which was given, about the beginning of the nineteenth century, to all works of piety and charity, may account to some extent for the marked advance made by the venerable society. But there is evidence from all quarters to show that it was specially stirred up to renewed vigour by the formation of the British and Foreign Bible Society. The very *raison d'être* of the younger society was a sort of challenge to the older. There was need, it was said, of a new society, because the old one was unable to meet the demand for Bibles in Wales. The old society distinctly denied its inability to do this, and girded itself up at once, so that there might not be the faintest suspicion of its inadequacy for such emergencies in the future. There certainly seems to have been some need of an awakening, for, by the admission of some of its most ardent supporters, it was little known. Now, the want of publicity in an institution which depended upon the public for the very continuance of its existence, to say nothing of its extension, was an obvious defect. We can understand, indeed, the feeling which prompted those who *did* know it to admire its "unforced dignity," "the silent unostentatious manner in which all its proceedings were carried on." "True charity," it was said, "is never ostentatious; this excellent society has made no noisy appeals to the passions or feelings of mankind on its own behalf."[1] No doubt this was the more excellent way, if only it was followed with success. But the very next sentence shows that it was not. "So far has this for-

[1] *Enquiry into the Claims of the British and Foreign Bible Society*, by the Rev. J. H. Spry.

bearance been carried that its very existence is unknown even to many of the Established Church, and some of the clergy have been induced to connect themselves with the Bible Society merely because they believe it to be the only institution which could furnish them with Bibles at a reduced price for distribution among the poor." The Bishop of London, Dr. Randolph, was "disgusted at the pomp and parade with which all the proceedings, and indeed all the meetings, of the new society were set forth in the public papers, and the more so when he contrasted it with the simplicity and modesty of the old society;"[1] but if the result of this simplicity and modesty was that the very existence of the old society was unknown to many of that very class which would naturally be most likely to know about it, it really was time that it should show itself a little less simple and modest in its operations.

It must not be supposed, however, that it was jealousy of a new agency doing the same work which it professed to do itself, that roused the S.P.C.K. to fresh efforts. It was not a case of two rivals in the same field. The real question at issue was, whether Churchmen ought to be content with helping to circulate the Bible alone, without the Prayer-book which is to them the authorized interpreter of the Bible. This was the point which was pressed with great force by Dr. Christopher Wordsworth, Archdeacon Daubeny, and, above all, Dr. Herbert Marsh, whose powerful and luminous statement will give the reader the best view of the question as it appeared to High Churchmen of that day. "The S.P.C.K.," he writes, "is the most ancient *Bible* Society in the kingdom, and was employed in the distribution of Bibles to the poor more than eighty years before any *other* Bible Society existed among us. Its title is well adapted to its *object;* for *Christian knowledge* is unquestionably promoted by circulation of the *Bible.* But as this society does not go by the *name* of a Bible Society, it has been strangely inferred that they who supported *this* Bible Society in preference to any other Bible Society are enemies to Bible Societies in general. Now, as I decidedly prefer the distribution of the Bible by *this* Bible Society to its distribution by means of

[1] Bishop Randolph's Letter to the Colchester clergy, 1804-5.

any other, I will briefly state to you the reasons of my preference. Though the use of the *Bible* makes us Christians, it is the use of the *Prayer-book* also which makes us *Churchmen*. The Bible is the sole *authority* on which Protestants found their articles of faith; whereas members of the Church of Rome found their articles of faith on the *joint* authority of Scripture and tradition. But when this maxim, which is true in respect to the *authority* of the Bible, is applied, as it has been, to the *distribution* of the Bible, the maxim is totally false. Though the Prayer-book has no *authority* but what it derives from the Bible, Churchmen must attend to its *distribution* with the Bible. Take away the Prayer-book, and, though we remain Christians, we cease to be Churchmen. Christians of *every* denomination appeal to the *Bible* in support of their faith and worship, however diversified that faith and worship may be. *Our* form of faith and worship is that which is prescribed in the Prayer-book, and as we have reason to believe that the faith and worship there prescribed is consonant with the tenets of the Bible, we must consistently, as good Churchmen, as good Protestants (whatever has been said to the contrary), regard the Prayer-book as a proper companion for the Bible. Now, the Bible Society which I recommend to your attention is the only Bible Society in this kingdom which distributes the Prayer-book, and it is chiefly on this ground that, as a faithful Churchman, I have earnestly laboured in its defence."[1]

This passage is interesting incidentally because it marks the difference between High Churchmen before, and High Churchmen after, the Oxford Movement. Of course, the latter would have agreed with Bishop Marsh, as against his opponents, but they would not have based their arguments on the same ground that he based his. The passage is, however, quoted here simply to show how the foundation and rapid success of the British and Foreign Bible Society gave an enormous stimulus to the S.P.C.K. The supporters of the latter could say to Churchmen, "You are asked to join a Bible Society of a mixed nature; but you have a Bible Society of your own, which, in loyalty to your Church, you are bound to support in preference." The appeal, though of

[1] Charge of Bishop Marsh at his Primary Visitation at Llandaff, 1817.

course it came home most closely to High Churchmen, yet touched others. Sydney Smith, for instance, though he thought "nothing could be more ridiculous than the whole contest"—an odd remark from a clergyman—yet agreed that "to a particular body of men [Churchmen] it was right to say, 'You are bound in consistency to circulate the Scriptures with the Prayer-book in preference to any other method.'"[1] S. T. Coleridge[2] and Southey[3] took quite the same view; and even Bishop Ryder, who was always reckoned as the first bishop who really and fully represented the Evangelicals, and was an early supporter of the Bible Society, distinctly and emphatically declares that "in cases where very contracted means would permit a parochial minister to subscribe only to one society, he should choose that which would enable him to provide the Liturgy as well as the Bible for his own people."[4]

One of the chief means by which the S.P.C.K. acquired additional support was through the establishment, in 1812, of district committees. Bishop Law, in his Charge to the diocese of Chester in 1814, says that before the formation of diocesan and district committees "the good which had been effected by the parent society was but little known in the more distant parts of the kingdom," and thinks that their formation is "an era that will be remembered." It is hardly necessary to say that the men who belonged to the "Hackney phalanx," notably Joshua Watson, Christopher Wordsworth, and John Bowdler, were most energetic in working up the S.P.C.K. generally, and the district committees' scheme in particular.[5]

The early part of the nineteenth century might be termed the age of societies. The *National Society*, founded in 1811, has already been noticed in connection with the subject of elementary education, and the *Church Building Society* in

---

[1] See Lady Holland's *Memoir*, ii. (Letters), 112.
[2] See his *Lay Sermons*, etc., published in 1817, the same year in which Bishop Marsh delivered his Charge.
[3] See *Life of Southey*, iii. 329. Southey thinks Marsh's arguments are unanswerable.
[4] Primary Charge delivered to the clergy of the diocese of Gloucester in 1816.
[5] See *Memoir of Joshua Watson*, i. 94, 95; *Life of Bishop Middleton*, i. 18, 19; *Memoir of John Bowdler*, p. 247.

connection with that of Church fabrics. But there still remain many others which date from this period. There was, for instance, a sort of minor missionary society called *The Society for the Conversion of the Negroes in the West Indies*, whose energies hardly came into operation before the commencement of the nineteenth century, though its actual foundation took place in 1794. It arose as follows. In 1691 the Hon. Robert Boyle left a sum of money "for pious uses," part of which, under the direction of the Court of Chancery, was applied to "the advancement of the Christian religion among infidels in Virginia." At the separation of the United States from the mother country, it was decreed by the same court that the fund should be applied to the conversion and religious instruction of negro slaves in the British West India Islands. The decree appears to have been made at the instance of Dr. Beilby Porteus, who, as Bishop of London, was a trustee for the property, and, when the society was founded, became its president. The spread of the colonial episcopate extended to the West Indies; and in 1825 the Bishops of Jamaica and Barbadoes arrived in their respective dioceses and gave a great impetus to the work of the society. It came slightly into collision with the abolitionists; but the dispute was of a temporary nature, and need not here be noticed.

Another society, of which Bishop Porteus was a chief promoter and the first president, was *The Society for the Suppression of Vice*. This, too, was founded before the eighteenth century ended, but did not come into working order until the nineteenth century had commenced. Its object was to enforce the king's proclamation against immorality and profaneness; and the means it took to effect this object were by inducing persons of rank and character to associate for putting the laws in force and convicting offenders. In this respect it exactly resembled those societies for the reformation of manners which had been founded a century before; but, unlike them, its members were exclusively confined to the Church of England. It fell into the same odium, and was liable to the same real abuses, as its predecessors. "It was, of course, assailed," says a writer in the *Quarterly Review* (March, 1812), "by low buffoonery and coarse abuse." Whether this was a hit at the great rival Review, I cannot say; but certain it is that in the *Edinburgh Review* (1809) Sydney Smith had directed the pointed shafts of his wit against the society. Unfortunately for it the attack has lived, while the defence has virtually perished. It must be admitted that the witty canon hits some blots which were almost inevitable in such an institution. From the days of the sycophants in Attica, informers have always been an unpopular race. "Private informers," says the reviewer, "are bad enough, but bands of them are worse." "The real thing," he goes on, "which calls for the sympathies and harrows up the soul, is to see a number of boisterous artisans baiting a bull or a bear; not a savage hare or a carnivorous stag, but a poor, innocent, timid bear; not pursued by magistrates and deputy-lieutenants, and men of education, but by those who must necessarily seek their relaxation in noise and tumultuous merriment, by men whose feelings are blunted and whose understanding is wholly devoid of refinement. The society details with great complacency the detection of a bear-baiting in Blackboy Alley, Chick Lane, and the prosecution of the offenders before a magistrate. A man of £10,000 a year may worry a fox as much as he pleases, and a poor labourer is carried before a magistrate for paying sixpence to see an exhibition of courage between a dog and a bear." But it is hardly an answer to those who were trying to check the demoralizing effects of the illegal recreations of one class, to say that the recreations of another class were cruel, though not illegal. And, at any rate, Bishop Porteus was never accused of hunting a savage hare or a carnivorous stag; nor yet was the excellent John Bowdler, who took up the cause of the society when it "had fallen very low through several unfortunate circumstances; was greatly instrumental in increasing its funds and the number of its active members; and greatly rejoiced in its successful endeavour (far beyond what its means would seem to admit) to check the alarming progress of infidelity and profaneness."[1]

Many of the societies of the period were connected with the Evangelical party. Among these was *The London Society for Promoting Christianity among the Jews*, founded in 1809. To this society Simeon "was pre-eminently attached. In

[1] *Memoir of John Bowdler*, p. 251.

truth, he was almost from the commencement the chief stay of that great cause;"[1] and one of the last things he wrote, or rather dictated, on his dying bed, was an address on the subject. In spite of his attachment, however, he was quite alive to one of its weaknesses, viz. the undue petting of converted Jews. "It was the want of caution," he writes with his usual quaint humour in 1830, "in the Jewish society at first, which brought such odium upon all its plans and upon all its promoters; and I would very earnestly recommend that as little as possible be said of our early converts. . . . Pharaoh was not more cruel to infant Hebrews than we are to adults. He drowned his victims, and we hug ours to death. Why are *they* to be introduced into higher company when converts from the ungodly world are not? It is a grievous mistake to imagine that the baptizing any by *a bishop* is at all likely to advance their spiritual welfare."[2]

So ardently was the cause taken up, that we actually hear of a *weekly* Jewish society meeting at the house of Mr. Budd, the London Evangelical clergyman whose church Edward Bickersteth attended when he was a layman in London, in 1811.[3] Some of Mr. Legh Richmond's most triumphant missionary tours were in behalf of this society. In 1812 he records how at Manchester Collegiate Church "the congregation was estimated at more than five thousand by the best judges," and adds, "the interest and popularity which the cause and preaching excite exceed all calculation;"[4] and many more such entries occur in his diary. The Duke of Kent became a patron of the society, through the influence, no doubt, of Legh Richmond, who was his chaplain.

Other societies especially connected with the Evangelical party in the Church of England were the *Prayer-book and Homily Society*, founded in 1812, in the first instance "to supply a deficiency in distributing Prayer-books in the Navy," but also because Prayer-books were frequently published without "the Articles, which are the appointed standard of doctrine and guide to her worshippers," and because "the Book of Homilies could not be obtained through the medium of any existing society in the Church of England;"[5] the

[1] Carus' *Memoir*, p. 597.   [2] *Id.*, p. 458.   [3] Birks' *Memoir*, i. 190.
[4] Grimshaw's *Life of Legh Richmond*, p. 238.   [5] *Id.*, p. 234.

Irish Society, the object of which was to distribute Bibles, Prayer-books, and other works in the Irish language, and to diffuse Churchmanship of an Evangelical type throughout Ireland; the *Newfoundland School Society*, which was intended to spread "Evangelical" in place of "Orthodox" views in that distant country; and the various *Clerical Education Societies*, for the purpose of helping young men of straitened means to pay the expenses of a University education, with a view to their becoming Evangelical clergymen. The first and most famous of these was the *Elland Society*, in Yorkshire; another was founded at Little Dunham, in Norfolk, by John Venn; another at Bristol; another in London; and another at Creaton, in Northamptonshire.

Besides these societies, which were confined to the Church of England, the Evangelicals also supported some of a mixed nature. First among these in point of date was the *Eclectic Society*, which was instituted in 1783 by a few London clergy "for mutual and religious intercourse and improvement, and for investigation of religious truth." John Newton, Richard Cecil, Henry Foster, and Eli Bates (a layman) were the original members. The first meeting was held at the Castle and Falcon Inn, Aldersgate Street, and afterwards the meetings took place fortnightly in the vestry of St. John's Chapel, Bedford Row. According to the original design, two or three laymen and Dissenting ministers were to be admitted, but by degrees the Dissenting appears to have swamped the Church element. A most interesting work, entitled "Eclectic Notes," was published by Josiah Pratt, which gives the fullest account of the Society's proceedings. The *Eclectic Review*, which was the organ of the society, having existed for ten years (1804-1814) as the joint production of Churchmen and Dissenters, came out in a new series in 1814, as the exclusive production of the latter.[1]

Next came the *Religious Tract Society*, founded in 1799 by members of the three denominations (Presbyterians, Independents, and Baptists), on the principle that there should be "nothing of sectarian shibboleths, nothing to recommend one denomination or to throw odium on another." It was almost from the first largely patronized by Evangelical

[1] See Advertisement to vol. i. of the *Eclectic Review*, new series, 1814.

Churchmen. Legh Richmond accepted the secretaryship of the society, thinking "that he might promote the interests of his own Church by preventing the circulation of tracts hostile to her opinions, as well as advance the common cause of true religion." "He required," adds his biographer, "a guarantee to this effect, and then accepted the post, and to the day of his death had no reason to complain that the engagement was violated in a single instance."[1]

Out of the Religious Tract Society sprang a far more extensive institution—the *British and Foreign Bible Society*. This was actually established in 1804, but the scheme was formed gradually. In December, 1802, Thomas Charles, of Bala, who was *really*, what many were called falsely, "a Methodist clergyman," first proposed "a contribution in aid of a plan for printing and distributing the Scriptures among his countrymen," the Welsh. At a committee-meeting of the Religious Tract Society, it was suggested by Joseph Hughes, a Baptist minister, that "as Wales was not the only part where the want might be supposed to prevail, it would be desirable to stir up the public mind to a general dispersion of the Scriptures." Mr. Hughes was "desired to prepare in writing an address, containing in more digested form the substance of his unpremeditated observations." Accordingly in May, 1803, he presented to the society an essay, entitled "The Excellence of the Holy Scriptures an Argument for their more General Circulation," in which he represented "the importance of an association of Christians at large with a view exclusively to the circulation of Holy Scripture." On March 7, 1804, a meeting was held at the London Tavern, Bishopsgate Street, Granville Sharp in the chair. This was followed by another meeting on March 12, at which Mr. Hughes was suggested as secretary of the new society. But Mr. John Owen, afterwards the historian of the society's early years, objected, because "it was desired to obtain the patronage and co-operation of the Established Church," and suggested the name of Josiah Pratt. The result was that Josiah Pratt and Joseph Hughes were appointed joint secretaries, and Mr. Steinkoff foreign secretary. But on April 23 Josiah Pratt resigned, and John Owen succeeded him as clerical

[1] *Life*, p. 366.

secretary. At the instance of Bishop Porteus, Lord Teignmouth was elected as first president of the society, and among the vice-presidents were the Bishops of London, Durham, Exeter, and St. David's. The society increased rapidly, throwing out by degrees various offshoots, which did much to strengthen the vitality of the parent stock. For instance, as early as 1805 people began to form themselves into voluntary associations for aiding the cause of the society. Glasgow, London, and Birmingham were the first places in which this was done ; but the first *regular* formation of an *Auxiliary Bible Society* was at Reading, on March 28, 1809 ; and its establishment was chiefly due to one whose name will awaken bitter recollections in the minds of some readers—Dr. Valpy, author of the "Delectus" and other school-books, at that time head-master of Reading Grammar School. The first *Juvenile Bible Society* is said to have been established at York in 1812, and the first *Ladies' Auxiliary Bible Societies* at Westminster and Dublin in the same year. In 1811 arose the first *Bible Association* at High Wycombe, for "distributing the Holy Scriptures among the lower orders of society chiefly through their own agency," though the principle had been recognized from the first—indeed, *before* the formal establishment of the society at all. These subsidiary organizations, though they were objected to by some—Reginald Heber among others—wonderfully strengthened and enlarged the parent society. Indeed, the society obtained so firm a footing that, before it had been in existence ten years, its ablest opponent, Professor Herbert Marsh, said in reply to its ablest defender, Dean Milner, "I have long since abandoned the thought of opposing the Bible Society. When an institution is supported with all the fervour of religious enthusiasm, and is aided by the weight of such powerful additional causes, an attempt to oppose it is like attempting to oppose a torrent of burning lava that issues from Etna or Vesuvius."[1] This was in 1813. In the same way Archdeacon Daubeny, in his "Reasons for declining Connection with the Bible Society" (1814), constantly refers to its great popularity.

Among so heterogeneous a group as the Bible Society

[1] Quoted in the *History of the Origin and First Ten Years of the British and Foreign Bible Society*, by the Rev. John Owen, ii. 560.

brought together, internal difficulties naturally arose; but it is wonderful how easily they were settled.

First came the controversy about the Apocrypha. It may seem strange, considering the source from whence the society sprang, that the Apocrypha should ever have been included in the Bibles circulated by it; but the reason is indicated by the name—"British *and Foreign* Bible Society." It had always been the custom on the Continent to print the Apocryphal with the Canonical Books. This "course of proceeding, at first imperceptibly adopted by the society, at length grew into a rule;"[1] and the foreign Protestants were "not prepared at once to relinquish the practice."[2] Scotland objected to the plan even more than England, and in 1825 it was resolved "that the funds of the society be applied to the printing and circulation of the Canonical Books of Scripture to the exclusion of the Apocrypha."[3] But the conclusion was not arrived at without arousing very bitter feelings; indeed, before it was settled, many of the Scotch Auxiliaries had seceded.[4]

In 1831 a very serious question arose as to whether all Socinians should be excluded from the management of the society, and also as to whether meetings should be opened with Scripture-reading and prayer. The two questions were closely connected, because any prayers would naturally end in a way which Socinians could scarcely accept. The proposal to institute a test to try the soundness of members on the doctrine of the Trinity was rejected by a large majority; but the minority seceded, and founded another society, termed the *Trinitarian Bible Society*.

So far as the Church of England was concerned, the controversy about the Bible Society brought to a head, more than any other question had done, the real point at issue between the "Evangelicals" and the "Orthodox." It was not merely a question as to the setting up of a rival society to the venerable S.P.C.K., nor as to whether the distribution of Prayer-books ought always to accompany that of Bibles,

---

[1] *Memoir of the Life and Correspondence of John, Lord Teignmouth*, p. 459.
[2] Owen's *History of the Bible Society*, p. 195.
[3] *Life of Lord Teignmouth*, p. 461.
[4] See *Life of Edward Bickersteth*, ii. 30.

nor even whether Churchmen could consistently join with
Dissenters in circulating the Holy Scriptures. Beneath all
these questions lay a still more fundamental one. The
famous dictum, "The Bible, and the Bible only, is the religion
of Protestants," again came to the front. The Evangelicals
to a man held this view, and supported the Bible Society,
heart and soul, accordingly. But on the part of High Churchmen and Broad Churchmen there was by no means the same
unanimity. Of course, as a rule, the High Churchmen held
aloof; but their attitude is curiously illustrative of what has
frequently been observed in these pages, viz. that during our
period they did not make generally clear their own position,
as the Evangelicals certainly did theirs. For instance, when
it was objected that the Bible Society was "dangerous to
the Establishment," the obvious answer was that the Establishment existed for the sake of religion, not religion for the sake
of the Establishment, to say nothing of the fact that the
Establishment was perfectly safe, Bible Society or no Bible
Society; when it was urged that the new society was calculated to injure the older and more Church-like one (S.P.C.K.),
the convincing reply was that, as a matter of fact, it did *not*
injure, but greatly helped the older one, by stirring up its
energies, and rousing sympathy in its behalf. Nor is it very
easy to see the force of the distinction which was drawn
between the home and foreign work of the society; as if the
latter was tolerable, the former intolerable.[1] There was more
force in the objection that the principle of the Bible Society
assumed that the Bible was intended to teach itself, and that,
as a necessary consequence, the work of learned interpreters
was superfluous. But, after all, the real point was hit by
Archdeacon Daubeny, and, so far as I am aware, by few
others on the High Church side—at least, in so direct and
unmistakable a way. "As every sect," he writes, "appeals
to the Bible for the standard of its religious views, therefore
every sect (so far, at least, as the parties in question are
qualified to judge) has the authority of that Bible for the
creed which it promulgates; and consequently, instead of

---

[1] This distinction was urged, among others, by Dr. Christopher Wordsworth
the elder, in his *Reasons for declining to become a Member of the British and
Foreign Bible Society*, and was answered by Lord Teignmouth.

the one only apostolical Church established in this country, from the lips of whose priests, as authoritatively commissioned for the purpose, the people are directed to seek knowledge, there are as many Churches as there are different meetings of associated religionists to be found among us. The obvious inference from this circumstance in *uninformed* minds will be, that God has left every man at liberty to make *his own Church and his own religion*, or, to make use of the absurd language of the day, 'Every man has a right to worship God in his own way.'"[1] Of course, there were other High Churchmen who took the same grounds, notably Dr. Christopher Wordsworth, whose memorable letter, dated from "Lambeth Palace,"[2] first stirred up the controversy; Dr. Randolph, Bishop Porteus' successor in the see of London; and Archdeacon (afterwards Bishop) Middleton; but none seem to me to have given so direct an expression to the real question at issue as Archdeacon Daubeny.

Outside the distinctly marked circles of the Evangelicals on the one side, and the pronounced High Churchmen on the other, there was a great divergence of opinion on the subject of the Bible Society. Alexander Knox, for instance, tells his friend Jebb in 1805 that he was busy with "an answer to a terrible kind of pamphlet against the Bible Society,"

---

[1] "The Substance of a Discourse at the Abbey Church, Bath, March 31, 1814, giving a Churchman's Reasons for declining a Connection with the Bible Society," by Charles Daubeny, Archdeacon of Sarum, published in the *Pamphleteer*, vol. v., No. ix., February, 1815.

[2] Dr. Wordsworth was very severely criticized for dating his letter from "Lambeth Palace;" but the criticism seems to me to have arisen from an entire ignorance of the characteristics of the Wordsworth family. "Lambeth Palace" was supposed to have been inserted to give "an adventitious importance" to the letter. I doubt whether the Dean of Bocking, the future Master of Trinity, and the brother of the great poet, would have considered the fact of his being with the archbishop on duty as domestic chaplain would give his letter any adventitious importance. Except in point of office he was a stronger man than the archbishop, and was much more likely to influence the archbishop than the archbishop was to influence him. It is not at all a Wordsworth characteristic to think that any adventitious prop is necessary to support his own opinion. On the other hand, courtesy and habits of business *are* Wordsworth characteristics; and as the letter was a reply to one which had been received three weeks earlier, it was necessary to explain the reason for the delay in answering. The heading "Lambeth Palace" and the first sentence of the letter *do* explain the delay.

and calls the pamphlet "an effusion of High Church bigotry;"[1] but, in later years, he clearly changed his opinion; for in 1816 he writes to the same correspondent on "the utter hopelessness of bringing home religious principles and truth to the mass of the people by the *distribution of Bibles*, which was the popular panacea for all spiritual ignorance;"[2] and when it was urged that the famous "Appendix to Bishop Jebb's Sermons" (in the composition of which Knox took a leading part) tended to excite doubts about the Bible Society, he owned that, though "its object was far deeper," yet "there was certainly no wish to preclude such an application, and that he himself could take no part in the Bible Society chiefly on the grounds set forth in that Appendix;" and then, assuming his favourite attitude of the calm and dispassionate observer, he adds, "But I have not the slightest wish to enter the lists against it. On the contrary, I am anxious to see it go on to the end of its course, and accomplish all it can. It is in my view a most interesting experiment; and though I am inclined to think it will not, in any respect, answer the purpose of its originators, it will assuredly serve some deep purpose of overruling Providence; for the sake of which, I should humbly think, the impulse was at first given, and the movement so long sustained and so surprisingly extended;"[3]—a line of defence, one would imagine, more exasperating to the advocates of the society than the most violent attacks upon it would be. Bishop Bathurst called it "that most excellent of all human institutions,"[4] and wrote to Lord Teignmouth in 1811, that he had promoted to the utmost of his power the institution of an Auxiliary Society in his diocese;[5] while, on the other hand, his devoted admirer, Sydney Smith, was against Churchmen supporting it.[6] Bishop Otter, who was a sort of quasi-High-Churchman, was in favour of it, and wrote a pamphlet in

[1] *Thirty Years' Correspondence between Bishop Jebb and A. Knox*, i. 211.
[2] See the article on "Alexander Knox and the Oxford Movement," by Professor G. T. Stokes, in the *Contemporary Review* for August, 1887.
[3] *Remains of A. Knox*, iv. 296.
[4] Charge to the diocese of Norwich, 1820; quoted in *Memoir of Bishop Bathurst*, ii. 68.
[5] See *Life of John, Lord Teignmouth*, ii. 185.
[6] See Lady Holland's *Memoir*, p. 112.

reply to Dr. Marsh in its defence;[1] but S. T. Coleridge, who may perhaps be similarly described, vehemently scouted the notion of distributing the Bible and the Bible only without note or comment among the poor,[2] on the ground that this was making light of "all the learning, sagacity, and unwearied labours of great and wise men, and eminent servants of Christ, during all the ages of Christianity;" and Bishop Maltby was against it on similar grounds, saying that "out of sixty-six books which form the contents of the Old and New Testaments, not above seven in the Old, and eleven in the New, were calculated for the study or comprehension of the unlearned."[3] Reginald Heber, though in many respects he acted with the High Churchmen, supported it; so did the *British Critic* in the interval between its earlier and its later High Church stage; and so, unless he very much altered his opinions in later years, did William Palmer, afterwards one of the chief precursors of the Oxford Movement.[4]

PRIVATE RELIGIOUS SOCIETIES

were during our period part of the equipment of an Evangelical clergyman's parish. When they were formed for some definite and practical object, such as those mentioned by Edward Bickersteth as existing in London under Mr. Budd and Mr. Pratt,[5] and such as Simeon formed at Stapleford, they were probably an unmixed good;[6] but when they were merely synonyms for prayer-meetings, that is, assemblies in which private Christians exercised their gift of extemporaneous prayer, they were liable to grave abuses, as some of the Evangelical leaders found to their cost. Simeon, as we have seen, sometimes found his societies at Cambridge quite

---

[1] See *Life of John, Lord Teignmouth*, ii. 201. This was some years before Otter became Bishop of Chichester.

[2] See his *Lay Sermons*, 1817.

[3] *Thoughts, etc., on the British and Foreign Bible Society, etc.*, 1812. (Dr. Maltby was not then a bishop.)

[4] See the almost rapturous account of the enormous good done by the Bible Society in Palmer's *Narrative of Events connected with the Publication of the Tracts for the Times*. This account occurs in the introduction, written in 1883, to the republication of the original *Narrative*, which was written in 1843.

[5] See Birks' *Memoir, etc.*, i. 171.

[6] See Carus' *Memoirs*, p. 128.

beyond his control, and complains bitterly of the self-conceit, the emulation, the lawlessness they engendered, though he winds up by saying that, after all, he considered them absolutely essential.[1] Thomas Scott condemns them point-blank, without any qualification whatever, and instances the evil effects which they had produced at Olney.[2] Legh Richmond, on the other hand, "formed a society at Brading which proved an occasion of much benefit."[3] Claudius Buchanan seems to have had a similar experience at Ouseham; and Edward Bickersteth writes gratefully of the advantage he derived from belonging to a society when he was a young layman in London.[4]

Outside the Evangelical circle they found no favour whatever. Reginald Heber writes very warmly against such societies as were formed only for the purpose of holding prayer-meetings.[5] Charles James Blomfield lifted up his voice against them in a visitation sermon at Saffron Walden in 1818.[6] Richard Mant steadily set his face against them at Great Coggeshall.[7]

It is characteristic of the two periods, that while in the old religious societies, originated by Dr. Horneck, Mr. Smythies, and Bishop Beveridge towards the close of the seventeenth century, the Church element was predominant, and the absolute control of the parish clergyman was enforced, the societies of the early nineteenth century were guarded by no such rigorous precautions. The result was that, while the earlier societies were a source of great strength to the Church, the later too often tended to weaken her hold and embarrass her work.

To sum up. The period before us seems to have been in danger of being a little over-stocked with societies. "I am not over-friendly," writes Bishop Jebb in 1824, "to the strong excitations of this age of societies."[8] It was not so

[1] Carus' *Memoirs*, pp. 238-240, 247, etc.
[2] Grimshaw's *Life, etc.*, p. 43.
[3] Pearson's *Memoirs, etc.*, ii. 218.
[4] Birks' *Memoir, etc.*, i. 254.
[5] See the *British Critic* for January, 1830, Art. iii.
[6] See *Memoirs of Bishop Blomfield*, p. 79.
[7] *Memoirs of Bishop Mant*.
[8] Forster's *Life and Letters of Bishop Jebb*, ii. 414.

much the "excitations" that were at fault. After the long torpor of the eighteenth century, the age required "excitations." The danger was lest this great multiplication of societies might result in their interfering with one another. However, it is better to have too much than too little of a good thing; and, on the whole, it must be hailed as a hopeful sign of reviving energy that the age could justly be termed "the age of societies."

CHAPTER IX.

CHURCH AND STATE.

THE relations between Church and State were far more intimate in the early part of the nineteenth century than they are at the present day. On the one hand, the Church looked to the State to support her in every way; there was a foolish sort of feeling that it was beneath the dignity of an "Establishment" to work through voluntary effort—that was what the "Methodists" did; and therefore she applied to the State in matters in which she would never dream now of making such application. On the other hand, the State still felt it its duty to stand by the Church as its natural ally. The argument that any measure would be injurious to the Church was one which was frequently used and always told. The State was proud of the Church, and in a vague kind of way felt the great advantage of having her in its midst. It regarded "Westminster Abbey as part of the British Constitution," as Mr. Croker said to Mr. Southey. At least, the party to which Mr. Croker belonged so regarded it; and his eloquent explanation of what he meant by his *bon-mot*[1] expresses what was generally felt at the beginning of the century, though far less generally in 1825, when he wrote it, and less generally still at the close of our period.

[1] "I do not mean the mere *political* connection of Church and State, but that mixture of veneration and love, of enthusiasm and good taste, of public liberty and self-control, of pride of our ancestors and hopes for our posterity, which affects every patriot and Christian mind at the contemplation of that glorious system which unites in such beautiful association and such profitable combination our civil and ecclesiastical constitutions, our ambition and our faith; the one thing needful and the all things ornamental; our well-being in this world and our salvation in the next,"—with much more to the same effect. See let'er from J. W. Croker to R. Southey, January 3, 1825, in *The Croker Papers*, i. 277.

For the history of Church and State during the first thirty-three years of the nineteenth century is the history of a growing alienation between the two, till at last the relations became so strained that it was almost universally believed that the Church, as a national establishment, must soon cease to exist. How the Church, deprived of her natural ally and thrown upon her own resources, more than recovered her hold upon the nation, does not fall within our province to record; but it may be said generally that the reverse of the Psalmist's utterance in this instance proved true, and that those things turned to her wealth which seemed to her an occasion of falling. The intimate connection between Church and State occasioned a very confused and often erroneous notion of what was the proper province of each. And that, far more so in the early part of the nineteenth than in the eighteenth century, for this very good reason. It was equally believed in the eighteenth century that what the Church did she must do through the State; but in that sleepy period she did very little at all. When she began to awake from her slumbers, and to be up and doing, events were of course perpetually occurring which affected the relationship between the two powers. Archdeacon Daubeny, who in this, as in many respects, was in advance of his age, made a wise and much-needed remark, when he wrote, just before the century began, "The jurisdictions of Church and State are like two parallel lines, which, so long as they are continued in their appointed directions, may be extended *in infinitum*, without the possibility of interfering with each other."[1] One of the great defects of the time we are considering was that the lines did *not* run parallel, and in consequence were constantly running into one another. At the same time, the State did make many laudable attempts to help the Church and render her work more effective, for which Churchmen ought to be grateful.

The first Act of Parliament which directly concerned the Church in the nineteenth century was one passed in 1801, enacting that in future no one in priest's orders should be a member of the House of Commons.[2] The subject was

---

[1] *Guide to the Church*, ii. 93.
[2] It would be wearisome and unnecessary to give references to Hansard's

brought forward in consequence of the persistent efforts of Horne Tooke, the famous clerical agitator, who, having twice contested Westminster in vain, obtained in this year a seat as member for Old Sarum through the influence of Lord Camelford. William Wilberforce has an entry in his diary on the subject: "Sad foolish work about the motion concerning clergy sitting in Parliament. More stir at Cambridge about clergy's ineligibility than ever before."[1] But the subject seems after all to have caused only a very slight and temporary excitement. The only publication on the subject with which I am acquainted is a foolish " Letter to Lord Porchester on the Degraded State of the Clergy," their degradation being chiefly their exclusion from Parliament.

Far more interest was taken by the clergy and by the Church generally in two Acts which, after much discussion, were passed in 1802, and which at least showed a laudable desire to elevate and purify the Church. One was an "*Act for restraining clerical farming ;*" the other an "*Act for enforcing the residence of incumbents on their cures, and encouraging the building of churches.*" As both Bills were introduced by Sir William Scott, M.P. for the University of Oxford, which was then an exclusively Church constituency, it may be presumed that they were not unacceptable to the Church at large. There was, however, considerable opposition to both. It was contended that "in this country the parish priest is, by the very constitution of his office, *in some degree* an agriculturist. He has to take care, undoubtedly, that the ecclesiastic shall not merge in the farmer ; but the moderated and subordinate practice of farming supplied many means of cheap subsistence for the clergyman and his family ;"[2] and so forth. One is carried back in thought to the times of Dr. Primrose and his son Moses, who worked in the fields from sunrise to sunset without causing any offence to the good doctor's little flock ; and to times when even a Parson Trulliber could be tolerated. But what did well enough in the easy-going days before the

Parliamentary Debates for the discussions in Parliament on the various Bills noticed in this chapter. They will all be found there under the dates of the different years.

[1] See *Life*, p. 220.
[2] See, *inter alia*, a tract entitled *Observations on the Speech of Sir William Scott*.

French Revolution, became unbearable when that event had cast a firebrand not only into its own, but into its neighbour's land. The fatal consequences "of permitting the clergy to hold farms," "of degrading the clergy into a set of dirty, puddling farmers," were never dreamt of when Goldsmith and Fielding wrote; but men were now beginning to take a higher standard of clerical duty. Still, there was something to be said about the hardships of both Acts, if their provisions were too rigorously enforced. The non-residence Act was really a revival of the statute of 21 Henry VIII.—a statute which, according to its adversaries, required to be *revised*, not *revived;* for "nothing could have concealed the vices and infirmities of this statute, but its having been consigned by almost general consent to almost general inefficiency, ever since its birth, till within the last two years, when it has been made the commercial bank of two or three trading attorneys."[1] Now, theoretically, it is quite right that the clergy should be required to reside on their cures, and to devote themselves exclusively to their proper work; but if so, their incomes should at least be raised above starvation-point. But this level was certainly not reached, if it be true that "after all the augmentations of Queen Anne's Bounty, there were still a thousand livings in England and Wales which did not on an average exceed £85, while a very large proportion did not amount to £30."[2] There was certainly some reason for the contention that the impoverished state of the Church prevented the literal obedience to a "law which demanded universal residence under one uniform penalty;" and the more so when that law was supplemented by another, which forbade the poor parson to eke out his scanty subsistence by one of the few employments which were open to him. It was also objected that the Bill gave too much power to the bishops; and some of the bishops them-

---

[1] *Observations, etc., ut supra.* See also *Anguis in Herbâ: a sketch of the true character of the Church of England and her clergy; as a caveat against the misconstruction on the subject of a Bill for the revival of certain ecclesiastical statutes concerning non-residence*, by James Hook (who, by the way, was himself a glaring pluralist). Also a tract by Dr. Sturges on the same subject, entitled *Thoughts on the Residence of the Clergy*, which had the distinction of being highly praised by Sydney Smith in the *Edinburgh Review*, 1803.

[2] *Observations, etc., ut supra.*

selves felt that an invidious duty was imposed upon them which they often could not fulfil without inflicting great hardship. The Bishop of London naturally felt this most, because he would have greater difficulty in enforcing residence in an expensive place like London. He therefore brought in a special Bill on July 19, 1804, called *The London Clergy Incumbents Bill*, in introducing which he said, " Many London clergy had no house on their livings; others had houses not habitable, fit only for greengrocers and cobblers. It was his duty to enforce residence within the city. From the population, and the value of houses, a clergyman could not get a house for less than £180 or £150 a year. How was this to be done with their incomes? It was all that most of them had. And once more, if the Act were strictly enforced, a number of worthy men would be thrown out of employment. What was to become of the stipendiary curate, who would be no longer required when the incumbent himself came into residence ? "

This last consideration drew attention to the position and circumstances of stipendiary curates generally, and led to the passing of two Bills in the autumn of 1803. One was called *The Stipendiary Curates' Bill;* it was introduced by Sir William Scott, and was intended to encourage the residence of stipendiary curates; the other was *The Curates' Relief Bill*, by which a sum not exceeding £8000 was granted for the relief of such curates as should be deprived of their cures in consequence of the Bill compelling the residence of the incumbents. The Earl of Suffolk might well complain, when the Bill came up to the House of Lords, that it did not go far enough, for the amount granted was but a drop in the ocean for the purpose for which it was intended.

In 1804 a Bill was very properly passed which enacted that "no person should be admissible to the sacred orders of deacon and priest till he should have attained his twenty-third or twenty-fourth year respectively." Of course this had previously been the canonical law of the Church, but it had not always been carefully adhered to, and the sanction of the legislature was desirable. The only complaint that can be made against the Bill is the inadequacy of its title, *Priests' Orders Bill;* but that is a minor matter. The debate on the subject in the House of Lords, on April 13, was valuable as eliciting from the Bishop of St. Asaph (Dr. Horsley) a much-needed reminder that "the sacerdotal character could not be done away by the secular power; the *sacerdotium Catholicum* was that which no secular power could either give or take away; it was derived from a higher source." Obvious as such truths may seem now, they were but scantily recognized in the early years of the nineteenth century.

The Clergy Residence Act of 1802-3 proved only a very partial remedy for the evils of non-residence. Another Clergy Residence Bill, therefore, was passed in 1808, through the exertions of Mr. Perceval. This was, no doubt, a much-needed and, in the end, successful measure; but it bore very hardly at first upon the existing clergy, many of whom had to build a residence before they could possibly comply with its requirements. For "one-third of the parsonages in England had gone to decay; and by the effects of this Bill, one generation of clergymen were compelled suddenly to atone for the accumulated sins of their predecessors."[1] Thus writes Lady Holland, whose father, Sydney Smith, was one of the first sufferers from the Bill. He was compelled to bury himself in a remote village in Yorkshire, and it is for this reason, among others, that he is perpetually vilifying Mr. Perceval. Mr. Perceval leaned to, if he did not actually identify himself with, the Evangelical party; hence we hear of "the odious vigour of the *Evangelical* Perceval;"[2] "that man who, instead of being a Methodist preacher, is for the curse of us become a legislator and a politician;"[3] "the little Methodist."[4]

In the same year (1808) Mr. Perceval also introduced a *Curates' Salary Bill*, which Sydney Smith also attacked in the *Edinburgh Review*, declaring that "a very great proportion of all the curacies in England were filled with men to whom the emolument was a matter of subordinate importance," and that "unless Mr. Perceval would raise an additional million or two for the Church, there must be poor curates—and poor rectors also." Mr. Perceval was not for-

[1] *Memoir of the Rev. Sydney Smith*, by Lady Holland, i. 153.
[2] "Peter Plymley's Letters:" *Works*, iii. 427.   [3] *Id.*, p. 385.
[4] Letter to Earl Grey in 1810, quoted by Lady Holland, ii. 53.

SERVICES OF MR. PERCEVAL AND LORD LIVERPOOL. 301

getful of the poor rectors any more than of the poor curates ; for, having carried a Bill for the improvement of curates' stipends, in the next year (1809), having meanwhile become Prime Minister, he successfully piloted through Parliament a measure for granting £100,000 a year to the governors of Queen Anne's Bounty for the augmentation of livings under £150 a year; and this grant was continued for several years. He was only prevented by his tragical death, in 1811, from bringing before Parliament the duty of making a better provision for public worship by the erection of new churches.

In treating of the relations between Church and State in the early years of the nineteenth century, it would be unjust not to express a grateful recognition of the services rendered to the Church by Mr. Perceval, both in his private and in his political capacity. We may not be able to go quite so far as S. T. Coleridge, who declares that he is "singular enough to regard Perceval as the best and wisest minister of this [George III.'s] reign;"[1] but a Churchman must own that he was a true and faithful friend to the Church, according to his lights, and gave a stimulus to the State in its laudable desire to help her, the effects of which continued to be seen some years after his death. "The attention," said Bishop Ryder in 1819, "which has been paid to the best interests of the Church, and the benefits which have been conferred upon her by the legislature during the last ten years, have exceeded all that had been accomplished for that object during the preceding century; and all these measures may be ascribed in their origin to him [Mr. Perceval]."[2] This may seem sweeping language, but those who are acquainted with the history of the Church in the eighteenth century will admit that it is literally true. At the same time, justice should be done to Mr. Perceval's successor in the Premiership, the Earl of Liverpool, who was an ardent and attached Churchman, and therefore quite ready to carry into effect all the projects which his predecessor had conceived.[3] The interval between Mr. Perceval's assassination in 1811 and the date of Bishop Ryder's Charge (1819) was indeed a busy time in the annals

[1] See *Biographia Literaria*, written in 1817.
[2] Second Charge to the clergy of the diocese of Gloucester.
[3] See *Memoirs of the Public Life, etc., of the Earl of Liverpool, sub finem*.

of ecclesiastical legislation; and though some Churchmen did not think so at the time, experience has shown that the measures passed were in the end beneficial to the Church.

For instance, the Act of 1812, which virtually repealed the old Conventicle and Five-Mile Acts, was undoubtedly to the advantage rather than the disadvantage of the Church. No one had ever dreamt of putting them into force for many years, and the only effect of retaining them in the Statute-Book was that it perpetuated the appearance of a persecuting spirit when the reality did not exist. Nor was it at all advantageous to the Church that the obsolete penalties which attached to those who denied the doctrine of the Blessed Trinity, and were, therefore, not included in the Toleration Act of William III., should be retained as a mere *brutum fulmen*. The Bill to remove them was passed without a debate in 1812, the Archbishop of Canterbury very properly reminding the House of Lords, on the third reading, that "it had not been called for by any attempt to inflict penalties upon, or to impede the worship of, Unitarians."[1]

In 1813 the irrepressible questions about curates' stipends and non-resident clergy reappeared. A *Bill for the Augmentation of Curates' Stipends* was introduced in the House of Lords by the Earl of Harrowby, and carried after much opposition. The debate brought out an argument which was painfully characteristic of the time. It was urged that if the Bill passed, the "subordination of different ranks, so necessary to the well-being of ecclesiastical government, would be destroyed; that the curate would be at variance with the incumbent, and an interference of the lower with the higher orders of that class of clergy would be perpetually recurring;" —as if the difference of orders consisted of incumbents and curates, and not of priests and deacons! And the Bishop of London, good Churchman though he was, used this argument! On this occasion occurred one of the first of those tirades against the clergy which, towards the close of our period, were the stock-in-trade of orators, inside and outside of Parliament. The speaker was Lord Redesdale, but he did not carry the House with him. This Act materially con-

[1] See *Annual Register* for 1813.

tributed to the residence of incumbents owing to the increase of expense in providing a substitute.

But the attempt to enforce their residence by the Act of 1803 had produced an effect which was not intended. The law was taken advantage of, among others, by a Mr. Wright, who had been secretary to three bishops and had thus learnt the ins and outs of ecclesiastical business, to institute a very serious persecution against many of the clergy. This led to the passing, in 1814, of *The Clergy Penalties' Suspension Bill.* The Bill of 1803 does not appear to have been drawn up with sufficient care—at any rate, the nature of residence had not been defined with sufficient accuracy ; and the consequence was that an unscrupulous person could, under the law which enacted very severe penalties, ruin an innocent man. "The Bill," said Sir William Scott, "had for its sole object to relieve the clergy from prosecutions under the Act of Henry VIII." It was unquestionably necessary, but the necessity was a most unfortunate one; for non-residence was still a crying abuse, and nothing tends more to perpetuate an abuse than an abortive attempt to remedy it. As a matter of fact, in spite of law after law, and warning after warning in bishops' Charges, non-residence continued to be a blot upon the Church almost up to the time of the present generation.

It will be better to finish the account of this wearisome but most important subject at once. So, passing over two years, we come to the *Clergy Bill* of 1816, which Bishop Herbert Marsh describes as "of greater consequence than any ecclesiastical law which has been made since the Reformation." " Bishops and clergy," he goes on, " will now find in one single Act a complete body of law, from which they may learn to regulate their conduct in everything relating to the *residence* of the clergy, the performance of their *spiritual* duties, the extent of their *temporal* engagements, and the payments to which the beneficed clergy are subjected when their duty is performed by a curate."[1] He then proceeds to give a full and most luminous account of this Act, which might well be called an "*Act of Consolidation,*" or "*Consolidated Act;*" for, as the bishop shows, it embraces what had been attempted by a great number of Acts in previous years. Finally, we have an

[1] Charge of Bishop Marsh at his Primary Visitation at Llandaff in 1817.

"*Act to restrain and regulate the holding of a plurality of dignities and benefices by spiritual persons*," which passed, first in the Lords, and then in the Commons, in 1832. This was the last Act during our period that was rendered necessary by the unfortunate Act of Mr. Bragg Bathurst in 1803, which has been so frequently referred to in these pages. After the repeal of the disabling clause of Act 21 Henry VIII., of the clauses of the same statute enabling certain persons to purchase dispensations, and of so much of the Act as enabled certain spiritual persons to accept any number of benefices, etc., it enacted that any spiritual person, having one or more benefices, and who shall obtain a licence or dispensation for the purpose, may hold another, provided the distance between them shall not exceed three miles, etc.

Enough has been said in the last chapter about the Act of 1813 for renewing the Charter of the East India Company, when provision was made for a bishop and three archdeacons for India. It need only be added that the debate in the House of Lords gave occasion for a noble utterance on the part of Lord Erskine. "Do not," he said, "forget, my lords, that this country holds her Indian provinces by the sole tenure of Christianity. And if she neglects to impart its blessings, she may lose them; and that tremendous storm which has burst upon Europe, from which we have mercifully escaped that we might propagate the Christian faith, may cross the Channel and fall on our guilty heads."

We come next to the most liberal instance in the whole history of the Church of England of help afforded to her by the State. In 1818, largely through the influence of Lord Liverpool, a Parliamentary grant of one million pounds was voted for the erection of new churches; in 1824 a further grant of half a million was made for the same purpose, and Exchequer loans were also given to about the same amount; and, finally, help was rendered by a remission of duty on the materials employed in sacred structures.

It may seem strange that this liberality should have been shown just at the time when the outcry against the Church generally and the clergy in particular was beginning to wax louder and louder, until it reached its height about the period of the Reform Bill. But, in point of fact, the liberality and the outcry were to a great extent due to the same cause. While the great war was going on, the nation had neither money to spend on building churches, nor leisure to devote to abusing the Church and the clergy. But the restoration of peace opened alike its purse-strings and its mouth.

We must now make rather an abrupt transition to a very different subject. The claim of the Roman Catholics to the full rights and liberties of citizens, or, as it was called, by an absurd misnomer, *Catholic Emancipation*, was a subject of agitation which was inherited from the eighteenth century, and continued until the final settlement of the question in 1829. It does not come within the province of this work to describe in detail how statesman after statesman took the matter up: Pitt in 1801, Canning in 1812, Grattan in 1813, Sir Francis Burdett in 1825,—on the last occasion the Relief Bill being actually passed by the House of Commons, but thrown out by the Lords. Up to the death of George III. the question was complicated by a feeling of loyalty to the good old king, who from first to last steadily set his face against Relief. So, for the matter of that, did his successor; but respect for the father did not extend itself to the son. Apart, however, from the royal disapproval, the measure was undoubtedly unpopular throughout the country; and the result of the attempt in 1825 was one of the few occasions on which the rejection by the Lords of a Liberal measure sent up to them by the Commons met with popular sympathy. So far as English Churchmen were concerned (and with these alone we have to do), opinion was curiously divided. Men who on most questions were agreed, now found themselves in opposite camps. The Evangelicals, for instance, generally presented a united front, which was one source of their strength. But on the Roman Catholic question there was a great divergence of opinion among them. The majority, as being sound Protestants, were, no doubt, against Relief; but some of their ablest leaders were "unsound" on the matter. William Wilberforce, for example, was sorely exercised when he felt himself bound to go against his party. "Meetings," he writes in 1813, "against Roman Catholics in all parts of England. I am very doubtful which way is right. Lord, direct me! All the religious people are on the other

x

side, but they are sadly prejudiced. It grieves me to separate from the dean and all my religious friends; but conscience must be obeyed."[1] "All the religious people," however, were not on the other side, or, at least, did not continue so. Daniel Wilson was at first with the majority, but went over heart and soul to the enemy, sacrificing some valued friendships by so doing. The Grants and Dr. Dealtry, all pillars of the Evangelical cause, were in favour of Relief. It was the same with other Church parties. Archdeacon Daubeny, perhaps the ablest and most prominent representative of the older form of High Churchmanship, was strongly against the measure; Alexander Knox, the precursor of the High Churchmanship of the future, was as strongly in its favour. Even among the Liberals, Bishop Copleston was against the Bill,[2] though as a rule his party was in its favour—Dr. (afterwards Bishop) Stanley, Bishop Bathurst, and, above all, Sydney Smith, being among its conspicuous champions. One of the most brilliant productions of the latter was a slashing article in the *Edinburgh Review* against Bishop Tomline's Charge against the claims of the Roman Catholics; and "Peter Plymley's Letters" are half filled with ridicule of the opposition to the Bill. Then, to make the entanglement complete, Mr. (afterwards Sir Robert) Peel, the chosen representative of the Oxford Tories and High Churchmen, who had long been an uncompromising opponent of the measure, executed a complete *volte de face*, passed it as a Government Bill in 1829, and lost his seat at Oxford in consequence.

The relief granted in one direction was preceded by relief in another, viz. the *Repeal of the Test and Corporation Acts* in 1828; or rather, as Bishop Kaye very properly pointed out, not the repeal of the Acts themselves, but of those clauses in them "by which all persons admitted to offices of power and trust in corporations, and to civil offices in general, were required to receive the Lord's Supper according to the rites of the Church of England."[3] The Test Act, indeed, had been originally passed to exclude Roman Catholics; but, like the

[1] *Life*, p. 336.
[2] But Bishop Copleston can only be called a Liberal in a very modified sense.
[3] Charge to the clergy of the diocese of Lincoln at Bishop Kaye's Primary Visitation, 1828.

Corporation Act, it pressed chiefly upon Protestant Dissenters. The measure of 1828 had not, like that of 1829, been a bone of contention all through the century, and its passing did not produce the same practical effects. For the clauses repealed had long been a dead letter, owing to the annual passing of an Indemnity Act which had virtually given the Dissenters all the privileges which in 1828 they received legally. Such being the case, it was desirable on all accounts that the disabling clauses should be expunged from the Statute-Book; and it is not at all surprising that many of the clergy should, for their own sakes, have desired to see them expunged. For if it was a grievance to the Dissenter to do violence to his conscience by communicating, simply in order to qualify for office, it was certainly no less a grievance to the conscientious clergyman to have to administer the Sacred Symbols to men whom he knew to have presented themselves from this motive. And so, again to quote Bishop Kaye, "the Repeal of the Sacramental Test was a concession, not exclusively to the feelings and wishes of our Dissenting brethren, but also to the conscientious scruples of many sincere Churchmen."[1] Sydney Smith, indeed, declared that he had "never met a parson in his life who did not consider the Corporation and Test Acts as the great bulwarks of the Church;"[2] but if he had extended his clerical acquaintance, he certainly might have met a few. Indeed, if we may judge from the debates in the House of Lords, many of the laity were less liberal than the clergy. To the infinite disgust of Lord Eldon and those who followed his lead, some bishops not only voted for the Bill, but also spoke in its favour from a Church point of view so admirably that their words deserve to be quoted. The Archbishop of York, premising that he expressed the Archbishop of Canterbury's opinion as well as his own, said he "felt bound, on every principle, to give his vote for the repeal of an Act which had, he feared, led in too many instances to the profanation of the most sacred ordinances of our religion. Religious tests imposed for political purposes must in themselves be always liable, more or less, to endanger religious sincerity." " I should," said the Bishop

[1] Charge of 1828, *ut supra*.
[2] " Peter Plymley's Letters: " *Works*, iii. 407.

of Lincoln, in words which deserve to be written in letters of gold, "feel it my bounden duty to resist the Repeal if I thought the safety of the Church of England would be compromised by it. I entertain no such apprehension; the best security of the Church of England is the hold which it possesses on the esteem and affections of the people. The legislature may, undoubtedly, contribute essentially to its stability and well-being; not, however, by throwing around it the external fences of restrictive laws, but by defining more accurately the privileges which belong to it as an Established Church, by improving its internal polity, and by providing it with less expensive and less circuitous modes of administering its discipline." The Bishops of Durham and Chester were equally explicit.

At the same time, it is fully admitted that throughout the Church at large there was great opposition to all these measures; and we cannot wonder at it, when we remember the *animus* in which they were passed. In fact, in the discussion of almost all the questions which have been noticed, even when they seemed to be most favourable to the Church, a growing bitterness of feeling against her had been displayed. The question of the non-residence of the clergy of course afforded an obvious opportunity for displaying this feeling; but no less did the debates on the augmentation of small livings, on the regulation of curates' stipends, and even on the grants for church-building. On these occasions there was a fine scope for orators to draw an invidious contrast between the wealthy pluralists, or drones, and the working bees of the hive, who did all the hard labour but got none of the honey; to exhibit through a strong magnifying-glass the enormous wealth of the Church and its unequal distribution; to dwell on the growth and popularity of Dissent, and the decay and unpopularity of the Church,—and so forth, and so forth.

The very closeness of the connection which then subsisted between the civil and ecclesiastical powers sometimes tended to increase the unpopularity of the latter, by placing the Church, through no fault of her own, on the unpopular side. This was notably the case in the unfortunate affair of Queen Caroline, wife of George IV. The history of this painful case furnishes a curious instance of the change of parties—which, however, is easily explained. During his father's lifetime, the Prince Regent was on the side of the Whigs, and in opposition to the Tories or "Church-and-King" men. Hence, in his early matrimonial troubles, the Whigs took the side of the Prince, the Tories that of the Princess.[1] But on the accession of George IV. to the throne, one of the first royal orders was that the name of the Queen Consort should be expunged from the Liturgy. As matters stood, it is difficult to see how the clergy could possibly have disobeyed the order, but they were furiously abused for not doing so. By this time "Hamlet and Laertes had changed rapiers." It was the Dissenters who were the stoutest advocates of the Queen; the Churchmen who, as a rule, were her opponents. But when Churchmen *were* on her side, as some were, what could they do? Dr. Parr made an interesting record in the Prayer-book of Hatton Church after the required erasure: "It is my duty as a subject and an ecclesiastic to read what is prescribed by my sovereign, as head of the Church, but it is not my duty to express my approbation."[2] It should be remembered that there was then no such thing as Convocation, except in name; and to what other authority could a clergyman appeal?

The odium against the clergy came to a head in the famous Durham episode. On the death of the Queen in 1822, the clergy of Durham were violently attacked by a local newspaper, because "in an episcopal city containing six churches besides the cathedral, not a single bell announced the departure of the magnanimous spirit of the most injured of Queens." "Thus," the writer goes on, "the brutal emnity of those who embittered her mortal existence pursues her in her shroud. . . . It is such conduct which renders the very name of our established clergy odious till it stinks in the nostrils, that makes our churches look like deserted sepulchres rather than temples of the living God. . . . It is impossible that such a system can last; it is at war with the spirit of the age, as well as with

---

[1] See this point well brought out in Lockhart's *Life of Sir Walter Scott* (in 2 vols.), i. 185.

[2] *Life of Samuel Parr, LL.D.*, by John Johnston; prefixed to the first volume of Dr. Parr's *Works*, p. 767.

justice and reason, and the beetles who crawl about its holes and crevices act as if they were striving to provoke and accelerate the blow which, sooner or later, will inevitably crush the whole fabric and level it with the dust." After the lapse of more than seventy years, it is impossible to judge fairly what ought to have been done. There may have been local circumstances which would alter the whole complexion of the case; and certainly great allowance ought to be made for change of times. But, speaking generally, one would have thought it wiser if the clergy had passed over the attack in dignified silence. However, they thought otherwise; and one is not surprised that they did so, when one finds that Henry Phillpotts, afterwards Bishop of Exeter, the very last man to sit down tamely under an insult, was then the ruling spirit among the Durham clergy. They prosecuted Mr. John Ambrose Williams, proprietor of the *Durham Chronicle*, in which the attack appeared, for a libel, in the Court of King's Bench; and, to the general surprise, gained their cause. But, so far as the popularity of the Church went, the victory was a Cadmean victory,—worse than a defeat. The popular sympathy was, as in a law case it generally is, against the parsons. The counsel for the defence, Mr. Brougham, carried the people with him, though he could not carry the jury; and, moreover, when he was beaten, he still had a terrible weapon in reserve, the *Edinburgh Review*, which published in its next number a fierce attack upon the Church in general, and the Durham clergy in particular. It was answered, and very ably answered, by many pens;[1] but the writers could not gain the ear of the

---

[1] *Letter to H. Brougham, Esq., on his Durham Speech, and Three Articles in the last " Edinburgh Review" on the Subject of the Clergy*, 1823; *An Appeal to the Gentlemen of England on behalf of the Church of England*, by Augustus Campbell, Rector of Wallasey, Cheshire, 1823; *The Seventy-fourth Number of the " Edinburgh Review's" Attack on the Church of England*, answered by the Rev. Francis Thackeray, 1823: supplementary to his *Defence of the Church of England* (1822); *A Vindication of the Church and Clergy of England from the Misrepresentations of the " Edinburgh Review,"* by a beneficed clergyman, 1823; *A Letter to F. Jeffrey, Esq., reputed Editor of the " Edinburgh Review,"* by H. Phillpotts, Rector of Stanhope; *A Defence of the Established Church*, by Alma Lux; *A Voice from St. Peter's and St. Paul's*, being a few Plain Words addressed to M.P.'s and Lords on the accusations against the Church Establishment, particularly those contained in No. 74 of the *Edinburgh Review*, by a member of the University of Oxford.

public, as the formidable *Review* could, and there is no doubt that this little episode added much to the already existing odium against the Church.

But the hostility to the Church in the political world did not rest upon any isolated episode. There was rising into power a political party whose vital principle was the destruction of the Church as a national establishment. This party was composed of men who were influenced by such writers as Jeremy Bentham [1] and James Mill,[2] who appealed to the more educated classes; while William Cobbett by his "Register" did the same kind office among the less educated. "I question," writes Dr. Stoughton, "whether in the present day any attacks on any institution are to be compared with those in reference to the Established Church between 1820 and 1830."[3] The Acts of 1828 and 1829 encouraged the assailants to hope that the days of the "Establishment" were numbered. The outworks had been taken; it only remained to take the citadel itself. "The year 1830," writes Dr. J. B. Mozley, "ushered in what was perhaps the most memorable and alarming struggle between the Church and her political and Dissenting opponents that had been seen for a century."[4] Friends were as despondent as foes were exultant. Dr. Miller, in his preface to his very striking sermons (1830), complains that it was scarcely possible for the friends of the Church to correct its abuses "by reason of the fierce, ungenerous clamour round about the sanctuary, and the variety of enemies all ready to rush in and build up their own visionary schemes, or schemes of selfishness, upon its ruins."[5] The bishops, as has been shown in a

[1] See Bentham's *Church-of-Englandism*, etc., etc.
[2] "Next to an aristocracy," writes John Stuart Mill, "an established Church, or corporation of priests, as being by position the great depravers of religion, and interested in opposing the progress of the human mind, was the object of my father's greatest detestation."
[3] *Religion in England*, 1800–1850, by John Stoughton, D.D., ii. 10.
[4] J. B. Mozley's *Essays*, vol. ii.: "Dr. Arnold."
[5] *Sermons intended to show a Sober Application of Scripture Principles to the Realities of Life*. With a Preface addressed to the Clergy. By John Miller, late Fellow of Worcester College, Oxford, 1830. To the same effect Connop Thirlwall wrote to Bunsen in 1832: "The Church of England contains many disinterested and devoted friends, who perceive its defects, and would wish to remedy them. But the present animosity about its temporal relations to the State so completely engrosses all other subjects connected with it, that it would be absurd

former chapter, began to "despair of the Republic." In fact, it was no cuckoo cry, as it had been in the eighteenth century, that "the Church was in danger;" and that danger was apparently increased tenfold by the passing of the Reform Bill in 1831. The clergy as a body, and the bishops in particular, were against it, while the great majority of the nation were in its favour. The episcopal vote in the House of Lords seemed to fill up the measure of the Church's iniquity.

Unfortunate as it may seem to us that the Church should have set itself against the State in this critical conjuncture, it can scarcely be a matter of surprise. The Reform Bill gave great power to just that class which was most hostile to the Church and most favourable to Dissent, which has always found its strongest supporters, not among the higher or the lower, but among the middle classes. It might justly be argued, that when the reform of the State was complete, the reform of the Church would come next; and that the reform of the Church by a reformed Parliament meant simply destruction. It was no imaginary fear that the next move would be fatal to the Church as a national establishment. But the thunder-clouds rolled harmlessly away, which at the period when this history closes seemed likely to burst, and to sweep away the most venerable part of the British constitution.

in any one to propose any scheme of internal reformation. The Church remains powerless for any new good, and at the utmost only able to preserve itself from ruin."—*Letters Literary and Theological*, p. 103.

CHAPTER X.

INTERCOURSE WITH SISTER CHURCHES.

IRELAND.

IT may not be strictly correct—at least from the statesman's point of view—to speak of the Church of Ireland as a "sister Church," because the same Acts which made England and Ireland, from January 1, 1801, one united kingdom, made also the two national Churches one united Church; but inasmuch as the union of the two Churches lasted barely seventy years, inasmuch as it was effected solely by the Acts of Parliament, or rather of both Parliaments, English and Irish, without any sort of reference to synod or convocation, that is, without consulting the spiritualty of either kingdom,[1] it is at least pardonable, as it is certainly more convenient, to speak of "the Irish Church," instead of using the awkward periphrasis of "the Irish branch of the United Church of England and Ireland." So accurate a writer and so sound a Churchman as Dr. Christopher Wordsworth, Bishop of Lincoln, makes no scruple about denominating it the Irish Church when he writes both *during* and *concerning* the time when the union was in force; and Bishop Wordsworth's is a good name for a Churchman to shelter himself under.[2]

Irish Churchmen, as a rule, anticipated with pleasure the closer connection with their brother Churchmen across the Channel which the union seemed to promise; nor were they, at any rate until the last year or two of the period, disappointed.

---
[1] See *The Reformed Church of Ireland*, by the Right Hon. J. T. Ball, p. 223; and *The Church of Ireland*, by the Rev. T. Olden (National Churches Series), p. 393.
[2] See Wordsworth's *History of the Church of Ireland, passim.*

It is a remarkable fact that, although the Oxford Movement found few sympathizers in Ireland, not a few of its most obvious precursors were connected with the Church of Ireland. It is, for example, an admitted fact that Dr. Percy, who was Bishop of Dromore from 1782 to 1811, contributed indirectly to the movement by the publication of his "Reliques of Ancient English Poetry," which drew men's attention to antiquity, and led them to be dissatisfied with modern systems.[1] Dr. Richard Mant, who also became Bishop of Dromore in 1820, was unquestionably "a Puseyite before Puseyism;" and as he was a very able and somewhat voluminous writer, his works must necessarily have drawn men in the same direction. Much more was this the case with Dr. John Jebb, Bishop of Limerick, who lived all his life in Ireland. His sermons, including the famous "Appendix," were naturally recommended by the early Tractarians, as one of many evidences that their views were not novelties; and the name of Bishop Jebb is generally cited as furnishing one of the links which connected the Oxford with the Caroline and the Nonjuring divines. Moreover, it was, as we have seen, to Bishop Jebb's ordination examination at Limerick that we owe a work which, beyond doubt, helped to prepare men's minds for the reception of the Tractarian tenets, viz. Palmer's "Origines Liturgicæ;" William Palmer is thus another name which connects Ireland with the Oxford Movement. But the most effective pioneer of all was Jebb's guide, philosopher, and friend, Mr. Knox, an Irishman born and bred, who never, except for an occasional visit across the Channel, left his native country.

All these, however, were exceptional cases; the general tone of the Church of Ireland was decidedly Evangelical; and this being so, it is somewhat strange that there was so little intercourse between the Evangelical Churchmen in England and those in the sister island. One of the most prominent among the latter was a clergyman named Walker, a Fellow of Trinity College, Dublin, and a man of great ability. He was an uncompromising Calvinist, and defended Mr. Overton's "True Churchman Ascertained." He had a considerable

---

[1] See, *inter alia*, Cardinal Newman's *Apologia pro Vitâ Suâ*. The researches of Joseph Ritson, which were more accurate and extensive than those of Bishop Percy, though his works never became so popular, would lead in the same direction.

following, and his followers were called "Walkerites;" but neither he nor they ever separated from the Established Church. Another able Evangelical clergyman was Dr. O'Brien, afterwards Bishop of Ossory, who wrote in defence of the doctrine of justification by faith.[1] But, as a body, the markedly Evangelical clergy of Ireland appear to have been, like their brethren in England, more distinguished by their piety and earnestness than by their intellectual power.[2]

A remarkable testimony to the excellence of one Evangelical household is given by Mr. J. A. Froude, who resided in it for some time. "Christianity," he says, "was part of the atmosphere which was breathed; it was the great fact of our existence, to which everything else was subordinated;" and much more to the same effect.[3] The once popular authoress who wrote under the name of "Charlotte Elizabeth" gives an equally enthusiastic account of a clerical household in Ireland which she visited in 1821—that of Dr. Hamilton, incumbent of Knocktopher, county Kilkenny. His father had been bishop of the diocese; and he himself is described by Charlotte Elizabeth as "a man of fine mind, deep erudition, unbounded benevolence, and Christian sweetness that endeared him to every one." He was rich, and "expended a large proportion of his income in works of charity; equally judicious, liberal, and impartial. He had under his roof thirteen poor girls, who were educated, maintained, taught in all the requisites of good household servants, and finally placed out in the families of his friends. Mrs. Hamilton seemed to have her heart in this school, over which a very competent mistress presided; and a more beautifully ordered little nursery of valuable domestics I never saw. Besides this, large benefactions were distributed in fuel, clothing, and other necessaries among the poor of the parish, without any regard to religious distinction; and as the Romanists amounted to above twelve hundred, while the Protestants could not muster one hundred, and the former were infinitely

---

[1] See Ball's *Reformed Church of Ireland*, pp. 250, 251. Dr. O'Brien's *Ten Sermons upon the Nature and Effects of Faith* were not published until 1834, but they were preached in the chapel of Trinity College, Dublin, in 1829 and 1831.

[2] Mr. Olden mentions the Revs. B. W. Matthias and P. Roe as prominent Evangelical clergy in the early days.—*The Church of Ireland*, p. 393.

[3] See *Short Studies on Great Subjects*, iv. 295.

more necessitous than the latter, of course nearly all went to them."[1] There is no reason to believe that these were exceptional cases; but, on the other hand, strong negative reason to believe that they were not. For it is a significant fact that amid all the complaints about the injustice of maintaining an endowed and established Church for the rich minority, while the poor majority were alienated from it, not one word of reproach, so far as I am aware, was uttered against the personal characters of the clergy as a body; they were generally recognized as blameless and benevolent Christian gentlemen. Nor were they deficient in learning.[2] Dr. Graves' (Dean of Ardagh) writings on the Pentateuch (1807), Dr. Magee's (afterwards Archbishop of Dublin) on the Atonement (1801), Dr. William Hales' on Prophecy and on the Chronology of the Bible (already noticed, p. 180), all became classics, and were all widely read and highly appreciated in England as well as Ireland. But, after all, by far the most interesting works bequeathed to us by Irish Churchmen of this period are the "*Remains of Alexander Knox*," and the "*Correspondence between Knox and Jebb.*" The latter commences with the beginning of the century, and is continued up to the time of Mr. Knox's death in 1831. It therefore covers almost the whole of our period; and besides being full of acute remarks (many of them being anticipations of a later school of thought), and containing unconscious pictures of two very striking men, it gives us some glimpses of the state of the Irish Church. It brings out both the strong and the weak side of the "Establishment" question, which soon afterwards became a burning one. It would be quite easy, on the one hand, for the agitator to find in this correspondence telling arguments in favour of disestablishment and disendowment. "Here," he might say, "you have a man with a professional income of £1000 a year, who, on his own showing, has little or nothing to do for it. Then he is transferred to a bishopric, from which he is frequently

---

[1] *Personal Recollections of Charlotte Elizabeth*, pp. 146, 147.

[2] That is, the Irish clergy generally. I do not think that any of the three mentioned below were decidedly Evangelicals, though Dr. Magee's work on *The Atonement* was most favourably reviewed in *The Christian Observer*, if I remember rightly.

absent for months together." That is one side of the question; but there is another. The residence of a highly cultured Christian gentleman in a remote part of Ireland could not fail to be beneficial to the whole neighbourhood, and £1000 a year was a cheap price to pay for it. The influence of John Jebb as Rector of Abington was very remarkable. In 1821, "while the whole surrounding country became a scene of fire and bloodshed, Abington continued, like Gideon's fleece, the only inviolate spot. A coachman passing through the village said to a barrister who was a passenger, 'That house is the residence of Archdeacon Jebb. The parish in which it stands is the only quiet district in the country, and its quiet is entirely owing to the character and exertions of the Protestant rector.'"[1] And so far from its being an undeserved honour when Archdeacon Jebb was promoted to the see of Limerick, it was most decidedly an honour to the see of Limerick (as it would have been to any see in England or Ireland) to have such a man as John Jebb to preside over it.

But so far as thought and intellect went, was not Jebb the mere puppet of which Knox pulled the strings? I am inclined to think that this view of their relationship has sometimes been stated a little too strongly. Jebb had a distinctly marked mind and character of his own; and though he was, of course, as he repeatedly owns, the disciple of Knox, he could do in some respects what his master could not do. He was more capable of sustained effort, more patient and painstaking, though a far less original genius. The admirable way in which, in his "*Sacred Literature*," he works out Bishop Lowth's theory of parallelisms in Hebrew poetry, and the infinite pains he evidently took in the composition of his printed sermons, are witnesses of this. And we must also not forget that if we had had no Jebb, we should probably have had no Knox; for Jebb was the whetstone on which Knox sharpened his intellect.

On the other hand, it is fully admitted that if we had had

[1] *Life of Bishop Jebb*, by the Rev. C. Forster, i. 214. See also *Correspondence between Knox and Jebb*, ii. 461, where Jebb writes to his friend Knox a similar account of the quiet of Abington and its riotous surroundings, but does not agree with the coachman that the result is solely due to himself.

no Knox, we should almost certainly have had no Jebb; that is to say, Jebb was one of those good and able men who do excellent work in their generation, but have not originality enough to preserve an undying name to posterity. It is in the "Remains" and the "Correspondence" and the "Appendix" (which was really Knox's work) that Jebb lives. It would be out of place, however, to say more about Knox in connection with the Irish Church; for he was cosmopolitan rather than Irish in his writings, and his recluse life kept him quite apart from the active side of Irish Church affairs. Far otherwise was it with his friend, Bishop Jebb, whose Charge to the clergy of the diocese of Limerick gives us so clear an insight into the state of the Irish Church, that it is worth quoting at some length. It should be premised that the circumstances of Jebb's life had made him equally acquainted with the north and the south of Ireland; for he was born and educated in the north, and there began his ministerial work; and then laboured for twenty years in the south before he became a bishop. It is so difficult for an Englishman to realize the strongly marked line which separates the north from the south, that his observations on this point are peculiarly valuable. He does not give a very favourable impression of the theological attainments of the clergy of the south. " I am pained to say, after no short or superficial acquaintance with the clergy of the south of Ireland, that, while many are most laudably diligent in other professional pursuits, some are but too apt to mistake the conclusion of their academical course for the completion of their theological studies. . . . While I rejoice to think that several individuals have derived incalculable benefit from the impulse given in the Divinity School of Dublin, I am obliged to state, from my own actual knowledge, that some who came forth from that school, clothed in its first honours, had, in the space of one short year, retrograded rather than advanced, and betrayed a degree of ignorance which it is painful to think upon."[1] But·

---

[1] To the same effect he writes about the whole of Ireland in his *Biographical Memoir of William Phelan, D.D.* (1832): "It must be confessed that hitherto, from unhappy circumstances, there has been in Ireland but little opportunity and, if possible, less encouragement for theological learning. . . . The flippant pamphlet and slight brochure (of merit, very different, indeed, from the slightest

he gives a much more favourable impression of their goodness and activity under trying circumstances. "The acknowledged smallness of our congregations in the south of Ireland has given rise to an imputation, most industriously circulated, that the established clergy are supine, inefficient, and superfluous. A less substantiated charge, or one which betrays a greater unacquaintance with the existing state of the country, cannot readily be imagined. . . . Bold as it may seem, I shrink not from saying that, in several important respects, the established clergy of the south are by no means a less useful, and incomparably a more influential body, than their brethren of the north of Ireland. What are the circumstances? In the north there is an affluent and educated resident gentry; an intelligent, industrious yeomanry; a general diffusion of knowledge through schools liberally maintained. In the south, the great aristocracy and the hereditary proprietors of the soil, absentees; a starving, ill-educated, unemployed, and most redundant peasantry; bad schools; and the clergy have the melancholy pre-eminence of being, I had almost said, the single class to whom the people look up for relief in their distresses, for counsel in their difficulties, and, in too many districts, for common honesty and civility in the ordinary transactions of life. Thus situated, their influence is of necessity very considerable; and in most parishes the poorer inhabitants feel that the rector is to them the most important individual in the neighbourhood. In the vast majority of instances our clergy are left alone and unsupported, with every unfavourable circumstance to counteract their exertions and to cripple their powers; and at this disadvantage are not only expected, but feel themselves conscientiously bound, to bear the whole burthen and heat of the day.

"I feel myself perfectly safe in the assertion that, while

efforts of Mr. Phelan) have been generally thought a far more marketable commodity than any solid work of genius, piety, and learning" (p. 36). In a speech in the House of Lords, delivered June 10, 1824, he gives a reason for the dearth of theological learning: "In Ireland we have unfortunately not abounded in magnificent patrons of learning. We have but one College, one Provost, and twenty-five Fellows, for the education of about fifteen hundred undergraduates. These twenty-six very learned men, thus occupied, have little time for the pleasures and the pains of authorship."

the clergy in the north of Ireland yield, perhaps, to no established clergy throughout Christendom in the efficient discharge of their *pastoral* duties, they have a comparatively narrow field of *economical* exertion; and that while the clergy in the south have, in most instances, but few claims upon them of a strictly professional kind, they are furnished with inexhaustible sources of employment, in supplying the wants, soothing the feelings, softening the animosities of a people redundant almost to mutual extinction. . . .

"If the enemies of the Church succeed in their unholy efforts, the people of this country will soon learn who have been their best benefactors."[1]

But such considerations would be little likely to have weight against the tangible facts which might be alleged against the Irish Church, when reform was in the air. There were churches practically without congregations; there were many clergy non-resident, though a publication of the "Abstracts of Numbers of Resident and Non-resident Incumbents, and Total Numbers of Curates in each Diocese in Ireland for 1829 and 1830," shows that there had been gross exaggerations and misstatements on that score. "The Reform Bill," it has been said, "placed three-fourths of the representation of Ireland in the hands of the priests and demagogues, whose power was based on the hostility to the religion and government of England;" and it is not surprising that one of the earliest acts of the Reformed Parliament was a drastic measure against the Church of Ireland, by which ten out of its twenty-two bishoprics were to be swept away. The immediate cause of the measure was this: The charge of maintaining the fabrics and providing for the expenses of Divine worship had been defrayed by an assessment imposed at the vestries, and to this assessment Roman Catholics and Protestant Dissenters had to pay. This was thought unjust, and therefore it was arranged by the Act of 1833, which was called the Church Temporalities Act, that henceforth the fund was to be provided from the property of

---

[1] Charge to the Clergy of the Diocese of Limerick, at his Primary Visitation, in the Cathedral Church of St. Mary, June 19, 1823, by John Jebb, Bishop of Limerick, Ardfert, and Aghadoe.

the Church. The money was to be forthcoming by the reduction of the archbishoprics to two and the bishoprics to ten,[1] which left a sum of about £60,000 a year disposable for the purpose.[2]

It is a curious instance of the irony of fate that this very measure, which was supposed to be one of the first direct blows levelled against the Church, was really the occasion of a complete turn of the tide in her favour. The measure was, of course, passed, and—"created the Oxford Movement."[3] Its immediate result was the formation of the "Association of the Friends of the Church," which called forth the real but latent sympathy with the cause of the Church to an extent which astonished her friends at least as much as her foes. To add to the anomaly, the framer of the measure was Mr. Stanley, who afterwards, as the Earl of Derby, was the trusted leader of exactly the opposite party to that of the reformers. The history of all this, however, belongs to a later period. So also does the episcopate of Archbishop Whately, who, to the dismay of many, was appointed to the archbishopric of Dublin in 1831.

But the episcopate of Bishop Mant comes well within our period, and as it gives us an interesting and characteristic illustration of the state of the Church in Ireland, strikingly confirming what has been quoted from Bishop Jebb, a few words on the subject will not be inappropriate. Richard Mant, who had already won a high reputation in England, was appointed, through Lord Liverpool, to the bishopric of Killaloe and Kilfenora in 1820. He found that there had only been one general confirmation in the diocese for the last sixteen or seventeen years, and in his Primary Charge, delivered August 3, 1820, he tells us that he finds from the reports before him that in most churches only a single Sunday service was performed, and he admits that "often more may not be practicable." The custom of having children baptized at home prevailed to a very great extent. There was a monthly

---

[1] See Ball's *Reformed Church of Ireland*, ch. xvi. p. 229.
[2] See Spencer Walpole's *History of England from the Conclusion of the Great War in* 1815, vol. iii. p. 152.
[3] *A Narrative of Events connected with the Publication of the Tracts for the Times*, by W. Palmer, Introduction (published in 1883), p. 45.

Y

celebration in some parishes, but in others only four times a year; the number of communicants, however, compared favourably with England. "The fact," he proceeds, "is notorious that a very large proportion of our population in this diocese is in a state of separation from the Church of Ireland;" and he forthwith impresses strongly upon his clergy the duty of exposing the errors of the Church of Rome. This part of his Charge gave offence in high quarters, and was one of the reasons why he was not sooner promoted to a better see; for "that," says his biographer, "was a time of conciliation, and it was the policy of the rulers of the State to discourage whatever was calculated, even remotely, to offend a Romanist." This was rather hard upon Bishop Mant, for "I was sent hither," he says, "as the Archbishop of Canterbury distinctly told me, to assist in infusing a more professional spirit in the clergy;" and how he was to do this without urging them to set forth boldly the principles of their Church, and to combat that which was the chief obstacle to its extension, it is difficult to see. The other reason which the Prime Minister (Lord Liverpool) alleged for not translating him has more force in it. Disturbances broke out in 1821, and the Established Church was an object of special attack. The bishop's life was threatened, and he retired for a while to England. No doubt it would have been more heroic if he had remained at his post; but he soon returned to it, and braved the danger. In 1822 the country was still in a state of alarm; outrages were frequent; there was one on a glebe-house close by, and soldiers had to be sent to the See-house itself to secure its safety. But in 1823 the bishop was, to his great delight, translated to Down and Connor. Here he had to do battle with the prevailing Presbyterianism of the north, instead of with the prevailing Romanism of the south. "He observed in the clergy rather a tendency to conciliate unduly the Presbyterians." An instance which he gives certainly bears out his observation. "Yesterday," he writes, December 26, 1823, "I preached at a church in ——, my practice being constantly to preach in some of the churches in my diocese. After I had read the Nicene Creed, what must the clergyman do but give notice of a charity sermon to be preached next Sunday at the Presbyterian meeting-house, and, in order to give his congregation the power of attending, added that 'there would be no sermon at the church.' This was done in the perfect simplicity of his heart." After the service the bishop, not without reason, remonstrated with him. It would perhaps have been well for the Irish Church if it had had more bishops of the type of Bishop Mant. The Roman Catholics understood perfectly well *their* position, and the Presbyterians *theirs*. It was highly important that the Established Church should have some firmer ground to stand upon than its establishment. There *was* such ground, and Bishop Mant stood upon it; but if he did not stand actually alone, there were, at any rate, few who made their position so clear as he did his.

SCOTLAND.

At the beginning of the nineteenth century the Episcopal Church of Scotland was an object of the deepest interest to one class of English Churchmen, because they saw in it a practical exemplification of a truth which they were most anxious to impress upon their countrymen. In the eighteenth century " the Church " and "the Establishment " were regarded as almost convertible terms; and we have already seen how Bishop Horsley, Archdeacon Daubeny, and others protested against this strange confusion of ideas. In order to see how forcible an illustration of their meaning Scotland supplied, we must go back to the period preceding our history. The very existence of the ancient, native Church of Scotland had become almost unknown across the border. After the Revolution of 1688 it had refused to recognize the Parliamentary title of William III. to the throne, and had thrown all its sympathies into the cause of the exiled Stuarts. It was deprived of its legal establishment as the national Church; and, after 1715, suffered severe persecution, which increased as years went on.[1] The Jacobite rising of 1745 led to the enactment of penal laws, which were nothing less than "an attempt to extirpate a whole communion by rendering their worship illegal."[2] It was enacted that "from and after the

[1] For a full account, see Mr. Abbey's *English Church and its Bishops* (1700–1800), ii. 175–185.
[2] *History of the Church in Scotland*, by the Rev. Michael Russell, ii. 404.

1st of September, 1746, every person exercising the function of a pastor or minister in any Episcopal meeting-house in Scotland, without registering his letters of orders and taking all the oaths required by law, and praying for his Majesty King George and the Royal Family by name, shall, for the first offence, suffer six months' imprisonment, and for the second be transported to some one of his Majesty's plantations for life." Every house in which five or more, besides the family, met for worship was declared to be a meeting-house within the meaning of the Act, and no letters of orders, except such as had been given by some bishop of the Church of England or of Ireland, were allowed to be registered after September 1. Another Act was passed against laymen worshipping in an Episcopal meeting-house, and in 1748 still more stringent enactments were made. It is fair to add that the Church of England, as a body, had no share in this deliberate attempt to stamp out a sister Church; on the contrary, all the English bishops voted, and three of the most eminent of them (Sherlock, Secker, and Maddox) spoke against the Bill of 1748, but in vain. The result was that "all appearance of public worship was avoided, and the clergy visited families in private, where a few met to celebrate the rites of the Church in the utmost secrecy;" and, outside its own body, the native Church of Scotland dropped out of notice, until a memorable event in 1784 called attention to it.[1] That event was the consecration of the first American bishop, Dr. Seabury. The consecration was canonical in every respect, and it not only drew the attention of English Churchmen to a depressed and struggling Church, but also made them feel that they owed to that Church a deep obligation for what she had done. There were difficulties in the way of consecrating an American bishop in England which did not exist in Scotland. The War of Independence was still fresh in the minds of the Americans, and made them regard with jealousy any English interference in the affairs of America. Oaths were required of every one who was raised to the episcopate through the

---

[1] Dean Luckock, however, says that "on the accession of George III., though a long time elapsed before the penal laws of the previous reign were erased from the Statute Book, their stringency was immediately relaxed."—*The Church in Scotland* (National Churches Series), p. 278.

English Church which an American could not take. Then the Scotch Church stepped in as a *Deus ex machinâ*, and cut the Gordian knot. The step had a most beneficial effect upon the English Church; it broke the hard crust of Erastianism which had long overlaid it, and supplied a want which good Churchmen had long felt, but knew not how to meet. No wonder the bold step which the Scotch bishops, chiefly through the influence of Bishop Skinner, took, made their southern brethren inclined to regard their Church with a favourable eye; and an opportunity soon occurred of enabling them to repay the obligation. The death of the last Stuart claimant to the throne in 1788 made all but the most fanatical and unreasonable of Scotch Episcopalians feel that they might now with a safe conscience pray publicly for the reigning family in the terms of the English Liturgy. This was accordingly done in all the chapels in Scotland except three. And now that they were loyal subjects, might they not fairly ask for a repeal of those penal laws, which had reduced them almost to the condition of those early Christians who had to worship in the dens and caves of the earth? So, in the spring of 1789, Bishop Skinner, who had taken the leading part in the matter of the consecration of Bishop Seabury, and was now Primus of the Scotch Church, was sent with two other bishops, Abernethy Drummond and Strahan, on a deputation to London to plead the cause of their oppressed communion. They had many good friends both in England and Scotland; a little knot of High Churchmen, of whom William Stevens, Jonathan Boucher, Dr. Gaskin, the Bowdlers, and James Allan Park (then a rising young lawyer) were the most prominent, were, and had long been, ready to help them with pen, tongue, and purse; they had a powerful ally in Henry Dundas, afterwards Lord Melville, who was so influential with the great premier, especially in Scotch affairs, that he was called "the Minister for Scotland," and who, though he himself belonged to an old Presbyterian family, threw himself heart and soul into their cause. Indeed, the Established Kirk generally, so far from being jealous of their pretensions, helped them actively, especially some of its most noted members, such as Principals Robertson and Campbell, and Drs. Beattie and Gerard. The English prelates were certainly not unfriendly; they were courteous, though (bishop-like) with one or two exceptions cautious. With these advantages it is no wonder that their case seemed to be progressing favourably and rapidly. The Bill for the removal of their disabilities passed all its readings in the House of Commons in fifteen days. But when it reached the House of Lords, it met with an apparently insurmountable obstacle in the determined opposition of the all-influential chancellor, Lord Thurlow. It is sad to think that mere petty, personal jealousy should have been sufficient to thwart an act of public justice; but it is more than probable that the fact that the Bill had been introduced in the Commons by the first-lieutenant of his rival and enemy, William Pitt, was at the bottom of the chancellor's hostility. At any rate, the deputation had to return to Scotland *re infectâ*, for the Bill was thrown out, and the Scotch Church had to wait for three weary years before it could obtain relief. It had, however, one friend on the English Bench, who was not faint-hearted in the cause, and was not afraid of the formidable chancellor himself. This was the greatest bishop then living, Samuel Horsley, who thoroughly understood (what few Englishmen then did) the position of the Scotch Episcopalians, and threw into their scale all the weight of his reputation and abilities. When the Bill came on for debate in 1792, he supported it in one of the greatest of his many great speeches, and it was probably to a large extent through his influence that it was carried. Another able supporter of the Scotch claims among the English prelates, Bishop Horne, had gone to his rest before the matter was settled.

The repeal of the penal laws was, after all, only a half-measure. It fully relieved all laymen from restrictions on their worship; but it left the clergy, in one respect, in worse plight than they were in before; for one clause provided "that no person exercising the function of a pastor in the Episcopal communion in Scotland should be capable of taking any benefice, curacy, or spiritual function in England and Wales unless ordained by some bishop of the Church of England or Ireland," whereas they were previously eligible to cures in the Church of England. The clergy were also still liable to penalties unless they took the oath of abjuration, which they could not, of course, do without casting a reflection upon their own past conduct, and that of their predecessors. Nor were they yet quite prepared to sign the Thirty-nine Articles, as they were required to do.[1]

All these matters, however, had begun to adjust themselves by the time when our history commences. A most important meeting, convention, convocation, or synod (it is called by all four names), was held at Laurencekirk in 1804, which affected permanently and beneficially the relations between the Scotch and English Churches. "The purpose of this meeting," as the circular stated, was "in the most solemn manner to exhibit a public testimony of our conformity in doctrine and discipline with the Church of England, and thereby to remove every remaining obstacle to the union of the Episcopalians in Scotland." To understand the force of this, it must be remembered that though the native Episcopal Church of Scotland had been all but stamped out, there had always been numbers of Episcopalians in Scotland. These had worshipped under ministers of English and Irish ordination; they were called "qualified congregations" and their ministers "qualified ministers;" and it is said that "the only active and declared opponents of the Bill" for the abrogation of the penal laws "belonged to the qualified Episcopalians in Scotland."[2] Their position was a most anomalous one; they were Episcopalians without a bishop, and their clergy were Episcopal clergy without the recognition of the proper Episcopal authority in the land where they ministered. It is no wonder that, after the repeal of the penal statutes especially, the better instructed and more right-minded among them should be dissatisfied with their status; and yet, what were they to do? They were members of the Church of England, and the Church of Scotland had not yet adopted the confessional of that Church. So, in 1803, the Rev. Daniel Sandford, one of the most weighty and distinguished of the English clergy in Scotland, suggested

---

[1] The "disabling clauses," as they were called, were insisted upon by the Lord Chancellor, Thurlow. See Luckock's *The Church in Scotland*, pp. 287, 288.

[2] *Life and Times of John Skinner, Bishop of Aberdeen and Primus of the Scottish Episcopal Church*, by the Rev. W. Walker, LL.D., p. 82.

to Primus Skinner that "were the Thirty-nine Articles made the permanent confessional of the Scotch Church, the continuance in separation of the English clergy could not be justified on ecclesiastical principles."[1] Hence arose the synod of Laurencekirk, at which, after some discussion, especially about the Seventeenth Article, all the forty-four clergy signed the Thirty-nine Articles.[2] A few weeks later (November 19, 1804) the primus received the submission of Dr. Sandford and his congregation at Edinburgh, Dr. Sandford declaring that it was "the happiest day in his life when he and his flock, without one dissentient voice, agreed to unite with the venerable Church." His example was followed by others, notably by the congregation of Cowgate Street Chapel, Edinburgh, of which Sir William Forbes was the main pillar. To Bishop Skinner on the one side, and Dr. Sandford and Sir William Forbes on the other, the muchneeded union between the native Church and the English congregations was chiefly due. The indefatigable primus determined to settle the matter by bringing about the appointment of an English clergyman to a Scotch bishopric; and shortly afterwards, when Dr. Abernethy Drummond resigned the bishopric of Edinburgh, Dr. Sandford, chiefly through the influence of Bishop Skinner, was elected to the vacant post. His acceptance of it caused some dismay to his English friends, who anticipated complications which never arose. The appointment highly gratified the qualified congregations, and caused no offence to the Scotch. Primus Skinner addressed a circular letter to the bishops of the English Church and two Irish archbishops, intimating "the progress made and making in the happy work of Episcopal union in Scotland, and the advancement to the Scotch episcopate of one of the English ordained clergymen in charge of a congregation in Scotland."[3] Some of the qualified congregations still held out in a state of separation, but they met with no sympathy from the best friends of

---

[1] *Remains of Daniel Sandford, Bishop of Edinburgh*, with a Memoir by the Rev. John Sandford, i. 47.

[2] See an account of this synod in Dean Luckock's *The Church in Scotland*, p. 288.

[3] Walker's *Life of Bishop Skinner*, p. 216.

Scotland across the border. Bishop Horsley, whose words carried weight with all parties, deliberately declared that "the clergymen of English or Irish ordination, exercising their functions in Scotland without uniting with the Scotch bishops, were, in his judgment, doing nothing better than keeping alive a schism."[1] Archdeacon Daubeny expressed himself to the same effect;[2] and, at any rate among English High Churchmen, this was the general opinion. Apart from the theoretical anomaly of having two Churches, an English and a Scotch Church in one land, the arrangement worked exceedingly ill in practice. "Sometimes," writes the biographer of Bishop Gleig, "in a small town two small congregations—one English and one Scotch—existed side by side, and personal antipathies or incompatibilities prevented their union into one strong congregation. Stonehaven had two: one, no doubt the qualified one, presided over by an old clergyman, a Churchman only in name; the other, the native Scotch."[3] When the repeal of the penal laws was being agitated, and the qualified congregations opposed it, Bishop Horsley "desired to be furnished with instances of persons being actually ordained by English bishops in order to officiate in Scotland;" to which Bishop Skinner promptly replied that "within the last forty or fifty years a great number of candidates for Holy Orders have gone from this country and obtained ordination in England, with no other view but that of officiating in Scotland," and illustrated it by a case which came very near home. " He himself, being collated by Bishop Gerard to the charge of an Episcopalian congregation at Ellon, two gentlemen wished to have a qualified clergyman set up in opposition. With this view, they agreed with a Mr. Blake, then a Presbyterian schoolmaster, who proceeded to London, and was ordained by the Archbishop of Canterbury;" and then he gives many other definite instances.[4]

The acceptance of the English standard of doctrine, the

[1] *Remains, etc., of Bishop Sandford,* i. 48.
[2] See *Annals of Scottish Episcopacy from* 1788 *to* 1816, by John Skinner, of Forfar, p. 293.
[3] Walker's *Life of Bishop Gleig,* p. 285.
[4] *Annals of Scottish Episcopacy,* p. 172.

appointment of an Englishman to the bishopric of Edinburgh, and the vigorous efforts of the Primus, soon began to tell. The " twenty-four congregations in a state of separation from the Scottish Episcopal Church, and supplied by clergymen of English or Irish ordination," were reduced to five by the close of Primus Skinner's administration—that is, by 1816. At the same time, all was not smooth sailing in the Scottish Church; and as the storms arose very much in connection with its relations to the English Church, it will be necessary to notice them. There had long been, not exactly two parties, but two rather different lines of thought and action in the Scottish Church itself; the one being chiefly prevalent in the north, having Aberdeen for its centre, the other in the south, with Edinburgh for its head-quarters; the one "holding firmly by the principles of the English Nonjurors, and, in matters of ritual, deviating considerably from the English Book of Common Prayer;" the other "holding generally the views of the then English High Church party, and in worship aiming at conformity with England and uniformity at home."[1] At first the northern party was by far the strongest, both numerically and intellectually; but the absorption of the qualified congregations, which would naturally have a leaning towards England, and still more the influence of the English High Churchmen of the Stevens and Bowdler type (who had a clear right to have a say in the matter, inasmuch as they had not only been Scotland's best friends in the time of her deliverance from persecution, but were still liberally supplying her with money), tended greatly to strengthen the southern party. In the early years of the present century the divergence between the two parties was exemplified by the different attitude which they took up in regard to the use of the Scottish Communion Office. The native Church naturally preferred its own native Office, which, apart from its associations, it considered as in itself superior to the English Office. Bishops Skinner and Gleig, who were not always in harmony, thoroughly agreed in this; but the English congregations and the Scotch of the south, who came under English influence, were all in favour of the English use. It was the indomitable perseverance of Bishop Skinner which

[1] Walker's *Life of Bishop Gleig*, p. 206.

succeeded in preserving the optional use of the Scottish Office. But all the English congregations were not satisfied with this; "though never called upon to use the Office, they held that, by union with a Church that tolerated it, they made themselves responsible for it."[1] The High Churchmen in England (Bowdler, Park, etc.) viewed with some dismay the publication of the Scottish Office—not, probably, because they objected to it, but because they feared it might alarm "the moderate men" whom they had persuaded to help the struggling Church in Scotland. "I told him [Dr. Dampier, Bishop of Rochester]," writes Bowdler to the primus in 1806, "every English-ordained clergyman who joined the Communion of the Scotch Episcopal Church had his option to use the English Eucharistic Liturgy, if he preferred it. The bishop said he thought it a sufficient answer." And so surely it was. At any rate, the primus insisted upon his point. He would not consecrate Dr. Gleig to the bishopric of Dunkeld, in 1808, without imposing a test upon him that he would "strenuously recommend, by his own practice and by every other means in his power, the use of the Scotch Office"—a test which the new bishop could abide with a safe conscience, for it accorded with his own sentiments and practice; and he steadily set himself against the Anglicizing junior clergy at Aberdeen, who would have given up the Office. In 1811 the matter was settled in a way which must have satisfied the native Church. By the fifteenth canon of the code, passed in a synod at Aberdeen in that year, the Scotch was put above the English Office, being made the primary and authorized Office, while the English held only the position of a tolerated one; and, oddly enough, it was two *English* dignitaries, one of them being the son of Scotland's best and most powerful friend, Bishop Horsley, who drew up the canon.[2]

There was, however, a very strong religious party in England, which would naturally view with anything but satisfaction what was going on over the border; and a few years later great excitement was raised by the appearance in Edinburgh of some clergymen of the Evangelical party, now at the climax of its reputation and influence. The first

[1] *Life of Bishop Skinner*, p. 221.
[2] See Luckock, *ut supra*, pp. 289, 290.

two were a Mr. Noel and a Mr. Craig, both said to have been eloquent and earnest men, who secured a following. "The Scotch Episcopalians," said Mr. Craig, "were perishing for lack of knowledge; they had looked for the bread of life in the pulpit ministrations of their own Church, and had not found it." This was the beginning of a controversy which did not reach its height until after our period closes; the rise of the Oxford movement in 1833 naturally tending to widen the breach between those who reflected the views of the old Nonjurors, and those who at all sympathized with the views of the Evangelicals in the Scotch Church. But the history of all this happily belongs to the forties, not the twenties or the thirties; so it need not here be dwelt upon.

The interest which English Churchmen took in the ancient Church of Scotland was intensified by the fact that there happened to be, during our period, among the Scotch bishops three exceptionally remarkable men, all of whom were, in different ways, brought into close relationship with England. These three were John Skinner, Bishop of Aberdeen; George Gleig, Bishop of Brechin; and Alexander Jolly, Bishop of Moray and Ross: the first, the greatest administrator; the second, the most variously accomplished; the third, the saintliest character the Scotch Church perhaps ever produced. The first attracted the attention of Englishmen by the leading part he took in the consecration of Bishop Seabury, in bringing about the repeal of the penal laws, and in uniting the qualified ministers and their congregations with the native Church of the country; the second, by his numerous and very able contributions to several English periodicals; the third, by his profound learning, apostolic simplicity, and purity of life, to which men of such different types as Dean Stanley, Dean Hook, Bishop Kaye, Bishop Hobart, and Dr. Routh bear testimony.

Into the details of the lives of Bishops Skinner, Gleig, and Jolly it is unnecessary to enter, as their biographies, all written by the same able hand, are easily accessible; but it was a happy accident—shall we not rather say, a providential arrangement?—that at a time when many Englishmen were only just beginning to be conscious of the very existence of Scotch bishops, there should have come to the front three men who would have been ornaments to any episcopate in any age of the church. There were others, such as Bishop Torry of Dunkeld, and Bishop Drummond of Edinburgh, who were more than worthy of their position; but these three stand pre-eminent.

It should be added in conclusion that, though the average Englishman had been strangely ignorant about the ancient Church of Scotland, well-read divines were not in such Cimmerian darkness. Dr. Routh paid it the compliment, which was highly appreciated, of dedicating the first volume of his "Reliquiæ Sacræ" "to the bishops and presbyters of the Episcopal Church of Scotland." Bishop Horne, in very early days, made the memorable remark that if St. Paul had been on earth, and had had to select the religious community to which he should belong, he would have chosen the Scotch Episcopal Church, as most like what he had been used to; and, of course, Bishop Horsley knew all about its struggles, and thoroughly realized the strength of its position.

AMERICA.

It is impossible for an English Churchman to look back without a feeling of shame to the wrong-headed and suicidal course which was taken by England in regard to ecclesiastical affairs in America in the eighteenth century. It seems almost incredible that any man of sense, not to say statesman, should have thought that the proper line to pursue was to encourage—indeed, practically to establish—one particular communion, and yet to deny that communion the one office which distinguished it from other communions. To a Churchman, a Church without a bishop is a body without a head; and yet in this headless condition did those who professed to be friends of the Church, obstinately keep the Church in America until the closing years of the eighteenth century. As there was thus no centre of unity, no *differentia*, it is not in the least surprising that, after petitioning the mother country again and again for the boon which she could not supply herself, the American Church should have gradually dwindled away until she almost reached the vanishing-point. How the episcopate first came to America has already been told. When it *did* come, it seemed at first as if it had come too late. It came just at a time when the complications and embarrassments of the Church were apparently hopeless. There can be no doubt that in the American struggle for independence the sympathies of the vast majority of Churchmen were in favour of the loyalists, and against the popular party. There can also be no doubt that royalty and episcopacy were inseparably connected in the American mind; and that an Episcopal Church in a republic seemed to it an anomaly.

In justice to our predecessors, it is only fair to remember the real difficulties under which they laboured. Many of them certainly felt the obligation of the mother Church to supply her eldest daughter with that which was necessary to rescue her from her strangely anomalous position. The learned Dr. Lowth, who, as Bishop of London, was supposed to hold the impossible office of diocesan of the whole Church in America, was not only in favour of an episcopate, but one of the most eloquent and forcible pleaders for it.[1] But what could he, or what could the Archbishop of Canterbury, to whom, as Primate of all England, application was made, do? The law forbade distinctly the consecration of any bishop who would not take the oath of allegiance; and it was, of course, absolutely impossible for citizens of the United States to do this. An attempt was made to obtain a special Act of Parliament to dispense with the obligation. Every one knows how tedious and cumbersome a process this is under any circumstances, but under the existing state of things it was all but impossible; for the English people were then smarting under the loss of their greatest colonies, after a fruitless struggle in which they had lost much money and many lives, and they were by no means in the frame of mind which would incline them to stretch a point in favour of "the rebels." The king's ministry refused to consent to such an act without an official assurance that it would not be offensive to the new government in America. It probably *would* have been offensive, if not to the government, at any rate to the people of America; for the prejudices against bishops were

---

[1] See his *Twelve Anniversary Sermons before the Society for the Propagation of the Gospel.*

very strong. We have an amusing instance of this forty years later, by which time one might have hoped that the prejudice would have been dispelled. But it was not so. Mr. Caswall, in his interesting book on "America and the American Church," tells us that when he was working in the diocese of Ohio under the excellent bishop, Philander Chase, he went about as an advocate for a sort of Church Bible Society in 1828; an old man, with whom he was pleading its cause, "when he found that the bishop was *ex-officio* its president, grew quite furious, and swore that the bishop wanted to make himself a king, or at least to introduce English power into Knox county." The bishop had lately been in England, and collected there more than £6000 for Kenyon College, an institution he had established for the education of American clergy; the old man "stated his firm conviction that the college was designed for an English fort; the bishop's object in going to England was, that he might make his own arrangements with the despotic government of that country. It was impossible that the English should have sent such vast sums to assist the bishop without a sinister motive; and he concluded by charging me with being a spy in the service of the British government, as well as an emissary hired by the bishop to make proselytes to his new religion."[1] If this sort of feeling lingered on in 1828, when the soreness of America had presumably had time to heal, what must it have been in 1783? "Episcopalians," writes Mr. Caswall, "were regarded with great dislike, being supposed to possess monarchical predilections." He is referring especially to Ohio, but there is no reason to suppose that the dislike was stronger there than in other States.

It is a remarkable fact, however, and creditable alike to both parties, that the strained relations between England and America do not seem to have affected seriously the regard which the daughter paid to the mother Church. She never seems to have forgotten that it was to the Society for the Propagation of the Gospel in Foreign Parts, founded and sustained by English Churchmen, that she owed almost her

---

[1] *America and the American Church*, by the Rev. H. Caswall, p. 47.

very existence and continued life.[1] Nor does the fact that, when American Independence was finally recognized by Great Britain, the society was compelled by the terms of its charter to withdraw its grants to missionaries in the United States, and thereby to cause much temporary distress, appear to have shaken the gratitude of Churchmen for past favours. Judge Hoffman represents the feelings of the American Church generally towards the society when he writes, "The story of its abundant labours and countless blessings is a proper theme for the historian; and when from the altars of the American Church the utterance of praise and prayer arises in the stately and flowing language of the Liturgy of Edward, let us remember that chiefly to that society we owe the inappreciable gift."[2] Of course, there was a little feeling of soreness in America at the failure of the attempts to gain that boon from England which it had succeeded in gaining from Scotland, and a disposition to contrast the conduct of the depressed Catholic remnant on the north of the border with that of the more powerful and wealthy Church on the south of it.[3] But it is surprising how soon this feeling seems

---

[1] "It would be more than ungrateful, it would be inexcusable, to omit here the recognition of the agency by which, under God, it came to pass that there were in what had been the colonies of Great Britain, and were now independent States, those who sought the episcopate as essential to the full organization of an autonomous Church. That agency is found in the venerable Society for the Propagation of the Gospel in Foreign Parts—a society to which American Churchmen must always look with undying gratitude; for to its noble labours they largely owe all that they were when Seabury was sent upon his mission of faith, and much of what they enjoy to-day. It was no fault of that society that there was not, in America, an episcopate before the war of the Revolution. Had the godly counsels and the strong appeals of the bishops, clergy, and faithful laity who shared in its plans and operations been listened to, American Churchmen would have had no need to seek the apostolic office outside the limits of their own country. . . . It is worthy of notice that where the labours of the society had been the most abundant, and its missionaries most numerous, then the need of the episcopate was most deeply felt, and the call for it was loudest."—Bishop Williams' sermon at the Seabury Commemoration at Aberdeen, October 7, 1884: *Seabury Centenary, etc.*, p. 158.

[2] Quoted by Mr. Caswall in his work on *The American Church and the American Union*, pp. 65, 66.

[3] On August 3, 1785, when Bishop Seabury held his first ordination, the clergy, in their address of welcome to their new bishop, said, "We hope that the successors of the Apostles in the Church of England have sufficient reasons to justify themselves to the world and to God [for not consecrating Dr. Seabury]. We,

to have passed away. We have many indications of the kindly feelings of the American Church towards the mother from which she sprang. In the Preface to the American Prayer-book it is declared that "this Church is far from intending to depart from the Church of England, to which, under God, she is indebted for her first foundation, and a long continuance of nursing care and protection, in any essential point of doctrine, discipline, or worship, or further than local circumstances require." In a Church meeting at New York, in 1784, it was agreed, among other things, "that the Episcopal Church of the United States shall maintain the doctrines of the Gospel as now held by the Church of England, and shall adhere to the Liturgy of the said Church, as far as shall be consistent with the American Revolution and the constitutions of the respective States." At the first General Convention held at Philadelphia in September, 1785, it was resolved that "though Dr. Seabury's consecration was doubtless valid, the succession should be sought from England rather than Scotland;" and the Convention addressed the archbishops and bishops of England, stating that "the Episcopal Church of the United States had been severed by a civil revolution from the jurisdiction of the parent Church of England;" acknowledging "the favours formerly received from the Bishop of London in particular, and from the Society for the Propagation of the Gospel;" declaring their desire to perpetuate among them the principles of the Church of England in doctrine, discipline, and worship; and "praying that their lordships would consecrate to the episcopate those who should be sent with that view from Churches in any State respectively."[1] Accordingly, in 1786, Dr. White and Dr. Provoost sailed for England, and on February 4, 1787, were consecrated at Lambeth by the two archbishops, and the Bishops of Bath and Wells and Peterborough; and in 1790 Dr. Madison was consecrated in England, as the first Bishop of Virginia. Still more markedly was this regard for

---

however, know of none such, nor can our imagination frame any." Of the Scotch bishops they said, "Wherever the American Episcopal Church shall be mentioned in the world, may this good deed which they have done for us be spoken of for a memorial of them." See *Seabury Centenary: Connecticut*, p. 118.

[1] See Caswall's *American Church and the American Union*, p. 133.

England shown in the case of Dr. Bass, who was elected Bishop of Massachusetts, and, as there was now a sufficient number of bishops in America, might have been consecrated by them; but Bishop White " conceived that he was pledged to the archbishop to hand on the English line unmixed;"[1] the consecration, therefore, was postponed "until this engagement should have been relaxed,"[2] and Bishop Bass was not consecrated until 1797, when there were three English-consecrated bishops to take part with Bishop Seabury. And once more; the proposed alterations in the American Prayer-book (many of them very undesirable[3]) were submitted to the English prelates, and at their desire some of them were withdrawn and others modified.

Many good Churchmen in England were ready to meet the advances of America half-way. They were always ready to give American prelates, and American Churchmen generally, a warm welcome when they visited the mother country, and helped them liberally with purse as well as counsel; as, indeed, they were bound to do, for their appeals were often in behalf of a population which consisted to a great extent of British emigrants.[4] But the way in which the English Church helped the American most effectively was by imbuing her with her own true principles at their best. In other words, it was not so much living Churchmen, as those who lived only in their writings, who gave the true life to the Church in America. This appears in the history of that man who, above all others, was the real reviver, we might almost say the real establisher, of the American Church.

It must be confessed that the immediate results of putting the Church on a proper footing were rather disappointing.

---

[1] This was before the consecration of Bishop Madison; but there were still three—Seabury, White, and Provoost—and the hesitation arose from the fact of Bishop Seabury having been consecrated in Scotland.

[2] Wilberforce's *History of the American Church*, p. 232.

[3] But some quite the reverse. In accordance with a promise to the Scotch bishops, Bishop Seabury procured that in the Communion Service the "Prayer of Consecration" should follow the Scotch model; and his successor remarks on this, "In giving us the primitive form of consecration, Scotland gave us a greater boon than when she gave us the episcopate." See *Luckock*, pp. 285, 286.

[4] This was notably the case with regard to the appeal of Bishop Philander Chase, which, as we have seen, was nobly responded to. See Wilberforce's *History of the American Church*, p. 318, *et seq.*

The twenty-five years which followed the consecration of its first bishop were the time when the Church reached its nadir. The present Bishop of Connecticut (Dr. Williams), in his "In Memoriam" sermon on Bishop Lee, of Delaware, who was born in the early part of this century, writes, "He was born at a time when our Church in these United States was reaching its lowest point of depression, and, as it seemed, hopelessness. That point was not touched, as is not unfrequently supposed, at the close of the war of the Revolution. At that period there were many who remained faithful to the order, doctrine, and worship in which they had been trained. But, as the years rolled on and these passed away, few came to fill the places they had left, and decrease rather than increase seemed to be the inevitable law." History fully bears out these remarks; and when we come to look into the matter, there is really nothing at all extraordinary in it. The inevitable result of the struggle for independence was to weaken men's attachment to that Church which was regarded as the symbol of British rule; the mere fact that it was spoken and thought of as the *English* Church was enough to set people against it, and it required time and tact to overcome the prejudice. Bishop Seabury had gone to his rest before the nineteenth century began, and therefore does not, strictly speaking, come within our range; but it may be permitted to say that, until late years, justice has scarcely been done to the great work he did in preparing the way. He certainly had a firmer grasp of Church principles than most of the early bishops in America; and that was above all what was needed, though of course it did not add to his popularity. Readers of Bishop Wilberforce and Mr. Anderson should certainly correct any unfavourable impression of Bishop Seabury they may have derived from those sources by reading Dr. Beardsley's "Life of Samuel Seabury," and "A Report of Commemoration Services, with the Sermons and Addresses at the Seabury Centenary." In fact, Bishop Seabury was the only American bishop before Bishop Hobart who represented the old historical school of English Churchmanship. Bishop Madison was a cultured scholar, but a man of no very definite opinions. Dr. William White, who lived to be a most interesting link between the ante-revolution and the post-revolution Church, was an excellent and lovable man. His long episcopate of forty-nine years was of immense benefit to the newly constituted Church; no man tended more by his conciliatory spirit and attractive character to dispel the prejudices against the name and office of bishop. His mild wisdom, his unselfishness, and his firmness on occasion were invaluable in the critical conjuncture; and he had the advantage of having been from the first a consistent republican. He had been chaplain to the Congress during the war; and George Washington (who was a consistent Churchman) had regularly worshipped under his ministry.[1] But he had not a sufficiently firm grasp of Church principles. Bishop Benjamin Moore, of New York, is said to have been distinguished for his "piety, simplicity, discretion, meekness, and love,"[2] admirable qualities in themselves, and calculated to advance the cause of the Church; but still compatible with a lack of that combination of qualities which was then needed. The man who above all others possessed this rare combination was Bishop B. Moore's successor, John Henry Hobart, who was appointed to the see of New York in 1811, and who found, as it were, his complement in Bishop Griswold, who became Bishop of "the Eastern Diocese"[3] in the same year. It is not at all too much to say that the appointment of Bishop Hobart was "a turning-point in the history of the Western Church."[4] He made, in fact, nothing less than a great revolution; and that, as much by his *de*structive as by his *con*structive work. He it was who more than any man, more even than Bishop White, dispelled the mischievous notion that episcopacy and monarchy were inseparable, and that therefore a patriotic American could not be a good Churchman. For he was himself an ardent republican; and partly to the dismay, partly to the amusement of his English friends, he had not the least

---

[1] Since the above was written, a *Life of Bishop White* has appeared in the "Makers of America" Series, which brings out these points more fully, and to which the reader is referred.
[2] Anderson's *History of the Colonial Church*, iii. 472.
[3] This included at that time all the New England States except Connecticut.
[4] Wilberforce's *American Church*, p. 295.

scruple about ventilating his republican sentiments in the heart of England, so it may be imagined that he would not be reticent about them in America.[1] He, again, it was who, both by precept and example, helped greatly to dispel the still more mischievous notion that "enthusiasm" (in other words, spiritual earnestness and activity) was inconsistent with Churchmanship. People hardly knew whether to call him a Methodist or a High Churchman.[2] In point of fact, he was both; that is to say, he had all the ardour and elasticity of the Methodist without his irregularities and extravagances; and all the definiteness of faith and sense of order of the Churchman without the cold, prim formalism of which some so-called Churchmen were not unjustly accused. And Hobart learnt his lesson in the English school. He had all the really great Anglican divines at his back; that gave him his strength. It was not his originality, but rather the want of it, that made him the force he was. "The gospel *in* the Church," "Evangelical doctrine combined with apostolic order,"—these were Hobart's watchwords; steadily acting on these principles, he was sure to make his mark. This is not the place to dwell on his excellent business habits, on his influence over young men, on his establishing successfully at New York a theological seminary for training clergy for the American Church.[3] These are details; the main, broad fact to be insisted on is, that he knew what he meant, and taught others to know what *they* meant—which was just what the American Churchmen, and perhaps other Churchmen, needed to learn; hence the period of his episcopate, from 1811 to 1830, was the period in which the real foundations of the American Church were laid. It need only be added that Hobart was on intimate terms, first by correspondence and then by a personal visit, with Churchmen of a similar type in England, such as H. H. Norris, the Watsons, and Hugh James Rose.

[1] "Oh, it was funny," wrote Mr. Sikes, of Guilsborough, "to see honest democracy and sincere episcopacy fast yoked in the man's mind, and perpetually struggling for his heart." "The good bishop," said Joshua Watson, "always avowed in this country the sentiments [in favour of a republic] which he published on his return."—Churton's *Memoir*, i. 244, 246.

[2] Curiously enough, people were exactly in the same perplexity about Bishop Seabury. See Beardsley's *Life, etc.*

[3] See *Life of Bishop Hobart*, by John M'Vicar, D.D., *passim*.

In attributing this importance to the work of Hobart, it is not meant to ignore that of others. Bishop Philander Chase, who may be regarded as the pioneer of American Church missions, and whose nobly unselfish life is beyond all praise; Bishop Richard Channing Moore, whose evangelistic labours were extraordinarily successful, and who made the Church in Virginia a reality; Bishop White, who, though a much older man, survived Hobart for nearly twenty years, and many others contributed their share; and if this were ever so slight a sketch of the history of the American Church, they would require more than the mere passing notice which is all that can be afforded to them in a chapter which only professes to touch upon the relationship between the Church of England and other Churches in communion with her. But the real epoch-making bishop was J. H. Hobart.

The general result of this survey is that a great advance was made in the range of English Churchmanship during our period. Looking back from our present standpoint, it may seem that we were still very insular; but looking forward from the standpoint of the eighteenth century, it will appear wonderful that we made the progress we did; and so this, the last of our subjects, gives one more illustration of the not sufficiently acknowledged fact that the early part of the nineteenth century was a period, not of stagnation, but of revival.

INDEX.

A

Aberdeen, synod of (1811), 331
Acland, Sir T. A., 92, 152
Act for excluding clergy from Parliament (1801), 296-297
Act for restraining clerical farming (1802), 297-298
Act to restrain and regulate pluralities (1832), 304
Acts for enforcing residence of incumbents, 297-300
"African Institution," the, 258
Alderley, parish of, 5, 114, 115
America, Church in, 333-337
American Prayer-book, 337
"Analysis of Chronology" (Hales), 182
"Anecdotes of my own Life" (Bishop R. Watson), 193
"Annals of the Poor" (Legh Richmond), 174
Ante-Communion Service from Prayer-desk, 130-131
Apocrypha, in connection with the Bible Society, 288
Apostolical succession, 26
Appendix to Bishop Jebb's sermons, 291, 314, 318
Architecture of new churches, 155-156
Arnold, Dr. Thomas, 120-124, 228, 229-231
"Association of the Friends of the Church," 321
Atkinson, Miles, 87
Augmentation of Curates' Stipends, Bill for, in 1813, 302
Augmentation of small livings in 1809, 301
Austen, Miss Jane, 95
Auxiliary Bible Societies, 287, 291

B

Babington, Thomas, 72, 258, 259
Baily, Archdeacon, 46, 135

Balliol College, Oxford, 220
Bampton Lectures, Hampden's, 124, 216; Mant's, 107, 190, 191; Nott's, 107; Van Mildert's, 26, 179-180; Whately's, 216
Baptismal Regeneration, 69, 190-192
Baptismal Service, mutilations of, 130
Barrington, Bishop Shute, 41, 89, 164
Bass, Bishop E., Massachusetts, 338
Bates, Eli, 285
Bathurst, Bishop Henry, 7, 113-114, 237, 247, 291, 306
Bathurst, Bragg, M.P., 304
Bell, Dr. Andrew, 114, 195, 233-239, 241, 242
Bell and Lancaster controversy, 233-239, 246, 247
Bentham, Jeremy, 125, 311
Bentinck Chapel, Marylebone, 81
Bible Associations, 287
Bible Society, British and Foreign, 39, 64, 71, 114, 267, 278, 286-292
Bickersteth, Edward, 85, 88, 99, 102, 107, 128, 133, 175, 176, 181, 186, 258, 260, 292
Biddulph, T. J., 191
"Biographia Evangelica" (Erasmus Middleton), 193-194
Biographical literature, 192-194
Bishop's College, Calcutta, 82, 275
"Black Book," 11
Blackwood's Magazine, 17
Blomfield, Bishop, C. J., 7, 42, 46, 130, 293
Blunt, Henry, 83, 175
Blunt, Professor J. J., 180, 196, 224
"Book of the Church" (Southey), 194-195
"Book of the Roman Catholic Church" (Butler), 199
Bowdler, John, the elder, 46, 145, 151, 152, 158, 193, 240, 281, 283, 331
Bowdler, John, the younger, 46, 70, 202
Bowdler, Thomas, 46
Bowles, John, 240

Bowles, Samuel, 203
Boyer, Dr., of Christ's Hospital, 229
Boyle Lectures, Van Mildert's, 169
Bradley, parish of North, 6, 40, 154
British and Foreign School Society, 238
British Critic, The, 36, 37, 44, 45, 127, 134, 140, 141, 186, 200, 201, 206, 292
British Magazine, The, 142, 203
Broad-bottom chapels, 148
Brougham, Henry, Lord, 67, 69, 243-245, 310
Brown, Canon Abner, 56, 250
Brown, David, 260
Buchanan, Dr. Claudius, 84, 101, 193, 201, 262, 265-269, 271, 293
Budd, Mr., 284, 292
Burgess, Bishop Thomas, 6, 21-22, 90, 202, 225
Burgon, Dean ("Lives of Twelve Good Men"), 43 *n.*, 87, 156, 251
Burton, Professor, 185
Buxton, Sir T. F., 78, 92
Byron, Lord, 214-215

C

Calcutta, bishopric of, 272
Calvinistic controversy, 185-190
Calvinistic Methodists in Wales, 19
Calvinists, 69
Cambridge, Archdeacon, 46, 178, 240
Cambridge architectural movement, 160
Cambridge Evangelicals, 52-66, 222
Cambridge University, state of, 222-224
Caroline, case of Queen, 308-311
Carus, Canon W., 54 and *passim* ("Life of Simeon")
Carwithen, J. B. S., 196
Catechizing in church, 233
Cecil, Richard, 51, 79, 102, 285
Charity Schools, 232, 239
Charles, Thomas, of Bala, 19
"Charlotte Elizabeth," 103, 223 *n.*, 315
Chase, Philander, Bishop of Ohio, 335, 343
"Cheap Repository Tracts" (H. More), 172, 173
Christ Church, Bath, 157
"Christian Morals" (H. More), 174
Christian Observer, The, 71, 81, 148, 201-202
Christian Remembrancer, The, 28, 44, 202-203
"Christian Year, The" (Keble). 35, 204
Church accommodation, want of, 144-146
Church and State, 295-312
Church-building after the war, 150
Church-building, difficulties of, 154
Church Building Society, 34, 151-153, 158

Church, Evangelicals' views of the, 97-98
Church history. 194-198
"Church History," Waddington's, 196-197
"Church in Danger, The" (Yates), 145, 147, 150
Church literature, 163-218
Church Missionary Society, 64, 66, 70, 73, 81, 82, 226, 255, 275, 276
"Church Reform," Arnold on, 217
Church services and fabrics, 127-162
Church Temporalities Act (Ireland), 320-321
Churton, Archdeacon E., 46 and *passim* ("Memoir of Joshua Watson")
"Clapham sect," the, 35, 66-79
"Clapton sect," the, 35, 44
Clarkson, Thomas, 77, 78
Clergy Orphan School, 31, 34
Clergy Penalties Suspension Bill in 1814, 303
"Clergyman's Work in 1825, A," 161-162
Clergymen excluded from Parliament, 296-297
Clerical Education Societies, 285
"Cœlebs in Search of a Wife" (H. More), 173
Coleridge, S. T., 47, 49, 116, 166, 183, 208-210, 213, 224, 229, 242, 274, 281, 292, 301
College chapel services, 225
Colonial Church, 34, 282
Colquhoun, J. C., 74, 173
Communicants, numbers of, 128-129
Confirmations at public schools, 229
Consolidated Act of 1816, 303
Conventicle and Five-Mile Acts, Repeal of, in 1812, 302
Conversation parties, Simeon's, 56
Copleston, Bishop E., 7, 20, 48, 117-118, 124, 160, 221, 306
Correspondence between A. Knox and J. Jebb, 316 and *passim*
Corrie, Bishop Daniel, 262, 273, 275
Country churches, squalor of, 158-160
Crabbe, George, 204
Croker, J. W., Right Hon., 295
Croly, Dr., 116, 254
Crouch, Dr. (Principal of St. Edmund's Hall), 86
Curates' Relief Bill (1803), 299
Curates' Salary Bill (1803), 300

D

"Dairyman's Daughter" (Legh Richmond), 174
Dale, Dr. R. W., 97

INDEX.   345

Dale, Thomas, 85
Dames' schools, 233
Daubeny, Archdeacon Charles, 6, 26–27, 34, 40–41, 148, 152, 157, 188, 199–200, 279, 287, 289, 296, 306
Davison, John, 124, 181–182, 252
Dealtry, William, 66, 74, 91, 106
"Discourses on Prophecy" (Davison), 182
"Dissertations on Prophecy" (Hales), 182
"Doctrine of the Greek Article" (Middleton), 170–172
D'Oyly, Dr., 46, 225
"D'Oyly and Mant's Family Bible," 178
Drummond, Abernethy, Bishop of Edinburgh, 325, 328, 333
Drury, Dr. J., of Harrow, 228 n.
Dundas, Henry (Lord Melville), 325
Durham clergy and death of Queen Caroline, 309–311
Durham University, 226
Dykes, T., 63, 64, 86

E

East India Company and Indian Missions, 261, 267, 271, 304
"Ecclesiastical Biography" (Christopher Wordsworth), 193–194
Eclectic Review, The, 192, 285
Eclectic Society, The, 80, 255, 257, 285
Edinburgh Review, The, 123, 237, 283, 306
Education grant, first, 252
Elland Society, the, 80, 257, 285
Elliott, Venn, 5, 147, 160
"End of Religious Controversy" (Bishop J. Milner), 198–199
English clergy in Scotland, 327, 328, 330–332
Erskine, Lord, 304
"Essay on St. Luke" (Schleiermacher), 183
Eton College, 227
Eucharist, the Holy, 127–129
"Evangelical," the name, 108
"Evangelicals," the, 15, 51–109 and passim
Eveleigh, Dr., Provost of Oriel, 220, 242
"Evidence of Christianity," etc. (J. B. Sumner), 169–170
"Evidences of Christianity" (Daniel Wilson), 168
Examinations at Oxford, 219–220
"Extraordinary Black Book," 11

F

Farish, Professor W., 63–65
"Fathers of the Church" (Legh Richmond), 174–175
Festivals and fasts, neglect of, 143
Fine arts, Evangelicals on the, 102
"Five chaplains" in Bengal, the, 262–266
Foreign missions, 253–278
Fort William College, Calcutta, 262, 265
Foster, Henry, 80, 285
Free Church, the first, 157
French Revolution, the, 1, 2, 107, 125, 172, 194, 207
French War, the, 2–3, 148–150
Friskin, J. (first pupil-teacher), 233
Froude, Professor J. A., 15–16, 315

G

German theology, 126, 176–177, 183–184
Gisborne, Thomas, 74–76, 147, 174–176, 201
Gladstone, Right Hon. W. E., 226, 230
Gleig, Bishop (Dunkeld), 329, 331, 332
Glenelg, Lord, 79
Goode, W., 81
Goodenough, Bishop S. (Carlisle), 62, 243, 247
Good Friday Communions, 129
Grammar schools, 232
Grant, Charles, 261, 266, 273
Grant, Sir Robert, 79
Graves, Dean, 316
Grenville, Lord, 222
Grey, Earl, 119
Griswold, Bishop A. V. ("Eastern Diocese"), 340
"Guesses at Truth" (A. and J. Hare), 212, 216
"Guide to the Church" (Daubeny), 41, 148
Gurney, J. J., 54–55

H

Hackney, parish of, 35
"Hackney phalanx," the, 37, 38, 44, 128, 242, 272, 281
Hales, Dr. William, 182
Half-million grant of 1824, 150, 304
Hamilton, Dr., of Knocktopher, co. Kilkenny, 315
Hampden, Bishop R. D., 124, 216
Hare, Augustus, 121, 216

Hare, Julius, 125, 183-184, 210, 212, 216, 224
Harrow parish church, 228
Harrow School, 227-228
Harrowby, Earl of, 92, 302
Hawkins, Dr. E., 121, 230
Hawtrey, Dr., 230
Heber, Bishop R., 68, 75, 116, 133, 135, 140, 193, 202, 203-204, 237, 243, 275-276, 287, 293, 298
Heslop, Archdeacon, 142
Hey, William, 108
Higgins, C. L., 250, 251
High Churchmen, 15, 24-50, and *passim*
"Hints for a Young Princess" (H. More), 173
"Historic Doubts Relative to Napoleon Buonaparte," 166-167
"History of the Church of England to the Revolution" (Carwithen), 196
—— (Vowler Short), 196
"History of the Jews" (Milman), 182-183
Hobart, Bishop J. H. (New York), 46, 217, 340-342
Holland, Lady, 113, 300
Hope, Right Hon. Beresford, 228
"Horæ Homileticæ" (Simeon), 186
"Horæ Solitariæ" (A. Searle), 176
Horne, Bishop, 28, 31, 246, 326, 333
Horne, Hartwell, 84, 100, 179
Horne, Melville, 256
Horsley, Bishop, 19-20, 25, 26, 29, 143, 163-164, 247-249, 300, 326, 329, 333
Hostility to the Church (1820-1833), 311
Howley, Bishop, 9, 36, 44, 133, 148, 179, 191, 194, 241
Hughes, Joseph (Sec. Bib. Soc.), 286
Human learning, Evangelical views of, 101-102
Hume, Joseph, 12
Hutchinsonians, 29, 30, 41
Hymns, prejudice against, 132

I

India, the Church in, 260-278
Infant schools, 252
Inglis, Bishop, 46
"Introduction to Critical Study of Holy Scripture" (H. Horne), 100, 179
Ireland, Church of, 120, 313-323
Iremonger, F., 202
Irish Society, the, 285
Islington, parish of, 85, 128, 144
Islington College (C.M.S.), 226

J

Jackson, Cyril, Dean of Christ Church, 220
Jacobinism, 2, 247-249
James, Dr., Bishop of Calcutta, 277
Jebb, J., Bishop of Limerick, 8, 37-38, 46, 49, 68, 94, 155, 173, 184, 220, 252, 293, 314, 316-320
Jennings, Archdeacon, 84
Jerram, Charles, 16, 55, 73, 91, 92, 104, 256 *n*.
Jesus Lane Sunday school, Cambridge, 249-251
Jewish converts, 284
Johnson, R. (missionary), 255
Jolly, Alexander, Bishop of Moray and Ross, 332
Jones, William, of Nayland, 28-29, 200
Jowett, Joseph, 65-66, 105 *n*.
Jowett, William, 65-66, 175
Julian's "Dictionary of Hymnology," 133
"Justin Martyr" (Kaye), 197
Juvenile Bible Societies, 287

K

Kaye, Bishop John, 10-11, 45-46, 140, 197, 306
Keats, John, 215
Keble, John, 35, 204, 206, 210
Kent, Edward, Duke of, 92, 284
Kenyon College, Ohio, 335
Kerr, Dr. (missionary), 268
King, John (of Hull), 73, 86
King's College, Cambridge, 52
King's College, London, 225
Kirby, William (naturalist), 47, 248
Knight, Samuel, 86, 256
Knight, William, 86
Knox, Alexander, 47-49, 75, 94, 137, 186, 192, 209, 218, 290-291, 306, 314, 316-318

L

Ladies' Auxiliary Bible Societies, 287
Lake Poets, the, 207
Lampeter, St. David's College, 21, 225
Lancaster, Joseph, 114, 235-239
Lancasterian system of education, 237, 247
Laurencekirk, synod of, 327
Law, Bishop E., 130, 281
Le Bas, William, 224, 273, 274
Leeke, William, 250
Lent, neglect of, 144

INDEX.   347

Lenten lectures, Bishop Porteus's, 4
"Letters to C. Butler, Esq." (Phillpotts), 199
"Liberals," the, 110-126 and *passim*
Life of Thomas Scott, 192 ; John Newton, 192 ; Joseph Milner, 192 ; John Wesley (Southey), 193 ; Daniel Waterland (Van Mildert), 193, 213 ; Jeremy Taylor (Heber), 193
Liturgy, mutilations of, 130
Liverpool, Earl of, 8, 150, 301
Llandaff, diocese of, 20, 21, 22-23
Lloyd, Bishop Charles (Oxford), 36, 45, 184
Lock Hospital Chapel, 80, 176
London Clerical Education Society, 80
London Clergy Incumbents' Bill (1804), 299
London Evangelicals, 78-86
London Missionary Society, 256, 257
London Society for Promoting Christianity among the Jews, 283-284
Lowth, Bishop, 112
Lyall, Dean, 46

M

Macaulay, Lord, 61, 71, 94, 95 *n.*, 102, 261
Macaulay, Zachary, 71, 74, 79, 95 *n.*, 102, 201, 258, 259
Macbride, Dr. (Magdalen Hall), 86
Madison, Bishop J. (Virginia), 337, 339
Madras system of education, 233-235, 247
Magdalen College, Cambridge, 63, 105, 261
Magee, Dr., on the Atonement, 316
Maitland, Dr. Samuel, 203
Maltby, Bishop (Durham), 292
Manners-Sutton, Archbishop, 6, 38, 39, 44, 133, 152, 178, 191, 240
Mant, Bishop R., 46, 131, 143, 185, 242, 293, 314, 321-323
Marsden, Samuel (missionary), 260
Marsh, Bishop Herbert, 21, 36, 44-45, 62, 66, 104, 132, 176-177, 187, 223, 224, 239, 241, 279, 287, 303
Marsh, Dr. William, 87, 107
Martyn, Henry, 201, 262-265
May, Sir Erskine, 77-78
Merivale, Dean, 227
Methodist, nickname of, 48, 54, 70, 75, 88, 105
Methodist communicants, 129
Michaelis' "Introduction to the New Testament" (H. Marsh), 177
Middleton, Erasmus, 176, 193
Middleton, Bishop T. F., 40, 45, 82, 170-172, 178, 193, 201, 272-275, 290
Mill, James, 311

Millennium, speculations about the, 180
Miller, Dr. John, 221, 311
Million grant of 1818, 150, 155, 304
Milman, Dean H. H., 116, 182-183, 204
Milner, Dean Isaac, 61-62, 72, 94, 101, 105 *n.*, 192, 223, 247, 287
Milner, Bishop John, 198-199
Milner, Joseph, 63, 197
Moberly, Bishop G., 230
Moore, Archbishop, 29, 257
Moore, Bishop B. (New York), 340
Moore, Bishop R. C. (Virginia), 343
More, Hannah, 4, 76, 88, 89, 91, 95, 172-174, 201

N

Nares, Archdeacon, 200
National Society, 33, 114, 151, 195, 238, 239-243
"Natural Theology" (Paley), 163-166
Nayland Vicarage, 29, 200
Neale, Cornelius, 85
New churches, ugliness and costliness of, 155, 156
New Zealand Mission, 260
Newfoundland School Society, 285
Newman, Cardinal, 34, 46 *n*, 118, 119, 207
Newton, John, 51, 55, 80, 83, 192, 265, 285
Niebuhr's " History of Rome " (Thirlwall and Hare), 184
"Nobody's Friends," club of, 31, 44
Noel, Hon. Baptist, 85
Noel, Hon. Gerard, 85
"Noetics," the Oriel, 117, 121, 124
Nonjurors, the, 33
Norris, Henry Handley, 35-38, 49, 128, 178, 200, 202, 221, 240, 341

O

O'Brien, Bishop (Ossory), 315
Obstructive incumbents, 153
Oliphant, Mrs., 95 *n.*
Olney, parish of, 5, 293
Organs in churches, 136
Oriel College, Oxford, 117, 220
"Origines Liturgicæ" (Palmer), 184, 314
"Orthodox," the, 24-50, 223-224
Otter, Bishop, 291
Overton, John, 87, 188, 201, 314
Owen, John (Sec. Bib. Soc.), 267, 271, 286
Oxford Movement, the, 25, 28, 38, 42-43, 49, 93, 185, 314, 321
Oxford University, the state of, 219-222, 306

P

Paley, Dr. William, 111, 164-166
Palmer, Sir Wm., 14, 17, 27, 292, 314
Park, Sir J. A., 47, 151, 240, 325
Parochial clergy's services to education, 242-245
Parr, Dr. Samuel, 111-112, 168 *n.*, 309
Parsons, Dr., Master of Balliol, 220, 242
Pearson, Dean Hugh, 94, 266, 270
Peel, Sir Robert, 222, 225, 306
Perceval, Right Hon. S., 71, 92, 145, 300, 301
Percy, Bishop (Dromore), 314
Periodicals, religious, 200-203
"Peter Plymley's Letters," 306
Pew system, 146-147
Philadelphia, Convention at, 337
Phillpotts, Bishop H., 7, 46, 199, 310
Pluralities and non-residence, 6-8
Poetry, religious, 203-204.
Poole, John, 245-246
Poole, Thomas, 246 *n.*
Pott, Archdeacon, 34 *n.*, 46, 178
Porteus, Bishop Beilby, 4, 45, 77, 88-89, 133-134, 144, 172, 187, 245, 249, 257, 266, 267, 282, 283, 287
Poverty of clergy, 298
"Practical Piety" (H. More), 174
Pratt, Josiah, 79 *n.*, 81-83, 95, 175, 192, 201, 258, 285, 286, 292
Prayer-book to be distributed with Bible, 280-281
Prayer-book and Homily Society, 284
Prayer-meetings, 57-58, 143
Preaching extempore, 138-141
Pretyman, Bishop, 45. *See* "Tomline"
Priests' Orders Bill (1804), 299
Private religious societies, 58, 292-294
Proprietary chapels, 197
"Protestant's Companion, The" (Daubeny), 200
Provoost, Bishop S. (New York), 337
Pryme, Professor ("Autobiographical Recollections"), 43 *n.*, 222, 223
Psalmody, 131-137
Public schools, 226-232
Pugh, Rector of Rauceby, 87, 256
Pupil-teachers, rise of, 233-234, 238-239
Pusey, Dr. E. B., 34, 42, 126

Q

Quarterly Review, 242, 282
Queen Anne's Bounty, 301
Queen's College, Cambridge, 62, 105, 249

R

Raikes, Chancellor, 115
Randolph, Bishop J., 45, 89, 177, 178, 242, 279, 290
Rationalism in Germany, 126
Rauceby Rectory, 87, 256
Record newspaper, 202
Redesdale, Lord, 302
Reform Bill, 13, 114, 311, 320
"Reformation in England, Sketch of the" (J. J. Blunt), 146
"Refutation of Calvinism" (Tomline), 187, 189-190
Religious Tract Society, 285-286
"Reliquiæ Sacræ" (Routh), 198, 333
"Remains of Alexander Knox," 316 and *passim*
"Remarks on 'The Refutation of Calvinism'" (T. Scott), 190
"Remarks on Scepticism, etc." (Rennell), 167
Rennell, Dean Thomas, 47, 167
Rennell, Thomas, the younger, 47, 167-168, 193, 201, 266
"Report from Lincolnshire Clergy" (1800), 4
Revolution, French, 1-2
Richardson, Sir John, 31-32, 240
Richardson, William, of York, 87
Richmond, Legh, 5, 87-88, 92, 94, 99, 107, 128, 136, 172, 174-175, 176, 201, 284, 286, 293
Robinson, T., of Leicester, 51, 87, 94, 193, 256
Roman Catholic Relief Bill, 305
Roman controversy, the, 198-200
Rose, Hugh James, 43, 44, 126, 171, 203, 224, 341
Routh, Dr. M., President of Magdalen, 46, 156, 185, 197-198
Royal Free Schools, Borough Road, 237
Royal Letters, 40
Rugby, Arnold's work at, 121-122, 229-232
Ryder, Bishop, 7, 90, 281, 301

S

"Sacred Dramas" (H. More), 174
Saints' days, 144
St. Ann's, Blackfriars, 81
St. Asaph, diocese of, 20
St. David's, diocese of, 19, 20, 21-22
St. Edmund's Hall, Oxford, 42, 86
St. John's, Bedford Row, 79-80, 128, 285
St. Nicholas', Yarmouth, 152
St. Pancras, London, 82, 145, 152, 153

INDEX. 349

St. Mary Woolnoth, 80, 83
Sandford, Bishop D. (Edinburgh), 327-328
Sawbridge, John, 5, 35, 128
"Scholar Armed, The," 200
Scholefield, Professor J., 65
Scotch Episcopal Church, 323-333, 336
Scott, John, of Hull, 86, 99, 191, 192, 201
Scott, Thomas, 51, 80, 99, 100, 108 n., 181, 192, 201, 258, 293
Scott, Sir Walter, 204-207, 214
Scott, Sir William, M.P., 297, 303
Scottish Communion Office, 330, 338 n.
"Scripture Help" (Bickersteth), 175
Seabury, Bishop S. (Connecticut), 324, 332, 337, 338, 339, 341
Serle, Ambrose, 136, 176
Sermons at Rugby (Arnold's), 217
Sermons, character of, 137-140
Sharp, Granville, 72, 78, 170-171, 193, 258, 259 286
Shelley, Percy Bysshe, 214
"Shepherd of Salisbury Plain, The" (H. More), 172
Sherwood, Mrs., 263-264
Short, Bishop T. Vowler, 196
Sierra Leone, colony of, 70, 258-259
Sikes, Thomas, of Guilsborough, 41-43, 142, 199
Simeon, Charles, 52-61, 72, 99, 117, 141, 146, 181, 186, 201, 251, 256, 257, 261, 283-284, 292
Simeonites, 60, 223 n., 251
Skinner, Bishop (Aberdeen), 325, 328, 332
Slave Trade, 70, 71, 72, 76-79, 105, 258
Slavery, abolition of, 77-79, 105
Smith, Abel, M.P., 88
Smith, Sydney, 112-113, 115, 136, 138, 139, 281, 283, 300
Society for Conversion of Negroes in West Indies, 282
Society for Promotion of Christian Knowledge, 30, 33, 34, 39, 52, 82, 178, 191, 278-281
Society for Propagation of the Gospel, 30, 34, 253-255, 257, 275, 335-336
Society for Reformation of Principles, 200
Society for Suppression of Vice, 282-283
Southey, Robert, 8, 10, 138, 185, 213, 214, 227, 242
Stanley, Bishop Edward, 5, 114-115, 243, 306
Stanley, Dean A. P., 122, 230, 231
Statute of 21 Henry VIII., 298, 303, 304
Stephen, James, 71, 76, 258, 272
Stephen, Sir James, 62, 74-75, 96 n.

Stevens, William, 29, 30-31, 325
Stipendiary Curates' Bill (1803), 299
Stoughton, Dr. John, 103-104, 156
Stretton, parish of, 128
Strickland, Miss Agnes, 47
Sumner, Archbishop J. B., 90, 169
Sumner, Bishop Charles, 90, 146, 156
Sunday evening services, 141
Sunday schools, 245-251
Swanage Rectory, 235
Symonds, Dr. B., of Wadham, 86
Syrian Christians of St. Thomas, Travancore, 267, 268

T

Teignmouth, John, Lord, 71-72, 76, 142, 201, 261, 269-271, 287
"Tertullian" (Kaye), 197
Test and Corporation Acts, Repeal of, 306
Thirlwall, Bishop Connop, 116, 121, 125, 183-184
Thomas, T., 58, 65, 262-263
Thornton, Henry, 69-71, 75, 76, 94, 99, 101, 201, 258, 259
Thornton, John, 55, 69, 79, 99
Thurlow, Lord Chancellor, 326
Tomline, Bishop, 45, 178, 306
Tooke, Horne, 296
Torry, Bishop (Dunkeld), 333
Training-schools for teachers, 251-252
"Treatise on Prayer" (Bickersteth), 175
Trimmer, Mrs., 47, 236-237, 248
Trinitarian Bible Society, 288
Trinity Church, Cambridge, 54, 128, 141
Trinity College, Cambridge, 46
"True Churchman ascertained" (Overton), 188
Tulloch, Principal, 100-101
Turner, Bishop (Calcutta), 277
Twining, Thomas, 267

U

Unfulfilled prophecy, writers on, 180-181
Union of England and Ireland (1801), 313
Union societies at Oxford and Cambridge, 224
Universities, state of the, 219-225

V

Valpy, Dr., 287
Van Mildert, Bishop W., 6, 9, 26, 33,

INDEX.

43, 44, 89, 169, 178, 179-180, 201, 202, 206, 226
Vansittart, Chancellor of Exchequer, 150
Vellore, mutiny at, 268, 269-270
Venn, Henry, the elder, 53-54, 72-73, 99, 160
Venn, Henry, the younger, 223 *n.*, 256 *n.*
Venn, John, 53, 72-74, 99, 193, 201, 257
"Village Politics by Will Chip" (H. More), 172, 173
"Vindiciæ Ecclesiæ Anglicanæ" (Daubeny), 188
Vitality of Evangelicals, five causes of, 104-108.

W

Waddington, Dean G., 196-197
Wakefield, Gilbert, 170-171
Wales, the Church in, 17-23
Walker, Fellow of Trinity College, Dublin, 314
Walmsley, T. T. (Sec. Nat. Soc.), 240
War with France, 2-3
Waring, Major Scott, 268-270
Washington, George, 340
Waterland, Daniel, Life of, 193
Watson, Archdeacon J. J., 35, 240
Watson, Joshua, 31-35, 39, 142, 152, 200, 202, 240, 243, 281
Watson, Bishop R., 116
Welbeck Chapel, Marylebone, 84
Week-day services, 142-144
Wellesley, Marquis, 262, 266
Wesley, John, Southey's Life of, 193
West Indies, Church in, 282

Westminster Review, 125
Whately, Archbishop R., 118-120, 121, 124, 166, 216, 321
Wheler Chapel, Spital Square, 83, 88
White, Blanco, 124
White, Henry Kirke, 154
White, Bishop W. (Pennsylvania), 337, 339-340, 343
Wilberforce, William, 5, 9, 52, 67-69, 74, 76, 94, 187, 201, 258, 261, 272, 273, 297, 305
Williams, Bishop (Connecticut), 339
Wilson, Carus, M. P., 92
Wilson, Bishop Daniel (Calcutta), 5, 56, 57, 79, 80, 85, 86, 128, 144, 168, 191, 277, 306
Woodd, Basil, 81, 99 *n.*, 175, 253 *n.*, 257
Wordsworth, Bishop Charles, 221, 229, 230
Wordsworth, Dr. Christopher, Master of Trinity, 38-40, 43, 171, 191, 193, 224, 229, 240, 279, 281, 290
Wordsworth, William, 207-208, 210-212, 224, 242
Wrangham, Archdeacon F., 27, 237, 266
Wright, James, 250

Y

Yates, Richard, 150
Yelling, Church of, 160

Z

"Zeal without Innovation," 76, 106, 134, 143, 155

THE END.

www.ingramcontent.com/pod-product-compliance
Lightning Source LLC
Chambersburg PA
CBHW020244240426
43672CB00006B/634